THE

POST-AMERICAN

PRESIDENCY

The Obama Administration's War on America

PAMELA GELLER

with Robert Spencer

Foreword by Ambassador John R. Bolton

THRESHOLD EDITIONS

NEW YORK   LONDON   TORONTO   SYDNEY

Threshold Editions
A Division of Simon & Schuster, Inc.
1230 Avenue of the Americas
New York, NY 10020

First Threshold Editions hardcover edition July 2010

THRESHOLD EDITIONS and colophon are
trademarks of Simon & Schuster, Inc.

For information about special discounts for bulk purchases,
please contact Simon & Schuster Special Sales at
1-866-506-1949 or business@simonandschuster.com.

The Simon & Schuster Speakers Bureau can bring authors to your live event.
For more information or to book an event contact the Simon & Schuster Speakers
Bureau at 1-866-248-3049 or visit our website at www.simonspeakers.com.

Designed by Ruth Lee-Mui

Manufactured in the United States of America

1   3   5   7   9   10   8   6   4   2

Library of Congress Cataloging-in-Publication Data

Geller, Pamela A.
The post-American presidency : the Obama administration's war on America / Pamela
Geller with Robert Spencer ; foreword by Ambassador John R. Bolton.
p.   cm.
1. Obama, Barack.   2. Presidents—United States.   3. Executive power—United
States.   4. Political culture—United States—Congresses.   5. Control (Psychology)—
Political aspects—United States.   I. Spencer, Robert, 1962–   II. Title.
JK516.G4 2010
973.932—dc22   2010005967
ISBN 978-1-4391-8930-6
ISBN 978-1-4391-8990-0 (ebook)

To my children and my children's children

C O N T E N T S

F O R E W O R D

BY AMBASSADOR JOHN R. BOLTON

Barack Obama is the first post-American president, as his statements and actions since his inauguration have proven beyond dispute. Central to his worldview is rejecting "American exceptionalism," and the consequences that flow from discarding this foundational belief so widely held by U.S. citizens. "Exceptionalism" is hard to define precisely, but it first appeared when John Winthrop, Governor of the Massachusetts Bay Colony, said "we must consider that we shall be as a city upon a hill." Ronald Reagan went one better, and called us "a shining city on a hill," and others have used the term "New Jerusalem." Alexis de Tocqueville, the gifted French observer of the early United States, laid the basis for the actual phrase when he said in *Democracy in America*: "The position of the Americans is therefore quite exceptional, and it may be believed that no democratic people will ever be placed in a similar one."

While most Americans have appreciated and prized our exceptionalism, that reaction has been far from universal overseas. It is no surprise, therefore, that since an overwhelming majority of the world's population would welcome the demise of American exceptionalism, they are just delighted with the Obama presidency.

One student interviewed after an Obama town hall meeting during his first presidential trip to Europe in 2009 said ecstatically, "He sounds just like a European." Indeed, he does. Of course, as a successful politician, Obama will never admit expressly that he rejects a unique U.S. role in the world. Asked during that visit to Europe about this very subject, Obama responded: "I believe in American exceptionalism, just as I suspect the Brits believe in British exceptionalism and the Greeks believe in Greek exceptionalism."

This answer, of course, proves exactly the opposite of what Obama is ostensibly saying in his opening words. If every country is exceptional—and there are 191 other United Nations members Obama could have referred to as believing in their own exceptionalism—none is. Obama is too smart not to know this, and just slick enough to hope that his U.S. listeners would tune out after his opening phrase.

It fell to an admiring media commentator to lift the cover more fully, and indeed unknowingly, since he intended a compliment. Following Obama's 2009 speech on the sixty-fifth anniversary of D-Day, *Newsweek* editor Evan Thomas contrasted his remarks with Ronald Reagan's address in 1984 at the fortieth anniversary:

> Well, we were the good guys in 1984, it felt that way. It hasn't felt that way in recent years. So Obama's had, really, a different task. . . . Reagan was all about America. . . . Obama is "we are above that now." We're not just parochial, we're not just chauvinistic, we're not just provincial. We stand for something. I mean in a way Obama's standing above the entire country, above—above the world, he's sort of God . . . he's going to bring all different sides together.

Thomas was dramatically wrong about Reagan's speech, which included sustained praise for America's wartime allies, and equating Obama with God is ring-kissingly breathtaking even for the U.S. press corps. But Thomas's central observation was unquestionably correct: Obama *is* above all that patriotism stuff.

Obama is not the first Democratic presidential nominee to hold these views, but he is the first to make it to the Oval Office. The then–vice president George H. W. Bush best described the type in 1988, contrasting himself with his opponent, Governor Michael Dukakis of Massachusetts: "He sees America as another pleasant country on the UN roll call, somewhere between Albania and Zimbabwe. I see America as the leader—a unique nation with a special role in the world." In 2004, the Democratic nominee, Sen. John Kerry, also of Massachusetts, argued that U.S. foreign policy had to pass what he called a "global test" of legitimacy to be fully acceptable, rather than simply resting on a basis acceptable to a majority of the American people.

The Dukakis/Kerry/Obama philosophy of near universal "moral equivalency" among the world's nations is widely held by European leaders and others, so, under Obama, we will now find out just how European we have become. During the opening acts of Obama's drama, the evidence is disturbingly robust across the spectrum of national security issues that we are well advanced in our post-American journey.

Take China as an important example. After Obama's November 2008 trip, the media highlighted how unyielding Beijing had been, thus confirming the conventional wisdom of a rising China and a declining America. But any objective analysis would show that it was in fact much more Obama's submissiveness and much less new Chinese assertiveness that made the difference. Take the apparently insignificant question of the staging aspects of the visit: where the president would speak, to whom, how it would be broadcast, and so on. The Chinese always fight hard to stage-manage such visits, but the difference this time is that Obama's team let them prevail. Multiply this snapshot many times on substantive policy, and the failures of Obama's visit become more understandable.

What happened in China has happened across the board: in the war against terrorism that is no longer a war, but a matter for law enforcement; in the weakness and indecisiveness demonstrated in presidential command of the wars in Iraq and Afghanistan; in dealing with the nuclear proliferation threats posed by North Korea and Iran; and in unilateral and multilateral steps to reduce the size and strength of America's nuclear deterrent capabilities.

This book carries forward the ongoing and increasingly widespread critique of Barack Obama as our first post-American president. What it recounts is disturbing, and its broader implications are more disturbing still. Most Americans believe they elect a president who will vigorously represent their global interest, rather than electing a Platonic guardian who defends them only when they comport with his grander visions of a just world. Foreign leaders, whether friend or foe, expect the same. If, by contrast, Obama continues to behave as a post-American president, our adversaries will know exactly what to do.

P R E F A C E

THE POST-AMERICAN PRESIDENT

America is being tested in a way that she has never been tested before.

America is under attack from within at the highest levels of power. Barack Hussein Obama's policies are bringing America to her knees.

With a consistency that can come only from deeply held conviction, Barack Hussein Obama is damaging the office of the presidency and compromising American sovereignty.

Domestically, Barack Obama is contemptuous of capitalism and rugged individualism. Internationally, Barack Obama is enabling Iran's Islamic bomb, is inveterately hostile to Israel, and generally appears intent on turning America's historical enemies into friends and friends into enemies. His dream seems to be to turn America into something like the Indonesia of his youth or the Pakistan he visited as a college student: at best, just another country, unexceptional in any way. At worst, a Third-World nation lagging far behind other global economic and cultural leaders.

Obama's perspective, his worldview, is of enormous import. It tells us who he is and why he is doing what he is doing. America did not shape Barack Obama. Instead, he was influenced and indoctrinated by many who despised America. These were his early influences, and many of them have been lifelong influences. Throughout his life and his political career, Obama has been consistent—right up to and into his presidency.

This book lays out in painstaking detail the political views of the people he has selected to help him govern this nation and the domestic and foreign policies he promotes. It is all a result of how he was brought up, of what shaped his mind and heart. It is all a result of what drives him.

What drives him is not American. He said it himself: "I was a little Jakarta street kid" who found the Islamic call to prayer to be "one of the prettiest sounds on Earth at sunset."[1] For the most part, Barack Obama has carefully distanced himself from any sign of patriotism or national pride throughout his political career and his presidency.

In his mind, apparently, to be a forthright believer in American exceptionalism would be unfair, chauvinistic, maybe even bigoted. On Barack Obama's playing field, there is no American exceptionalism. (The irony here, of course, is that his presidency would have been impossible without it.) There are, in the appointments he has made and the policies he has chosen, many indications that for Barack Obama, there is no good, no evil, only equivocation and moral relativism.

Unlike Obama's childhood homeland of Indonesia, America is not tribal. American identity is not based on race or creed or color. It is a shared value system. The idea of America is freedom and individual rights—a historical first.

Ayn Rand articulated the essence of American exceptionalism when she wrote in a letter: "America's founding ideal was the principle of individual rights. Nothing more—nothing less. The rest—everything America achieved, everything she became, everything 'noble and just' and heroic and great, and unprecedented in human history—was the logical consequence of fidelity to that one principle."[2]

This is anathema to Barack Hussein Obama. Witness his sanction of Ahmadinejad and the bloody putdown of the Iranians yearning to be free. Witness his abandonment of democracy in Honduras. Witness his betrayal of Eastern Europe by scrapping the essential missile defense program. Witness the ethnic cleansing of Jews from parts of Israel. Obama does not subscribe to the principle of man's individual rights—and this is the key, the key to this country and its very nature. The United States is the nation of enlightenment, of the power of the individual.

But this is not Barack Obama's point of reference.

Barack Hussein Obama did not grow up breathing these ideas. He spent a good portion of his childhood in Indonesia, and when he did move to the States to live with his grandparents when he was twelve, it was not to the continental United States, but off the mainland in Hawaii. Hawaii had only just become a state two years prior to his birth, and many on the island were not happy about it. So not only was it a nascent state, but many within it were hostile to the idea of America.

Obama's absentee father, Barack Hussein Obama, Sr., was a member of Kenya's Luo tribe.[3] Obama, Jr., went so far as to oppose our ally in Kenya, President Mwai Kibaki, and to campaign for his fellow Luo tribesman, Raila Odinga, a violent socialist who claimed to be Obama's cousin.

You have to grow up in America to *get* America. Or you have to escape tyranny, oppression, and suppression and live the dream by emigrating to America. Obama is missing the DNA of the USA. It's just not in him—through no fault of his own.

Barack Obama's "third-grade teacher Fermina Katarina Sinaga, now sixty-seven, has perhaps the most telling story. In an essay about what he wanted to be when he grew up, Obama 'wrote he wanted to be president,' Sinaga recalled. *'He didn't say what country he wanted to be president of.'"*[4]

Barack Obama has no desire for America to win—hence his refusal to use the word "victory" in any of his remarks concerning the military operations in which the United States is currently engaged. His desire to make peace with the Islamic world was a legitimate goal in this age of jihad. But he seemed to have no effective way to attain this goal in light of Islamic intransigence—and so his every move made matters worse.

Obama sees himself not just as another American president. He announced during his Inaugural Address that he had far more sweeping plans: "Starting today, we must pick ourselves up, dust ourselves off, and begin again the work of remaking America."[5] Remaking America? Into what?

Since he has taken office he has been hard at work to do just that: destroying the free-market system and nationalizing major segments of the U.S. economy, restricting dissent and the freedom of speech in general, turning against longtime friends of the United States, and above all subjecting America to the determinations of foreign authorities.

This is a deeply troubling presidency—and a dangerous period in American history.

The period of the post-American presidency.

He himself said it in April 2009. During a visit to London for a summit of the Group of Twenty Finance Ministers and Central Bank Governors (G-20), a reporter asked Obama: "[C]ould I ask you whether you subscribe, as many of your predecessors have, to the school of 'American exceptionalism' that sees America as uniquely qualified to lead the world, or do you have a slightly different philosophy?"

It was a question Ronald Reagan once answered without ever

having been asked it. He said: "With all its flaws, America remains a unique achievement for human dignity on a scale unequaled anywhere in the world."

But Obama offered no similar avowal of American uniqueness. Instead, he equated American exceptionalism with the national pride that a citizen of any nation could feel: "I believe in American exceptionalism, just as I suspect that the Brits believe in British exceptionalism and the Greeks believe in Greek exceptionalism."

Then, perhaps realizing how much he had just trivialized the achievements of the greatest republic and most magnanimous nation the world had ever known, Obama avowed: "I'm enormously proud of my country and its role and history in the world." He even allowed for the possibility that there were some reasons that Americans should not be embarrassed by their nation's history: "If you think about the site of this summit and what it means, I don't think America should be embarrassed to see evidence of the sacrifices of our troops, the enormous amount of resources that were put into Europe postwar, and our leadership in crafting an Alliance that ultimately led to the unification of Europe. We should take great pride in that."

Embarrassed? Who would even think such a thing? Except someone who *is* embarrassed by America. It's as if the most beautiful girl in the world walks into the best party, bedecked in the most magnificent dress and finest jewels, and someone whispers to her, "Don't be embarrassed."

Obama even acknowledged that "we have a core set of values that are enshrined in our Constitution, in our body of law, in our democratic practices, in our belief in free speech and equality, that, though imperfect, are exceptional." But in saying that he may have sensed that he was venturing into areas where he didn't want to go, so he backtracked: "Now, the fact that I am very proud of my country and I think that we've got a whole lot to offer the world does not lessen my interest in recognizing the value and wonderful qualities of other countries, or recognizing that we're not always going to be right, or that other people may have good ideas, or that in order for us to work collectively, all parties have to compromise and that includes us."

It was a defining moment. Barack Obama could find some praise-worthy aspects of America—but in saying that he was careful to say also that every country could say the same, apparently in equal measure, and while the U.S. Constitution and system of government—"though imperfect"—had some "exceptional" features, well, other countries also had "wonderful qualities."

In other words, America was nothing special. Just another country. Former vice president Dick Cheney summed it up: "There's never been a nation like the United States of America in world history, and yet when you have a president who goes around and bows to his hosts and then proceeds to apologize profusely for the United States, I find that deeply disturbing. That says to me this is a guy who doesn't fully understand or share that view of American exceptionalism that I think most of us believe in."[6]

Even when Obama does refer to America's essential goodness, as he did in his 2010 State of the Union address, it is only to advance his commitment to socialist internationalism and redistribution of American wealth: he wields Americans' empathy and compassion like a club to manipulate us into funding bad foreign policy and despotic regimes.

In a seminal moment for modern historians and active political observers like myself, a snapshot came across the newswires, showing presidential candidate Barack Hussein Obama crossing an airplane tarmac, mid-gait, and holding Fareed Zakaria's American epitaph, *The Post-American World*. In the photo, Obama is holding his place in the book with his finger, as if he didn't dare put it down and wanted to dive back into it as soon as he could.

Zakaria describes his book this way: "This is not a book about the decline of America, but rather about the rise of everyone else." In it, he details the era he hopes we are entering now—a world in which the United States would "no longer dominate the global economy, orchestrate geopolitics, or overwhelm cultures." He asserts that the "rise of the rest" is the "great story of our time, and one that will reshape the world. The tallest buildings, biggest dams, largest-selling movies, and most advanced cell phones are all being built outside the United States. This economic growth is producing political confidence, national pride, and potentially international problems."[7]

It was at the moment that photo went out over the wires, back in May 2008, that I began calling him "post-American Obama" and, subsequent to the election, the "post-American president." The book predicting America's inevitable decline turned out to be a veritable blueprint for Obama's presidency. Obama seems determined to make it a self-fulfilling prophecy. Obama went to work from his first day in office to make Zakaria's wishful thinking about America's decline become a reality. As the most powerful man in the world, he would level the playing field, even if it meant cutting America off at the knees. Good and evil would be made equivalent, with evil sanctioned by the world's only remaining superpower: democracy and tyranny, dictator and elected leader would be given the same moral sanction.

Obama has been working fast. He was elected president by a wide margin. If he had governed as a left-of-center president in the mold of Bill Clinton, he would have been certain of reelection. Most observers saw him as another Democrat politician in this mode. Cheney remarked: "I saw him when he got elected as a liberal Democrat, but conventional in the sense of sort of falling within the parameters of the national Democratic Party. I think he's demonstrated pretty conclusively now during his first year in office that he's more radical than that, that he's farther outside the parameters if you will of what we've traditionally had in Democratic presidents in years past."[8]

He could have in due time repaid the many favors he owed to his various special interest constituencies—including trial lawyers, labor unions, banks, and insurance companies—and governed as a successful president, boosting our country's stature worldwide, and waving the flag proudly. This doesn't mean he couldn't have found success implementing his plan to change the nation radically—but everyone expected that he would go about it slowly, careful not to alienate any of his supporters or cause undue alarm among his opponents.

Instead, he traveled around the world and denigrated American achievements and American uniqueness. He reached out in friendship to our enemies and the enemies of freedom and individual rights, including Hugo Chávez and even Fidel Castro, and offered Russia a significant boost on its way to returning to superpower status by selling out Eastern Europe. He catered to—and fawned shamelessly over—Islam and Muslim countries, making preposterous statements about how much the United States owes Islam, and even about how America was a Muslim country.[9]

Obama clearly believed that doing all this would bolster his image in other countries. But he was taking a calculated risk: that his apparent lack of concern for American national security, and for America's historical achievements and place in the world, would backfire and anger Americans. Nonetheless, he took the risk. He must have believed that he was powerful enough and popular enough to neutralize any domestic political backlash that may result—and he certainly had the mainstream media on his side, as he did during his presidential campaign, to cover for him, make excuses for him when he failed, and obscure the full scope of what he was doing.

Barack Hussein Obama had chosen the path of the post-American presidency. He seemed to envision himself as more than just the president of the United States, but as a shaper of the new world order, an internationalist energetically laying the groundwork for global government: the president of the world.

The problem for Americans was that in his quest for internationalism and global socialism, Obama was leaving the United States twisting in the wind. He was treating America as a stepping-stone to help get him where he wanted to go, and he seemed willing to do anything to destroy America's prestige in the world.

Domestically he is just as destructive. Americans worry about the extraordinary national debt that he has helped increase exponentially, and which is leading us to economic ruin. Obama doesn't seem concerned about this at all: his plans include a $200 billion second stimulus program and various socialist programs that will further drain the nation's resources, including nationalized health care and the cap-and-trade plan.

One common thread running through all of Obama's Orwellian-sounding proposals to "remake America" is that they all give much greater power to the government.

The difficulty in writing this book was keeping up with the speed at which Obama set about radically transforming both the global and the national landscape in favor of our enemies. In this book we have sketched out how he has set out to do this in the first year of his presidency. He sought to gain control of health care (20 percent of the American economy), energy, and education. His foreign policy is breathtaking in its betrayal of the rational self-interest of all Americans. In working to bring socialism and internationalism to America, appeasing Iran, betraying Israel, and infringing upon our freedoms, Obama is setting America on the path to ruin.

We have mapped out how he has begun here. Nothing is more certain than that he will continue on the same course.

The Shining City on a Hill has gone dark. The United States has entered the age of the post-American presidency.

And Barack Hussein Obama is the first post-American president.

THE POST-AMERICAN PRESIDENCY

ONE

OBAMA AND AMERICAN EXCEPTIONALISM

No one nation can or should try to dominate another nation. . . .

—Barack Obama[1]

BARACK HUSSEIN OBAMA ABDICATED. HE ABDICATED THAT WHICH WAS NOT HIS TO ABDICATE.

In his first months as president he showed himself ready to give up American sovereignty for the primacy of international law; regulations on climate change, gun control, and free speech (including speech on the Internet); and the replacement of the dollar as the basic international currency.

During his campaign, Obama declared his affinity for international law. "Since the founding of our nation, the United States has championed international law because we benefit from it. Promoting—and respecting—clear rules that are consistent with our values allows us to hold all nations to a high standard of behavior, and to mobilize friends and allies against those nations that break the rules. Promoting strong international norms helps us advance many interests, including non-proliferation, free and fair trade, a clean environment, and protecting our troops in wartime. Respect for international legal norms also plays a vital role in fighting terrorism. Because the administration cast aside international norms that reflect American values, such as the Geneva Conventions, we are less able to promote those values abroad."[2]

It sounded great—until it became clear that promoting international norms meant compromising American sovereignty. Ambassador John Bolton warned in his book *Surrender Is Not an Option* of the dangers of what is known as "norming." Norming, Bolton explained in an interview, "is a term that's applied to international agreements that affect the behavior of individual governments." When leftist activists fail in pushing their domestic agendas, "such as on gun issues in Congress or state legislatures, they stop fighting there and try and take the issue internationally."[3]

"This approach," Bolton explained, "often called 'norming,' meaning, in a neutral sense, creating international norms of behavior, could be helpful, especially if it meant raising standards in intolerable regimes. What it increasingly came to mean, however, was whipping the United States into line with leftist views of the way the world should look."[4]

What would be the good of subjecting America to international norms? America has always been a light to the world.

It is essential that we understand the importance and singular greatness of America, and not give in to internationalist gobbledygook that amounts to nothing more than transnational serfdom.

In May 2009, the United States joined the notorious cabal of evildoers, the United Nations Human Rights Council—which the Bush administration had boycotted for its relentless defamation and demonization of Israel and refusal to condemn human-rights violations in Islamic countries, notably Sudan. Ironically, the United States would sit on the council with four notorious human-rights violators: China, Cuba, Russia, and Saudi Arabia.[5] In December 2009 the watchdog group UN Watch issued a report showing that the Human Rights Council had effectively become an enabler for human-rights violators, rather than a genuine defender of human rights. Hillel Neuer, UN Watch's executive director, remarked: "Paradoxically, as our report today shows, the U.N.'s main human rights body has turned into the world's leading sponsor of impunity for gross human rights abuses worldwide. It's a case of the foxes guarding the chickens, with countries like China, Russia, Pakistan, Cuba and Saudi Arabia shielding each other's abuses. Democracies should send a signal by opposing the council's resolutions, even if they will be outvoted."

That was something Barack Obama was extremely unlikely to do.

Then on September 24, 2009, Obama became the first president of the United States to serve as chairman of the United Nations Security Council. Harry Truman, who oversaw the establishment of the UN, never did it. Neither did Eisenhower, the general who defeated Nazism in Europe. No other president did either—not even Ronald Reagan after he called upon Mikhail Gorbachev to tear down the Berlin Wall, or George H. W. Bush with his new world order.

But Barack Hussein Obama was a new kind of American president.

The media hailed the move as signaling a "new co-operative relationship between the US and the United Nations."[6] Gone were the days when the United States would stand against the initiatives restricting free speech sponsored by the Organization of the Islamic Conference. Gone were the days when the United States would stand with Israel against the hypocritical condemnations that would rain down upon it from the communist and Islamic blocs. By chairing the

Security Council session, Barack Obama was signaling that America was no longer singular in the world, no longer the lodestar of free people around the globe, no more exceptional than any other country.

Barack Obama's America was just another country, a large and still strong country, to be sure, but not one that stood any longer against authoritarianism—no longer the leader of the free world, but now the leader of the globalist initiative to unify the world's government and economy, and enforce a drab uniformity.

Obama's chairing of the Security Council session only put an official stamp on a series of initiatives he had been pursuing in this direction since long before he became president. As soon as he became president, he took decisive steps to submit American sovereignty to the will of international bodies.

THE INTERNATIONAL CRIMINAL COURT CLAIMS JURISDICTION

In March 2009, the Obama administration dropped the term "enemy combatant" for the prisoners still being held at the Guantánamo Bay detention center, and instead adopted international laws of war as the basis for holding the accused jihad terrorists there. Attorney General Eric Holder explained: "As we work towards developing a new policy to govern detainees, it is essential that we operate in a manner that strengthens our national security, is consistent with our values, and is governed by law."

Not American law, international law. Norming. The Justice Department announced proudly that its new policy "draws on the international laws of war to inform the statutory authority conferred by Congress."[7]

Several months later, the Obama administration opened the door to extending the norms of international law not only to jihadists in Gitmo, but to the American troops who had put them there.

In August 2009, according to *The Wall Street Journal*, Secretary of State Hillary Clinton "expressed 'great regret' . . . that the U.S. is not a signatory to the International Criminal Court (ICC). This has fueled speculation that the Obama administration may reverse another Bush policy and sign up for what could lead to the trial of Americans for war crimes in The Hague."[8] George W. Bush had refused in May 2002 to accept the jurisdiction of the ICC—precisely because of the prospect of American troops being tried for war crimes on highly politicized grounds.[9]

Whether Obama signed on to the court or not, the ICC itself seemed determined to assert jurisdiction over Americans. The chief prosecutor of the ICC, Luis Moreno-Ocampo, claimed that he had the authority to investigate allegations of American war crimes in Afghanistan, and to prosecute American military personnel accordingly, even if the Obama administration did not agree. "I prosecute whoever is in my jurisdiction," Ocampo insisted. "I cannot allow that we are a court just for the Third World. If the First World commits crimes, they have to investigate, if they don't, I shall investigate. That's the rule and we have one rule for everyone."[10] Not coincidentally, on the windowsill in Ocampo's office is a photograph of himself with the head of the Arab League, Amr Moussa.[11]

The idea that American troops might have committed war crimes in Afghanistan that warranted their being placed into the same category as Sudan's Omar Bashir was one that could have occurred only to a rabid anti-American ideologue. Bashir, after all, murdered hundreds of thousands of people in a jihad-inspired genocide.

The Obama administration further opened the door to war-crimes prosecutions of American troops by praising the ICC's work in other areas. Obama's ambassador to the United Nations, Susan Rice, praised the court as an "important and credible instrument for trying to hold accountable the senior leadership responsible for atrocities committed in the Congo, Uganda and Darfur." Ben Chang, spokesman for Obama's national security advisor, General James Jones, agreed: "We support the ICC in its pursuit of those who've perpetrated war crimes."[12] Obama himself has said that "it is in America's interests that these most heinous of criminals, like the perpetrators of the genocide in Darfur, are held accountable. These actions are a credit to the cause of justice and deserve full American support and cooperation."[13]

The Bush administration had also praised the prosecution of Bashir, but at the same time Bush championed the American Service-members Protection Act, which expressed disapproval of the ICC.[14]

Would Obama likewise stand up for America and her defenders? Unlikely. The British author and columnist Gerald Warner observed correctly that joining the ICC would "flatter Obama's ego as the conscience of the world. It would also put US servicemen at the mercy of any American-hating opportunists who might choose to arraign them on trumped-up charges before an alien court whose judges are likely to be ill-disposed towards America too." Some of those "American-hating opportunists" would be Americans themselves: "So, vengeful Democrats could facilitate the indictment of President George W. Bush and all his senior commanders in Iraq."[15]

What's more, such war-crimes trials would be enormously popular in the Islamic world—the very region that the post-American president was so anxious to accommodate.

In pursuit of that accommodation, Obama's internationalism also quickly manifested itself as a distaste for the freedom of speech.

THE WAR ON FREE SPEECH AND OBAMA'S INTERNATIONAL AGENDA

In a crushing blow to the freedom of speech worldwide, the United Nations Human Rights Council in March 2009 approved a resolution calling upon member states to provide legal "protection against acts of hatred, discrimination, intimidation and coercion resulting from defamation of religions and incitement to religious hatred in general."[16]

Hatred, discrimination, intimidation, coercion, defamation, and incitement according to whom? In whose eyes?

To ask the question was to reveal the authoritarian nature of the resolution. It was designed to be a tool in the hands of the powerful, enabling them to silence the powerless.

While the resolution speaks of religion in general, the proposal came from Pakistan and had the backing of the powerful fifty-seven-government Organization of the Islamic Conference (OIC). (It also bears noting that there is no Organization of the Jewish Conference or Organization of the Christian Conference at the UN.) The OIC is the UN's largest, most powerful, and most influential voting bloc—so it was clear that Islam was the only religion the drafters of the resolution had in mind. In fact, it was the only one specifically mentioned. This was underscored by the fact that Muslim states worked energetically to make "Islamophobia" the focus of Durban II—the UN's second World Conference against Racism, Racial Discrimination, Xenophobia and Related Intolerance.

The conference "outcome document" deplored "Islamophobia, anti-Semitism, Christianophobia and anti-Arabism manifested in particular by the derogatory stereotyping and stigmatization of persons based on their religion or belief," and insisted that the criminalizing of speech deemed to be "religious hatred" was consistent with "freedom of opinion and expression."[17]

But of course, what constituted "religious hatred" was in the eye of the beholder, and this could open the door for criminalization of any speech about Islam that the Islamic bloc disliked. Abdoulaye Wade, president of Senegal and chairman of the Organization of the Islamic Conference, commented: "I don't think freedom of expression should mean freedom from blasphemy. There can be no freedom without limits."[18] Is reporting on Islamic jihad, gender apartheid, clitorectomies, beheadings, child marriage, polygamy, absence of women's rights, honor killings, Islamic expansionism, and Islamic supremacism also to be considered defamation of Islam?

If the Organization of the Islamic Conference and the drafters of the Durban declaration had their way, any honest examination of how jihadists use Islamic texts and teachings to make recruits would be illegal. This would herald the death of the freedom of speech, leaving us mute and defenseless before the advancing global jihad.

The United Nations was putting itself in the position of policing Sharia rules on blasphemy. The West had accepted the Islamic narrative of victimization and intimidation to such a degree that large segments of the Western elites seemed ready to accept the proposition that it was blasphemy to criticize Islam.

Barack Obama was putting the world's only superpower behind this outrage. The Obama administration took a decidedly friendly attitude toward this initiative. *The Weekly Standard* noted that "in order to please our European allies and our Third World critics, the Obama administration may be tempted to surrender one particular manifestation of American 'dominance': central management of key aspects of the Internet by the U.S. Department of Commerce"—and that some countries are already agitating for this. And not just countries: "If we give control of the Internet naming infrastructure to an international organization, we must expect attempts to censor the Internet. The Organization of the Islamic Conference will doubtless demand the suppression of websites that 'insult Islam' or 'encourage hatred,' and a number of European countries may well go along."[19]

Meanwhile, the Obama administration moved swiftly to show a conciliatory face to the OIC. Within two weeks of taking office, Obama wrote to the secretary-general of the OIC, Ekmeleddin Ihsanoglu, seeking improved relations.[20] Ihsanoglu visited Washington on June 23, 2009—the same day that the State Department announced the establishment of the Office of the United States Special Representative to Muslim Communities, as Ihsanoglu had urged.[21] This office is so important that the special representative to Muslim communities reports directly to the secretary of state.[22]

With the OIC engaged in its all-out international effort to restrict free speech about Islam, including speech designed to alert non-Muslims to the motives and goals of the global jihad movement, Obama's outreach to the OIC had ominous overtones—especially in light of the other indications that his administration had been giving that the defense of free speech was not exactly high on its list of priorities.

THE UNITED STATES BECOMES AN ENEMY OF FREE SPEECH

Ominous overtones became ominous reality in October 2009, when the Obama administration actually cosponsored (with Egypt, itself not a bastion of free inquiry and free expression) an anti–free speech resolution at the United Nations. Approved by the UN Human Rights Council, the resolution calls on states to condemn and criminalize "any advocacy of national, racial or religious hatred that constitutes incitement to discrimination, hostility or violence."[23]

What could be wrong with that? Everything.

There is, after all, the First Amendment, which preserves Americans' right to free speech and freedom of the press.

"Incitement" and "hatred" are in the eye of the beholder—or more precisely, in the eye of those who make such determinations. The powerful can decide to silence the powerless by classifying their views as "hate speech." The Founding Fathers knew that the freedom of speech was an essential safeguard against tyranny: the ability to dissent, freely and publicly and without fear of imprisonment or other reprisal, is a cornerstone of any genuine republic. If some ideas cannot be heard and are proscribed from above, the ones in control are tyrants, however benevolent they may be.

Now no less distinguished a personage than the president of the United States has given his imprimatur to this tyranny.

The resolution also condemns "negative stereotyping of religions and racial groups," which is, of course, an oblique reference to accurate reporting about the jihad doctrine and Islamic supremacism—for that, not actual negative stereotyping or hateful language, is always the focus of complaints by the Organization of the Islamic Conference and allied groups. They never say anything when people like Osama bin Laden and Khalid Sheikh Mohammed issue detailed Qur'anic expositions justifying violence and hatred; but when people like Dutch politician Geert Wilders and others report about such expositions, that's "negative stereotyping."

Eugene Volokh explained why even the First Amendment may not be able to stand up against Obama's assault on free speech. "If the U.S. backs a resolution that urges the suppression of some speech," he explains, "presumably we are taking the view that all countries—including the U.S.—should adhere to this resolution. If we are constitutionally barred from adhering to it by our domestic constitution, then we're implicitly criticizing that constitution, and committing ourselves to do what we can to change it."[24]

Volokh added that in order to be consistent, "the Administration would presumably have to take what steps it can to ensure that supposed 'hate speech' that incites hostility will indeed be punished. It would presumably be committed to filing amicus briefs supporting changes in First Amendment law to allow such punishment, and in principle perhaps the appointment of Justices who would endorse such changes (or even the proposal of express constitutional amendments that would work such changes)."[25]

In 2008 the secretary-general of the OIC, Ekmeleddin Ihsanoglu, issued a warning: "We sent a clear message to the West regarding the red lines that should not be crossed" regarding free speech about Islam and terrorism. And he reported success: "The official West and its public opinion are all now well-aware of the sensitivities of these issues. They have also started to look seriously into the question of freedom of expression from the perspective of its inherent responsibility, which should not be overlooked."[26]

No American president had ever taken more seriously his "responsibility" to restrict the freedom of speech and bow to Muslim demands than Barack Hussein Obama. When he said during his Nobel Peace Prize acceptance speech that "peace is unstable where citizens are denied the right to speak freely," the irony was blistering.[27]

And he worked to erode American sovereignty in other ways as well.

GIVING UP AMERICAN SOVEREIGNTY
AT THE G-20 LEADERS' SUMMIT

Obama scored a major victory for his internationalist agenda in April 2009 at the G-20 Leaders' Summit on Financial Markets and the World Economy in London.

Dick Morris, the author, columnist, and former aide to Bill Clinton, explained it to Greta Van Susteren of Fox News: "Literally from April 2nd of this year, that is, today," said Morris, "it's a whole new world of financial regulation in which, essentially, all of the U.S. regulatory bodies and all U.S. companies are put under international regulation, international supervision. It really amounts to a global economic government."

At the G-20 summit Obama helped establish this global economic government by signing off on the establishment of an international Financial Stability Board (FSB). The assembled world leaders agreed to "a framework of internationally agreed upon high standards. We will set up a financial stability board with a strengthened mandate to extend regulation and oversight to all systemically important financial institutions, instruments and markets to endorse and implement tough new principles on paying compensation and to support sustainable compensation schemes and the corporate social responsibility of all firms." [28]

Thus American financial institutions, instruments, and markets would be subjected to international regulation and oversight, including regulation on salaries and the "corporate social responsibility" of "all" firms. Not just some of them, but all of them. "Just when Obama is accused of socialism," Morris said, "he's essentially creating world economic governments." This was no exaggeration: the FSB would have authority over regulations on salaries for executives and other issues that the U.S. Federal Reserve Board could apply to major American companies. American economic life would be institutionally made subject to international supervision and control.

The G-20 leaders, according to Morris, slipped this in "under the radar, which is absolutely creating an international economic union." He noted that Obama, oddly enough, "was the one pressing for less regulation and more spending, and he had to convince the Europeans." But this wasn't done out of conviction, in Morris's opinion: "Obama himself is a socialist, I believe, and he had no problem really with this. This truly created a global economic system. From now on don't look to Washington for the rule making, look to Brussels. . . . European socialists are going to be making the regulatory rules concerning compensation for all, all, systematically important US firms. All."

A global economic system: just the thing fondly envisioned by many Marxist theorists Obama studied with and learned from.

And now he was the one poised to bring their dreams to fruition.

THE LISBON TREATY

Those same European socialists, meanwhile, had already been moving to consolidate their own power. The Lisbon Treaty significantly strengthened the power of the Brussels bureaucracy that oversees the European Union. Ireland held out against this treaty for a long while, rejecting it in June 2008 but finally voting to approve it in a second vote in early October 2009. Shortly after that, Polish president Lech Kacynski ratified the treaty, remarking: "The fact that the Irish people changed their minds meant the revival of the treaty, and there are no longer any obstacles to its ratification." The Czech Republic remained the lone holdout.[29]

Obama applauded the Lisbon Treaty, saying: "I believe that a strengthened and renewed EU will be an even better transatlantic partner with the United States."[30] Not surprisingly, the treaty he was praising was one that provided for centralization, increased government control, and the weakening of democracy in Europe. The post-American president was happy to see an internationalist, socialist partner on the global horizon.

In fact, the EU could never have brought the treaty back to a vote so soon after Ireland had voted it down had it not been for the weak, globalist U.S. president.

The treaty creates the position of President of the European Union and removes member nations' right to veto EU legislation. The former U.S. ambassador to the United Nations, John Bolton, warned Dubliners about it just before the 2008 Irish vote: "The only people you elect have a very limited role and I think this treaty will further enhance the power of institutions in Brussels without extending democratic authority to people." He added that the treaty could also undercut NATO.[31]

This strengthened Brussels bureaucracy, on the verge of being given the power to override the will of majorities in EU member states, could now also gain oversight of the American economy—courtesy of Barack Hussein Obama, with the creation of the Financial Stability Board.

Internationalism and socialism run as consistent strains through Barack Obama's associations and policies.

But Americans can't say they hadn't been warned. They should have noticed that the charismatic young Democratic presidential candidate had numerous socialist associations, going back to a childhood spent among internationalists. And even as recently as nine months before he was elected president, he sponsored a bill in the Senate that would compromise American sovereignty. Even if Obama and his associates would deny that they are socialists (and it is an open question as to whether or not they actually would), their commitment to the redistribution of wealth is a core socialist principle—and is abundantly documented.

SENATOR OBAMA AND THE GLOBAL POVERTY ACT

A year before he took the oath of office to preserve, protect, and defend the Constitution of the United States, Barack Obama, senator from Illinois, sponsored the "Global Poverty Act," which was passed by the Foreign Relations Committee in February 2008. Ultimately the bill never came to a vote and died with the end of that session of Congress, but it is telling for what it reveals about the post-American president. According to Accuracy in Media editor Cliff Kincaid, if the bill had become law it could have meant the "imposition of a global tax on the United States." Even worse, the Global Poverty Act made "levels of U.S. foreign aid spending subservient to the dictates of the United Nations."

Significantly, Senator and future vice president Joe Biden (D-DE), said Kincaid, as chairman of the Senate Foreign Relations Committee "was trying to rush Obama's 'Global Poverty Act' (S. 2433) through his committee without hearings." The costs would have been prohibitive. "The legislation," according to Kincaid, "would commit the U.S. to spending 0.7 percent of gross national product on foreign aid, which amounts to a phenomenal 13-year total of $845 billion over and above what the U.S. already spends."[32]

And that spending would have been at the discretion of UN officials, not representatives accountable to the American people.

A socialist, internationalist bill subverting American sovereignty and burdening the American economy through the forced redistribution of wealth. This was not just your run-of-the-mill Marxism: this was redistribution of wealth on a global scale. Productive and wealth-producing countries would be enslaved and forced to give up their hard-earned money to impoverished nations. Most disturbingly, the chief beneficiaries of the redistribution of our wealth would be one continent and one religion: Africa and Islam.

GIVING UP AMERICAN SOVEREIGNTY
FOR CLIMATE CHANGE?

Toward the end of his first year in office, Barack Hussein Obama again laid plans to sign away American sovereignty and accept international supervision of American affairs. He had initially planned to travel to Copenhagen in December 2009 for the United Nations Climate Change Conference, where he would sign the United Nations Climate Change Treaty. The United Nations Framework Convention on Climate Change, on which that treaty was based, had ominous implications for American sovereignty. It provided for the establishment of what was essentially a governmental body, which would have the power of enforcement over the states that signed the treaty.

"It is a blueprint to save the world," wrote environmental journalist David Adam in *The Guardian*. "And yet it is long, confusing and contradictory."[33]

But its internationalist and socialist aspects are unmistakable.

The Framework Convention document includes regulations for climate control; for "mitigation," which is money that the developed world pays to the underdeveloped world for all the carbon and resources it has consumed, ostensibly to the detriment of the world's poor nations; and "adaptation"—money developed countries pay to underdeveloped nations to aid in their development. A large portion of the treaty is devoted to scaling back Western development and "consumption" to a level that will supposedly enable the Third World to catch up industrially and technologically with the First—whereupon all will march together into the glorious socialist future.

It is the same socialist vision that the post-American president is pursuing domestically: the rich give to the poor, so that we can all be poor, and all just alike.

Justice! Climate justice, the new and improved Orwellian lexicon for a warming that was more chilly than warm.

The climate agreement stipulated that the nations that signed on to the treaty would meet in a conference, where they would "identify elements, including the economic development stages, response capabilities and shares of greenhouse gas emissions in the world, to be considered as criteria for changes in circumstances of the Parties." In other words, the conference itself would examine the various factors and decide on their basis whether to change the requirements of any particular nation that was a signer of the treaty.

So in effect, the nations themselves would no longer have the power to determine their own degree of compliance with recommendations to combat global warming; instead, they would cede this right to this new supranational body. And this conference would in turn give way to a new international governing body: an "institutional arrangement and legal framework" would be established after 2012 "for the implementation, monitoring, reporting and verification of the global cooperative action." This would "include a financial mechanism and a facilitative mechanism drawn up to facilitate the design, adoption and carrying out of public policies"—and to this mechanism, "market rules and related dynamics should be subordinate, in order to assure the full, effective and sustained implementation of the Convention."

In other words, the free market would be subordinate to the oversight and direction of this new governing body. The new international governing body would regulate markets and trade worldwide, subordinate to the Copenhagen accords.

This new body would, quite explicitly, be a "government"—so it is termed in the document. This government would oversee the enforcement of international socialism, establishing "an international registry for the monitoring, reporting and verification of compliance of emission reduction commitments, and the transfer of technical and financial resources from developed countries to developing countries."

The document envisions a government on the model of the current European Union, with nations subordinating themselves to a secretariat, and the citizens of those nations having absolutely no elective voice, nor any other monitoring or governing authority over that secretariat. This secretariat would set global standards on emissions controls, on carbon dioxide levels, on trade rates, and most likely also on currency exchange and value rates. It will, in short, determine who pays, and who receives.

This is, plainly and simply, world government.

Given the complexities of the regulations delineated in the UN Framework Convention on Climate Change, nothing less than world government would be necessary: only a huge international bureaucracy could monitor, implement, and enforce these regulations.

Ironically, the developing nations, the chief beneficiaries of this global government and attendant transfer of wealth, are hopelessly ill equipped to establish and maintain the giant bureaucracy and enforcement apparatus that the climate agreement would entail. So the treaty would effectively induce the West to create and enforce a huge government apparatus for the transfer of its own wealth to other countries, the emasculation of its economies, and the surrender of its political independence.

Is this the suicide of the West? Perhaps—but Western European and American leaders don't see it that way. At first glance, the climate change treaty looks as if the West is imposing a horrible burden on itself. And certainly the new global climate change order will be prohibitively expensive, both financially and in terms of loss of sovereignty. But in exchange the West is buying the status quo. As with welfare systems in America and Europe, the new world order will pay the poor to be poor—and when the poor buy into it, they will be poor forever. By accepting payoffs instead of developing ways to earn money on their own, they exchange subsistence levels for achievement, and the fathers and mothers who buy into it simply ensure that their children will never rise above it, for they will not raise their children with the values necessary to enable them to do so.

After decades of the failed policy of throwing hard-earned American currency at despots, dictators, and bureaucrats of failed nations, what we should have been exporting was political freedom. What we should have been insisting upon was individual rights, entrepreneurship, and self-governance. And only nations that upheld such standards would qualify for the ample bounty of American largesse.

But instead, the end result of all this transfer of wealth and sovereignty will be neither climate justice nor economic equality. The West will retain its technical and technological superiority, although its further growth will be hamstrung by the new climate regulations. The developing countries will remain developing countries, because the riches they will receive via the climate treaty will do nothing to develop their economies. They will get rich by doing nothing, and as they continue to do nothing and the largesse from the West dries up, they will return to their former poverty. The developing nations are on the brink of ensuring their "developing" status for generations to come—simply by "forcing" these concessions from the West and its willing post-American leader.

It is also noteworthy that there is virtually nothing in the document forcing the developing nations to adhere to any standards of reporting or compliance or wisdom in the way the money is spent.

In reality, it is all about assuaging Western guilt and establishing a transnational socialist regime. And for the Islamic world, the climate change treaty is a sweet deal. We buy the oil from them. We burn the oil. We pay them reparations for having consumed the oil. We pay them "adaptations" for not burning their trees. At every step, they gain.

LORD MONCKTON BLOWS THE WHISTLE

Several weeks before Obama was scheduled to leave for Copenhagen, the internationalist aspect of his plans was exposed. On October 14, 2009, Lord Christopher Monckton, a former science adviser for Margaret Thatcher and noted critic of Al Gore's climate change dogma, spoke at Bethel University in St. Paul, Minnesota, about the threat to American sovereignty that was posed by the United Nations Climate Change Treaty, which was set for Obama and others to sign at a conference in Copenhagen.

Monckton told his audience that at that conference, "a treaty will be signed. Your president will sign it. Most of the third world countries will sign it, because they think they're going to get money out of it. Most of the left-wing regimes from the European Union will rubber stamp it. Virtually nobody won't sign it." And he issued a warning: "I have read that treaty. And what it says is this: that a world government is going to be created. The word 'government' actually appears as the first of three purposes of the new entity. The second purpose is the transfer of wealth from the countries of the West to third world countries, in satisfaction of what is called, coyly, 'climate debt'— because we've been burning CO2 and they haven't. We've been screwing up the climate and they haven't. And the third purpose of this new entity, this government, is enforcement."

While Monckton's words were greeted with skepticism, in fact the United Nations Framework Convention on Climate Change backed him up completely. And Barack Obama, with all his hard-line socialist associations and policies, was hardly one to stand up in opposition to a measure that embodied so many of his core beliefs. Monckton explained the nature of the government envisioned in the climate change treaty—and it sounded like the government of Obama's dreams. He pointed out that the words "election," "democracy," "vote," and "ballot" do not appear in the treaty, and declared that this treaty would "impose a communist world government on the world. You have a president who has very strong sympathies with that point of view. He's going to sign it. He'll sign anything. He's a Nobel Peace Prize [winner]; of course he'll sign it."

Monckton declared that this treaty would supersede U.S. law and eclipse American sovereignty: "And the trouble is this; if that treaty is signed, your Constitution says that it takes precedence over your Constitution, and you can't resign from that treaty unless you get agreement from all the other state parties—And because you'll be the biggest paying country, they're not going to let you out of it." He apparently based this view on Article VI of the U.S. Constitution, which stipulates: "This Constitution, and the Laws of the United States which shall be made in Pursuance thereof; and all Treaties made, or which shall be made, under the Authority of the United States, shall be the supreme Law of the Land; and the Judges in every State shall be bound thereby, any Thing in the Constitution or Laws of any State to the Contrary notwithstanding." If "Treaties" are to be the "supreme Law of the Land," theoretically Obama's climate treaty could supersede U.S. laws that may contradict it.

Accordingly Monckton concluded with a warning: "In the next few weeks, unless you stop it, your president will sign your freedom, your democracy, and your humanity away forever. And neither you nor any subsequent government you may elect will have any power whatsoever to take it back. That is how serious it is. I've read the treaty. I've seen this stuff about [world] government and climate debt and enforcement. They are going to do this to you whether you like it or not." [34]

As Herman Van Rompuy, the first Lisbon Treaty–era president of Europe, put it: "2009 is the first year of global governance." [35]

Perhaps stung by the publicity that Monckton's warning received, an Obama administration official announced ten days later, on October 24, that the post-American president was "leaning toward not going" to Copenhagen. He said that Obama would instead address climate change issues during his Nobel Prize acceptance speech. But the treaty would remain unsigned.

For the time being.

Climategate, the explosive revelations that the evidence of manmade global warming was largely fabricated, should have changed all that. But genuine science seemed to have little to do with the international environmental-global-industrial complex.

Obama, meanwhile, had made appointments in line with his overall internationalist goals.

INTERNATIONALIST ON THE SUPREME COURT

When Justice David Souter retired from the Supreme Court, Obama chose Sonia Sotomayor, judge of the United States Court of Appeals for the Second Circuit, as his replacement. Quickly approved, Sotomayor joined the high court on August 6, 2009.

An internationalist had joined the Supreme Court.

In 2007, Sotomayor contributed a foreword to a book entitled *The International Judge*, by Daniel Terris, Cesare P. R. Romano, and Leigh Swigart. In it, Sotomayor emphasized how important it was to consider "how much we have to learn from foreign law and the international community when interpreting our Constitution. . . ." She added: "We should also question how much we have to learn from international courts and from their male and female judges about the process of judging and the factors outside of the law that influence our decisions." [36]

This was Sotomayor's consistent line of thought. In April 2009, addressing the American Civil Liberties Union of Puerto Rico, Judge

Sotomayor again declared in effect her support for a role for international law in deciding cases stateside: "international law and foreign law," she said, "will be very important in the discussion of how to think about the unsettled issues in our own legal system." Opponents of the consideration of international laws and foreign laws to decide cases in the United States were "asking American judges to close their minds to good ideas." She referred to cases in American courts where foreign precedents were used to "help us understand what the concepts meant to other countries and . . . whether our understanding of our own constitutional rights fell into the mainstream of human thinking."

Would the concepts of the freedom of speech and legal equality of women with men fall into "the mainstream of human thinking" today? Not with the rapid advance of Sharia norms in Islamic countries (as well as in the West). Not with the increase of authoritarian governments in countries all over the world. And not with the post-American president paying only the vaguest lip service to the freedom of speech, while working in all sorts of ways to undermine it.

The hazards of Sotomayor's approach were many. *The Wall Street Journal* asked a pointed question in an editorial published just as Sotomayor's confirmation hearings were about to begin: "If one judge may look to the courts of Western Europe for expansion of liberal thoughts on human rights, why may another not look to decidedly less liberal ideas? Iran allows women who appear without a hijab on the streets to be lashed 74 times. China limits families to bearing one child. Even the democracies of Western Europe have laws that differ broadly from ours. Few countries, for instance, share our rules protecting the rights of the accused, or have the U.S.'s constitutionally mandated separation of church and state."[37]

Besides her internationalism, Sotomayor had something else in common with the president who appointed her: a predilection for racial grievance mongering and manipulation. While studying law at Princeton, Sotomayor's writings demonstrated a preoccupation with racial politics: she was the author of *Race in the American Classroom* and *Undying Injustice: American "Exceptionalism" and Permanent Bigotry*. She saw the distinctive features of America, the things that made this nation powerful and free, as liabilities rather than virtues. Instead of Ronald Reagan's "shining city on a hill," America in the reign of the post-American president and his post-American advisers and colleagues would become less and less exceptional, less and less distinctive, less and less different from the rest of the world.

And in so doing, it would cease to be the refuge to which those yearning to breathe free would turn. For the tired, the poor, the huddled masses would soon come to know that there was no freedom, no prosperity, no legal protection for them in the United States of America. Not anymore.

Sonia Sotomayor also showed a distaste for the Second Amendment similar to that of the president, who derided those who "cling" to their guns. In *Deadly Obsession: American Gun Culture*, she argued that the very idea that private citizens could own guns in the United States was based on a misunderstanding. There was, she claimed, actually no right to bear arms that was guaranteed to citizens by the Second Amendment. Rather, she said, this right pertained to militias only.[38]

Not surprisingly, Sotomayor was not the only Obama appointment that struck at the very principle of American sovereignty.

TRANSNATIONALISM, SHARIA, AND AMERICAN LAW

Obama seemed determined to turn over the Land of the Free to global forces with interests decidedly different from the best interests of Americans. And that included Islamic supremacists—whose attachment to Sharia was apparently just fine by Harold Koh, the internationalist lawyer whom Obama tabbed in April 2009 to become the legal adviser for the State Department.

Obama should have abandoned the climate warming hoax as soon as "the miracle" happened. But this would never happen. Global warming is a tool to "level the playing field," to weaken America, and to burden her with crippling taxes while enriching her enemies and competitors.

Superficially, Koh had impressive enough credentials. He served as a law clerk for Supreme Court Justice Harry Blackmun in 1981 and 1982, and then worked in the Justice Department's Office of Legal Council (OLC) from 1983 to 1985. He became a professor at Yale Law School in 1985 and dean in 2004, and from 1998 to 2001 he was assistant secretary of state for democracy, human rights, and labor. He has written many books, including *Transnational Legal Problems* (with Harry Steiner and Detlev Vagts) and *Transnational Litigation in United States Courts*, as well as numerous articles and monographs, including one entitled *International Law as Part of Our Law*, which was published in *The American Journal of International Law*.

The titles reveal a substantial, focus of Harold Koh's legal scholarship—one that raised concerns among Obama's critics that he was appointing an internationalist, someone who would not necessarily have America's best interests at heart, to a key position at State. Koh's own words confirm this: "As American lawyers, scholars, and activists," he wrote in 2003, "we should make better use of transnational legal process to press our own government to avoid the most negative and damaging features of American exceptionalism." These "negative and damaging features" include "U.S. insistence upon double standards," including having the effrontery to think that "a different rule" should "apply to itself than applies to the rest of the world."

Koh zeroes in on the freedom of speech, warning that "our exceptional free speech tradition can cause problems abroad, as, for example, may occur when hate speech is disseminated over the Internet." What can be done to solve these "problems"? The Supreme Court "can moderate these conflicts by applying more consistently the transnationalist approach to judicial interpretation."[39]

In a world that generally values the freedom of speech, as well as the freedom of conscience and the legal equality of all people, far less than does the United States of America, the implications of this are clear: erasing the distinctions between American law and international law would mean an erosion of the rights and freedoms of Americans, and a concomitant deterioration of American society.

Referring to the implications of Koh's appointment, Glenn Beck thundered: "Once we sign our rights over to international law, the Constitution is officially dead." However, Obama's defenders were dismissive: Pamela S. Karlan, a professor at Stanford Law School, said that concern over Koh's internationalism was "all just an attempt to whip up hysteria." White House spokesman Reid Cherlin said it was all an invention of the right-wing attack machine out to discredit Obama by misrepresenting one of his key appointees: "You have political opponents of the president who are motivated by their opposition to his agenda who are mischaracterizing or fabricating statements by Dean Koh."[40]

In reality, however, none of the genuine concerns about Harold Koh's internationalism and slight attachment (at best) to American sovereignty were fabricated. Koh really was a committed transnationalist who believed that American law should be subject to foreign authorities and informed by foreign precedents—a fact that should make every American demand that Barack Obama fire him. But, of course, Obama will never do that: there is no indication that the post-American president's views on transnationalism differ in any serious way from Koh's.

Legal expert M. Edward Whelan III explains that transnationalism "challenges the traditional American understanding that (in the summary, which I slightly adapt, of Duke law professor Curtis A. Bradley) 'international and domestic law are distinct, [the United States] determines for itself [through its political branches] when and to what extent international law is incorporated into its legal system, and the status of international law in the domestic system is determined by domestic law.' Transnationalists aim in particular to use American courts to import international law to override the policies adopted through the processes of representative government."

Whelan is the president of the Ethics and Public Policy Center, the former general counsel to the U.S. Senate Committee on the Judiciary, former principal deputy assistant attorney general for the Office of Legal Counsel in the U.S. Department of Justice, and like Koh a former law clerk for a Supreme Court justice (in Whelan's case, Antonin Scalia). "Harold Koh's transnationalist legal views," he declared before Koh's nomination as State Department legal adviser was approved, "threaten fundamental American principles of representative government and . . . Koh would be particularly well positioned as State Department legal adviser to implement his views and to inflict severe and lasting damage. . . . Among other things, he would be advising on the legal positions that the United States should be taking in federal courts on issues arguably implicating international law and before international bodies; he would be counseling State Department officials on international negotiations, treaty interpretation, and treaty implementation; and he would be a major player in interagency disputes on all these matters."

"What transnationalism, at bottom, is all about," Whelan explains, "is depriving American citizens of their powers of representative government by selectively imposing on them the favored policies of Europe's leftist elites." In contrast, "proponents of a nationalist jurisprudence view 'foreign legal precedents' as 'an impermissible imposition on the exercise of American sovereignty.'"

And Harold Koh is a "leading advocate of transnationalism. Further, on the spectrum of transnationalists, ranging from those who are more modest and Americanist in their objectives and sympathies to those who are more extreme and internationalist (or Europeanist), Koh is definitely in the latter category. He is also very smart, savvy, determined, and dogmatic."

Whelan sees Koh's embrace of transnationalism as essentially absolute: "If there are any limits—beyond intrusions on recognized individual constitutional rights—that Koh would place on the legitimate and desirable use of the treaty power to regulate domestic social and economic policy, I have not yet run across them in his writings."

Resistance to this internationalism would be very difficult. Whelan explains: "The only available recourse for pesky citizens who still believe in the system of representative government that our Constitution creates will be congressional action to override the new CIL [customary international law] norms, action that would require a veto-proof majority in both houses of Congress while President Obama or any Europeanist successors of his are in office. Such action will be made all the more difficult as the cultural elites clamor for Americans to show proper deference to international law and the federal judiciary."[41]

Among numerous questionable and controversial statements, Koh had said that the "war on terror"—a term that the Obama administration had by then already quietly abandoned—was "obsessive." And in a 2007 speech that became notorious when Obama nominated him, Koh opined (according to a lawyer who was in the audience, as reported in the *New York Post*) that "in an appropriate case, he didn't see any reason why sharia law would not be applied to govern a case in the United States."[42]

Asked for comment, a spokeswoman for Koh waved the incident

away: "I had heard that some guy . . . had asked a question about sharia law, and that Dean Koh had said something about that while there are obvious differences among the many different legal systems, they also share some common legal concepts."[43] What's more, Robin Reeves Zorthian, president of the Yale Alumni Association of Greenwich, Connecticut, said that the *Post*'s account was "totally fictitious and inaccurate. I was in the room with my husband and several fellow alumni, and we are all adamant that Koh never said or suggested that sharia law could be used to govern cases in US courts. The subject of his talk was Globalization and Yale Law School, so, of course, other forms of law were mentioned. But never did Koh state or suggest that other forms of law should govern or dictate the American legal system."[44]

What was at issue, however, was not whether Koh had said that Sharia should "govern or dictate the American legal system." The question was whether he said it could be used to determine the outcome of a particular case in an American courtroom. And given Koh's demonstrable affinity for the use of international legal principles and precedents in American courts, there was no reason why he would not have said something like this, and certainly no indication that he would oppose such a practice.

Perhaps Koh had something in mind akin to what the Archbishop of Canterbury, Rowan Williams, was thinking when he made a notorious statement in 2008 that Islamic law was "unavoidable" in Britain. Williams didn't mean that Britain would become a Sharia state, but only that Muslims could have recourse to private Sharia arbitration for marital disputes, inheritance matters, and the like. Stonings and amputations? Of course not. "Nobody in their right mind," said Williams, "would want to see in this country the kind of inhumanity that's sometimes been associated with the practice of the law in some Islamic states; the extreme punishments, the attitudes to women as well." But, he concluded, the idea that "there's one law for everybody . . . I think that's a bit of a danger."[45]

Equality of treatment and equality of rights for all people? A dangerous concept!

One may have hoped that Koh wouldn't go that far, but in saying that "in an appropriate case" Sharia legal principles could be applied in the United States, he seems to be opening the door to Sharia courts in the United States, instituted after the pattern already established in Britain.

Sharia courts are already operating there, and multiculturalists dismiss concerns about them by insisting that they're just private, voluntary arbitration tribunals, like similar arbitration panels for Jews and Catholics. The analogy, however, is not exact. Jewish family courts and Catholic marriage tribunals claim authority only over those who accept that authority, i.e., those who believe in the tenets of those faiths. What's more, such courts claim no authority beyond their narrow purview, such that most legal matters are beyond their scope. Islamic law, by contrast, asserts itself as the only legitimate law for all areas of human life—not just marriage and family law, and by no means just religious law, but as the sole legal foundation for every aspect of social and political life.

As such, Sharia claims jurisdiction over non-Muslims as well as Muslims. The great Pakistani Islamic theorist of the twentieth century, Sayyid Abul Ala Maududi, whose writings remain internationally influential among Muslims today, wrote that non-Muslims have "absolutely no right to seize the reins of power in any part of God's earth, nor to direct the collective affairs of human beings according to their own misconceived doctrines." If they do, "the believers would be under an obligation to do their utmost to dislodge them from political power and to make them live in subservience to the Islamic way of life." In accord with this, there is no concept in the Qur'an, Islamic tradition, or Islamic law of non-Muslims living as equals with Muslims in an Islamic state: Muslims must be in a superior position.

And so it comes as no surprise that those private Sharia courts in Britain are already coming into conflict with British law. Recently Sharia courts in Britain have been allowed to adjudicate cases of domestic violence rather than have those cases referred to the criminal courts, even though the Qur'an directs men to beat disobedient women (4:34)—a directive likely to find the battered woman's complaint falling on deaf ears in a Sharia court.

Sharia is a complex and comprehensive unity that traditional Muslims believe to be the unalterable law of Allah. To open the door to one aspect of it is only to open the door to the rest—which inevitably will result in the institutionalized subjugation of women and non-Muslims, and the extinguishing of freedom of speech and freedom of conscience. Consequently, all free people may have hoped that Koh would reconsider his earlier naïve approval of the coming of Sharia to the Land of the Free.

But given Barack Obama's warm praise for all things Islamic and thoroughgoing commitment to internationalism, nothing seemed less likely.

GIVING UP SOVEREIGNTY FOR GUN CONTROL

Obama was also actively engaged in efforts to extend the authority of United Nations gun control initiatives to the United States, using them to limit the freedoms guaranteed by the Second Amendment.

"In most cases," according to the National Rifle Association, "agendas for the elimination of private ownership of firearms are disguised as calls for international arms control to stem the flow of illicit military weapons. These instruments are generally promoted by a small group of nations and a large number of Non-Governmental Organizations

(NGOs) working in conjunction with departmental bureaucracies in multi-national institutions such as the UN and European Union."

While the Bush administration had opposed such initiatives, Obama reversed course, actively cooperating with the UN and the EU on the development of the Arms Trade Treaty (ATT), which would severely restrict Second Amendment rights within the United States.[46]

Would the Second Amendment stop the importation of weapons restrictions laws into the United States? The question was the same as for the First Amendment and free speech: all Obama needed to circumvent the Constitutional protections was a pliant Supreme Court, aided and abetted by an ideologically driven media. He had the media, and with a few retirements would have the Supreme Court as well.

John Bolton observed that Obama might use "norming" to impose gun control laws on America. "I think it would work this way: They know, for example, that legislation restricting gun rights—infringing on the Second Amendment—would be very unpopular and very hard to get through Congress. They may want to do it to repay certain of their constituencies, but they know there would be a fight. If it comes in through the back door, where they can say, 'Well, look, this is an international agreement,' then it's a lot easier to say we're simply going along with something else that may have other benefits for the U.S."

Bolton said that UN internationalists were just waiting for Bush to leave in order to try to force the United States to accept international protocols. "People in the U.N. system, the Non-Governmental Organizations, basically concluded they weren't going to get anything through while Bush was president. So they've been waiting, they've been holding back, and it's precisely what they've been waiting for—the right guy to get in the White House. I think they believe they have found him. And that's why I think groups that care about Second Amendment rights—groups like the NRA and all of its members—really have to pay very close attention to what's going on in the State

Department and New York for the next four years. In a diplomatic world, a lot takes place below the radar screen. You don't see it until it's essentially a done deal, when it's much harder to oppose."

Groups lobbying at the UN for international arms control legislation restricting weapons distribution in combat zones have a "hidden agenda," said Bolton. "In fact it's not so hidden to many of these groups," and it "is not weapons flowing to conflict zones. It's imposing their domestic agenda, particularly on the United States, to get gun laws enacted here in ways they couldn't possibly be successful in doing in Congress. They'd much rather lobby the U.N. than our own Congress."[47]

Apparently, so would Barack Obama.

WHAT'S WRONG WITH INTERNATIONALISM?

As Barack Obama made significant moves during his first year in office to subject the United States to the authority of the UN and the OIC, Americans remained largely indifferent. Of course, the mainstream media did not report on these initiatives. But informed citizens knew what was at stake.

Decades before the post-American president took office, Ayn Rand saw the UN for what it was, and what every free person should have known it was—and it has only gotten worse since then: "Psychologically, the U.N. has contributed a great deal to the gray swamp of demoralization—of cynicism, bitterness, hopelessness, fear and nameless guilt—which is swallowing the Western world."[48] That, of course, was just the kind of guilt Obama and his cronies were playing upon. This guilt and demoralization was largely due to Communism in those days; now the "gray swamp" is still there, but it stems from Islam.

The similarities between Communism and Islam are many. French sociologist Jules Monnerot, in his 1949 *Sociologie du communisme*, which was published in English as *Sociology and Psychology of Communism*, concluded that "Bolshevism combines the characteristics of the French Revolution with those of the rise of Islam."[49] And today Islam is enjoying the same success in intimidating the West and keeping it off balance that Communism once did—and in the same way, with willing help from subjugated Westerners. "The communist world," Rand continued, in words that apply equally to the Islamic world today, "has gained a moral sanction, a stamp of civilized respectability from the Western world—it has gained the status and prestige of an equal partner, thus establishing the notion that the difference between human rights and mass slaughter is merely a difference of political opinion."

Whether Obama thought that making such concessions to thugs would pacify them, or whether he actively favored their cause, or both, was unclear. In any case, he seemed determined to feed the beast, to the detriment of those he had sworn to protect.

And to the detriment of the free and sovereign nation he was supposed to be leading.

So the question comes to mind yet again: Who is this guy?

TWO

THE INDOCTRINATION
OF BARACK OBAMA

HOW DID BARACK OBAMA BECOME THE LEADER OF A NATION WHOSE POWER HE SEEMED DETERMINED TO DIMINISH?

Some assumed that he must not have known what he was doing, but was carried along by inexperience and naïveté into embracing policies that were disastrous for the nation and the world. But this view was at odds with the assessment of his political rivals and colleagues, who during the rough and tumble of the 2008 presidential campaign increasingly regarded him—according to a July 2008 *New Yorker* profile—as a "pure political animal": after Obama outfoxed John McCain on the issue of campaign finance reform, "commentators abruptly stopped using the words 'callow' and 'naïve.'"[1]

The key to Barack Obama's policies and activities as president lies in beliefs and assumptions that he began to absorb in his earliest upbringing—often in associations and events that he has done his best to obscure. But they must be explored. Before understanding why Obama does what he does, it's important to review his schooling, his parents' social mores, their political beliefs, his gurus, his mentors, his friends, and his associations. Essentially, these things are what made Obama what he is.

The unique and singular beauty of America is that we are not a single race, creed, or color. Ours is a shared value system. Rugged individualism, property rights, intellectual property rights, freedom of speech and religion and the right to assemble—we are wet-nursed on such basic unalienable human freedoms. We assume these freedoms, like we assume the very air we breathe. No other country can say such a thing. This is what makes America exceptional, an historic anomaly, blessed and gifted. This is how America is built.

But Barack Obama was not built this way. He did not grow up this way. Since America is not an ethnicity, but a value system, in order to *be* American, in order to "get" America, one has to have grown up in America, and to have soaked in the idea of living free—growing up under the righteous glow of the Declaration of Independence and the Constitution. This is neither tribal nor collective. It is singular and individual—America is the place where one man is not at the mercy of mob rule or minority plotting.

But Barack Hussein Obama wasn't always Barack Hussein Obama. From 1967 to 1971, he was Barry Soetoro, an elementary school student in Jakarta, Indonesia. Barack Hussein Obama spent four of his crucial formative years, from the ages of six to ten, outside the United States, in the largest Muslim country in the world. His father was a Muslim from Kenya; his stepfather a Muslim from Indonesia. Even when he moved to the United States, he came to a place that was far from the American heartland both geographically and culturally. "Hawaii," according to the *Chicago Tribune*, "had become a state only two years before Obama's birth, and there were plenty of native Hawaiians still deeply unhappy about it. . . . The arc of Obama's personal journey took him to places and situations far removed from the experience of most Americans."[2]

While in Indonesia also, Obama's family lived "as Indonesians lived." Much later, he recalled that the family lived what in America would have been considered a life of poverty: "We lived in a modest house on the outskirts of town, without air-conditioning, refrigeration, or flush toilets. We had no car—my stepfather rode a motorcycle, while my mother took the local jitney service every morning to the US embassy, where she worked as an English teacher. Without the money to go to the international school that most expatriate children attended, I went to local Indonesian schools and ran the streets with the children of farmers, servants, tailors and clerks."

The future president recalled a decidedly Indonesian childhood, saying he spent his days "chasing down chickens and running from water buffalo."[3] He recounted much later: "When I think of (Bali) and all of Indonesia, I am haunted by memories—the feel of packed mud under bare feet as I wander through paddy fields; the sight of day breaking behind volcanic peaks; the muezzin's call at night and the smell of wood smoke; the dickering at the fruit stands alongside the road; the frenzied sound of a gamelan orchestra, the musicians' faces lit by fire."[4]

Occasionally his mother would take him to the American Club, "where I could jump in the pool and watch cartoons and sip Coca-Cola to my heart's content." Obama said in his second autobiography, *The Audacity of Hope*, that he knew that he and his mother were "citizens of the United States, beneficiaries of its power, safe and secure under the blanket of its protection."[5]

Yet his mother appeared dedicated to undermining that power and stripping American citizens of that safety and security. For Barack Obama's mother, Stanley Ann Dunham, was a communist. She moved in communist circles and had communist friends. Her parents put her in a high school run by a self-proclaimed communist who had been hauled before the House Un-American Activities Committee. A high school friend described her as a "fellow traveler," and in both high school and college she moved in the most radical circles in her area.[6]

Stanley Ann Dunham met Barack Hussein Obama, Sr., in 1960, at the height of the Cold War, in a Russian class at the University of Hawaii.[7] It was, no doubt, a meeting of the minds: Obama, Sr., according to journalist Andrew Walden, "left behind a published record of an embrace of communist policies."[8] And why was Obama's mother taking Russian-language classes in 1960—the height of communist antagonism toward the West? Stanley Ann Dunham had no interest in becoming a diplomat.

Obama recalled that when Lolo Soetoro got a job with an American oil company in Indonesia, the family's standard of living improved considerably. They moved to a better house and bought a car, a television, and a record player. But instead of being pleased, Stanley Ann Dunham Obama Soetoro's Marxist consciousness was offended. "Looking back," Obama writes in his first autobiography, *Dreams from My Father*, "I'm not sure that Lolo ever fully understood what my mother was going through during these years, why the things he was working so hard to provide for her seemed only to increase the distance between them." As if there was something normal, right, and logical about his mother's reaction.

Apparently no one had clued Lolo in on white guilt, middle-class guilt, and the agony of a socialist consciousness that has been raised. Obama recalled later that his mother argued with Lolo Soetoro over her refusal to go to dinner parties at the oil company. Obama describes these as dinner parties from hell, choked with crude, boorish Ugly Americans: "American businessmen from Texas and Louisiana would slap Lolo's back and boast about the palms they had greased to obtain the new offshore drilling rights, while their wives complained to my mother about the quality of Indonesian help." Lolo asked Stanley Ann to consider "how it would look for him to go alone, and remind her that these were her own people."

In response, Obama remembered, "my mother's voice would rise to almost a shout. They are *not* my people."[9]

Yet that was far from the picture Obama painted of her as he ran for president. "My mother, whose parents were nonpracticing Baptists and Methodists," said Obama during the campaign, "was one of the most spiritual souls I ever knew. . . . She believed that people were all basically the same under their skin, that bigotry of any sort was wrong and that the goal was then to treat everybody as unique individuals."[10]

He said nothing about her radical leftism and Marxism.

Yet this was the milieu in which young Barack Obama grew up. This was the early air he breathed, the early intellectual food he feasted upon. He has called his mother "the dominant figure in my formative years. . . . The values she taught me continue to be my touchstone when it comes to how I go about the world of politics."[11] Certainly he has maintained and strengthened associations that his mother made in those years: Morgan Reynolds, a professor emeritus at Texas A&M University and former chief economist for the Department of Labor, reports that "Peter Geithner oversaw the 'microfinance' programs developed in Indonesia by Ann Dunham-Soetoro, Barack Obama's mother."[12]

Barack Obama appointed Peter Geithner's son, Timothy Geithner, secretary of the Treasury.

Once in Hawaii, Obama's radical associations continued. He went to Sunday school at the First Unitarian Church of Honolulu, a highly politicized church that aligned during the 1970s with the radical group Students for a Democratic Society (SDS)—a group in which a future Obama comrade played a significant role: Bill Ayers.[13]

FRANK MARSHALL DAVIS

In *Dreams from My Father*, Obama writes affectionately about "Frank," whose full name he never gives.[14] During the 2008 campaign, the Obama camp acknowledged that "Frank" was poet, journalist, and activist Frank Marshall Davis.[15]

Davis was yet another communist—indeed, a Communist Party member.[16] According to Gerald Horne, a contributing editor of the Communist Party, USA magazine *Political Affairs*, Davis lived in the same places as Obama and his family, but not always at the same time: he "was born in Kansas and spent a good deal of his adult life in Chicago, before decamping to Honolulu in 1948 at the suggestion of his good friend Paul Robeson."[17] (Robeson, of course, was another communist.) Once in Hawaii, Horne explained that Davis eventually "befriended another family—a Euro-American family—that had migrated to Honolulu from Kansas and a young woman from this family eventually had a child with a young student from Kenya East Africa who goes by the name of Barack Obama, who retracing the steps of Davis eventually decamped to Chicago."[18] Maya Soetoro-Ng, Obama's half sister, recalled that their grandfather, Stanley Dunham, encouraged Davis and Obama to form a bond, regarding Davis as "a point of connection, a bridge if you will, to the larger African-American experience for my brother."[19]

Davis was hardly a wholesome acquaintance. He wrote a pseudonymous pornographic book, *Sex Rebel: Black* in which he stated in an introduction that "all incidents I have described have been taken from actual experiences." He said that "under certain circumstances I am bisexual," as well as being a "voyeur and an exhibitionist" with an interest in "sado-masochism." He mused: "I have often wished I had two penises to enjoy simultaneously the double—but different—sensations of oral and genital copulation." In the book Davis describes how he and his wife bedded a thirteen-year-old girl named Anne. He portrayed this as a favor to the girl.[20]

And this pedophile and child rapist was an overwhelming and warmly remembered influence on the future post-American president.

But for Obama, of course, Davis was not an instructor in unconventional sexual practices. He seems to have instructed young Barack Obama in leftism and racial grievance mongering. Horne recalled that in *Dreams from My Father*, Obama "speaks warmly of an older black poet, he identifies simply as 'Frank' as being a decisive influence in helping him to find his present identity as an African-American, a people who have been the least anticommunist and the most left-leaning of any constituency in this nation."[21]

From the looks of his portrayal in *Dreams from My Father*, Frank Marshall Davis was a principal influence on the race-baiting and polarization that Barack Obama would make a centerpiece of his presidency. This is no surprise: *Dreams from My Father* is itself a political manifesto cast as a first-person narrative in order to make the ideologies of internationalism, socialism, and race hate palatable to left-leaning Americans.

OBAMA AND ISLAM

One of the most peculiar lessons of the presidential campaign of 2008 was that you could disparage someone merely by saying his name. During the campaign of 2008, to speak of Barack Obama's Muslim roots and ties suddenly became akin to disparaging and insulting him, and engaging in bigotry and innuendo. I had written about these links early on and for doing so was called bigot, racist, and Islamophobe.

Obama went to extraordinary measures to obfuscate his Muslim background. The more proof that bloggers like me produced, the more we were marginalized. So secretive was Obama that he refused to release his long-form birth certificate, his school records, his thesis, his school records, his passport on which he traveled as a teen . . . the list itself was a looming red flag.

And then suddenly, after the election, in 2009, it was no longer "racism" to point out Obama's Muslim roots. They became a point of pride for him and a centerpiece of his outreach to the Muslim world. It was a curious turnabout, and one with important implications.

ISLAMIC LAW OR A CONSTITUTIONAL REPUBLIC?

In 2008, Obama's evident embarrassment over his early Muslim connections was a tacit acknowledgment of the legitimacy of many Americans' concerns about Islam's supremacist and violent elements. But his turnabout made clear that he had no such concerns himself, and would do little or nothing as president to address them.

Yet those concerns were of immense import. Islamic law and democracy, Islamic law and a free constitutional republic, are incompatible. Every precious freedom that is protected by the American rule of law is prohibited in Islam. And Islam traditionally allows for no competition. The influential twentieth-century Pakistani jihad theorist Sayyid Abul Ala Maududi (1903–1979) explained it forthrightly: "Islam wishes to destroy all States and Governments anywhere on the face of the earth which are opposed to the ideology and programme of Islam regardless of the country or the Nation which rules it."

According to Maududi, at that point Sharia law will be put in their place: "The purpose of Islam is to set up a State on the basis of its own ideology and programme, regardless of which Nation assumes the role of the standard-bearer of Islam or the rule of which nation is undermined in the process of the establishment of an ideological Islamic State."[22]

The First Amendment to the Constitution stipulates that "Congress shall make no law respecting an establishment of religion, or prohibiting the free exercise thereof." This was one of the most masterful achievements of the Founding Fathers: providing the foundation for a society in which people may differ from one another in conscience but live together as equals without one group trying to gain hegemony over the other.

This is a far cry from the 1998 statement by Omar Ahmad, the cofounder and longtime board chairman of America's foremost Islamic pressure group, the Council on American-Islamic Relations (CAIR). "Islam," said Ahmad, "isn't in America to be equal to any other faith, but to become dominant. The Koran should be the highest authority in America, and Islam the only accepted religion on Earth."

After he received unwelcome publicity as a result of this statement, Ahmad denied saying it, several years after the fact. However, the original reporter, Lisa Gardiner of the *Fremont Argus*, stands by her story. Art Moore of *WorldNetDaily* asked Gardiner in December 2006 about Ahmad's statement, and reported: "Gardiner, who now works for a non-profit group, told WND last week she's 100-percent sure Ahmad was the speaker and that he made those statements, pointing out nobody challenged the story at the time it was published eight years ago." In response, Ahmad snapped: "She's lying. Absolutely, she's lying. How could you remember something from so long ago? I don't even remember her in the audience." But he failed to come up with any explanation of why a reporter for an obscure local paper would fabricate such an egregious falsehood about him. What's more,

CAIR's spokesman, the acerbic and combative American convert Ibrahim Hooper, once said in a similar vein: "I wouldn't want to create the impression that I wouldn't like the government of the United States to be Islamic sometime in the future."[23]

In service of this aim, the international Islamic organization known as the Muslim Brotherhood, which operates in the United States under a variety of names and organizational umbrellas, describes its own mission in this country (according to a document captured in a raid and released by law enforcement in 2007) as "a kind of grand Jihad in eliminating and destroying the Western civilization from within and 'sabotaging' its miserable house by their hands and the hands of the believers so that it is eliminated and God's religion is made victorious over all other religions."[24]

The goal of "God's religion"—Islam—being made "victorious over other religions" was a political, not solely a religious one. The Islamic law that the Muslim Brotherhood wanted to impose was a comprehensive system covering every aspect of society—and restricting many freedoms that Americans cherished. Chief among these was the freedom of speech: while the First Amendment protects not only the freedom of religion but also the freedom of speech and of the press, Islamic law stipulates that non-Muslims are forbidden to say "something impermissible about Allah, the Prophet . . . or Islam."[25]

In line with this, riots broke out in several Muslim countries in 2006 over cartoons of the Islamic prophet Muhammad that appeared in a Danish newspaper. That became the impetus for an all-out effort by the fifty-seven-nation Organization of the Islamic Conference (OIC), the largest voting bloc at the United Nations, to try to compel Western nations to restrict the freedom of speech when it came to Islam—including antiterror analyses that discussed the Islamic texts and teachings that jihadists used to make recruits and justify their actions among peaceful Muslims.

Ekmeleddin Ihsanoglu, secretary-general of the OIC (whom Obama has since had to the White House), made it clear that he was the one dictating terms: "In confronting the Danish cartoons and the Dutch film 'Fitna' [a film critical of Islam made by the Dutch politician Geert Wilders], we sent a clear message to the West regarding the red lines that should not be crossed. As we speak, the official West and its public opinion are all now well-aware of the sensitivities of these issues. They have also started to look seriously into the question of freedom of expression from the perspective of its inherent responsibility, which should not be overlooked."

The OIC's influence is considerable. Historian Bat Ye'or explains that the OIC is "one of the largest intergovernmental organizations in the world. It encompasses 56 Muslim states plus the Palestinian Authority. Spread over four continents, it claims to speak in the name of the *Ummah* (the universal Muslim community), which numbers about 1.3 billion. The OIC's mission is to unite all Muslims worldwide by rooting them in the Koran and the Sunnah—the core of traditional Islamic civilization and values. It aims at strengthening solidarity and cooperation among all its members, in order to protect the interests of Muslims everywhere and to galvanize the ummah into a unified body. The OIC is a unique organization—one that has no equivalent in the world. It unites the religious, economic, military, and political strength of 56 states."

And it is a sworn enemy of the freedom of speech. "In its efforts to defend the 'true image' of Islam and combat its defamation," Bat Ye'or explains, "the organization has requested the UN and the Western countries to punish 'Islamophobia' and blasphemy. Among the manifestations of Islamophobia, in the OIC's view, are European opposition to illegal immigration, anti-terrorist measures, criticism of multiculturalism, and indeed any efforts to defend Western cultural and national identities."[26]

The OIC had an ally in Barack Hussein Obama. As we shall see later, when he became president, Barack Obama, in a sharp departure from the policy of his predecessor, showed an eagerness not to cross those "red lines." He even went so far as recommending criminal penalties for those who did.

Strange behavior for a man who swore to preserve, protect, and defend the Constitution of the United States—including the freedom of speech.

Islamic law is also incompatible with the ringing words of the Declaration of Independence: "We hold these truths to be self-evident, that all men are created equal, that they are endowed by their Creator with certain unalienable Rights, that among these are Life, Liberty and the pursuit of Happiness."

In Islam, the idea that all are not equal, and do not share unalienable rights, arises from the sharp dichotomy between believer and unbeliever that runs through the Qur'an and the religion as a whole. A manual of Islamic law endorsed by Al-Azhar University in Cairo, Egypt, the most respected and prestigious institution in Sunni Islam (which comprises 85 to 90 percent of Muslims worldwide), elaborates a system of blood money payments in restitution for a killing—but the payments are less if the victim was a woman or a non-Muslim: "The indemnity for the death or injury of a woman is one-half the indemnity paid for a man. The indemnity paid for a Jew or Christian is one-third the indemnity paid for a Muslim. The indemnity paid for a Zoroastrian is one-fifteenth that of a Muslim."[27]

Perhaps most importantly of all, the Declaration of Independence asserts that governments derive their "just powers from the consent of the governed." By contrast, in Islamic law all authority derives from Allah alone—and accordingly, non-Muslims have no right to hold political power, at any time, in any place. The internationally influential Pakistani jihad theorist Sayyid Abul Ala Maududi explained that non-

Muslims have "absolutely no right to seize the reins of power in any part of God's earth nor to direct the collective affairs of human beings according to their own misconceived doctrines." If they did this, "the believers would be under an obligation to do their utmost to dislodge them from political power and to make them live in subservience to the Islamic way of life."

THE HUSSEIN WARS

On February 26, 2008, Bill Cunningham, a popular radio host in Cincinnati, spoke at a rally there for Republican candidate John McCain. Cunningham referred at least three times to "Barack Hussein Obama." McCain repudiated Cunningham and his remarks even before anyone asked him to do so.[28] When asked later if using Obama's middle name was appropriate, McCain responded, "No, it is not. Any comment that is disparaging of either Senator Clinton or Senator Obama is totally inappropriate."[29]

It was "disparaging" Obama and taking the low road simply to call him by his full name? Apparently so. Leftist professor Juan Cole huffed in *Salon* that Obama's name was "a name to be proud of. It is an American name. It is a blessed name. It is a heroic name, as heroic and American in its own way as the name of Gen. Omar Nelson Bradley or the name of Benjamin Franklin. And denigrating that name is a form of racial and religious bigotry of the most vile and debased sort."[30]

It is worth pointing out, however, that Cunningham did not in fact speak disparagingly of Obama's name, or denigrate it. He just used it, without explicit commentary upon it. Of course, McCain, Obama, and the others who took umbrage at this usage were noting the subtext: that Obama's middle name of Hussein, so unfortunately shared with the Iraqi dictator recently toppled by American troops, could imply to some that the Democratic candidate was not quite American, not quite as Christian as he claimed, and possibly holding loyalties to entities at war with the United States.

These implications were what made the usage so offensive—and so throughout the presidential campaign of 2008, commentators on both sides of the political divide studiously avoided even mentioning Obama's middle name, tacitly accepting the contention that Cole articulated, that to do so would be "racial and religious bigotry of the most vile and debased sort."

Obama himself played up this idea, suggesting in June 2008 that the Republicans would run against him by exploiting that bigotry: "The choice is clear. Most of all we can choose between hope and fear. It is going to be very difficult for Republicans to run on their stewardship of the economy or their outstanding foreign policy. We know what kind of campaign they're going to run. They're going to try to make you afraid. They're going to try to make you afraid of me. He's young and inexperienced and he's got a funny name. And did I mention he's black?"[31]

And in September 2008, he expanded upon this theme, telling a crowd in Pennsylvania: "I know that I'm not your typical presidential candidate and I just want to be honest with you. I know that the temptation is to say, 'You know what? The guy hasn't been there that long in Washington. You know, he's got a funny name. You know, we're not sure about him.' And that's what the Republicans when they say this isn't about issues, it's about personalities, what they're really saying is, 'We're going to try to scare people about Barack. So we're going to say that, you know, maybe he's got Muslim connections.' . . . Just making stuff up."[32]

Thus it was all the more surprising when, once elected, Obama began to use that same "funny name" and even to speak about his "Muslim connections." He announced in an interview with the *Chi-*

cago Tribune in December 2008 that he would be sworn in as president as "Barack Hussein Obama," but disclaimed any agenda in doing so: "I think the tradition is that they use all three names, and I will follow the tradition. I'm not trying to make a statement one way or another. I'll do what everybody else does."

However, in the same interview, he gave voice to a desire that would lead to his proudly proclaiming his middle name a few months later: "I think we've got a unique opportunity," he told the *Tribune*, "to reboot America's image around the world and also in the Muslim world in particular." He said he wanted to "create a relationship of mutual respect and partnership in countries and with peoples of good will who want their citizens and ours to prosper together."[33]

OBAMA THE BELIEVER

In pursuit of these goals, when Obama made his much-anticipated major address to the Islamic world from Cairo on June 4, 2009, he proclaimed proudly that "much has been made of the fact that an African-American with the name Barack Hussein Obama could be elected President."[34] In the same speech, he invoked the "Muslim connections" that he had derided during his campaign as dirty tactics from his political opponents: "I am a Christian, but my father came from a Kenyan family that includes generations of Muslims."

However, so anxious was he to appeal to the Islamic world that he made several statements in the speech that Muslims would understand as indicating that he himself was a believer in Islam. He referred several times to the "Holy" Qur'an, and referred to "Moses, Jesus, and Muhammad (peace be upon them)." Muslims generally say "peace be upon him" after mentioning the name of a prophet.

Did Obama mean to imply, then, that he accepted Muhammad as a prophet? And, given the Islamic flavor of his locution here, did he mean to imply also that he accepted the Islamic understanding of Moses and Jesus not as the cardinal figures of Judaism and Christianity, respectively, but as two prophets on the roster of Muslim prophets?

It was a momentous phrase—one that could have been the subject of some intense and revealing questioning from the international media. But, of course, no such questioning was forthcoming.

Obama also extended to Muslims worldwide "a greeting of peace from Muslim communities in my country: assalaamu alaykum." While he characterized this as a greeting from Muslims in America and not from him personally, his usage was significant, since *assalaamu alaykum*, peace be upon you, is the greeting that a Muslim extends to a fellow Muslim. And most tellingly of all, Obama said: "I have known Islam on three continents before coming to the region where it was first revealed." Not "where Muslims believe it was first revealed," or "where it began," or "where it was founded," but "where it was first *revealed*."

The choice of words was telling. Did Obama really believe, then, despite his proclamation of his Christian faith, that Islam was *revealed*—that is, revealed by Allah to Muhammad, not developed out of human experience? Did he mean to signal to Muslims worldwide that he believed that Muhammad, the prophet of Islam, received divine revelations that were collected in the Qur'an? Or was he a Christian of an unorthodox variety, accepting both Jesus and Muhammad, the New Testament and the Qur'an, despite the many contradictions between them?

And most important of all, what would his apparent acceptance of Muhammad and the Qur'an—at least in some form—indicate about both the veracity of statements made by his campaign in the run-up to the election? Also, what would his positive view of Islam indicate about his policies toward Israel, Iran, and the Islamic world in general, given the deeply ingrained nature of Islamic anti-Semitism and the intransigent bellicosity of traditional Islamic theology and law regarding non-Muslims?

No reporter was willing to follow up with such questions in the wake of the Cairo speech. No one seemed to pick up on just how remarkable Obama's statements were in light of the campaign he had run.

OBAMA THE CHRISTIAN AT THE FIGHT THE SMEARS WEB SITE

"Let's not play games," said Barack Obama to George Stephanopoulos in a September 2008 interview. "What I was suggesting—you're absolutely right that John McCain has not talked about my Muslim faith. And you're absolutely right that that has not come."

Stephanopoulos quickly interjected a correction: "Christian faith."[35]

Slip of the tongue?

Many who were skeptical about Obama's campaign-era version of his early life seized upon this as evidence that he wasn't being honest about his Muslim upbringing. And indeed, whether or not this was a slip of the tongue, there was plenty of evidence to fuel their skepticism.

"My father was from Kenya," Barack Obama explained in December 2007, "and a lot of people in his village were Muslim. He didn't practice Islam. Truth is he wasn't very religious."[36] And on May 22, 2008, he said: "My father was basically agnostic, as far as I can tell, and I didn't know him."[37]

Yet as Obama prepared to deliver his major address on America and the Islamic world in Cairo in June 2009, Denis McDonough, Obama's deputy national security adviser for strategic communications, said that "the President himself experienced Islam on three continents before he was able to—or before he's been able to visit, really, the heart of the Islamic world—you know, growing up in Indonesia, having a Muslim father. . . ."[38]

A Muslim father? So was Barack Obama, Sr., a practicing Muslim or not? And why was the president's father, who died in 1982, an agnostic in 2008 and a Muslim in 2009?

The curiosities, discrepancies, deceptions, and mysteries just begin there.

Obama further stated in December 2007: "I was raised by my mother. So, I've always been a Christian. The only connection I've had to Islam is that my grandfather on my father's side came from that country. But I've never practiced Islam. For a while, I lived in Indonesia because my mother was teaching there. And that's a Muslim country. And I went to school. But I didn't practice."[39]

In line with this, in June 2008 the Obama campaign launched FightTheSmears.com, a Web site devoted to debunking purported lies and distortions about the candidate. Prominent among the "smears" to be debunked was the widely circulating claim that Obama was a Muslim, or at very least had been a Muslim in his youth. "Obama never prayed in a mosque," the Web site stated. "He has never been a Muslim, was not raised a Muslim, and is a committed Christian who attends the United Church of Christ."[40]

Yet there is an abundance of evidence to contradict the claims that Obama never prayed in a mosque, was never a Muslim, and was not raised a Muslim. Nicholas Kristof of *The New York Times* wrote in March 2007—before Obama's religious background became a point of controversy—that Obama remembered quite fondly some of his childhood lessons in Islam. "Mr. Obama recalled the opening lines of the Arabic call to prayer, reciting them with a first-rate accent. In a remark that seemed delightfully uncalculated (it'll give Alabama voters heart attacks), Mr. Obama described the call to prayer as 'one of the prettiest sounds on Earth at sunset.'"[41]

Kristof also notes that Obama "once got in trouble for making faces during Koran study classes in his elementary school"—an incident Obama himself recalls in his first autobiography, *Dreams from My Father*: "In the Muslim school," the future president recalled, "the teacher wrote to tell my mother that I made faces during Koranic studies."[42]

This was apparently at Public Elementary School Menteng No. 1, which Obama attended for fourth grade. In 1971 in Indonesia, when Barack Obama was in that grade, only Muslim children studied Islam in school. Christian students were in another room studying Christianity.[43] According to Hardi Priyono, the vice principal for curriculum, "the Muslims learn about Islam, prayer and religious activity, and for the Christians, during the religious class, they also have a special room teaching Christianity. It's always been like that."[44]

A teacher in the school, Tine Hahiyary (1971–1989), said of young Barry Soetoro: "I remembered that he had studied 'mengaji' (recitation of the Qur'an)."[45] The American blogger in Indonesia who uncovered this information explained: "While the word 'mengaji' means to either learn or study, however, the actual usage of the word 'mengaji' in Indonesian and Malaysian societies means the study of learning to recite the Qur'an in the Arabic language rather than the native tongue. . . . To put it quite simply, 'mengaji classes' are not something that a non-practicing or so-called moderate Muslim family would ever send their child to. To put this in perhaps a Christian context, this is something above and beyond simply enrolling your child in Sunday school classes. The fact that Obama had attended mengaji classes is well known in Indonesia and has left many there wondering just when Obama is going to come out of the closet."[46]

So if Barry Soetoro attended Qur'an classes in his Indonesian elementary school, was Barry Soetoro a Muslim? Barry Soetoro was registered in Assisi Primary School in Jakarta, Indonesia, in 1968, as an Indonesian citizen whose religion was Islam.[47] Assisi was a Catholic school, and according to Israella Dharmawan, Obama's first-grade teacher, "Barry was also praying in a Catholic way, but Barry was Muslim." This may, however, have simply been a formality based on his stepfather's religion: "He was registered as a Muslim," Dharmawan continued, "because his father, Lolo Soetoro, was Muslim."[48] Maya Soetoro-Ng recalled: "My whole family was Muslim, and most of the people I knew were Muslim."[49]

"American Expat in Southeast Asia," the American blogger in Indonesia who uncovered much of what we know about Obama's Indonesia years, concludes that "the evidence seems to quite clearly show that both Ann Dunham and her husband Lolo Soetoro Mangunharjo" were actually "devout Muslims themselves and they raised their son as such."[50]

Thus the available evidence indicates that, contrary to the Obama campaign's claims, Barack Obama was known to be a Muslim, was raised a Muslim for at least part of his childhood, and attended a mosque on at least a few occasions (whether or not he actually prayed in it, which was the specific claim that the Web site denied).

But he has explained nothing.

If Barack Obama was raised a Muslim, why lie on his Fight The Smears Web site? The idea that the American people, after hearing for seven years after 9/11 that Islam was a religion of peace, would reject Obama because as a child he was briefly a Muslim, is hard to believe. But Obama, instead of coming clean, has obfuscated and denied the facts. He claimed during his campaign to have been a practicing Christian for twenty years. He was, at the time, forty-seven years old. What was happening in his life prior to age twenty-seven?

Faced with the evidence of Obama's Muslim upbringing, by October 2008 the Obama camp had revised the Web site's statement to remove the initial sweeping claims.[51] As of July 2009, the Fight The Smears site contained this much more easily defensible statement:

"Barack Obama is a committed Christian. He was sworn into the Senate on his family Bible. He has regularly attended church with his wife and daughters for years. But shameful, shadowy attackers have been lying about Barack's religion, claiming he is a Muslim instead of a committed Christian."[52]

However, the original statement—"Obama never prayed in a mosque. He has never been a Muslim, was not raised a Muslim, and is a committed Christian who attends the United Church of Christ"— still appears, also as of July 2009, on a page on the BarackObama.com Web site.[53]

The deceptions didn't stop there.

OBAMA'S GRANDMOTHER:
A CHRISTIAN IN 2008, A MUSLIM IN 2009

Sarah Hussein Obama, eighty-six, Barack Obama's Kenyan grandmother, was angry. In March 2008, when asked about the rumors that her illustrious grandson was or had been a Muslim, she replied: "Untruths are told that don't have anything to do with what Barack is about. I am very against it." A photo was circulating of Obama in Muslim garb, and his grandmother was fuming. "Bringing such pictures that are trying to imply that not only is he a foreigner, he is a Muslim, is wrong, because that is not what he is." But wasn't the candidate's father a Muslim? That didn't matter, said Sarah Obama: "In the world of today, children have different religions from their parents." The Associated Press added: "She, too, is a Christian."[54]

Yet in May 2009, the *Daily Times* of Pakistan reported that Sarah Obama would "perform haj this year along with her son Syed Obama, a private TV channel reported on Saturday. . . . The channel said performing haj is one of the most desired wishes of the US president's grandmother."[55]

The haj is the pilgrimage to Mecca that all Muslims are obliged to make at least once in their lives if they are able. Non-Muslims are not permitted to make the haj or even to enter Mecca, the site of the pilgrimage and the holiest city in Islam. The highway in Saudi Arabia that leads to Mecca even has an exit labeled: "Non-Muslims must exit here." Thus Sarah Obama's performance of the haj means that she must be a Muslim, and that she was actually a Muslim in March 2008 (just when the presidential race was heating up) when the AP reported that she was a Christian—unless we are expected to believe that this octogenarian woman converted to Islam between March 2008 and May 2009 without attracting any attention from the international media.

Why was Obama's grandmother represented as a Christian when she wasn't? Who was responsible for the deception? Why didn't the Obama campaign, in the interests of openness and full disclosure, correct the false report about the candidate's grandmother when it circulated around the world?

And why wasn't anyone in the mainstream media asking such questions?

Nor did Obama's Muslim connections—connections he denied having while he was on the campaign trail—end even there.

Investor's Business Daily reported in January 2008 that one of Obama's half brothers, Abongo "Roy" Obama, who lives in Kenya and now goes by the name Malik, "is a Luo activist and a militant Muslim who argues that the black man must 'liberate himself from the poisoning influences of European culture.' He urges his younger brother to embrace his African heritage." [56]

WHY IT MATTERS

In October 2008, former secretary of state Colin Powell expressed the mainstream view when he said on *Meet the Press*: "I'm also troubled by not what Senator McCain says, but what members of the party say. And it is permitted to be said such things as, 'Well, you know that Mr. Obama is a Muslim.' Well, the correct answer is, he is not a Muslim, he's a Christian. He's always been a Christian. But the really right answer is, what if he is? Is there something wrong with being a Muslim in this country? The answer's no, that's not America. Is there something wrong with some seven-year-old Muslim-American kid believing that he or she could be president? Yet I have heard senior members of my own party drop the suggestion, 'He's a Muslim and he might be associated with terrorists.' This is not the way we should be doing it in America."[57]

Powell was assuming, however, that if Obama had a Muslim identity, or identified with Muslims or Islam in anyway, that this was of no greater significance than if he identified with Baptists or Methodists. Powell appeared unaware that Islam has since its inception had a political and expansionist character, and that that would mean that ties to Islam had a greater significance than simply allegiance to this or that religious group.

And Obama himself, with his Muslim father and stepfather and Muslim upbringing in Indonesia, knows the stakes involved.

It is impossible in our post-9/11 world to be a leader and not know what Islam means, or at the very least know the hell being wreaked upon the free and not-so-free world by the warriors of Islamic jihad. And Obama has already told us which side he will be on when the lines are fully drawn: "In the wake of 9/11," he wrote in *The Audacity of Hope*, "my meetings with Arab and Pakistani Americans, for example, have a more urgent quality, for the stories of detentions and FBI questioning and hard stares from neighbors have shaken their sense of security and belonging. They have been reminded that the history of immigration in this country has a dark underbelly; they need specific reassurances that their citizenship really means something, that America has learned the right lessons from the Japanese internments during World War II, and that I will stand with them should the political winds shift in an ugly direction."[58]

In the first year of his presidency, he showed in numerous ways that he would indeed stand with them.

It must also be noted that Islamic anti-Semitism is part of the Qur'anic imperative. The pervasive influence of Islamic Jew-hatred cannot be ignored when assessing the impact of Barack Obama's early life experiences upon the later trajectory of his career. If a devout Muslim prays the obligatory five daily prayers, he will repeat the Fatihah, the first chapter of the Qur'an, seventeen times; that chapter concludes with prayers that Muslims generally understand as asking Allah not to make the believer like the Jews ("those who have earned Allah's anger") or the Christians ("those who have gone astray").[59] The prayers generally conclude with the *dua qunoot*, a prayer that Allah's wrath would overtake infidels.

Imagine the influence that all this—inculcating contempt for Jews and Christians seventeen times a day—might have on a young mind and a future president. Troubling psychological wiring might have been set in place for a lifetime.

Yet Obama has never spoken about the influence his early experiences with Islam had upon his mind and heart—in sharp contrast to others who were raised in Islam and left the faith. Obama would have had to make a decision to reject Islam.

If so, when did he make that decision? How?

Muslims who have left Islam are generally vocal about why they left: Wafa Sultan, Ibn Warraq, Ayaan Hirsi Ali, Walid Shoebat, and others have spoken out fearlessly on these issues. Obama may not wish to engage in critiques of Islam, but if he left Islam, he must have very definite thoughts about it. And even if this is simply not an important issue to him, then he can still appreciate how important it is—knowing what he knows about Islam and apostasy.

Apostasy is punishable by death in Islam. Yet there have been no calls for Obama's death from the Islamic world. Why is this? Islam gives no free passes.

Obama's posture on this is hard to define or understand—all the more so because this is a critical issue.

Transformational issues facing this nation and the world at large—the world at war, creeping Sharia, the perversion of the rights of free men—hang in the balance during the Obama administration as never before. The stakes could not be higher. On foreign policy, Europe has lain down. The political elites have capitulated to Islamists and to multiculturalists. Europe is committing slow cultural and demographic suicide. It seems unclear that they could hold up their end even if America did the heavy lifting. As far as Israel is concerned, Obama has already made it clear that while he is in the White House, Israel is on its own.

As Obama continues to pursue his pro-Islamic and anti-Israel policies, this will only get worse. And so his deception about his Islamic ties must be explored. The potential damage to this country is incalculable.

These are dangerous times. Those consequences are, in this post-American presidency, already becoming apparent.

OBAMA AND THE LEFT

As a young man, Barack Hussein Obama cultivated a persona, one steeped in hard-left and racial grievance mongering. At Occidental

College, "to avoid being mistaken for a sellout, I chose my friends carefully. The more politically active black students. The foreign students. The Chicanos. The Marxist professors and structural feminists and punk-rock performance poets." So he recalled about his college years in his first autobiography, *Dreams from My Father*.[60]

Obama dived headfirst into radical chic:

> We smoked cigarettes and wore leather jackets. At night, in the dorms, we discussed neocolonialism, Franz [sic] Fanon, Eurocentrism, and patriarchy. When we ground out our cigarettes in the hallway carpet or set our stereos so loud that the walls began to shake, we were resisting bourgeois society's stifling conventions. We weren't indifferent or careless or insecure. We were alienated.[61]

Incidentally, I can't help but note the misspelling of Frantz Fanon's name: no media made mention of this or any of Obama's endless flow of gaffes during his 2008 campaign. But the misspelling was the least of it: Obama's heralding Fanon was disturbing. Fanon was a bloodthirsty Hard Leftist. "Violence," he proclaimed, "is man re-creating himself." Fanon's publisher described his book *The Wretched of the Earth* as "the handbook for the black revolution." It was full of slogans exhorting readers to revolution: "Violence," Fanon asserted in one famous formulation, "is a cleansing force."[62]

Was Obama's infatuation with Fanon part of a young man's college pose? Not according to John C. Drew, a former political science professor and former Marxist. Drew met Obama at Occidental College, where the future president drove a BMW (paid for by whom?) and counted as his best friend another Occidental student named Mohammed Hasan Chandoo. "We all went out to dinner," recalled Drew, "partied and drank, smoked cigarettes—and we did what young Marxists do—we basically argued politics." Drew said that it was clear that Obama was "on our team . . . a blood brother . . . a fellow revo-lutionary . . . he was a Marxist-Leninist dedicated to the overthrow of the capitalist system."

Obama thought, according to Drew, that "America was definitely the enemy, and American elites were the enemy, and whatever Amer-ica was doing was definitely wrong and bad. He thought that perhaps the Soviet Union was misunderstood, and it was doing a better job for its people than most people realized."

Obama's doctrinaire Marxism, Drew said, was why he was able to gain the enthusiastic support and aid of other Marxists such as Bill Ayers, Bernardine Dohrn, and the woman he replaced in the Illinois State Senate, Alice Palmer.[63] And indeed, Obama's hard-left polariz-ing and resentment were to remain with him. All his post-college as-sociations only reinforced it.

At Columbia University, Obama attended Socialist Scholars Con-ferences (SSC), which featured guest speakers from the Communist Party USA, even more radical communists adhering to the Maoist line, radical black nationalists, and the like.[64]

After leaving Columbia University, Obama spent three years in Chicago. And when he left Harvard Law School, he returned to Chi-cago. How Obama paid for Harvard is not known. Who financed Obama's education still remains shrouded in mystery. If he did apply for financial aid, those documents remain under seal—adding fuel to speculation that perhaps he filed for aid as a foreign student.

Unlike the majority of Harvard Law grads, Obama did not take a position with a prestigious law firm. Instead, he went back to Chi-cago and got a job with the Developing Communities Project (DCP) as a "community organizer." Stanford University sociologist Thomas Sowell explains that for community organizers, "racial resentments are a stock in trade. . . . What he organizes are the resentments and paranoia within a community, directing those feelings against other communities, from whom either benefits or revenge are to be gotten, using whatever rhetoric or tactics will accomplish that purpose."[65]

According to David Moberg, writing in *The Nation* in 2007, "Obama worked in the organizing tradition of Saul Alinsky, who made Chicago the birthplace of modern community organizing."[66] This was no surprise: Obama's teachers, according to investigative journalist Ryan Lizza in *The New Republic*, "were schooled in a style of organizing devised by Saul Alinsky, the radical University of Chicago trained social scientist."[67] Alinsky was the famous communist agitator who inspired Hillary Clinton and left an enduring mark on leftist political discourse—initially only that of the totalitarian Far Left, but increasingly on the liberal mainstream as the Hard Left became ever more respectable. That drive toward the mainstream for the Hard Left reached its culmination with the election of Barack Obama as president of the United States. But the victorious Left had not discarded its extreme views to become mainstream. In the age of Obama, the Hard Left *was* now the mainstream.

ENTERING POLITICS FROM STAGE LEFT

Obama's hard-left connections came into play once again in 1996, when he made his first political run—for a seat in the Illinois State Senate. Alice Palmer, the outgoing state senator from Obama's district, personally chose him as her successor. According to journalist Andrew Walden, "Palmer was an executive board member of the US Peace Council, US affiliate of the World Peace Council, a communist front group founded by Stalin in 1948 and funded by the USSR."[68]

Yet Palmer was not the most radical of young Barack Obama's Chicago associates.

In the sixties, Bill Ayers and his wife, Bernardine Dohrn, were members of the Weather Underground, a communist terrorist group that planted bombs at the Pentagon, the Capitol building, and other government buildings. Ayers himself planted a bomb at a statue commemorating police casualties during the 1886 Haymarket riots in Chicago. When a bomb he was hoping to use to kill American soldiers in New Jersey exploded prematurely in a house, Ayers became for ten years a fugitive from justice, but all charges against him were dropped in 1980 when an FBI program that was investigating the Weathermen was accused of improprieties.

Ayers, however, remains unrepentant, saying in 2001: "I don't regret setting bombs . . . I feel we didn't do enough."[69]

Leaving his terrorist activities behind, Ayers served his cause as part of the Left's long march into the institutions. He became a respectable professor at the University of Chicago. One of his neighbors was an ambitious young man named Barack Hussein Obama. In 1995, Obama launched his political career with a run for the Illinois State Senate, and he began his campaign with a fundraising event at the Chicago home of Bill Ayers and Bernardine Dohrn.[70]

Later, State Senator Obama wrote a glowing endorsement of Ayers's book *A Kind and Just Parent: The Children of Juvenile Court*.[71] And when Obama served as board chairman of a philanthropic group known as the Chicago Annenberg Challenge, that group gave over $600,000 in grants to the Small Schools Workshop, an organization founded by Ayers and headed by Mike Klonsky, leader of the Communist Party (Marxist-Leninist) (CP-ML), a Maoist party in the United States.[72]

For his part, Obama was dishonest about the significance of this association, dismissing the aging terrorist as a casual acquaintance: Ayers, said Obama, was merely "a guy who lives in my neighborhood, who's a professor of English in Chicago, who I know and who I have not received an official endorsement from. He's not somebody who I exchange ideas from [*sic*] on a regular basis." The terrorist attacks? "Now, Mr. Ayers is a 60 plus year old individual who lives in my neighborhood, who did something I deplore 40 years ago when I was six or seven years old. By the time I met him, he was a professor of education at the University of Illinois."

Yet records don't justify his having been so dismissive. Ayers and Obama were also both board members of Chicago's Wood Fund between December 1999 and December 2002. According to the *Chicago Sun-Times*, "that board met four times a year, and members would see each other at occasional dinners the group hosted."[73]

The old terrorist Bill Ayers, who just happens to live in Barack Obama's old neighborhood, but who hardly knows the president and has had only the slightest casual contact with him over the years, visited the White House twice between January and October 2009.

House Speaker Nancy Pelosi visited only once during that span.[74]

In late January 2010, the White House denied that Ayers, Wright, and Farrakhan had visited the White House:

> Also, as we have previously noted, sometimes rather than providing clear information, transparency can have confusing or amusing results. Given the significant number of visitors to the White House, many visitors share the same name. Today's release includes the names of some notable figures (for example, Louis Farrakhan and James Taylor appear in this disclosure). The well-known individuals with those names have not visited the White House, but we have included the records of the individuals that did.[75]

But reports that the White House visitors list featured William Ayers and Jeremiah Wright were circulating as early as October 2009. And even at that time, many people claimed that these visitors were other people with the same name. Yes, if you do an Intelius search for William Ayers or Jeremiah Wright, there are a lot of them. It is easy to dismiss. But Louis Farrakhan? There aren't too many Louis Farra-khans in America, especially with a family member by the name of Nasir Farrakhan, who is also on the visitors list. Nasir Farrakhan is Louis Farrakhan's son. Every family member supposedly went on a "tour." Louis Farrakhan met with "someone" in the East Room.

And remember, Obama blocked access to the visitors list.[76] The White House had to be sued for the records to be released.[77]

JEREMIAH WRIGHT AND BARACK OBAMA

The Reverend Jeremiah Wright of Trinity United Church of Christ, of which Obama was a member for twenty years, had roots in both Islam and economic radicalism: "But Wright was a former Muslim and black nationalist who had studied at Howard and Chicago, and Trinity United's guiding principles—what the church calls the 'Black Value System'—included a 'Disavowal of the Pursuit of Middleclass-ness.'"[78] Wright was also a close associate of Nation of Islam leader Louis Farrakhan, who in November 2009 offered a doggerel version of Obama's lofty post-American internationalism: "America," he de-clared, "has run out of time. It is the time of the setting of the sun on the Western world."[79]

Jeremiah Wright was a committed Marxist, as he himself con-firmed in an address in September 2009: "My work with liberation theology, with Latin American theologians, with the Black Theology Project and with the Cuban Council of Churches taught me 30 years ago the importance of Marx and the Marxist analysis of the social real-ities of the vulnerable and the oppressed who were trying desperately to break free of the political economics undergirded by this country that were choking them and cutting off any hope of a possible future where all of the people would benefit."[80]

The Fight The Smears Web site says that Obama "has never been a Muslim, was not raised a Muslim, and is a committed Christian who attends the United Church of Christ."[81] *The New York Times* reported in 2007 that Obama was baptized at Chicago's Trinity United Church of Christ in 1988.[82] Details, however, are sketchy and contradictory: a year later, *Newsweek* stated that Obama was baptized "in the early 1990s."[83] Was Obama baptized at all? The truth of this matter is elusive. However, the positions of the Trinity United Church of Christ, which Obama attended for twenty years, are not elusive in the least: black nationalism and socialism were always on the agenda—and it is significant that the Christianity preached in the Trinity United Church of Christ is a far-left variety that focuses upon few of the features of Christianity that distinguish it from Islam, or at least from the black nationalist amalgam of Islam, Christianity, and racial identity that is the hallmark of that peculiarly American brand of Islam, the Nation of Islam.

When Obama became a member of Trinity United Church in 1991, he accepted what the church calls "the Black Value System," a race-based code of ethics that encourages black separatism, warning black Americans to shun the middle-class life as a white trap, and to patronize only black-owned businesses. As Jeremiah Wright put it, "We are an African people, and remain true to our native land, the mother continent."[84]

Not to America.

Wright, of course, drew controversy during the campaign for his exaggerated race-baiting and hateful statements in support of his protégé's presidential campaign. And Obama, after a good deal of hesitation, ultimately threw Wright under the bus for these and other statements:

The government gives them the drugs, builds bigger prisons, passes a three-strike law and then wants us to sing God Bless America, no no no, not God Bless America, GOD DAMN AMERICA, that's in the Bible for killing innocent people. . . .

Ohhh, I am so glad that I got a god who knows what it is to be a poor black man, and in a country and a culture that is controlled by and run by rich white people!

Obama's repudiation of this race hate was welcome, albeit tardy and politically motivated. Wright's remarks during the campaign, however, were not likely to have differed significantly in philosophy from remarks he had made over the course of twenty years—while Barack Obama sat and listened.

And there were signs that Obama did listen. Wright preached after 9/11 that America had gotten what it deserved—that the attacks were just desserts for the atomic bombs exploded in Japan: "We bombed Hiroshima, we bombed Nagasaki and we nuked far more than the thousands in New York and the Pentagon, and we never batted an eye. We have supported state terrorism against the Palestinians and the black South Africans, and now we are indignant. Because the stuff we have done overseas has now been brought back into our own front yard. America's chickens are coming home to roost."[85]

This was Obama's spiritual adviser. The man whose sermon inspired the title of Obama's second autobiography, *The Audacity of Hope*.

Asked during a visit to Japan in November 2009 whether he thought the bombings of Hiroshima and Nagasaki were justified, Obama ducked the question. Were Wright's condemnations of those bombings still ringing in his ears? Of course, there were plenty of other radical Leftists from whom Obama might have picked up this idea. But the coincidence was notable.[86]

Now it certainly seems as if Barack Obama, with his schemes to nationalize health care, the auto industry, and more, has absorbed and adopted as his own some of Wright's principal preoccupations—and is intent on making the nation as a whole disavow the "pursuit of middleclassness."

These are not just insignificant associations. Obama and Wright are still close; despite Obama's public repudiation of Trinity United Church of Christ during his presidential campaign, and bitter words from Wright about the severing of their relationship, Wright has visited the White House at least once since his onetime protégé became president.[87]

And Wright's race-baiting Christianity of resentment has also left its mark on Obama's handling of racial issues as president.

OBAMA AND ODINGA

In an August 2006 campaign stop, Illinois senator Barack Obama thundered against corruption: "My own city of Chicago, Illinois, has been the home of some of the most corrupt local politics in American history over the years, from patronage machines to questionable elections."

But he wasn't speaking in Chicago. Barack Obama was in Kenya.

"Here in Kenya, there is a crisis," Obama said, "a crisis that's robbing an honest people of the opportunities they fought for."[88] Although he didn't mention him by name, he was attacking the president of Kenya, Mwai Kibaki, and appeared with Kibaki's chief opponent, Raila Odinga. Foreshadowing his own presidential campaign slogan, Obama declared, "Kenyans are now yearning for change."[89] Alfred Mutua, a spokesman for the Kibaki government, accused Odinga of "using Senator Obama as his stooge, as his puppet."[90]

Mutua was magnanimous about Obama's apparent naïveté: "It is now clear that he was speaking out of ignorance and does not understand Kenyan politics, we earlier thought he was mature in his assessment of Kenyan and African politics. We forgive him because it is his first time in the Senate and he is yet to mature into understanding issues of foreign policy."[91]

So if Obama's grasp of Kenyan politics was weak at best, what might have moved him to campaign for Raila Odinga? Odinga and Obama's father were both Luos from the same area of Kenya, and Odinga claimed to be Obama's cousin; however, Obama's uncle contradicted him, saying that there was no blood relationship between the two men.[92] Blood no, but ideology yes: Obama's support for Odinga is consistent with his other associations: Odinga is a socialist who is enough of a hard-core true believer to have named his son Fidel.[93] Odinga's history suggests that he is more of a Marxist than a social democrat: his father, longtime Kenyan opposition leader Oginga Odinga, was a communist. The East German government gave Raila Odinga a scholarship to Technical University Magdeburg, from which he graduated in 1970.[94]

Odinga also had troubling ties to Islamic hard-liners, although the exact nature of those ties was hotly disputed. Odinga reportedly made a fortune in the oil industry by making a deal with the Al-Bakri Group of Saudi Arabia; Abdulkader al-Bakri, the CEO of the Al-Bakri Group, has been identified as a sponsor of Al-Qaeda.[95] Odinga also cultivated ties with Libyan strongman Muammar Gaddafi.[96]

Odinga campaigned against the Kibaki government's cooperation with the U.S. war on terror, making an issue out of the extradition of a group of accused Al-Qaeda operatives, some of whom the Odinga camp maintained were innocent. "Our government will not be held at ransom to extradite Muslims to foreign lands," thundered Odinga at a campaign rally.[97] And with Muslim Kenyans, the message resonated: "Islamic outrage," observed Joshua Hammer of *The New York Times*, "had placed the incumbent, Kibaki, on the defensive and provided Raila Odinga with a tool to rally the support of Kenya's Muslims."[98]

Nor was that all. Just a month before the December 27 election, controversy broke out over a Memorandum of Understanding that Odinga had purportedly signed on August 29, 2007, with Sheikh Abdullahi Abdi, chairman of the National Muslim Leaders Forum (NAMLEF), an umbrella organization comprised of the nation's principal Islamic groups.[99] The memorandum had Odinga promising "within six months" to "rewrite the Constitution of Kenya to recognize Sharia as the only true law sanctioned by the Holy Qur'an for Muslim declared regions."[100] Odinga, according to the memorandum, would recognize "Islam as the only true religion" and give Islamic leaders an "oversight role to monitor activities of ALL other religions." Christian preaching, alcohol, and pork would be banned.[101]

Darara Gubo, the regional manager for Africa of International Christian Concern, denounced the agreement for undermining "the secular nature of Kenya and open[ing] a Pandora's box of chaos and conflict similar to what happened in Nigeria and Sudan." Gubo added: "This is not a stand-alone incident; rather, it is part of strategy to Islamize Eastern Africa and the Horn of Africa, through the introduction of Sharia law."[102]

Odinga denounced the leaked memorandum as a forgery, and the next day released what he said was the genuine Memorandum of Understanding that he really had signed with Abdi—a substantially more innocuous document that Odinga termed "very innocent."[103] Abdi sought to reassure the public: "The objective was to safeguard the interests of a section of the Kenyan community (Muslims) that has undergone atrocities over the last 44 years. Fears that Muslims want to introduce Sharia law and make Islam the supreme religion in this country are false and only meant to generate hostility between us and our Christian and Hindu brothers. Islam does not suppress other religions."[104]

Not everyone was mollified, however. The human-rights group International Christian Concern, which monitors persecution of Christians worldwide, concluded that the pro-Sharia version of the memorandum was in fact not a forgery at all, but an authentic secret agreement made between Abdi and Odinga.[105] The Evangelical Alliance of Kenya said that in both versions of the memorandum Odinga "comes across as a presumptive Muslim president bent on forcing Islamic law, religion and culture down the throats of the Kenyan people in total disregard of the Constitutionally guaranteed rights of freedom of worship and equal protection of the law."[106]

Whatever the truth of the matter, Kenyan Christians remained concerned that with Odinga would come Sharia, with its institutionalized discrimination against non-Muslims—but ultimately there proved to be no way to tell whether their fears were justified. For despite Barack Obama's help, Odinga lost the Kenyan presidential election—and then the violence began.

Amid widespread charges that Kibaki had stolen the election, Odinga supporters staged bloody reprisals, killing 700 and displacing 250,000 within a month after the election.[107] By the middle of February 2008, just over six weeks after the election, the death toll had risen to 1,500, with 500,000 homeless.[108] Two hundred people were burned alive when Odinga supporters torched a church in which they had taken refuge.[109]

A Human Rights Watch report stated that "several leaders involved in anti-Kikuyu violence" had said that "they were merely doing by force what they had been denied a chance to do through the ballot box." A Kenyan tribal elder said that the Odinga camp planned the unrest beforehand: "[The elders] said that if there is any sign that Kibaki is winning, then the war should break [sic]. They were coaching the young people how to go on the war [sic]."[110] Stanley Kamau, who campaigned for Kibaki, declared: "It was definitely as if it had all been planned. Before the elections they (the Luos) said: 'It is our turn.' They told us no matter what, they were going to take power."[111]

Barack Obama was so concerned about the violence in Kenya that he took time out of his hectic schedule during the New Hampshire primary to call . . . Raila Odinga.[112] Twice.[113] *Time* reported in January 2008 that "in the days since his Iowa victory, Obama has had near daily conversations with the U.S. ambassador in Nairobi, Michael Ranneberger, or with Kenya's opposition leader, Raila Odinga. Obama was trying to reach Kibaki as well."[114]

Kibaki doesn't seem to have taken Obama's calls, but in an attempt to quell the rioting and murder, Kibaki named Odinga prime minister—in which role Odinga realized a long-standing dream of his friend, supporter, and possible relative Barack Obama: in February 2009, he met with Iranian president Mahmoud Ahmadinejad.[115]

Ayers, Wright, Odinga—communists, socialists, race baiters. All the people close to Barack Hussein Obama throughout his life and into his presidency seemed to be cut from the same ideological cloth. As was, of course, their star-crossed friend who became the 44th president of the United States.

THREE

OBAMA AND JEWS

BARACK OBAMA IS THE MOST ANTI-ISRAEL PRESIDENT OF THE UNITED STATES SINCE THE STATE OF ISRAEL WAS FORMED, YET AMERICAN Jews voted in large numbers for him.

After Obama gave his first speech to the United Nations, former UN ambassador John Bolton on *The Glenn Beck Program* lamented that "this is the most radical anti-Israel speech I can recall any president making . . . I have to say I was very shaken by this speech."

Yet even after he became president, many continued to support and defend him with Stockholm syndrome–like fervor. Even as he betrayed his pro-Israel supporters and sold Israel down the river, they continued to love him. He assuaged their liberal guilt. He made them feel as if they were right-thinking, high-minded, and free of racism and bigotry.

They loved him—even as he worked for the destruction of Israel, even as he grew more hostile toward Israel as his first year in office drew to its close. The Israeli pundit Caroline Glick described Obama's hostility toward Israeli prime minister Binyamin Netanyahu in November 2009 as "breathtaking." Glick noted that "it isn't every day that you can see an American President leaving the Prime Minister of an allied government twisting in the wind for weeks before deciding to grant him an audience at the White House."

But it wasn't just the wait. Glick reported that Netanyahu was "brought into the White House in an unmarked van in the middle of the night rather than greeted like a friend at the front door"; was "forbidden to have his picture taken with the President"; was "forced to leave the White House alone, through a side exit"; and finally, was "ordered to keep the contents of his meeting with the President secret."[1]

The oddest and most puzzling thing about it all was that the American Jews who voted so overwhelmingly for Obama could have seen it coming all along. It never dawned on Jews, Christians, or Americans that a presidential candidate would be so patently dishonest. But he was more than just a skillful dancer. In hindsight, Barack Hussein Obama turns out to have been a bald-faced liar.

Yet those of us who were aware of Obama's troubling past met his newly minted pro-Israel sentiments with grave skepticism. Sarah Silverman and the other pro-Obama Jews should have been aware, for example, of a March 2007 account by the pro-Palestinian blogger Ali Abunimah at a Web site called *The Electronic Intifada*. Abunimah alleged that Obama adopted a pro-Israel position as a matter of political expediency as his national aspirations developed. "The last time I spoke to Obama," Abunimah recalled, "was in the winter of 2004 at a gathering in Chicago's Hyde Park neighborhood. He was in the midst of a primary campaign to secure the Democratic nomination for the United States Senate seat he now occupies. But at that time polls showed him trailing."

When Abunimah greeted him, Obama "responded warmly," and volunteered an apology for not being more outspoken against Israel: "Hey," said the candidate to Abunimah, "I'm sorry I haven't said more about Palestine right now, but we are in a tough primary race. I'm hoping when things calm down I can be more up front." Abunimah added: "He referred to my activism, including columns I was contributing to the *Chicago Tribune* critical of Israeli and US policy, 'Keep up the good work!'"[2]

As the various Democratic rivals for the 2008 presidential nomination competed for Jewish support, major pro-Israel donors should have seen Abunimah's account. A false supporter for Israel was the last thing the free world needed in the fight against the global jihad. But his ruse was dazzling the eyes of men who should have seen clearly.

Abunimah's piece—and Obama's anti-Semitic associations—got little attention. The Jewish people and lovers of our most important strategic ally missed a big opportunity. But it wasn't just Abunimah. Voters had only to scratch the surface and look into his background to see through Barack Obama's deception—and find not one, not two, not three, but numerous associations with virulent anti-Semites and haters of Israel. (I reject the leftist/Islamic supremacist claim that one can be anti-Israel but not anti-Semitic. The two are essentially related and inseparable; in fact, the claim that they can be separated is part of the modern anti-Semitic narrative.) Throughout his life Barack Obama has been close friends with numerous virulent anti-Semites: Jeremiah Wright, Bill Ayers, Khalid al-Mansour, Rashid Khalidi, and others.

It may be an old cliché, but it's true: show me your friends, and I'll show you who and what you are.

American Jews should have noted this, and noted it well. Instead, they fell for Obama's smooth talk at the American Israel Public

Affairs Committee (AIPAC). One speech became the litmus test. And a lifetime of anti-Semitic associations, alliances, mentors, and troubling actions were summarily dismissed.

The mainstream media, of course, took little notice, either.

BILL AYERS: ANTI-SEMITISM IN THE WEATHER UNDERGROUND

Obama's association with Ayers became well-known during the campaign of 2008, although predictably enough, the real background of it never got a great deal of attention from the mainstream media. What was not as well-known as their Weathermen activities was Bill Ayers and Bernardine Dohrn's virulent anti-Semitism in the 1960s and 1970s—including the hatred for Jews and Israel expressed in Ayers's 1974 book *Prairie Fire: The Politics of Revolutionary Anti-Imperialism*— the "Political Statement of the Weather Underground," which he coauthored with Dohrn.

The book's dedication page lists numerous "victims of imperialism," including Sirhan Sirhan, who assassinated Robert F. Kennedy in 1968 because of Kennedy's support for the State of Israel. RFK's murder is thought to have been the first "Palestinian" terrorist attack in the United States of America. In *Prairie Fire* itself, Ayers and Dohrn characterize Israel as an "expansionist power, based on Zionist colonialism." They assert that "from its inception, Zionism has been an imperial ideology, presented as an alternative to communism," and claims that "the Zionist state is clearly the aggressor, the source of violence and war in the Mideast, the occupier of stolen lands. . . . It is racist and expansionist—the enemy of the Palestinians, the Arab people, and the Jewish people."

Ayers and Dohrn end their condemnation of Israel with a ringing peroration: "The U.S. people have been seriously deceived about the

Palestinians and Israel. . . . SELF-DETERMINATION FOR THE PALESTINIAN PEOPLE! U.S. OUT OF THE MIDEAST! END AID TO ISRAEL!"[3]

WRIGHT AND FARRAKHAN

During the campaign, when unwelcome attention began to focus on the Rev. Jeremiah Wright and his anti-American and anti-Semitic statements at the Trinity United Church of Christ, a church Obama faithfully attended for twenty years, the candidate claimed not to have heard or approved of the offending statements.

That's hard to believe. Twenty years is a long time to sit regularly in a pew, listening to a man preach, and never hear anything he says.

Wright married Barack and Michelle Obama and baptized his children. Obama's children attended school in Wright's church of hate.

On one occasion Wright was railing against Israel and then stopped himself, saying: "I said that dirty word again, *Israel*."[4]

The New Republic reported in March 2007 that Wright was "a former Muslim and black nationalist."[5] The Christianity preached in the United Church of Christ is a far-left variety that focuses upon few of the features of Christianity that distinguish it from Islam, or at least from the black nationalist amalgam of Islam, Christianity, and the racial anger that is the hallmark of that peculiarly American brand of Islam, the Nation of Islam.

Wright defended the church's award to Farrakhan by saying: "When Minister Farrakhan speaks, Black America listens. Everybody may not agree with him, but they listen. . . . His depth of analysis when it comes to the racial ills of this nation is astounding and eye opening. He brings a perspective that is helpful and honest. Minister Farrakhan will be remembered as one of the 20th and 21st century giants of the African American religious experience. His integrity and honesty have secured him a place in history as one of the nation's most powerful critics. His love for Africa and African American people has made him an unforgettable force, a catalyst for change and a religious leader who is sincere about his faith and his purpose."[6]

The church's *Trumpet Newsmagazine* said that Farrakhan "truly epitomized greatness."[7]

In an infamous March 1984 radio broadcast, Farrakhan said: "Hitler was a very great man. He wasn't great for me as a black person but he was a very great German. . . . He rose Germany up from nothing. Well, in a sense you could say there's a similarity in that we are raising our people up from nothing." Three months after that he embroidered on this, saying that "Hitler was great, but wickedly great," and that he had made a deal with Zionist Jews that allowed them to "take the land away from the Palestinian people." Judaism, said Farrakhan, was a "gutter religion." Israel was the product of the Jews' "old naked scheming, plotting and planning against the lives of a people there in Palestine," and the ultimate result of all that scheming would be that America, as Israel's ally, would be "drawn into the heat of the third world war, which is called Armageddon."[8]

Farrakhan has also referred to "satanic Jews," and has railed against "these false Jews" who "promote the filth of Hollywood." He has repeatedly denounced "the wicked Jews," echoing mainstream Islamic theology by asserting that the "Koran says that the Jews have altered the word of God out of its place. They did not want the masters of the people to know what Jesus really said, what Moses really said, because then you wouldn't have a yardstick to measure their deviations."[9]

Of course, Farrakhan has disclaimed anti-Semitism: "You say I hate Jews. I don't hate the Jewish people, I never have. But there [are] some things I don't like. 'What is it you don't like, Farrakhan?' I don't like the way you leech on us. See a leech is somebody that sucks your blood, takes from you and don't give you a damn thing. See, I don't

like that kind of arrangement." He has called Jews "the greatest con-
trollers of Black minds, Black intelligence," and has warned them that
"Allah will punish you. You are wicked deceivers of the American
people. You have sucked their blood. You are not real Jews, those of
you that are not real Jews. You are the synagogue of Satan, and you
have wrapped your tentacles around the U.S. government, and you are
deceiving and sending this nation to hell. But I warn you in the name
of Allah, you would be wise to leave me alone. But if you choose to
crucify me, know that Allah will crucify you."

"As I said over 20 years ago," Farrakhan said in 2008, "there will be
no peace for Israel, because there can be no peace as long as that peace
is based on lying, stealing, murder, and using God's name to shield a
wicked, unjust practice that is not in harmony with the Will of God." [10]

Wright copublished a book defending Farrakhan's Million Man
March, *When Black Men Stand Up for God: Reflections on the Million
Man March.* In it, Wright continues to defend Farrakhan, saying that
"The enemy is not white people, but white supremacy. The enemy
isn't Farrakhan. The enemy is still white supremacy." [11]

Wright's association with Farrakhan is long-standing. In April
2008, when he appeared at the National Press Club in order to address
the controversy that had engulfed the Obama campaign because of his
incendiary anti-American remarks from the pulpit, his security detail
was made of members of the Nation of Islam. [12] He and Farrakhan
even once traveled to Libya to confer with Libyan strongman Muammar Gaddafi—as Wright recalled during the 2008 campaign: "When
[Obama's] enemies find out that in 1984 I went to Tripoli to visit [Gad-
dafi] with Farrakhan, a lot of his Jewish support will dry up quicker
than a snowball in hell." [13]

Surprisingly, it didn't, but Wright had good reason to suspect that
it might. Wright's anti-Semitism matches Farrakhan's, as is clear from
his "War on Iraq IQ Test," which purported to answer the question,

"Do you know enough to justify going to war with Iraq?" It was clear from Wright's questions and answers that he believed that the Iraq venture was all about protecting Israel—and that Wright's slant was all about demonizing Israel:

41. Q: How many UN resolutions did Israel violate by 1992?
    A: Over 65

42. Q: How many UN resolutions on Israel did America veto between 1972 and 1990?
    A: 30+

43. Q: How much does the U.S. fund Israel a year?
    A: $5 billion

48. Q: How many nuclear warheads does Israel have?
    A: Over 400

49. Q: Has Israel every [*sic*] allowed UN weapon inspections?
    A: No

50. Q: What percentage of the Palestinian territories are controlled by Israeli settlements?
    A: 42%

51. Q: Is Israel illegally occupying Palestinian land?
    A: Yes.[14]

Wright demonstrated his own anti-Semitism anew when he complained in June 2009 that "them Jews ain't going to let [Obama] talk to me." In the same interview, Wright echoed jihadist propaganda regarding Israel: "Ethnic cleansing is going on in Gaza. Ethnic cleansing of the Zionist is a sin and a crime against humanity, and they don't want Barack talking like that because that's anti-Israel."[15]

In fact, it was Obama's new rigid and strident policies toward restricting Jews from living in parts of Israel that mandated ethnic cleansing: the ethnic cleansing of Jews from parts of the Jewish homeland. He pressed Israel to freeze construction of settlements on land that belonged rightly to Israel, and in November 2009 issued a veiled warning: settlement construction, he said, "embitters the Palestinians in a way that could end up being very dangerous."[16] In other words, Jews had to clear out of Jewish land, or risk terror attack.

During the campaign, the mainstream media yawned and generally did not publicize information about Wright's anti-Semitism or ties to Farrakhan. One thing is certain: if Barack Obama had been a Republican presidential candidate with analogous ties to pro-Israel spokesmen and groups, the mainstream media would not have considered this story a matter of indifference.

During the campaign, Obama aide David Axelrod said that Obama disagreed with Wright about Farrakhan.[17] But after a year of the post-American presidency, the question of Obama's ideological kinship with these anti-Semites cannot be so easily dismissed. It should come as no surprise to anyone that an Obama presidency would prove lethal for Israel. It is not an illegitimate question to ask whether the views of Wright and Farrakhan influenced Obama and formed his opinion of Jews and Israel, and helped form in turn the policies of Obama's administration toward Israel. Wright was his spiritual mentor.

And Obama has other ties to anti-Israel entities that the liberal media generally found unworthy of notice. Obama's mentors, friends, and comrades tell us *his story*. These associations show us who he is. And his record during the first year of his presidency demonstrates that these associations were not casual and tangential to his intellectual and ideological development.

KHALID AL-MANSOUR

In September 2008, the eighty-seven-year-old Percy Sutton, former Manhattan borough president and lawyer for Malcolm X, reminisced in a New York 1 television interview about when he first met Barack Obama: "I was introduced to (Obama) by a friend who was raising money for him," he recalled. "The friend's name is Dr. Khalid al-Mansour, from Texas. He is the principal adviser to one of the world's richest men. He told me about Obama."

Al-Mansour, said Sutton, wanted a favor from him—he wanted Sutton to write young Obama a letter of recommendation for Harvard Law School. "He wrote to me about him. And his introduction was there is a young man that has applied to Harvard. I know that you have a few friends up there because you used to go up there to speak. Would you please write a letter in support of him?" Sutton complied: "I wrote a letter of support of him to my friends at Harvard, saying to them I thought there was a genius that was going to be available and I certainly hoped they would treat him kindly."

But why was Khalid Abdullah Tariq al-Mansour, who was already winning renown as a lawyer and black nationalist and would later become notorious as an associate of Saudi prince Al-Waleed bin Talal and unabashed anti-Semite, taking such a keen interest in a promising but anonymous law school aspirant? That crucial part of the story Sutton left unexplained, and al-Mansour himself declined to elucidate; how and why Obama caught his eye and became the object of his patronage remains mysterious.

Not mysterious at all, however, is al-Mansour's fervent anti-Semitism. "Today," he once declared in a speech in South Africa, "the Palestinians are being brutalized like savages. If you protest you will go to jail, and you may be killed. And they say they are the only democratic country in the Middle East. . . . They are lying on God." The Jews, he said, were "stealing the land the same way the Christians stole the land from the Indians in America."[18] He is the author of a nineteen-page booklet entitled "Americans Beware! The Zionist Plot Against Saudi Arabia."

Khalid al-Mansour is also featured in a DVD with a title that fore-shadowed the internationalism of the Obama administration: *Will the West Rule Forever?*

RASHID KHALIDI

In 2005, Columbia University professor Rashid Khalidi taught a fifteen-week course on Middle Eastern politics at Columbia's Middle East Institute. *The New York Sun* reported that the Saudis "funneled tens of thousands of dollars" into the institute's programs.[19] However, New York City's schools chancellor, Joel Klein, removed Khalidi from the program after it came to light that Khalidi had justified jihad terror attacks against Israeli civilians: "Killing civilians is a war crime, whoever does it. But resistance to occupation is legitimate in international law."[20] Martin Kramer, a trenchant critic of the anti-Israel and pro-jihad bias that prevails in American academia, explained: "If you're a Saudi, it's very convenient for Rashid Khalidi to claim that the source of America's problems in the region is not their special relationship with Saudi Arabia, but their special relationship with Israel. All he has to do is say it's Palestine, stupid."[21]

That wasn't all. Reports indicate that Khalidi was a director of WAFA, the official press agency of the Palestine Liberation Organization, in Beirut from 1976 to 1982. According to journalist Aaron Klein, "Rashid Khalidi at times has denied working directly for the PLO but Palestinian diplomatic sources in Ramallah told *WorldNetDaily* he indeed worked on behalf of WAFA. Khalidi also advised the Palestinian delegation to the Madrid Conference in 1991." What's more, "during documented speeches and public events, Khalidi has called Israel an 'apartheid system in creation' and a destructive 'racist' state. He has multiple times expressed support for Palestinian terror, calling suicide bombings a response to 'Israeli aggression.' He dedicated his 1986 book, 'Under Siege,' to 'those who gave their lives . . . in defense of the cause of Palestine and independence of Lebanon.' Critics assailed the book as excusing Palestinian terrorism."[22]

In 2001 and 2002, the fiercely anti-Israeli Arab American Action Network (AAAN), headed by Khalidi's wife, Mona, received $110,000 in grants from the Woods Fund, a Chicago-based nonprofit organization.[23] One of the members of the Woods Fund board of directors at that time was Barack Obama, Khalidi's former colleague back in the 1990s, when they both taught at the University of Chicago. Like Ayers, Khalidi also took a financial interest in Obama's political career: in 2000, he held a fund-raiser for Obama's unsuccessful run for a seat in the House of Representatives.[24] In October 2008, the *Los Angeles Times* obtained a video of a 2003 AAAN dinner attended by Obama, Ayers, Dohrn, and Khalidi. The *Times* refused to release the video, leading to angry accusations of journalistic bias from the McCain campaign, since it was widely rumored that the video showed Obama making or at very least assenting to anti-Israel statements.[25]

One thing that the *Times* did reveal was that Obama spoke warmly at the banquet about his numerous conversations with Rashid and Mona Khalidi, saying that they had served for him as "consistent reminders to me of my own blind spots and my own biases. . . . It's for that reason that I'm hoping that, for many years to come, we continue that conversation—a conversation that is necessary not just around Mona and Rashid's dinner table," but on the big stage of "this entire world."[26]

Times reporter Peter Wallsten noted that "the warm embrace Obama gave to Khalidi, and words like those at the professor's going-away party, have left some Palestinian American leaders believing that Obama is more receptive to their viewpoint than he is willing to say. Their belief is not drawn from Obama's speeches or campaign literature, but from comments that some say Obama made in private and from his association with the Palestinian American community in his hometown of Chicago, including his presence at events where anger at Israeli and U.S. Middle East policy was freely expressed."

One of those was the 2003 AAAN dinner, at which "a young Palestinian American recited a poem accusing the Israeli government of terrorism in its treatment of Palestinians and sharply criticizing U.S. support of Israel. If Palestinians cannot secure their own land, she said, 'then you will never see a day of peace.'" Another speaker compared the "Zionist settlers on the West Bank"—to whom Obama as president has been notoriously hostile—to Osama bin Laden. Obama is not recorded as having contradicted these remarks, although he did, according to Wallsten, adopt "a different tone in his comments and called for finding common ground."[27]

In any case, whatever was said on this notorious video, no smoking-gun videotape was really necessary to establish Obama's close ties to haters of Israel.

The evidence was already there in abundance.

CAMPAIGN MONEY FROM GAZA

Obama's 2008 campaign finance records are full of riddles, mysteries, and unanswered questions. Contributing nearly $25,000 to the Obama campaign was Monir Edwan, who was listed on FEC documents as contributing from the city of Rafah in the state "GA." Georgia? No—there is no Rafah in the Peach State. Monir Edwan sent money to Obama from Rafah, *Gaza*.

Rafah is a Gaza refugee camp.

The Federal Election Campaign Act (FECA) "prohibits any foreign national from contributing, donating or spending funds in connection with any federal, state, or local election in the United States, either directly or indirectly. It is also unlawful to help foreign nationals violate that ban or to solicit, receive or accept contributions or donations from them. Persons who knowingly and willfully engage in these activities may be subject to fines and/or imprisonment."[28]

Yet no one has found it noteworthy that Barack Hussein Obama himself appears to be in violation of this statute.

According to the FEC, contributions to the Obama campaign from three brothers, Osama, Monir, and Hosam Edwan, all from Rafah, totaled $33,000.[29] And they weren't alone. Al-Jazeera reported on March 31, 2008, that Gazans were manning phone banks for the Obama campaign.[30]

The brothers were vocal in their "love" for Obama—which in itself spoke volumes to Obama's campaign. The media showed no interest, but Obama pricked up his ears. He smelled trouble; even though no reporters asked him about these contributions, he answered anyway. The Obama campaign contended in the summer of 2008 that they had returned $33,500 in illegal contributions from Palestinians in Hamas-controlled Gaza—despite the fact that records do not show that it was returned, and the brothers said they did not receive any money. And indeed, Obama's refunds and redesignations on file with the FEC show no refund to Osama, Hosam, or Monir Edwan in the Rafah refugee camp.

One of the Gazan brothers, Monir Edwan, claimed that he bought "Obama for President" T-shirts off Obama's Web site, and then sold the shirts in Gaza for a profit. All purchases on the Barack Obama Web site are considered contributions. The brothers allegedly claimed that they were American citizens—so said the Obama camp. They listed their address with the zip code 972 (ironically, the area code for Israel) and entered "GA," the state abbreviation for Georgia, as their location, while actually living, as we have seen, in a Hamas-controlled refugee camp. If Obama's people thought they were dealing with American citizens from Georgia, why did they ship the T-shirts that

Monir Edwan ordered to the correct address in Gaza? Shipping overseas to a Gaza refugee camp is vastly different from sending a package to the state next door.

On Watchdog.net, a site that monitors campaign contributions, Monir Edwan is listed as Barack Obama's Top Contributor, giving $24,313 between October 27, 2007, and November 11, 2007.[31] Intriguingly, however, although it gives zip codes and other details for the other four of Obama's top five individual contributors, it provides no additional information at all for Monir Edwan—and Edwan's link is the only dead one on the Watchdog page.

Why did Palestinians in a Gaza refugee camp have such love for Obama in the summer of 2008? Did they know he was going to run a jihad presidency?

Did Jamal M. Barzinji know the same thing?

Jamal M. Barzinji gave the Obama campaign $1,000.

Dr. Jamal M. al-Barzinji is a noted American businessman and political operative. He has most recently been associated with, notably, the International Institute of Islamic Thought (IIIT) and the World Assembly of Muslim Youth (WAMY). The IIIT is linked to the international Islamic organization known as the Muslim Brotherhood. In a May 22, 1991, document entitled "An Explanatory Memorandum on the General Strategic Goal for the Group in North America," the Brotherhood lays out a plan to do nothing less than conquer and Islamize the United States. The Brotherhood's success in America would ultimately further the even larger goal of establishing "the global Islamic state."[32]

The Brotherhood memorandum includes "a list of our organizations and the organizations of our friends," with the appended note: "Imagine if they all march according to one plan!!!" Among these organizations are some of the most prominent "moderate Muslim" organizations in the United States today, including the IIIT as well as the Islamic

Society of North America (ISNA); the Muslim Students Association (MSA); the North American Islamic Trust (NAIT); the Muslim Arab Youth Association (MAYA); the Islamic Association for Palestine (IAP), out of which emerged in 1994 the most prominent Muslim group in the United States, the Council on American-Islamic Relations (CAIR); the Islamic Circle of North America (ICNA); and many others.

The memorandum also explains that Muslim Brotherhood operatives "must understand that their work in America is a kind of grand jihad in eliminating and destroying the Western civilization from within and 'sabotaging' its miserable house by their hands and the hands of the believers so that it is eliminated and Allah's religion is made victorious over all other religions."[33]

According to *The Wall Street Journal,* Jamal Barzinji also has business ties to a Muslim Brotherhood activist, Youssef Nada.[34] And the destruction of Israel is high on the jihadist agenda. After 9/11, federal agents raided Barzinji's office and home. An affidavit filed in federal court charges that "Barzinji is not only closely associated with PIJ (as evidenced by ties to al-Arian, including documents seized in Tampa), but also with Hamas."[35]

PIJ is the jihad terror group Palestinian Islamic Jihad.

Just as disturbing were the phone banks in Gaza campaigning for Obama. Muslims in Gaza methodically worked the phones in Internet cafes, calling Americans and doing everything they could to influence the vote.[36]

When New York congressman Jerrold Nadler was confronted with the Gaza phone banks issue while campaigning for Obama in South Florida in early November 2008 he said that if there "really were phone banks in Gaza, that would be a major campaign issue." He said it would be all over the media and be a major problem for the campaign. And he laughed at the idea that Obama was receiving campaign contributions from Gaza. The mainstream media laughed along with him, continuing its refusal to cover this explosive story.

If there had been just one questionable tie, one link to jihadist entities, one link to groups advocating the destruction of Israel, Barack Obama might have merited the free pass he got from the mainstream media about this. But there were so many.

And to this day they have never been explained.

SAMANTHA POWER

Some say, of course, that Barack Hussein Obama should not be held responsible for associations he made years or even decades ago. It's unclear why that should be if he has never adequately renounced or repudiated these associations. But even if he has in some cases, as a candidate and as president he has surrounded himself with advisers who have distinguished themselves by their anti-Israel positions.

One Obama foreign policy adviser, Samantha Power, resigned from the Obama campaign team under fire in March 2008 after calling Hillary Clinton a "monster." Obama never seemed fazed by her calling, in a 2002 interview with Harry Kreisler of the Institute for International Studies at Berkeley, for military action against Israel to secure the creation of a Palestinian state.[37]

Power said that establishing a Palestinian state would mean "sacrificing—or investing, I think, more than sacrificing—billions of dollars, not in servicing Israel's military, but actually investing in the new state of Palestine, in investing the billions of dollars it would probably take, also, to support what will have to be a mammoth protection force, not of the old Rwanda kind, but a meaningful military presence." She said that this would "require external intervention."

Many observers quite reasonably concluded that in this Power meant that the United States should invade Israel in order to secure the creation and protection of a Palestinian state. Confronted about this during the Obama presidential campaign, Power made no attempt to explain or excuse her statement: "Even I don't understand it. . . . This makes no sense to me. . . . The quote seems so weird." She assured supporters of Israel that she did not believe in "imposing a settlement."[38]

Power's anti-Israel bias was not limited to that one statement. When the much-hyped "Jenin Massacre" of 2002 turned out to have been a Palestinian propaganda operation rather than an actual massacre, Power remained skeptical, saying at a conference funded by George Soros: "I was struck by a [*New York Times*] headline that accompanied a news story on the publication of the Human Rights Watch report. The headline was, I believe: 'Human Rights Reports Finds Massacre Did Not Occur in Jenin.' The second paragraph said, 'Oh, but lots of war crimes did.' Why wouldn't they make the war crimes the headline and the non-massacre the second paragraph?" *National Review*'s Michael Rubin commented: "It is questionable whether any war crimes occurred in Jenin, except of course the war crimes associated with Palestinian assembly of suicide bombs which Palestinian terrorists—not uniformed officials—used to target civilians on buses and elderly in hotels. But, that does not seem to be what Samantha Power means."[39]

Indeed not. The *New Statesman* noted in March 2008 that Power "has been fiercely attacked by bloggers objecting to her questioning the US's axiomatic support for Israel on security matters. 'So much of it is about: "Is he going to be good for the Jews?" ' "[40]

She didn't explain what she found wrong with that question.

Yet despite all this, Barack Obama hired her first for his campaign team and then rehired her in November 2008 as part of his transition team for the State Department; then once in office, he appointed her to the National Security Council as senior director for multilateral affairs and human rights. And in August 2009 he demonstrated his confidence in Samantha Power yet again. The White House announced that she would "coordinate the efforts of the many parts of the U.S. government on Iraqi refugees and internally displaced persons (IDPs), including the Department of State, U.S. Agency for International Development, Department of Homeland Security, and Department of Defense."[41]

ROBERT MALLEY

The anti-Israel statements of Robert Malley, whom Obama tabbed for an important mission right after he was elected president, were even worse than Power's.

Early on in his campaign, Obama named Robert Malley one of his primary foreign policy advisers—to the immediate consternation of Israeli officials. One Israeli security official noted in February 2008: "We are noting with concern some of Obama's picks as advisers, particularly Robert Malley, who has expressed sympathy to Hamas and Hizbullah and offered accounts of Israeli-Palestinian negotiations that don't jibe with the facts."[42]

Malley's sympathy was too much for the dancing Obama of the presidential campaign: he dropped Malley in May 2008 after it came to light that he had met with representatives of the jihad terror group Hamas.[43]

However, this turned out to be only a trial separation, not a divorce. Meeting with an Islamic terrorist group was not a disqualifying résumé item for Barack Hussein Obama. Only six months after Obama had dismissed him, the now-President Obama sent Malley to Egypt and Syria. "The tenor of the messages," explained an aide to Malley, "was that the Obama administration would take into greater account Egyptian and Syrian interests."[44]

Malley was a good choice to convey such a message. He has coauthored opinion pieces with a former adviser to Yasir Arafat and has repeatedly called upon the United States to hold talks with Hamas. His anti-Israel record was perfect; he even blamed Israel for the failure of the Camp David talks of 2000, when Arafat shocked the world by rejecting an offer to establish a Palestinian state in Gaza, the West Bank, and East Jerusalem and beginning another bloody intifada instead. When Hamas won the Palestinian elections in the winter of 2006, Malley explained the result as stemming from "anger at years of humiliation and loss of self-respect because of Israeli settlement expansion, Arafat's imprisonment, Israel's incursions, Western lecturing and, most recently and tellingly, the threat of an aid cut off in the event of an Islamist success."

Jihadist intransigence and Islamic anti-Semitism? Malley had nothing to say about either.

Malley has continued to defend Hamas and call for its acceptance by the United States, saying that "a renewed national compact and the return of Hamas to the political fold would upset Israel's strategy of perpetuating Palestinian geographic and political division."[45]

ZBIGNIEW BRZEZINSKI

In devising plans to frustrate Israel's self-defense, however, Malley had nothing on Zbigniew Brzezinski, the national security adviser during the Carter administration. Obama consulted Brzezinski for advice during his campaign, calling the octogenarian Brzezinski "one of our most outstanding scholars and thinkers" and saying that he was "someone I have learned an immense amount from."

This came at a time when Brzezinski raised eyebrows with his claim that the "Jewish lobby" in the United States was "too powerful." Brzezinski complained that "there is a McCarthy-ite tendency among some people in the Jewish community. They operate not by arguing but by slandering, vilifying, demonising. They very promptly wheel out anti-Semitism. There is an element of paranoia in this inclination to view any serious attempt at a compromised peace as somehow directed against Israel."[46]

Yet Brzezinski himself was not an unwavering advocate of a "compromised peace"—he recognized the need for force under some circumstances. But he envisioned that force being used not in Israel's defense, but against Israel. Bizarrely, he even called for the United States to protect *Iran* from an Israeli strike against Iranian nuclear facilities. "We are not exactly impotent little babies," he declared in a September 2009 interview. If the Israelis struck Iran, he said, "they have to fly over our airspace in Iraq. Are we just going to sit there and watch?" Brzezinski advocated military action against Israel to stop it from striking Iran: "If they fly over, you go up and confront them. They have the choice of turning back or not."[47]

Brzezinski, of course, holds no official position in the Obama administration, and there was no indication in the fall of 2009 that Obama was contemplating calling out the Air Force against Israel if it tried to destroy Iran's nuclear installations. But Brzezinski's was not the only anti-Israel voice associated with Obama. There was Power. There was Malley. Before that, there were Wright and al-Mansour and the rest.

There was no comparable group of defenders of Israel around Obama.

ROSA BROOKS

As if Power, Malley, and Brzezinski weren't enough, there were more haters of Israel on the Obama team as well.

Obama named *Los Angeles Times* columnist Rosa Brooks as an

adviser to the undersecretary of defense for policy. Brooks is venomously anti-Israel. During Israel's defensive action in Gaza in January 2009, Brooks wrote an op-ed in the *Times* entitled "Israel can't bomb its way to peace."[48] Stephen A. Silver of the media watchdog Committee for Accuracy in Middle East Reporting in America pointed out that while Brooks gave the number of Palestinian casualties in this conflict, she didn't mention that most of these were combatants, not innocent civilians. "She also takes no interest," noted Silver, "in the fact that Hamas fires missiles at Israeli civilians from the midst of Palestinian population centers—a double war crime specifically intended by Hamas to manufacture Palestinian civilian casualties for public relations purposes whenever Israel tries to defend itself from Hamas terror."

Silver also observed that "Brooks does not bother to note that Israel goes to such lengths to avoid civilian casualties that it often gives up the element of surprise in order to warn Palestinian civilians who may be in harm's way before Israel targets nearby Hamas terrorists."

Like Brzezinski, Brooks also indulged in the familiar anti-Semite's complaint: that a few simple criticisms of Israel got one slapped with accusations of . . . anti-Semitism. (Neither, of course, seemed inclined to own up to how they had prejudged the case and stacked the deck against Israel.) Brooks enunciated this complaint in this way in 2006: "Publish something sharply critical of Israeli government policies and you'll find out. If you're lucky, you'll merely discover that you've been uninvited to some dinner parties. If you're less lucky, you'll be the subject of an all-out attack by neoconservative pundits and accused of rabid anti-Semitism."[49]

CHUCK HAGEL

Former senator Chuck Hagel (R-NE) would probably have agreed with Brooks. According to *The Jerusalem Post*, he was "one of a handful of senators who frequently didn't sign AIPAC-backed letters related to Israel and the peace process during his time in the Senate and opposed additional sanctions on Iran."

Apparently, like Brooks, he has faced criticism for these anti-Israel stances—and has complained that "the Jewish lobby intimidates a lot of people."[50]

Yet Hagel himself doesn't seem to have been particularly intimidated. In the Senate he amassed a significant track record as one of a hard-line hater of Israel who would not affix his name even to the most innocuous pro-Israel initiative. When all but four senators signed a pro-Israel statement in 2000, Hagel was one of the holdouts. The next year, he was again among the few senators—eleven this time—who refused to add their names to a statement urging George W. Bush not to meet with Yasir Arafat as long as the Palestinian groups under his control continued to pursue violence against Israel. In 2005, Hagel, along with twenty-six other senators, opposed a call to the Palestinian Authority to disqualify terror groups from participating in elections. And when twelve senators wrote to the European Union in 2006 asking that the EU join the United States in classifying Hizbullah as a terrorist organization, Hagel was once again one of the few.[51]

Hagel wasn't intimidated, and Barack Hussein Obama wasn't either. In late October 2009 he appointed Hagel cochair of his Intelligence Advisory Board.[52] And in a particularly piquant symbolic move, the appointment was announced at the anti-Israel Jewish group J Street's first annual conference—by Steve Clemons of George Soros's New America Foundation.[53]

And the effect of all this showed in his policies, beginning almost immediately when he took office.

It bodes ill for Jews just how comfortable and at ease Obama obviously is with proud anti-Semites and Israel haters. Obama has appointed all these people, but has concealed their true natures.

THEN THERE IS OBAMA HIMSELF

During the 2008 presidential election, Barack Obama's Web site, Organizing for America, hosted a series of vile anti-American, Jew-hating posts and pieces.

The anti-Semitic onslaught was overwhelming. It included numerous heinous calls for Jewish genocide and incitement to hatred. And it continued after the election, into the fall of 2009—on the official Web site of the man who supposedly is the leader of the free world, and who has editorial control over the Web site.

The site was and is policed closely. It now cautions, "Content posted on our Website by our users is not guaranteed by us as to accuracy, completeness, or usefulness, and we do not endorse any content posted by our users." However, the Web site operators say that they "reserve the right, in our sole discretion," to "discontinue, change, improve or correct" material on the site.[54]

On what basis would they make such judgments? During the campaign, the site moderators said that they removed material they considered to be "disrespectful to our other users" and to "detract from a welcoming community where all people can engage in positive discourse."[55]

What they found disrespectful and removed, and what they allowed to stay on the site, were interesting. Once during the campaign a conservative blogger, Bill Levinson, posted a blog on Obama's Web site consisting entirely of a series of quotations from Obama's own book, *Dreams from My Father*. Obama's people did not approve of their standard-bearer's words, so Levinson's blog and account were deleted from the Obama site in less than forty-eight hours.[56]

That's right: Barack Obama's Web site banned Obama's own words.

But the most disgusting anti-Semitic ravings remained on the site—along with blogs advocating anarchy and the overthrow of the United States Congress.

In April 2008 a post appeared claiming that "Jews owe Africa and Africans everything they have today because if Africa did not shelter them when they were homeless and starving, they would not be here today."[57]

When such things went up on Obama's Web site (and often stayed there for long periods), the Jewish lay leadership in this country said nothing, did nothing, and supported this man. When he became president of the United States, there was even more ugly Jew hatred and incitement to kill Jews on Obama's Web site.

It harked back to Jewish blood libels. Obama's Web site became a hub for Islamic anti-Semitism.

On October 5, 2009, a post went up on Obama's Web site entitled "Nazi Israel . . . Indeed." It quoted a Princeton professor, Richard Falk, referring to Israel's "war crimes," "genocidal tendencies," "holocaust implications," and "holocaust-in-the-making." It spoke about Israel's "Nazi-like crimes and human rights violation."

It claimed: "Comparing the present-day Israel with Nazi Germany one discovers that the majority of the Israeli policies are the exact copies of the Nazi policies. Nazi Germany had invaded its European neighbors extending from England to Russia. Israel had also invaded all its neighboring countries: Egypt, Jordan, Syria, and Lebanon. It is also heavily involved in the invasion of Iraq and Afghanistan. Its tentacles had also reached African countries as far as South Africa, Somalia, Sudan, Angola, and Sierra Leone."

Continuing the lies and blood libels, the post also asserted: "Worse than the Nazis Israeli forces used to invade peaceful Palestinian towns, execute men, women and children in cold blood everywhere and anywhere they encounter them, dynamite their homes on top of their residents, and finally demolish the whole town making room for new

Israeli colonies." It charged that Israel pursued "a pre-meditated geno-cidal plan" against the Palestinian Arabs.[58]

Suffice to say that this entry passed muster with Obama's mod-erators and was clearly acceptable to Obama for America: it was not taken down.

There appeared to be a campaign of sorts to normalize this hatred, as if it were not so bad. Otherwise, why did this poison go up and stay up at Obama's Web site under his name for months? Why didn't Obama stop the terrible hate speech he was hosting on his site?

He must have known that anti-Semites were posting these blood libels on his Web site. So why did he retain the platform as president of the United States?

Why did he encourage it with his silence? By creating an Obama-sanctioned forum that continued to be updated and maintained after his election, a state-sanctioned Web site for such incitement to hate, Obama gave his silent assent to those sentiments.

It is increasingly clear that the Islamic anti-Semitism taught in the Qur'anic classes of Obama's youth in Indonesia and the subsequent adult years he spent with the likes of demagogues and Jew haters like Jeremiah Wright, Bill Ayers, and Louis Farrakhan have made him the man he is.

One Israeli intelligence official summed up Obama's policy toward his country in a nutshell: "Obama wants to make friends with our worst enemies and until now the worst enemies of the United States. Under this policy, we are more than irrelevant. We have become an obstacle."[59]

An obstacle . . . but to what goal?

FOUR

OBAMA AND ISRAEL

THE OBAMA POLICY TOWARD ISRAEL SEEMED TO PROCEED FROM THE ASSUMPTION THAT THE RESPONSIBILITY FOR THE CONFLICT BETWEEN Israel and the Palestinians lay entirely with Israel. It was only three weeks after Barack Hussein Obama took office when Israeli pundit Caroline Glick noted that "since it came into office a month ago, every single Middle East policy the Obama administration has announced has been antithetical to Israel's national security interests." She listed them:

> From President Barack Obama's intense desire to appease Iran's mullahs in open discussions; to his stated commitment to establish a Palestinian state as quickly as possible despite the Palestinians' open rejection of Israel's right to exist and support for terrorism; to his

expressed support for the so-called Saudi peace plan, which would require Israel to commit national suicide by contracting to within indefensible borders and accepting millions of hostile, foreign-born Arabs as citizens and residents of the rump Jewish state; to his decision to end US sanctions against Syria and return the US ambassador to Damascus; to his plan to withdraw US forces from Iraq and so give Iran an arc of uninterrupted control extending from Iran to Lebanon, every single concrete policy Obama has enunciated harms Israel.[1]

Glick could have added the 900 million dollars that the Obama administration announced in February 2009 that it would be giving to the Palestinians in Gaza in order to help them rebuild after the Israeli action in Gaza that winter. "None of the money will go to Hamas, it will be funneled through NGOs and U.N. groups," an administration official insisted.[2]

Reality was not so easy. This bestowal of American largesse came only weeks after the UN Relief and Works Agency announced that it was suspending aid to the Palestinians because Hamas kept hijacking the aid packages.[3] What safeguards did the United States put into place to make sure that this $900 million would not likewise find its way into Hamas coffers?

None.

Three months after Obama took office, his administration launched what Glick termed "its harshest onslaught against Israel to date."[4] Obama's national security adviser, Gen. James L. Jones, stated that "the new administration will convince Israel to compromise on the Palestinian question. We will not push Israel under the wheels of a bus, but we will be more forceful toward Israel than we have been under Bush."[5]

"More forceful" in what way?

Glick reported that that same week, "acting on behalf of Obama,

Jordanian King Abdullah II urged the Arab League to update the so-called Arab peace plan from 2002. That plan, which calls for Israel to withdraw from Jerusalem, Judea, Samaria and the Golan Heights and accept millions of foreign Arabs as citizens as part of the so-called 'right of return' in exchange for 'natural' relations with the Arab world, has been rejected by successive Israeli governments as a diplomatic subterfuge whose goal is Israel's destruction."

How would the destruction of Israel result from this? "By accepting millions of so-called Palestinian refugees," Glick explained, "Israel would effectively cease to be a Jewish state. By shrinking into the 1949 armistice lines, Israel would be unable to defend itself against foreign invasion. And since 'natural relations' is a meaningless term both in international legal discourse and in diplomatic discourse, Israel would have committed national suicide for nothing."[6]

Also during the first week of May 2009, Assistant Secretary of State Rose Gottemoeller broke sharply from precedent by calling upon Israel to join the nuclear Non-Proliferation Treaty: "Universal adherence to the NPT itself, including by India, Israel, Pakistan and North Korea," she asserted, "remains a fundamental objective of the United States."[7]

The Obama administration had made history. This was the first open acknowledgment by a U.S. official that Israel had nuclear weapons at all. Israel itself had never confirmed that it had any, and its American ally had always recognized that to disclose the full nature and extent of Israeli armaments could seriously harm the Jewish state's ability to defend itself against its neighbors.

Its American ally had always recognized this, that is, until the administration of Barack Hussein Obama.

SOUNDING LIKE A ZIONIST

Barack Hussein Obama had a disturbing track record from the beginning. He knew he couldn't win with a background filled with Jew-haters and support for Palestinians. So he did what any politician does when faced with troublesome facts—he began a cover-up. He began an elaborate game of pretending that his positions were other than what they were.

When he began his campaign for president, Obama pursued the Jewish vote in earnest.

Suddenly, without warning, he started sounding like . . . a Zionist.

On January 22, 2008, as the jihad terrorist group Hamas in Gaza was raining rockets upon schools, homes, and residential areas in southern Israel, Senator Barack Obama began to position himself as a defender of Israel. He wrote this to Zalmay Khalilzad, the permanent U.S. representative to the United Nations:

> Gaza is governed by Hamas, which is a terrorist organization sworn to Israel's destruction, and Israeli civilians are being bombarded by rockets on an almost daily basis. This is unacceptable and Israel has the right to respond while seeking to minimize any impact on civilians.
>
> The Security Council should clearly and unequivocally condemn the rocket attacks against Israel, and should make clear that Israel has the right to defend itself against such actions. If it cannot bring itself to make these common sense points, I urge you to ensure that it does not speak at all.[8]

Those of us, like me, who had been studying him for years were taken aback. Others were pleasantly surprised. He was standing up for Israel's right to defend itself just months after claiming that "nobody is suffering more than the Palestinian people."[9] Many people, especially on the Far Left, didn't like the bright young senator's shift one bit. *Mother Jones* huffed that Obama's endorsement of Israeli self-defense was "an object lesson in the intense pressure under which presidential candidates stake out ground on the Israeli-Palestinian conflict, and the extraordinary effectiveness of the self-styled 'pro-Israel' movement."[10]

But Barack Hussein Obama kept moving toward Israel.

On June 4, 2008, in a major address to the American Israel Public Affairs Committee (AIPAC), he called himself a "true friend of Israel." He warned his audience not to take seriously mass e-mails that were circulating warning American Jews that he was just the opposite. He spoke of his "strong commitment to make sure that the bond between the United States and Israel is unbreakable today, tomorrow and forever."

Obama decried the existence of "terrorist groups and political leaders committed to Israel's destruction," and "maps across the Middle East that don't even acknowledge Israel's existence, and government-funded textbooks filled with hatred toward Jews." He lamented the "rockets raining down on Sderot" and the fact that "Israeli children have to take a deep breath and summon uncommon courage every time they board a bus or walk to school."

Obama even claimed—with a straight face—to have been a proud "part of a strong, bipartisan consensus that has stood by Israel in the face of all threats," and stated disapprovingly: "I don't think any of us can be satisfied that America's recent foreign policy has made Israel more secure." He denounced Hamas, Hizbullah, and Iran, saying that the latter "always posed a greater threat to Israel than Iraq." He shed crocodile tears over "the heavy burdens borne by the Israeli people." Obama even criticized "those who would lay all of the problems of the Middle East at the doorstep of Israel and its supporters, as if the

Israeli-Palestinian conflict is the root of all trouble in the region" and those who "blame the Middle East's only democracy for the region's extremism."

Spoken like a real mensch!

Americans are, by and large, big supporters of Israel. They thought Obama was, too. His shift in stance gave many people that impression. Barack Hussein Obama made a solemn promise: "Our alliance is based on shared interests and shared values. Those who threaten Israel threaten us. Israel has always faced these threats on the front lines. And I will bring to the White House an unshakeable commitment to Israel's security." He declared that as president he would ensure "Israel's qualitative military advantage" and its ability to "defend itself from any threat—from Gaza to Tehran." He said that he would "always stand up for Israel's right to defend itself in the United Nations and around the world."

What about the Palestinians? He didn't entirely abandon his old friends. He called for a two-state solution, but even then Obama said: "We must isolate Hamas unless and until they renounce terrorism, recognize Israel's right to exist, and abide by past agreements. There is no room at the negotiating table for terrorist organizations." He warned that "the Palestinian people must understand that progress will not come through the false prophets of extremism or the corrupt use of foreign aid."

The expertness of Obama's performance raised questions about his inconsistency and disingenuousness.

And when he offered explanations, he usually just made matters worse. After all, when he spoke at AIPAC in 2007, he made "a clear and strong commitment to the security of Israel: our strongest ally in the region and its only established democracy."[11]

I was there. The Jews at AIPAC gave him rock-star treatment. They couldn't get enough of him. They loved him. Kissed his ring.

He was swarmed by well-wishers. Yet only nine days later, he made his infamous claim that "nobody is suffering more than the Palestinian people."[12] When confronted about this odd and incendiary remark, Obama offered an unconvincing explanation: "Well, keep in mind what the remark actually, if you had the whole thing, said. And what I said is nobody has suffered more than the Palestinian people from the failure of the Palestinian leadership to recognize Israel, to renounce violence, and to get serious about negotiating peace and security for the region."

But actually, Thomas Beaumont of *The Des Moines Register* reported on March 12, 2007, that Obama attributed the allegedly unique suffering of the Palestinian people to the "stalled peace efforts with Israel," and said nothing about failures of the Palestinian leadership or violence on the part of the Palestinians.[13]

No one, no matter how nimble minded, can explain away such duplicity.

And even in the midst of all his pro-Israel statements of 2008, there were warning signs. The Rev. Jesse Jackson (who described his relationship with Obama as that of "a neighbor or, better still, a member of the family") said forthrightly in October 2008, as Obama appeared poised for victory, that the "Zionists who have controlled American policy for decades" would find that control loosening. "Obama is about change," Jackson asserted. "And the change that Obama promises is not limited to what we do in America itself. It is a change of the way America looks at the world and its place in it."

But most Americans who supported Israel paid no heed. Nor did they stir when Obama himself, while proclaiming that "Israel's security is sacrosanct" and "non-negotiable," in practically that same breath declared that "the Palestinians need a state that is contiguous and cohesive." Contiguous? A contiguous Palestinian state comprising both Gaza and Judea and Samaria ("the West Bank") would necessitate either a noncontiguous, bisected Israel, or a severely reduced Jewish state. Yet at the same time Obama also promised that Jerusalem would "remain the capital of Israel," and would "remain undivided."

It would take a Solomon—or maybe a Suleiman the Magnificent—to make sense of all of Obama's contradictory recommendations.

Yet above all, despite expounding upon his desire to negotiate with Iran, Barack Obama promised: "I will always keep the threat of military action on the table to defend our security and our ally Israel."[14]

High-sounding words, and most Jews believed those words. Jewish comedienne Sarah Silverman expressed the prevailing tendency among American Jews to keep their heads firmly in the sand in September 2008 when she exhorted Jews to make "the Great Schlep" to visit their grandparents and urge them to vote for Obama: "If Barack Obama does not become the next president of the United States," she declared, "I'm going to blame the Jews." She asserted that "Barack Obama's foreign policy is much more stabilizing than John McCain's, and much better for Israel."[15]

On what did she base that claim? Wishful thinking.

I traveled to South Florida days before the election to debunk the mythology of the Obama brand and Silverman's demands that Jewish grandchildren bully bubbe and zayde into voting for Obama, but it was for naught. Video clips of Sarah's rant and my Florida trek are still available on YouTube for viewing. Watch them. It's an eye-opener. But alas, the spell was not broken—no thanks to a media completely and utterly in the tank for this mysterious, charismatic chameleon. The spell ultimately got shattered, but not until after the election. Seventy-eight percent of American Jews voted for Barack Hussein Obama to become president. And once he became president, that's all they had: words. As a famous Jew, Jesus of Nazareth, once said, it is not by words, but "by their fruits you shall know them."

And so we know him.

For despite everything he said at AIPAC, when Barack Obama became president of the United States, he began a relentlessly anti-Israel course, treating America's foremost ally in the Middle East like an enemy, and its enemies—including jihad-enabling terror states such as Syria—like allies.

COZYING UP TO HAMAS

For all the Jews who voted for him, Barack Hussein Obama had an inauguration present: he selected the leader of a group that had been named an unindicted coconspirator in a Hamas terror funding case to present a prayer during his inauguration festivities. Ingrid Mattson, president of ISNA, offered a prayer at the National Cathedral during inaugural festivities on January 20, 2009.

Superficially, Obama's choice was understandable: Ingrid Mattson was a Canadian convert to Islam who carefully cultivated the image of a moderate spokesperson. Yet her organization's record is far from clean. Federal prosecutors in summer 2008 rejected claims that ISNA was unfairly named an unindicted coconspirator in the Holy Land Foundation terror funding case.[16]

ISNA has even admitted prior ties to the Muslim Brotherhood and Hamas.[17] The Muslim Brotherhood is an international Islamic organization dedicated to establishing the rule of Islamic law everywhere on earth. Hamas identified itself in its charter as "one of the wings of Muslim Brotherhood in Palestine." The charter also quotes the founder of the Muslim Brotherhood, Hassan Al-Banna: "Israel will exist and will continue to exist until Islam will obliterate it, just as it obliterated others before it."[18]

The Brotherhood has designs on the United States, too. In a memorandum on the Muslim Brotherhood's strategy in the United States, a

Muslim Brotherhood operative named ISNA as an allied organization in what it called "a kind of grand Jihad in eliminating and destroying the Western civilization from within and 'sabotaging' its miserable house by their hands and the hands of the believers so that it is eliminated and God's religion is made victorious over all other religions."[19]

Mattson has also tried to set Jews and Christians against one another. Speaking at Harvard's Kennedy School of Government in March 2007, Mattson said: "Right-wing Christians are very risky allies for American Jews, because they [the Christians] are really anti-Semitic. They do not like Jews."[20]

Neither Obama nor the media ever asked Mattson to explain ISNA's ties to the Muslim Brotherhood and Hamas.

And so she prayed for Barack Hussein Obama on January 20, 2009. After that, Valerie Jarrett, Obama's senior advisor for public engagement and international affairs and a longtime, close Obama aide, asked Mattson to join the White House Council on Women and Girls, which is dedicated to "advancing women's leadership in all communities and sectors—up to the U.S. presidency—by filling the leadership pipeline with a richly diverse, critical mass of women."[21]

A hijab-wearing leader of a group with ties to terrorists and Islamic supremacists—that's diverse, all right!

But prayers and largely symbolic appointments were the least of Israel's worries. When Obama became president, he began to act, and to show his true colors.

MAKING FRIENDS WITH A STATE SPONSOR OF TERRORISM

One of Israel's chief enemies is, of course, Syria. It partners with Iran in aiding the terror group Hizbullah that likewise is determined to wipe Israel off the map. Syria has given assistance to Al-Qaeda in Iraq;

today, it is building a nuclear reactor on the sly—with North Korean assistance. Israel bombed the site of a suspected Syrian nuclear reactor in September 2007. Many suspected even then that the reactor bombed by the IDF was not the only nuclear activity going on in Syria. Still smarting over its loss of the Golan Heights in the Six-Day War of 1967, Syria plays host to jihad terror organizations and individuals that have vowed to destroy Israel.

The U.S. State Department named Syria a State Sponsor of Terrorism on December 29, 1979. Syria has been on that list ever since—the longest tenure of any of the world's rogue states. Cuba didn't make the list until 1982; Iran was added in 1984; and Sudan in 1993. This designation results, according to the State Department Web site, in "restrictions on U.S. foreign assistance; a ban on defense exports and sales; certain controls over exports of dual use items; and miscellaneous financial and other restrictions."[22]

The designation was richly deserved. Damascus is a cosmopolitan hub of the global Islamic jihad, and has been the site of numerous summit meetings between jihadist leaders. Hassan Nasrallah of the terrorist group Hizbullah met there in July 2007 with President Mahmoud Ahmadinejad of Iran.[23] The terrorist group Hamas maintains an office in Damascus, and Hamas leader Khaled Meshaal met there in early 2009 with Ali Larijani, the speaker of the Iranian parliament and one of the most powerful politicians in the Islamic Republic of Iran.[24]

The United States has taken Syria to task for supporting jihad terror groups including Hizbullah and Hamas. And in February 2005, the Bush administration recalled its ambassador from Damascus as an expression of "profound outrage" over the murder of the prime minister of Lebanon, Rafik Hariri, an opponent of Syria.[25]

Within weeks of taking office, Obama announced plans to ease sanctions that had been put into place against Syria because of its involvement in enabling the global jihad. "The Obama administration," reported the *World Tribune*, "was expected to suspend U.S. sanctions on Syria's military and energy programs."[26] On June 24, 2009, he announced that he was returning an American ambassador to Damascus. "This strongly reflects the administration's recognition of the role Syria plays," explained White House press secretary Robert Gibbs, "and the hope of the role that the Syrian government can play constructively to promote peace and stability in the region."[27]

What had Syria done to convince Obama that it could play a constructive role "to promote peace and stability in the region"?

Nothing.

Syrian president Basher Assad hadn't kicked Hamas out of Damascus. He hadn't cut ties with the bloodthirsty mullahs of the Islamic Republic of Iran, or their equally bloodthirsty clients in Lebanon, Hizbullah. Syria was still one of the four nations designated as State Sponsors of Terrorism.

So what made Barack Obama think that it would be a good time to approach Syria with arms outstretched, fists unclenched? Well, he had promised to do so in his Inaugural Address. But his gestures of goodwill were never reciprocated.

And given the consistent streak of hostility toward Israel that runs through his associations, his appointments, and his actions during his first months as president, maybe he never expected them to be. For without removing Syria from the State Department list of State Sponsors of Terrorism—or having any reason to do so—according to Syria's ambassador in Washington, Imad Mustafa, the Obama administration in July 2009 lifted a ban on selling to Syria's aviation industry, as well as a prohibition on selling information technology to Syria.

More easing of restrictions was to come, said Mustafa, despite the restrictions on "defense exports" and more to a State Sponsor of Terrorism.[28] And despite Syria's fanatical hatred of Israel.

Mustafa was right. In October 2009 it came to light that the Obama administration had played a key role in smoothing the progress of a trade agreement between Syria and the European Union that would mean as much as 7 billion dollars a year for the slumping Syrian economy. The deal had been in the offing since 2004, but the Bush administration had opposed it because of Syria's ties to Hizbullah and Iran. Without asking for anything but promises in return, Obama dropped American opposition to the deal, and it went through.[29]

OBAMA AND ABBAS VS. NETANYAHU

During their press conference on May 18, 2009, Israeli prime minister Binyamin Netanyahu called Barack Obama a "great friend of Israel" and a "true friend of Israel." He thanked him for "your friendship to Israel and your friendship to me." He even praised Obama as a "great leader: a great leader of the United States, a great leader of the world."

Netanyahu sounded like a man who was trying to convince himself of something. Perhaps he thought he might convince Obama of Israel's historic loyalty and importance as America's most important strategic ally in the Middle East. After Obama's performance at that press conference, it was understandable that the Israeli prime minister would feel the need to do that. It became clear at the meeting, which Obama had initially postponed, that Israel was being relegated to second-class status as far as its relationship with the United States was concerned.

In his remarks Obama was far less effusive than was Netanyahu. Obama did not call Netanyahu a "friend of the United States," or confirm Netanyahu's effusions about his alleged pro-Israel sentiments. He praised the Israeli leader's "political skills" and said that he was confident the prime minister would "rise to the occasion" as he would be "confronted with as many important decisions about the long-term strategic interests of Israel as any prime minister that we've seen in a very long time." He declared, as if his solicitude for the Palestinians was quite understandable but that his concern for the Israelis was unusual, that it was "in the interests not only of the Palestinians but also the Israelis and the United States and the international community to achieve a two-state solution in which Israelis and Palestinians are living side by side in peace and security."

Obama then noted, correctly, that "we have seen progress stalled on this front." But just as he has consistently acted since he has been president as if the conflict between the United States and the Islamic world is entirely the fault of the United States and within America's power to end, so he seemed to assume that it was entirely up to Netanyahu and Israel to get progress moving toward this vaunted two-state solution: "And I suggested to the prime minister that he has a historic opportunity to get a serious movement on this issue during his tenure."

To be sure, Obama did say that "there is no reason why we should not seize this opportunity and this moment for all the parties concerned to take seriously those obligations and to move forward in a way that assures Israel's security, that stops the terrorist attacks that have been such a source of pain and hardship, and that we can stop rocket attacks on Israel, but that also allows Palestinians to govern themselves as an independent state that allows economic development to take place, that allows them to make serious progress in meeting the aspirations of their people."[30]

However, while calling upon Netanyahu to rise to the occasion, Obama issued no similar call to Palestinian Arab leaders. Yet the weekend before Obama met with Netanyahu, Hamas, in control of the Gaza Strip and a significant presence in the West Bank, had repeated that it would never recognize Israel's right to exist—in other words, it was still dedicated to Israel's total destruction.[31] Hamas chief Khaled Meshaal said also, nine days before Obama met with Netanyahu, that Hamas would never accept a two-state solution, either.[32]

And what if it did, anyway? The PLO's ambassador to Lebanon, Abbas Zaki, said in April 2009 that "with the two-state solution, in my opinion, Israel will collapse, because if they get out of Jerusalem, what will become of all the talk about the Promised Land and the Chosen People? What will become of all the sacrifices they made—just to be told to leave? They consider Jerusalem to have a spiritual status. The Jews consider Judea and Samaria to be their historic dream. If the Jews leave those places, the Zionist idea will begin to collapse. It will regress of its own accord. Then we will move forward."[33]

Was this the kind of attitude that Obama wanted to encourage? Certainly if he didn't, he did nothing to discourage it.

And his take on Iran's threat to Israel was no better. Obama declared during his meeting with Netanyahu that "it is in U.S. national security interests to assure that Israel's security as an independent Jewish state is maintained." But in speaking of Iran's nuclear threat, he said that he wanted Iran to be "in a position to provide opportunities and prosperity for their people, but that the way to achieve those goals is not through the pursuit of a nuclear weapon"—as if Iran was pursuing nukes to alleviate some economic distress than can be relieved in some other way.

Fanatical Shi'ite messianism and genocidal hatred for Israel? Nothing that a few good talks couldn't cure!

Obama also said: "It's not clear to me why my outstretched hand would be interpreted as weakness." But it wasn't just reporters who saw it as weakness, it was the Iranian mullahs, who stepped up their demands and ratcheted up the bellicosity of their rhetoric considerably once Obama took office. Still, Israel's "great friend," and the nominal standard-bearer of the free world against the global jihad, did not adjust his course.

The jihad against Israel stayed on course also. Obama said during his press conference with Netanyahu that he supported "a two-state solution in which Israelis and Palestinians are living side by side in peace and security." Hamas, unimpressed—or even emboldened—by Obama's concessions and overtures, responded by sending rockets into Israel again on the next day, severely damaging a home in Sderot and wounding several people. As the rockets fell, Senator and 2004 Democratic presidential candidate John Kerry (D-MA) was meeting with Netanyahu to discuss the finer points of Obama's plan for peace between Israel and the Palestinians.[34]

Ten days after Obama met with Netanyahu, he welcomed Palestinian Authority president Mahmoud Abbas to the White House. The contrast with the chilly atmosphere of the Netanyahu meeting couldn't have been more stark. Obama met Abbas bearing a gift: a firm U.S. demand that Israel stop the settlements in what it called Palestinian territories.[35] He had met Netanyahu with no corresponding gift: no call to the Palestinians to stop the rocket attacks into Israel, or to tone down the genocidal and hate-filled anti-Semitic rhetoric that filled their airwaves even on children's programs, or to recognize Israel in a definitive and honest way.

MILITARY TRAINING FOR THE PALESTINIANS

In May 2009 came the revelation that the United States and allied military, under the command of Lt. Gen. Keith Dayton, was training 1,500 Palestinian troops. "We also have something in our pocket," Dayton explained, "called the West Bank Training Initiative where we have plans to continue a series of courses in the West Bank on logistics, leadership, first aid, maintenance, English language, battalion staff training and driver education. These are led by our British and Turkish officers with an eye to eventually turning this over to the Palestinians themselves."[36]

Would American-trained Palestinian troops one day go into

battle against the forces of American ally Israel? It was a distinct possibility.

But, of course, that was not why Lieutenant General Dayton and his aides were training the Palestinians. American officials were evidently hoping that the Palestinians trained in logistics, leadership, and battalion staff training would use this knowledge to fight against Hamas. That was fanciful enough. It reflected the widespread fantasy in Washington that Fatah represented a "moderate" alternative to Hamas and, once it prevailed in the Palestinian Authority, would establish a Palestinian state that would recognize Israel's right to exist and live in peace side by side with the Jewish state. No one could have held this fantasy without ignoring numerous indications to the contrary, such as this July 2009 statement by Rafik Natsheh of the Fatah Central Committee:

> Fatah does not recognize Israel's right to exist nor have we ever asked others to do so. All these reports about recognizing Israel are false. It's all media nonsense. We don't ask other factions to recognize Israel because we in Fatah have never recognized Israel.[37]

Even aside from its Fatah fantasy, however, there were indications that the U.S. government under Barack Hussein Obama no longer had much of a problem with Hamas participating in the government of the new Palestinian state Obama so longed to establish. He had talked tough during his campaign about isolating Hamas and compelling it to renounce terrorism, but once he took the Oath of Office, he seemed to forget everything he had ever said about the terrorist group.

THE RENEGING BEGINS

Even before his meeting with Netanyahu, and even before the fateful week in May 2009 that Glick saw as marking the Obama administration's "harshest onslaught against Israel to date,"[38] Obama's pro-Israel pose was a distant memory. He was working hard to renege on his 2008 AIPAC promise to "isolate Hamas unless and until they renounce terrorism, recognize Israel's right to exist, and abide by past agreements."[39]

He said at that time that "there is no room at the negotiating table for terrorist organizations," but as president, in April 2009, he was singing a different tune. He asked Congress to revise American laws preventing financial aid to terrorist organizations so that the United States could keep funding the Palestinian Authority even with Hamas as part of the government.[40]

Rep. Mark Steven Kirk (R-IL) had an eye for the outrage of legitimizing a group that celebrated the murders of Israeli civilians in pizza parlors and on buses. He remarked drily to Secretary of State Hillary Clinton that this was tantamount to supporting a government that "only has a few Nazis in it."[41]

The Obama administration did not ask the Palestinians to meet any conditions whatsoever, despite the conditions Obama had promised he would insist upon while he was campaigning for president. In October 2009, national security adviser Gen. James Jones declared that nothing was going to stand in the way of the creation of a Palestinian state. Speaking of the Israeli-Palestinian conflict at the Fourth Annual Gala of the American Task Force on Palestine (ATFP), Jones said, "The time has come to relaunch negotiations without preconditions to reach a final status agreement on two states."[42]

Jones emphasized the president's personal commitment to this resolution: "President Obama's dedication to achieve these goals is unshaken, is committed, and we will be relentless in our pursuit of achieving these." Belying Obama's AIPAC promises, Jones said nothing about isolating Hamas until they renounce terrorism. Not a word about the need for Hamas or any other Palestinian entity to recognize

Israel's right to exist. Nothing about compelling the Palestinians to abide by past agreements, which they have routinely violated. And Jones was entirely mum about the necessity for the Palestinians to renounce "the false prophets of extremism," of which they are obviously still quite enamored.

History is full of ironies. And the Palestinians had more in store.

Just as Hamas fired rockets into Israel the day after Obama spoke confidently, at his press conference with Netanyahu, about Israel living peacefully side by side with a Palestinian state, so also the day after General Jones assured the ATFP crowd that the state would be established, Hamas made sure that no one got the impression that the Palestinians really had any intention at all of living in peace with the Israelis. Hamas's Al-Aqsa TV broadcast a children's program, "Tomorrow's Pioneers," that featured a Palestinian child expressing a desire to become an English teacher in order "to teach children the language of their enemy." Then a recurring character on the program, Nassur the bear, chimed in: "Like me! Just like I know the Zionist enemy's language."[43]

That Palestinian children were being taught that the United States and Israel are the "enemy" is no surprise. Still, coming at the same time as Jones's remarks, it provided yet another indication of just how disconnected from reality was the Obama administration's policy. General Jones, according to an ATFP press release, "said that ending the conflict and the occupation is essential because what is at stake is 'nothing less than the dignity and the security of all human beings.'"

But Obama and Jones never quite seemed to grasp the fact that only one side was teaching its children that the other was the "enemy." And that sentiment was in any case hardly compatible with the new era of peace that was supposed to dawn with the establishment of this state. Would the Palestinians cease to regard Israel and the United States as their "enemies" once this state was established? Would they begin to teach their children peace and tolerance? Would they renounce the jihad doctrine that settles for nothing less than the entire destruction of Israel, as their leaders have repeated on numerous occasions?

The real answer to all those questions and others like them is "no." But even worse, Obama and Jones weren't asking them. They were determined to establish a Palestinian state despite the abundant evidence that the Palestinians have not renounced their jihadist intransigence, and would use a new Palestinian state as a terror base from which to launch new attacks against the "Zionist entity"—just as Israel's withdrawal from Gaza did not usher in the promised new era of peace, but only more jihad.

Obama and Jones should have known better. And they probably did. For they knew Hamas. Apparently, they liked Hamas. For as he made concessions to Hamas in Gaza, Obama pursued the same policy stateside, making numerous overtures to dubious Hamas-linked entities.

As we have seen, the promise of Israel's destruction is in the first paragraph of the Hamas charter. This is no secret. And Hamas refuses to alter it or change its mission.

"Israel will exist and will continue to exist until Islam will obliterate it, just as it obliterated others before it."

But Obama didn't just sidle up to Jew-haters abroad. He sought to legitimize them here as well. For one thing, he wasn't through cozying up to the Islamic Society of North America.

THE JEW-HATING ISNA CONVENTION

His eye—as always—on outreach to Muslims, Barack Obama on July 3, 2009, sent Valerie Jarrett, his senior advisor and assistant to President Obama for public engagement and intergovernmental affairs, to speak at the 46th Annual Convention of the Islamic Society of North America (ISNA).

Jarrett ended up addressing a racist hate-fest. At the ISNA conference, pure hate speech and Islamic anti-Semitism were promoted—and the Obama administration was there.

Imam Warith-Deen Umar spoke about his books, *Jews for Salaam: The Straight Path to Global Peace* and *Judaiology*. Umar, the former head of New York prisons' Muslim chaplain program, repeatedly described Jewish conspiracies to control the world: "Why do this small number of people," he asked, "have control of the world? . . . There's some people in the world says no Holocaust even happened. Some of their leaders say no Holocaust even happened. Well it did happen. These people were punished. They were punished for a reason, because they were serially disobedient to Allah." [44] He means that the Jews, who are portrayed as "serially disobedient to Allah" in the Qur'an, deserved all they got in the Holocaust.

Valerie Jarrett was there. She was apparently right at home, uttering nary a word of protest.

HAMAS TV IN WASHINGTON

That's not all. In July 2009, Obama invited the propaganda television station of Hamas, Al-Quds TV, to film propaganda in the United States—on the American taxpayer's dime.

The proposal came from the U.S. Consulate in Jerusalem: Al-Quds TV, the mouthpiece for Hamas, would film "several documentaries on the life of Muslims in America.

The nominated 2–3 person TV crew will conduct interviews with local Muslim leaders and individuals, visit Muslim institutions and organizations, and meet with USG officials." All at U.S. taxpayers' expense. [45]

The stated goal of this venture was to "improve attitudes of Palestinian public and leaders toward U.S. policies, principles, and people." It would try to accomplish this by showing Muslims in America as "active participants in civil society" and highlighting their "contributions to U.S. society overall." The documentaries would show that Muslims in the United States enjoyed "equal and full exercise of guaranteed civil rights and full protection under the law to practice their religion freely," and would "help counter numerous local press reports of alleged discrimination against Muslims living in the United States."[46]

Why did the State Department think it necessary to appeal to the Palestinians in this way? Why wasn't it calling upon them to improve their *own* human-rights situation, and to end the endless vilification of Israel on the same TV stations that were slated to run these documentaries?

Why was it trying to improve the image of the United States, as if we were the guilty party, instead of challenging the oppressive and bloody rule of Hamas in Gaza?

In fact, this attempt to "improve the image of the United States" became official policy of the U.S. government. The State Department commissioned a confidential survey of Palestinians in the West Bank, East Jerusalem, and the Gaza Strip. The Department of State's Office of Opinion Research, the official pollster for the U.S. government outside the United States, is designed to gauge foreign public opinion so as to help diplomats in their missions. This office commissioned a "reputable local research firm" that conducted "face-to-face interviews" with "a representative sample of 2,000 adult Palestinians, age 18" to ascertain what could be done to "improve the image of the U.S." in the minds of jihadist barbarians who celebrate the murders of people going about their business in buses and restaurants.

The results of the poll were hardly surprising. The respondents demanded more money (in line with the Qur'an's demand that non-

Muslims pay tribute to Islamic rulers), more respect for Islam, and more pressure on Israel.

Was a survey like this one taken in Israel?[47]

HONORING AN ANTI-SEMITE

In August 2009, the Obama administration announced that Mary Robinson would be given the Presidential Medal of Freedom—the highest honor given to civilians in the United States.

Superficially, it seemed like a reasonable choice. Mary Robinson had been president of Ireland and United Nations High Commissioner for Human Rights. But—unsurprisingly, given Obama's other appointments and associations—she has also been consistent in her virulent opposition to Israel. Gil Troy, a professor of history at McGill University in Toronto, notes that "she was one of the people most responsible for the great debacle at Durban, 2001, when a conference convened to fight racism became a UN-sponsored hate-fest against Jews." Troy points out that "in her closing remarks Robinson declared 'we . . . succeeded,' a shocking statement considering that anti-Zionists hijacked the conference, demonizing Israel, bullying Jewish participants and distributing crude anti-Semitic images of hooked-nose Jews at the parallel NGO [Non-Governmental Organizations] forum."[48]

Robinson also displayed a thoroughgoing pro-Palestinian bias and tendency to demonize Israel while serving as UN High Commissioner for Human Rights. And her Medal of Freedom was no mistake, no oversight—for when Obama started looking for a Jewish group with which he could talk, he sought one out that held views about the Palestinians and Israel that were virtually identical to those of Mary Robinson.

J STREET

Obama kept finding new ways to go from bad to worse. He gave his official sanction to one Jewish group—J Street. J Street was unique among Jewish groups in being anti-Israel. Isi Liebler, former chairman of the Governing Board of the World Jewish Congress, challenged J Street's "duplicity in trying to masquerade as a Jewish mainstream 'pro-Israel' organisation while consistently campaigning against the Jewish state."[49]

Philip Klein, *The American Spectator*'s Washington correspondent, says that "while the group bills itself as the 'pro Israel' and 'pro peace' alternative to the American Israel Public Affairs Committee, in reality it is a liberal organization actively campaigning against Israel's right to defend itself."[50]

Just how extreme and anti-Israel is J Street? According to Liebler, as of October 2009 "Arab and pro-Iranian elements were providing approximately 10% of J Street funding, a somewhat bizarre situation for a genuinely 'pro-Israel' organisation."[51] Federal Election Commission records showed that tens of thousands of dollars flowed into J Street from Arabs and Muslims, including some donations from groups involved in agitating for the Palestinian cause.[52]

Liebler pointed out that J Street seemed to attract support from groups that have always opposed Israel. Genevieve Lynch, a lobbyist for the National Iranian American Council, which has numerous ties to the bloody Iranian government, is a member of J Street's finance committee. Judith Barnett, whom Liebler calls "a former registered agent for Saudi Arabia," donates to J Street and is a member of its advisory council. Another donor to J Street is Nancy Dutton, a former lawyer for the Saudi Arabian embassy.[53]

In no other era would this radical group of self-hating Jewish sell-outs have been anything but a fringe group.

But in Barack Obama's America, this transparent front group became a darling of the White House. James Jones, the national security adviser, was the keynote speaker at the group's very first annual convention in 2009. Other speakers included the former director of the hard-left group MoveOn.org, as well as Salam al-Marayati of the Muslim Public Affairs Council (MPAC), who in the aftermath of 9/11 accused Israel of complicity in the attacks.

"If we're going to look at suspects, we should look to the groups that benefit the most from these kinds of incidents, and I think we should put the state of Israel on the suspect list because I think this diverts attention from what's happening in the Palestinian territories so that they can go on with their aggression and occupation and apartheid policies."[54]

J Street was inevitable in the hostile climate for Israel that Obama has created in Washington. Once Obama was elected president, it was only a matter of time before a leftist Jewish group associated with anti-Semitic ideologies would emerge—particularly when those were the people the administration would meet with when choosing "Jewish groups" with which to confer.

As president, Obama could have chosen to meet and work with any Jewish group in the United States. He didn't choose the Zionist Organization of America (ZOA). He didn't even choose AIPAC.

Instead, Obama decided to work with J Street.

THE MISSING CZAR

During Obama's first six months in office, his administration appointed upward of forty "czars." But there was one czar appointment on which Obama dragged his feet for months—and it was an omission that spoke volumes. While he worked with relentless energy to create and fill new positions by the dozens, he suddenly seemed overcome with lassitude when it came to appointing an Anti-Semitism Czar—and this was one appointment that was actually called for by law. The *Jerusalem Post* reported on July 30, 2009, that 'the Obama administration has failed to name an envoy for monitoring and combating anti-Semitism around the world, as mandated by US law, since the previous ambassador was relieved of his duties at the start of the president's term more than six months ago.' Rafael Medoff, director of the Washington D.C.–based David S. Wyman Institute for Holocaust Studies, explained: 'Foot-dragging on the selection sends a message that anti-Semitism is not of great importance to the United States.'"[55]

Obama finally filled the position in mid-November 2009, but his choice was hardly comforting. For Obama's new anti-Semitism czar was Hannah Rosenthal, former chief of the Jewish Council for Public Affairs (JCPA) and a current board member of none other than J Street. In April 2008 Rosenthal recalled the National Israel Solidarity Rally in Washington in 2002: "I recall much of that day with fondness and pride. I also recall the many rally attendees who pulled me aside to ask why the word 'peace' was so absent from the proceedings. How could we talk security without talking peace? . . . How did we arrive at a place where pro-Israel events had come to be dominated by narrow, ultra-conservative views of what it means to be pro-Israel?"[56]

Abraham H. Foxman, president of the Anti-Defamation League, shot back at Rosenthal: My memory of what happened at the event that day is quite different from yours. I remember many of the speakers delivering "pro-peace" messages. There was Rep. Richard Gephardt ("We must not waver in our commitment to those—Israelis and Arabs alike—who have chosen the path of peace"), as well as Sen. Harry Reid ("I call on all who share our vision and hopes to continue to spread a message of peace: shalom, salaam, peace"). There was also Paul Wolfowitz, representing the Bush administration ("Peace in the

Middle East is the only way to end the suffering of Palestinians and Israelis, of Arabs and Jews"), as well as Natan Sharansky ("Real peace, dear friends, depends on us"). And there was Mayor Rudy Giuliani ("All of us, all of you good people who have come here today, all of us wish for peace. We pray for it."). I remember you introducing Hugh Price, then president of the National Urban League, and I remember Mr. Price closing his remarks with a call to world leaders "to give lasting peace a chance in the Middle East."[57]

Apparently Rosenthal heard only what she wanted to hear: that defenders of Israel were "narrow, ultra-conservative" warmongers. Journalist Ed Lasky observed of her appointment as anti-Semitism czar: "This is just one more pick by the president that has led many (especially the Israelis) to wonder about his claim to be pro-Israel. It is also one more step forward by J Street, a group with ties to George Soros, in their reach for power in Washington, D.C."[58]

Other constituencies appeared to be more important to the post-American president. While extremely slow to appoint an envoy to monitor anti-Semitism, Obama swiftly instructed the State Department to create a Muslim outreach czar—a U.S. special representative for Muslim (*Ummah*) outreach, who reports directly to the secretary of state. This was at the urging of the head of the Organization of the Islamic Conference, Ekmeleddin Ihsanoglu. According to CNS News, when Ihsanoglu visited the White House on June 23, 2009, he "urged the US to quickly appoint an envoy to the Islamic bloc." Obama promptly created the "new office that is responsible for outreach with Muslims around the world."[59]

Priorities are priorities.

"THE MOST RADICAL ANTI-ISRAEL SPEECH
I CAN RECALL ANY PRESIDENT MAKING"

Cozying up to Hamas domestically and internationally, and leaving a pro-Israel position unfilled for months, were the least of it.

The Obama administration from its first days began to press Israel for concessions, while making no corresponding demands upon the Palestinians. Obama demanded that Israelis withdraw from "settlements"—which were in reality often established communities—in "occupied Palestinian territory." No other president had ever made such harsh demands. He never took note of the fact that the "Palestinian territory" in question was ruled by Jordan from 1948 to 1967, during which time there was never a single complaint from Palestinians about "occupation."

The "settlements," moreover, were on land to which Israel had a perfectly legitimate historical and legal claim. "Settler" was a derogatory term for a Jew in the Jewish homeland. But Obama made the "settlements" the latest concession that the Israelis had to make for a promise of peace with the Palestinians that never seemed to materialize after earlier territorial concessions in the Sinai and Gaza and elsewhere.

Thus, on September 23, 2009, Barack Obama declared at the UN: "We continue to emphasize that America does not accept the legitimacy of continued Israeli settlements." He called for the establishment of a "viable, independent Palestinian state with contiguous territory that ends the occupation that began in 1967, and realizes the potential of the Palestinian people."[60]

When, three weeks later, not much progress had been made on this front, it was reported that officials leaked the news that Obama was "disgusted" with Israel for not moving more quickly to dismantle the settlements.[61] A few weeks after this, Secretary of State Hillary Clinton took a somewhat softer line than that of her boss when she praised Israeli concessions on the construction of new settlements as "unprecedented."[62] By contrast, Obama, like the Palestinians, had never publicly acknowledged that Israel had taken any steps toward peace at all.

Former UN ambassador John Bolton pointed out that Obama didn't say that "new Israeli settlements" were illegitimate, but that "continued Israeli settlements" were illegitimate and unacceptable. Said Bolton: "That calls into question in my mind all Israeli settlements."

And a "contiguous" Palestinian state would cut Israel in two. Bolton commented: "Do you think that matters to the Palestinians? That is the kind of approach to an issue that is attempting to decide the outcome to the negotiations, before the negotiations, that's why I think that the Israelis should be worried. He's laid it out where he wants it to end up."

Bolton added: "The important thing is, when you have the Palestinians in as weak a position as they are now, and to have Barack Obama be their lawyer, in effect, puts them in a very strong bargaining place." And Obama, said Bolton, has "made it very clear how much he wants to do through the UN." How much? "An overwhelming percentage of our policy."[63]

Around the same time, the results of Obama's policies toward Israel began to appear.

STRANGE FRUIT

Obama's policies toward Israel began to bear poisonous fruit around the same time that Jones declared that the United States wanted to give the Palestinians a state "without preconditions."

Late in September 2009, an Israeli was shot in his car while traveling north of Jerusalem. A local Israeli leader, Avi Roeh, commented:

"This attack is a direct result of the removal of roadblocks. It's only by some miracle that the outcome of these attacks has been no worse than injuries, but you cannot base security policies on miracles." [64]

Maybe Israelis really were expecting miracles in September 2009, when the Israeli army began removing one hundred roadblocks in Judea and Samaria. *The Jerusalem Post* said this was "an effort to make life easier for Palestinians." [65] They were all gone by the week before the shooting took place north of Jerusalem.

The official line was that the roadblock removal wasn't related to Obama envoy George Mitchell's meeting with Israeli prime minister Binyamin Netanyahu, which took place around the same time, but the *Post* said, "While Israeli sources said there was no direct link with Mitchell's visit, they added there was an indirect connection because an improved West Bank economy was good for the diplomatic process."

This attempt to show goodwill was met only with increased pressure on Israel from the United States. The same day that the shooting took place, U.S. assistant secretary of state Michael Posner said that Israel should investigate war-crimes charges that the Palestinians (in reality the world's worst human-rights violators) had made in the UN Human Rights Council's Goldstone Report, prepared by the head of the UN fact finding mission, Justice Richard Goldstone: "We encourage Israel to utilise appropriate domestic (judicial) review and meaningful accountability mechanisms to investigate and follow-up on credible allegations. If undertaken properly and fairly, these reviews can serve as important confidence-building measures that will support the larger essential objective which is a shared quest for justice and lasting peace." [66]

So the United States had put itself into the position of pressuring Israel to plead guilty to something it did not do, so as to "build confidence" with the jihadis in Gaza.

That same day, at the UN Human Rights Council in Geneva, Anne

Bayefsky delivered a statement on behalf of both the Touro Institute on Human Rights and the Holocaust and the Hudson Institute. She said: "The Goldstone mission will go down in history as the 21st century's equivalent to the Protocols of the Elders of Zion—a notorious work of fiction which spun a conspiratorial web of deceit and distortion that has fueled hatred of Jews ever since. At its core, the Goldstone report repeats the ancient blood libel against the Jewish people—the allegation of bloodthirsty Jews intent on butchering the innocent."[67]

It came as no surprise, then, in October 2009, when the secretary-general of the OIC, Ekmeleddin Ihsanoglu, revealed that his organization was the driving force behind the Goldstone Report. Speaking of the Goldstone Report in an interview with Al-Jazeera, Ihsanoglu said: "What I would like to put on record is that the OIC was the initiator of this process." He explained that the whole idea of such a report was hatched during a meeting of the OIC's executive committee at the time of the Israeli defensive incursion into Gaza of January 2009.[68]

The OIC is one of the principal enemies of the freedom of speech internationally today—and it is no friend of Israel. On November 1, 2009, the fifty-seven-member organization issued a stern warning to Israel over unrest at Jerusalem's Temple Mount that had broken out in October: "Al-Aqsa represents the red line . . . Causing any harm to this mosque will have dangerous consequences"—although the idea that Israel had any plans to tamper with the Al-Aqsa was overheated rumor in the first place. The OIC's communiqué also called for the creation of a Palestinian state with Jerusalem as its capital, action by the UN Security Council against Jewish settlements in Jerusalem and elsewhere, and for an end to Israel's "policy of ethnic cleansing."[69]

THE NEW GOAL OF AMERICAN POLICY

After all this it came as no surprise in November 2009 when William J. Burns, the State Department's undersecretary for political affairs, announced: "Our goal in the region is clear: two states living side by side in peace and security; a Jewish state of Israel, with which America retains unbreakable bonds, and with true security for all Israelis; and a viable, independent Palestinian state with contiguous territory that ends the occupation that began in 1967, that ends the daily humiliations of Palestinians under occupation, and that realizes the full and remarkable potential of the Palestinian people."

How would all this be accomplished? Why, by pressuring the Israelis for more concessions, of course. "We do not accept the legitimacy of continued Israeli settlements," declared Burns. "We consider the Israeli offer to restrain settlement activity to be a potentially important step, but it obviously falls short of the continuing Roadmap obligation for a full settlement freeze." [70]

And what would the Palestinians have to do in order to get free from these "daily humiliations" and claim their "viable, independent" state "with contiguous territory"? Nothing at all. True to the continued pattern of the Obama administration, he made no demands upon the Palestinians at all.

The Palestinians seemed to be well aware of this, and reacted by making no secret of their ultimate intentions. After all, what did they have to lose? Palestinian Authority prime minister Salam Fayad met in August 2009 with over fifty senators and representatives, telling them that the new Palestinian state would be an Islamic state, devoted to "developing and implementing programs of Shari'a education as derived from the science of the Holy Qur'an and Prophet's heritage." [71]

A Palestinian Islamic state would not be a democracy, it would be Gaza tenfold, a terror state—and Obama wanted to set it up.

Significantly, in September 2009 on the Jewish New Year, Rosh Hashana, Obama sent greetings—to Muslims on the occasion of the Eid al-Fitr holiday marking the end of Ramadan. He sent Jews Rosh Hashana greetings also, including a veiled jab reflecting his acceptance of Palestinian propaganda: "Let's reject the impulse to harden ourselves to others' suffering."[72]

Obama apparently thought that the trouble between Israel and the Palestinians stemmed entirely from the alleged evils committed by Israel against the Palestinians; it mirrored his diagnosis of the causes of the conflict between the West and the Islamic world. At Cairo in June 2009, he identified several root causes of the Islamic world's hatred of the West and America in particular; all were the West's fault. It never seemed to enter his mind—much less influence his policy—that possibly Israel and the United States were facing foes who hated them for their own reasons, and were not just passively reacting to the evils perpetrated upon them by the Western powers.

And so he was determined to make the Israelis give, and give, and give, in exchange for nothing more than airy promises.

The Israelis began to notice—and to act. In July 2009, for the first time in decades, there was an anti-U.S., pro-Israel rally in the heart of Jerusalem. Knesset member Yaakov Katz, chairman of the National Union party, explained: "Not since the days of Kissinger has there been such a protest against American policies. The pressure that Barack Hussein Obama is exerting against us to simply stop growing and stop living will not work."[73]

But Obama's antipathy toward Israel has been a disaster for the Jewish state. With great speed during Obama's first months as president, Israel became more and more isolated in an increasingly hostile world—a world that was leaning toward capitulating to an OIC-driven UN.

But nothing was more dangerous, reckless, and lethal than Obama's tacit sanction of Iran's nuclear program. It changed the balance of power and the course of human events.

FIVE

OBAMA AND IRAN

THE OBAMA ADMINISTRATION SEEMED INTENT IN SO MANY WAYS ON DISMAYING AMER- ICA'S FRIENDS AND ENCOURAGING OUR ENEMIES. IN A breathtaking surrender to Russia in August 2009, Obama abandoned our allies Poland and the Czech Republic, scrapping their missile- defense shield.

Ostensibly Obama made a deal with Russia: he would scrap the missile-defense plans for Eastern Europe in exchange for Russian help in blocking Iran's quest for nuclear weapons.[1] With his attempts to bring the Iranians to the negotiating table having already failed, Obama certainly needed help with Iran. But he was effectively ex- changing a reality (the missile-defense shield) for a hope (the possibil- ity that the Russians would be able to stop Iran from gaining nuclear weapons, or would even care to if they could).

It was stunning in its betrayal of good, reliable allies who had unfalteringly stood by us. The immediate effect was the weakening of American allies. Former United Nations ambassador John Bolton commented: "I think this is a near catastrophe for American relations with Eastern European countries and many in NATO. It was the kind of unilateral decision that the Bush administration was always criticized for, and I think the clear winners are in Russia and Iran."[2]

Even Obama's old presidential rival John McCain was unhappy with the decision: "Given the serious and growing threats posed by Iran's missile and nuclear programs, now is the time when we should look to strengthen our defenses, and those of our allies. Missile defense in Europe has been a key component of this approach. I believe the decision to abandon it unilaterally is seriously misguided. This decision calls into question security and diplomatic commitments the United States has made to Poland and the Czech Republic and has the potential to undermine perceived American leadership in Eastern Europe."[3]

BETRAYING HONDURAS

"Coup" was the word du jour in June and July 2009, when the Obama administration at its most Orwellian used it to define, or defame, the healthy functioning of democracy in Honduras.

Superficially, it did look like a coup. Honduran president Manuel Zelaya was rudely awakened in the middle of the night: "I was awakened by shots, and the yells of my guards, who resisted for about 20 minutes. I came out in my pajamas, I'm still in my pajamas. . . . When (the soldiers) came in, they pointed their guns at me and told me they would shoot if I didn't put down my cellphone." Zelaya put it down. The soldiers, still holding their guns on him, then exiled him from the country.[4]

What really happened in Honduras? A military coup, destroying democratic rule? No. The United Nations, the leftopaths in the mainstream media, and the radical U.S. president tried to paint what happened in Honduras as a coup, but it was not a coup. What happened in Honduras was in reality an example of how democracy works—and constituted yet more confirmation that Barack Obama was not on the side of freedom, but of tyranny. What happened in Honduras was democracy at work: a free nation saving itself from a Hugo Chávez–backed takeover.

The real story behind the chaos in Honduras was that Barack Obama got it wrong, *again*.

Take this hypothetical: imagine that Barack Obama announced that he was going to hold a referendum on legalizing a third term for himself. Imagine that even his attorney general, Eric Holder, advised him that it was illegal. Imagine that the Supreme Court ruled that in light of the Twenty-second Amendment, holding the referendum was unconstitutional. Imagine that in spite of that, Obama coerced the FEC into holding the referendum anyway.

Then—let's further imagine—it came to light that the Venezuelan strongman Chávez (who has pulled off a similar power grab in his own country) was financing Obama's referendum. What should the Joint Chiefs do in such a case? And if they removed Obama from office, would they be destroying the Constitution or preserving it?

That was exactly the situation in Honduras. The Honduran Supreme Court and attorney general ruled that Zelaya's referendum was unconstitutional. The Honduran generals did what they had to do. But then Hugo Chávez, Zelaya's friend and ally, announced that he had put the armed forces of Venezuela on alert.

And at that point Barack Obama spoke out—to side with Zelaya, Chávez, and dictatorship. Obama said he was "deeply concerned" about what was happening in Honduras and called upon that nation to "respect democratic norms."[5]

Obama had put himself, and America, on the same side as Chávez, Ortega, and the Castro brothers. It is a testimony to the Honduran people's love for freedom that despite all the pressure Obama and Chávez brought to bear upon them, they still voted out Zelaya and the Leftists in the November 2009 elections.[6]

HIDING A DAGGER BEHIND THEIR BACK

On November 4, 2009, the thirtieth anniversary of the storming of the U.S. embassy in Tehran, Obama struck an appeasing tone toward the Iranian mullahs, as he had so many times before. As he did so, the brave, brutally beaten people of Iran chanted in the streets, "you're either with us, or you're with them!"[7] This was directed straight at Obama, who had abandoned them in their marches for freedom and free elections. Instead of talking about the need to confront international jihad terrorism and the thuggish intimidation increasingly practiced by rogue states, Obama again kissed the fists of the mullahs: "This event helped set the United States and Iran on a path of sustained suspicion, mistrust and confrontation. I have made it clear that the United States of America wants to move beyond this past, and seeks a relationship with the Islamic Republic of Iran based upon mutual interests and mutual respect."[8]

The mullahs laughed. And they set about building their nuclear weapons program. And slaughtering their people. It was one of history's terrible ironies, that the people of Iran rose in a desperate plea for freedom and there should be a U.S. president who had effectively discarded the very idea of democracy—at least for the Iranians—as some ancient relic of a past age.

Instead of helping those Iranians who loved freedom, Obama reached out personally to Iran's Supreme Leader, Ayatollah Ali

Khamenei—several times. Khamenei described the messages he was getting from the president: "The new U.S. president has said nice things," Khamenei recounted amid celebrations in Tehran of the embassy takeover. "He has given us many spoken and written messages and said: 'Let's turn the page and create a new situation. Let's cooperate with each other in resolving world problems.'"

Khamenei, however, thought Obama was being duplicitous. "On the face of things, they say, 'Let's negotiate.' But alongside this, they threaten us and say that if these negotiations do not achieve a desirable result, they will do this and that. . . . Whenever they smile at the officials of the Islamic revolution, when we carefully look at the situation, we notice that they are hiding a dagger behind their back. They have not changed their intentions."[9]

However, long before Khamenei batted away Obama's outstretched hand, the former U.S. ambassador to the United Nations, John Bolton, saw through the ruse. He observed that "Tehran welcomes direct negotiations with Washington. Why not, given the enormous benefits its nuclear programs have accrued during five and a half years of negotiations with Europe? Why not, with America at the table, buy even more time to marry its impending nuclear weapons with its satellite-launching ballistic missile capability?"

Bolton pointed out that the negotiations that Obama so dearly longed to begin could actually hurt the United States rather than help it. "First," he said, "diplomacy has not and will not reduce Iran's nuclear program." European leaders, according to Bolton, were "belatedly feeling hollow in the pits of their diplomatic stomachs, now that their failed diplomacy has left us with almost no alternatives to a nuclear Iran." Bolton said that they were dismayed that Obama was trying to reopen the negotiations that they had been trying tentatively to bring to a close before it was too late and too much was lost.

Meanwhile, the West's supine and confused response to the Iranian nuclear threat, Bolton noted, only emboldened the Iranians in other areas also.[10]

Certainly they showed themselves ever bolder toward Obama and the United States as 2009 wore on. During the celebrations of the takeover of the embassy in November, the head of security forces in Tehran announced: "Only anti-American rallies in front of the former American Embassy in Tehran are legal. Other gatherings or rallies on Wednesday are illegal and will be strongly confronted by the police."[11]

"Only anti-American rallies" were legal. And this after Barack Hussein Obama wrote letters, and sent spoken messages, and smiled, and entreated. "Only anti-American rallies" are legal.

The mullahs had never made any secret of their anti-Americanism and hostility to Washington, but Barack Obama was undaunted. His conciliatory message on the thirtieth anniversary of the storming of the U.S. embassy was only one of many such messages.

SLAPPING THE EXTENDED HAND

Obama appeared anxious to sanction the evil of the Iranian mullahcracy.

He had done all he could to demonstrate his goodwill to the Iranian mullahs, and to bring them to the negotiating table. He started in his Inaugural Address, offering to "extend a hand if you are willing to unclench your fist."[12]

As is the lot of appeasers throughout history, all he received in return was disdain and renewed bellicosity. They knew a beggar when they saw one, and accorded him the respect they believed he merited. Virtually from the beginning of the Obama administration, the Iranian leadership reacted to his overtures with gleeful contempt.

Iranian president Mahmoud Ahmadinejad demanded just over a week after Obama took office that the United States "must apologize to the Iranian people and try to repair their past bad acts and the crimes they committed against Iran."[13] Government spokesman Gholam Hossein Elham crowed days later that the new president's request for talks "means Western ideology has become passive, that capitalist thought and the system of domination have failed."[14] Not long after that, the speaker of the Iranian Parliament, Ali Larijani, said that "in the past years, the U.S. has burned many bridges, but the new White House can rebuild them"—if, that is, it "accepts its mistakes and changes its policies."[15]

Likewise when Obama set a deadline of the end of September for Iran to begin talks over its nuclear program, Ahmadinejad was again contemptuous—although those talks did ultimately take place. "From our point of view," said the Iranian president, "Iran's nuclear issue is over. We continue our work within the framework of global regulations and in close interaction with the International Atomic Energy Agency. . . . We will never negotiate over obvious rights of the Iranian nation."[16] And when Iran's nuclear representative sat down with the American negotiator, Ahmadinejad turned out to be entirely correct: the Iranians budged not one inch.

Barack Obama didn't ask them to.

HAPPY NEW YEAR, MULLAHS

Obama was undaunted. Late in March 2009, he stretched out his hand to Tehran again, issuing a videotaped greeting to "people and leaders of the Islamic Republic of Iran" on the occasion of Nowruz, the Iranian New Year.

He praised Iranian culture: "Over many centuries your art, your music, literature and innovation have made the world a better and more beautiful place." He praised Iranian immigrants: "Here in the United States our own communities have been enhanced by the contributions of Iranian Americans." He praised Iranian civilization: "We know that you are a great civilization, and your accomplishments have earned the respect of the United States and the world."

Obama acknowledged that relations between Iran and the United States had been "strained." But he stressed the "common humanity" of Iranians and Americans. To the mullahs and Ahmadinejad he declared: "My administration is now committed to diplomacy that addresses the full range of issues before us, and to pursuing constructive ties among the United States, Iran and the international community. This process will not be advanced by threats. We seek instead engagement that is honest and grounded in mutual respect."

The new president spoke glowingly of "a future with renewed exchanges among our people, and greater opportunities for partnership and commerce. It's a future where the old divisions are overcome, where you and all of your neighbors and the wider world can live in greater security and greater peace."[17]

But in response to these high-minded words, Mahmoud Ahmadinejad was again scornful and threatening. He referred to the United States as "the arrogant ones, those who speak through violence, the [most] corrupt people in history." He took issue with the manners of the superpower: "We advise you to correct your behavior, since the world is changing. . . . Stop the egotism, the aggression, and the lack of manners. Speak to the [world's] nations in a correct manner and politely. . . ."

Iran, he said, is "a nation that cannot be defeated," and "no power in the world entertains the notion of taking action against the Iranian nation. Even if someone were to entertain this notion and want to undertake any act of aggression against the nation . . . he should know that the Iranian nation is ready, and any hand outstretched in order to attack will be cut off."[18]

Two weeks after that, Ahmadinejad sneered at Barack Obama's desire to sit down and talk it out. While saying that "we welcome" Obama's invitation to dialogue, he added: "We say to you that you yourselves know that you are today in a position of weakness. Your hands are empty, and you can no longer promote your affairs from a position of strength. We recommend that you amend your rhetoric towards the rest of the nations, respect them, and not talk with the Iranian nation from the position of egocentric people."[19]

Again and again, Barack Obama extended his hand. And again and again, the Iranians slapped his face. In May 2009, for example, Iran's government-run media announced that the Iranians had successfully tested a missile that could reach not only Israel, but also southern Europe and U.S. military bases in Iraq and elsewhere in the Middle East.[20]

Iran was clearly emboldened by Barack Obama's weakness—at the worst possible time for it to be emboldened.

BEGGING IN CAIRO

Yet Barack Obama came begging yet again during his major address to the Islamic world, delivered in Cairo on June 4, 2009. Obama noted there that "our shared interest in the rights and responsibilities of nations on nuclear weapons" had been "a source of tension between the United States and the Islamic Republic of Iran." At issue now, he said, "is not what Iran is against, but rather what future it wants to build."

And he repeated yet again: "We are willing to move forward without preconditions on the basis of mutual respect." Part of that mutuality, as far as he was concerned, was a disarmed and vulnerable United

States: "No single nation should pick and choose which nations hold nuclear weapons. That is why I strongly reaffirmed America's commitment to seek a world in which no nations hold nuclear weapons. And any nation—including Iran—should have the right to access peaceful nuclear power if it complies with its responsibilities under the nuclear Non-Proliferation Treaty."[21]

A world in which the most powerful nation has voluntarily divested itself of nuclear weapons, while granting nuclear power to rogue states in exchange for promises that they will not use nuclear energy for weapons, is a world that will soon have a new most powerful nation—and nuclear weaponry proliferating like never before.

IRAN SPINNING OUT OF CONTROL

For through the summer and fall of 2009, while Barack Obama begged for an audience with the Supreme Leader Khamenei and his henchman Mahmoud Ahmadinejad, the Islamic Republic—the regime of the Ayatollah Khomeini, the regime that trampled upon international law and stormed the U.S. embassy in 1979, holding American hostages for over four hundred days—faced the biggest challenge of its thirty-year existence. In 2009, demonstrators filled the streets of Iran, denouncing the regime and crying out for freedom.

It was a glorious opportunity for the leader of the free world to demonstrate his support for free people everywhere, and strike a decisive blow against the bloody regime that had considered itself at war with the United States for three decades.

But Barack Obama didn't help them. Quite the contrary. The leader of the free world was too busy extending his hand to those same mullahs.

As Mahmoud Ahmadinejad declared victory in the June 2009 Iranian elections, riots broke out in Tehran. Iran was spinning out of control. The government tried to clamp down—opposition candidates were placed under house arrest and then released—but the unrest did not die down for weeks, and flared up again on November 4 during the celebrations of the storming of the embassy: crowds that shouted "Death to America" faced competition from others who shouted "Death to the dictator"—Khamenei—instead.[22]

From the beginning of the unrest, the CIA should have been at work inside Iran, helping the dissidents and reformers, and strategizing about the removal of the country's nuclear weapons. And the president of the United States should have spoken out strongly in favor of the demonstrators, and freedom. But instead, Obama said that "it is up to Iranians to make decisions about who Iran's leaders will be," and that he was "deeply troubled by the violence" in Iran.[23] In a press conference on June 23, Obama said: "I've made it clear that the United States respects the sovereignty of the Islamic Republic of Iran, and is not interfering with Iran's affairs."[24]

Obama offered only the most lukewarm criticism of the regime's bloody crackdown: "I think that the democratic process, free speech, the ability of people to peacefully dissent—all of those are universal values, and need to be respected." (I hope he will remember to respect them in the United States.) "And whenever I see violence perpetrated on people who are peacefully dissenting, and whenever the American people see that, I think they're, rightfully, troubled."[25]

All right, so he was "troubled." Or the American people were. Many were not only troubled, but horrified at the murder of Neda Agha-Soltan, the beautiful young woman who was shot dead by the mullahs' thugs on a street in Tehran. But in fact there were many Neda Agha-Soltans. The most visible feature of the Iranian protest movement was the leadership role of the women in Iran. They were the heart, soul, and fuel of that defiance in the face of crushing repression.

But Barack Obama did not stand with Neda Agha-Soltan. He did not stand with any of the Iranian women who put their lives on the line for freedom during that first summer of his presidency.

What did Obama choose to do when he became "troubled" by the ferocious crackdown on political dissent in Iran? Give his public support to the democracy movement? Call for restraint from the mullahs in dealing with the protesters, and justice in the Iranian election?

Barack Hussein Obama chose to do none of those things.

Instead, he reiterated his desire to talk with the Iranian leaders who were coordinating the bloody crackdown against their own people: "We will continue to pursue a tough direct dialogue between our two countries." [26]

And those terrified, courageous souls marched through Tehran, acting out in hope that it might effect any change. They were engaged in an exercise in futility, courtesy of Barack Hussein Obama. It was an opportunity missed.

Not that the Iranian elections really would have changed anything in and of themselves. The allegations of fixed elections came after polls showed that half of the electorate wanted Ahmadinejad. But if half of the electorate wanted this bloodthirsty jihadi annihilationist, then what led to all the unrest? Hundreds of thousands of people turned out at rallies *for* Ahmadinejad before the election. The election was a ruse. As Christopher Booker wrote in *The Telegraph*, "The reality is that this was a completely sham battle between rival factions of a regime as ruthless as any in the world, in which the real power is exercised by the gang of hard-line mullahs round the 'Supreme Leader', Ali Khamenei. In an election riddled with fraud (six million more ballot papers were printed than there are Iranians eligible to vote), all four regime-approved candidates had long been personally involved in the regime's murderous reign of terror." [27]

Opposition candidate Mir Hussein Mousavi, although he had always been a faithful servant of the mullahcracy, positioned himself as a reformer. It was shaping up to be a first-class piece of political theater: the "reformer" would win, and would con the UN and the president while finishing their extensive, comprehensive nuclear-weapons program. Not one nuke, not two nukes. Many nukes. The world wanted so desperately to be fooled. And so the "new" Iranian president would "engage" in a "new era," "new dialogue," and "diplomacy," to Obama's delight.

Many people (including Barack Obama) pointed out that Mousavi was in reality scarcely different from Ahmadinejad. After his numerous overtures to the mullahs, it wasn't hard to know why Obama appeared to be hoping the opposition would be crushed.

But there were numerous signs that many of the Iranian protesters were not fighting for Mir Hussein Mousavi.

The resistance to the Iranian regime that the world witnessed in the summer and fall of 2009, with young people risking torture and death, was not about installing Mousavi as president. The Iranians were given four choices; it was not as if they could write in Ronald Reagan's name. But what might a regime change, or even a modification of the regime with someone like Mousavi as president, have meant to Iran's nuclear program? If the Iranian demonstrators had not been crushed, it is anyone's guess how many of the strictures of the Islamic Republic they might ultimately have thrown off—after all, Iran was a relatively secular state until 1979.

Clearly a significant number of the protesters have been fighting for freedom from the Islamic Republic and the stifling restrictions of Sharia itself. Some attitudes are entrenched in people and cultures, but I do not believe that people fight bullets with rocks and bricks for more of the same. They already had Sharia rule, without the suffering and horror that came with the demonstrations. Even Sheikh Naim Qassem, the deputy leader of Hizbullah, the jihad terror group that is Iran's client in Lebanon, noticed that. "What is going on in Iran," he said in June 2009, "is not a simple protest against the results of the presidential election. There are riots and attacks in the streets that are orchestrated from the outside in a bid to destabilize the country's Islamic regime."[28]

Would people who are fighting simply to install a different president in a strict Sharia state that is viciously hostile to Israel appeal for help from the country they hate the most? Yet Iranian dissident Arash Irandoost asked for help from . . . Israel: "Dear Israeli Brothers and Sisters, Iran needs your help more than ever now." He argued that Israel and the Iranian freedom fighters faced a common foe: "The unjust treatment and brutal massacre of the brave Iranians in the hands of the mullahs' paid terrorist Hamas and Hizbullah gangs are not seen by the majority of the Iranians."[29]

The Iranian people were dying for their aspirations. As Arash Irandoost's appeal suggests, those aspirations do not include the destruction of America or Israel. The freedom fighters were trying to travel an uphill road against a cruel, vicious theocracy and a huge fundamentalist peasantry. They fought and they died tragically—and magnificently and bravely, trying to better their society.

It is a stain on America's great history as a force for good that we elected a president who gave tacit support to murderers and savages, and abandoned those dying for freedom.

If Obama had thrown his support to the demonstrators and the Islamic regime had been toppled, the new president would need the West as a bulwark in his defenses against a resurgence of Islamic supremacism. He might have bowed to pressure from the Iranian people for a relaxation of Sharia rule and a return to something like the way Iranian society was under the shah. This could have led him to moderate Iran's foreign adventures also: no bomb, and perhaps no Syria, Hizbullah, and Abbas as proxies by which to wage terrorism.

A moderate Iran could have been an enormously stabilizing force in the region. This was why Obama's failure to seize the moment was so shortsighted and stupid.

The Green Revolution, like the Cedar Revolution (Lebanon), the Rose Revolution (Georgia), and all those purple fingers were the manifestation of an idea, an idea that men yearned for: liberty and freedom. And while not everyone wants freedom, those who do ought to be given their inalienable human rights: life, liberty, and the pursuit of happiness. The Iranians who were taking bullets, axe blows, and the crushing blows of batons were those very people. And these courageous and desperately isolated people deserved the wholehearted support of all free people.

CHANGE, BUT NO HOPE: ENDING FUNDING FOR IRANIAN FREEDOM

According to "Iran: U.S. Concerns and Policy Responses," a Congressional Research Service report dated May 19, 2009, Barack Obama hung the Iranian democracy protesters out to dry in the 2010 budget.[30] The report detailed $67 million that was set aside during the Bush administration to promote democracy in Iran. "Of that, as of October 2008," according to the report, "$42.7 million has been obligated, and $20.8 million disbursed." It adds that more money had also been "appropriated for cultural exchanges, public diplomacy, and broadcasting to Iran."

But all that changed when Barack Obama became president: "However, the Obama Administration did not request funding for democracy promotion in Iran in its FY2010 budget request, an indication that the new Administration views this effort as inconsistent with its belief in dialogue with Iran."[31]

Could the mullahs have asked for a better friend?

Obama not only passed up a chance to speak up for the brave Iranian citizens who dared to take their lives in their hands and protest the Iranian regime. He not only ended funding for the promotion of democracy in Iran. He also abandoned them to their fate by cutting off funding for a watchdog group that monitored human-rights violations inside Iran, the Iran Human Rights Documentation Center.[32]

The Iran Human Rights Documentation Center had received over $3 million from the State Department between 2004 and 2009, and used it to document the human-rights abuses—notably the torture of political prisoners and the murder of pro-democracy activists and dissenters—perpetrated by the Islamic Republic. Executive Director Renee Redman had requested $2.7 million to fund the group's work for two more years, only to find the request summarily and inexplicably denied.

Redman was shocked, since the denial came just as the whole world had seen the Iranian regime's brutality and ruthlessness in dealing with the election protesters. "If there is one time that I expected to get funding, this was it," said Redman. "I was surprised, because the world was watching human rights violations right there on television."

But with no funding, the Iran Human Rights Documentation Center was set to shut its doors in May 2010.

The Obama administration also cut off funds to at least three other Iranian organizations that opposed the Islamic Republic and had received funding during the Bush administration. Roya Boroumand of the Boroumand Foundation, an anti–death penalty group, articulated why the Obama approach was so spectacularly wrong: "If the rationale is that we are going to stop funding human rights–related work in Iran because we don't want to provoke the government, it is absolutely the wrong message to send. That means that we don't really believe in human rights, that the American government just looks into it when it is convenient."[33]

Indeed. And for whatever reason, Barack Obama never seemed to find it convenient to confront Iran's Islamic regime about its miserable human-rights record.

IRAN'S MAN IN WASHINGTON

In November 2009, Obama appointed John Limbert as deputy assistant secretary for Iran in the Bureau of Near Eastern Affairs. According to a report at Politico, an unnamed State Department official with twenty years of service in the department said that before Limbert's appointment, "we've never had a DAS for Iran." Limbert, he said, would be "the most senior official at State who deals exclusively with Iran."[34]

At first glance it seemed like a savvy appointment. Limbert was a hostage in the U.S. embassy in Tehran in 1979, and a fluent Farsi speaker. There is video of Limbert discussing the hostages' plight with the future Supreme Leader, Ayatollah Khamenei. A career diplomat, Limbert has received the highest award that the State Department gives out, the Distinguished Service Award. He is the author of a book entitled *Negotiating with Iran: Wrestling with the Ghosts of History*.

Who, then, would be better to navigate the twists and turns of dealing with the mullahs for a president who is intent on negotiating with them, and will not be dissuaded from this goal?

There was just one catch: Limbert was a member of the advisory board of the George Soros–funded National Iranian American Council (NIAC), a powerful Iranian lobbying group in Washington that boasts of its connections in high places: "Throughout the recent crisis," the NIAC announced in July 2009, at the height of the bloody crackdown on the demonstrators in Tehran, "NIAC has been in contact with the White House almost daily to convey the views of our community, and policymakers have been listening." It "strongly condemned the crackdown" in Iran "and called for new elections as the best way to end the violence." It has also called upon the mullahs to "immediately release opposition figures, human rights defenders, and all other persons arrested for contesting the election results," as well as "immediately halt state-sanctioned violence against the Iranian people."[35]

The NIAC's boasting was not misplaced. As the organization itself put it, "since its inception in 2002, NIAC has grown to become the largest Iranian-American grassroots organization in the country, with supporters in all 50 states."[36]

That the largest Iranian-American advocacy group in the country would stand against the Iranian regime's repression of the Iranian demonstrations was welcome. However, for all its apparent advocacy of freedom for Iranians, the NIAC consistently opposed the tough measures that would truly aid genuine fighters for freedom in Iran—and also opposed the steps that the United States, Israel, and the West must take to defend themselves against the increasingly bellicose and brutal Islamic Republic.

The NIAC has consistently followed a line indicating that while it opposes the mullahs' excesses, it does not oppose the Islamic regime itself. For example, some time ago it published statements from an Islamic cleric and former government official under Khomeini, Haddi Ghaffari. "Khamenei," Ghaffari wrote, addressing Iran's Supreme Leader, "your recent actions and behavior has brought shame to us clerics. . . . Khamenei, you are wrong, your actions are wrong."

Sounds great, right? Sure. But then Ghaffari added: "I'm not preaching these messages so that I could be associated with the West. I loathe the West and will fight to the last drop of my blood before I or my land succumbs to the West."[37] In other words, he would fight to the last drop of his blood to make sure that the bloody Sharia rule of the mullahs does not end.

This is the organization that John Limbert serves as a member of its advisory board.

The NIAC has also criticized journalist Kenneth Timmerman for equating "opposition to a U.S.-Iran war with support for the Iranian government. Nothing could be further from the truth," the group proclaims. "NIAC believes that Iranian Americans are double-stakeholders in attempts to avoid war—as Americans, they don't want to see a single American life lost, and as Americans of Iranian descent, they don't want to see their friends and family in Iran getting bombed." [38]

Did German-Americans complain in 1943 that they didn't want to see their friends and family back in the old Nazi homeland getting bombed? "The images of the devastation in Iraq," NIAC maintained, "should serve as a deterrent against prospective wars in the region. In this, NIAC agrees with the Iraq Study Group's recommendations that diplomacy, not military confrontation should be the way to resolve U.S.-Iran tensions." [39]

Of course, Barack Obama couldn't have agreed more. And as we have seen, he also agreed that, as NIAC's Trita Parsi put it, "imposing new sanctions prior to diplomacy having begun will only decrease the chances of successful diplomacy." [40]

The NIAC has opposed sanctions for quite some time. Iranian dissident Hassan Daioleslam notes that "in 2008, when [the] U.S. Congress was showing some teeth to the Iranian regime," a coalition of Islamic groups, antiwar groups, and others founded the Campaign for New American Policy on Iran to fight against new sanctions against Iran called for by the advisory resolution H.R. 362. This resolution was not passed, and "NIAC and Parsi," says Daioleslam, "were on top of this event." [41]

No strike on Iran. No sanctions. Just diplomacy—with a genocidally inclined and fanatically intransigent regime whose contempt for Obama's overtures made the president look increasingly beggarly as the first year of his presidency wore on.

It was no mystery why many wondered which side the NIAC is really on. But as long as it continued to wield such influence in Washington and held the ear of Barack Obama and John Limbert, the freedom fighters in Tehran didn't stand a chance.

SANCTIONS? WHAT SANCTIONS?

The Congressional Research Service report notes that "the Bush Administration characterized Iran as a 'profound threat to U.S. national security interests,' a perception generated primarily by Iran's nuclear program and its military assistance to armed groups in Iraq and Afghanistan, to the Palestinian group Hamas, and to Lebanese Hezbollah."

"The U.S. approach," the report goes on, "was to try to prevent a nuclear breakout by Iran by applying multilateral economic pressure on Iran while also offering it potential cooperation should it comply with the international demands to suspend its enrichment of uranium."

Whether or not the sanctions worked, they were the only weapon the West was using to try to put pressure on the mullahs. However, "the Obama Administration has not pushed assertively for new sanctions, pending the results of its outreach to Iran." [42]

In fact, not only did the post-American president not push for new sanctions; he actively opposed them. In October 2009, Jonathan Schanzer, a former Treasury Department terror expert, noted that "legislators are growing increasingly frustrated with President Barack Obama's seeming unwillingness to pull the trigger on an Iran sanctions package that is already locked and loaded." Schanzer was referring to the Iran Refined Petroleum Sanctions Act (IRPSA), which would have impeded foreign oil companies from helping Iran with oil production. "In short," Schanzer explained, "IRPSA could deal a fiscal body blow to Iran and destabilize the regime, as a means to derail its nuclear ambitions."[43]

Obama, however, dragged his feet, despite overwhelming support for the measure in Congress—perhaps because if the IRPSA failed, the only remaining option would be to deal with the Iranians with military force.

And that was one option that Barack Hussein Obama absolutely refused to consider.

Apparently Obama believed that simply by showing the Iranians some love, he could persuade them to drop their genocidal bellicosity and join the ranks of free nations. And no amount of rejection and scorn would disabuse him of this notion.

That was bad enough. But Obama's dithering about the Iranian nuclear program was even worse.

LETTING IRAN GET AWAY WITH MURDER

In late September 2009 the United States, in conjunction with Britain and France, revealed that Iran was building a nuclear-fuel plant that the Iranians had up to that point kept secret. Several weeks later, International Atomic Energy Agency (IAEA) inspectors were given a look inside the facility.

American diplomat Marc Ginsberg, the former U.S. ambassador to Morocco, remarked acidly: "We now have definitive confirmation from IAEA and European diplomats that the nuclear installation was too small for peaceful nuclear enrichment, but large enough to hold enough centrifuges to convert low grade enriched uranium into enough weapons-grade uranium needed to make nuclear warheads. In other words, the Qum nuclear facility appears to be *the* smoking gun in Iran's secret nuclear weapons construction program. If the neutral IAEA has come to that conclusion, I can't wait to hear from those who would love to spin it as nothing more than an innocent doughnut factory."[44]

Barack Obama was almost certainly one of them, but such spin wasn't possible in the face of such flagrant flouting of international law. A clearly annoyed Obama talked tough: "The size and configuration of this facility is inconsistent with a peaceful (nuclear) program," he said, in remarks more critical of Iran than he had ever made before. "Iran is breaking rules that all nations must follow, endangering the global nonproliferation regime, denying its own people access to the opportunity they deserve, and threatening the stability and security of the region and the world."[45] He thundered that this secret plant constituted "a serious challenge to the global nonproliferation regime, and continues a disturbing pattern of Iranian evasion." He said that Iran "must pursue a new course or face consequences."

What kind of consequences? A strike on its nuclear facilities? No. A defiant Iran, predicted Obama, will put the mullahs in a situation in which they "will face increased pressure and isolation, and deny opportunity to their own people." He invited the Iranian leadership to a "serious, meaningful dialogue," provided that Iran "take actions to demonstrate its peaceful intentions." And he begged once again, intoning plaintively: "My offer of a serious, meaningful dialogue to resolve this issue remains open."[46]

When asked at a press conference about the disclosure of the existence of this second Iranian nuclear facility, which some of Obama's advisers were terming a "victory," Obama was dismissive: "This isn't a football game," he declared, "so I'm not interested in victory; I'm interested in resolving the problem."[47]

Of course, Obama considered himself to be an enlightened sophisticate who has moved beyond the primitive warlike tendencies of bygone cultures and civilizations. He is a twenty-first-century man, and he is confident that underneath it all, Khamenei and Ahmadinejad are too, and aren't any more interested in victory than Barack Obama is.

A rude awakening was certain to come.

GENEVA: OBAMA SURRENDERS TO THE MULLAHS

Iran's Supreme Leader, Ayatollah Khamenei, and its president, Mahmoud Ahmadinejad, responded to Barack Obama's overtures with scorn and contempt. But that didn't mean that Iran had no interest whatsoever in talking. The mullahs were happy to send their representatives to talk to the infidels when they perceived a clear advantage in doing so. But they signaled their continuing defiance by testing a few short-range missiles just before the talks. On that occasion the leader of the Revolutionary Guard Air Force, Gen. Hossein Salami, issued a general threat: "We are going to respond to any military action in a crushing manner, and it doesn't make any difference which country or regime has launched the aggression."[48]

With Iran's in-your-face stance thus established, on October 1, 2009, Iran's chief nuclear negotiator, Saeed Jalili, went to Geneva for talks on Iran's nuclear ambitions with negotiators from the United States, Russia, China, Great Britain, France, and Germany.

At the same time, a high-level U.S. diplomat, whose identity was not revealed, met one-on-one with Jalili to discuss Tehran's nuclear ambitions.[49] The results of the meeting were not disclosed, but enough damage was done by the fact of the meeting itself. The signal this meeting sent was nothing less than disastrous: what do you get for being a rogue regime that builds renegade nuclear weapons, slaughters its own people, hijacks an election and illegally seizes power, sows the seeds of war and destruction in neighboring countries, uses foreign proxies to attack free nations, kills U.S. soldiers in Lebanon, Iraq, and

Afghanistan, creates Hizbullah, funds and backs Hamas, and promises a second holocaust?

With Barack Obama as president, you get a clampdown on those who are reporting your nefarious activities, and a one-on-one with the United States for the first time in decades.

The meeting with the six nations was even worse. Significantly, during the seven-and-a-half-hour meeting with the six powers, none of those powers asked Jalili what they had asked Iran to do before: give up its nuclear ambitions. No one said a word about sanctions, either.

The Iranians were, understandably, jubilant. And they did not see the meeting as movement toward a compromise, but as the humiliation of their powerful enemies. The influential Ayatollah Seyyed Ahmad Khatami said in a Friday sermon: "The meeting was a great victory for the Islamic Republic of Iran to such an extent that even the Western and Zionist media had to admit defeat."[50]

Ambassador Bolton agreed with Khatami: "In fact, the agreement constitutes another in the long string of Iranian negotiating victories over the West. Any momentum toward stricter sanctions has been dissipated, and Iran's fraudulent, repressive regime again hobnobs with the U.N. Security Council's permanent members."

Bolton also pointed out that the meeting had facilitated Iran's violation of UN Security Council resolutions. "In Resolution 1696, adopted July 31, 2006," Bolton explained, "the Security Council required Iran to 'suspend all enrichment-related and reprocessing activities, including research and development.'" But in Geneva, Iran and the six powers came to an "'agreement in principle' to send approximately one nuclear-weapon's worth of Iran's low enriched uranium (LEU) to Russia for enrichment to 19.75% and fabrication into fuel rods for Tehran's research reactor."

And despite his internationalist respect for the United Nations,

Obama did not reject the "agreement in principle" between Iran and Russia. Instead, said Bolton, "Obama says the deal represents progress, a significant confidence-building measure."[51]

Whose confidence was being built? "The issue with most rogue states, like Iran, like North Korea, is that by talking to them you are giving them legitimacy and you're also giving them time, which proliferators need," said Bolton back in March 2008.[52]

Ultimately Iran rejected the deal that the UN brokered on its nuke program, although Obama remained mum about the rejection for understandable reasons. He knew what it would show about his determination to negotiate with the Iranians "without preconditions." One colossal failure after another.

But why would Iran have endorsed this deal?

WOULD ISRAEL BOMB IRAN?

Barack Obama in May 2009 warned Israeli prime minister Binyamin Netanyahu not to launch a surprise attack on Iran.[53] This was an attempt to ensnare Israel in a particularly difficult catch-22, for it was extremely unlikely that Obama would approve of or lend his support to an Israeli strike against Iran before the fact, while a surprise attack could jeopardize Israel's alliance with the United States.

The Israelis, however, unlike Obama, were prepared to make hard choices. The chief of staff of the Israeli Defense Force, Gabi Ashkenazi, declared in September 2009: "Israel has the right to defend itself, and all options are open."[54]

Including the option of taking out Iran's nuclear installations.

Israel had to act, because a focal point of Iran's increasing bellicosity was its hatred of Israel. In November 2009, the Israelis intercepted a ship bound for Lebanon, laden with missiles and ammunition sent from Iran to the jihad terrorist group Hizbullah. Former Israeli defense minister Shaul Mofaz explained: "As of now, what we know is that this was a smuggling attempt to arm Hezbollah with terrorist means against civilians. The intent was to send arms, mainly missiles and launchers, meant to strike civilian targets."[55]

The incident underscored the urgency of stopping Iran's nuclear ambitions. A country that would smuggle conventional weapons to a terrorist group would smuggle nuclear weapons to that terror group as well. But with Barack Obama in the White House, Israel faced hard choices.

On October 23, 2009, the American Enterprise Institute held a panel discussion entitled "Should Israel Attack Iran?" Dictating the choice of topic was the obvious fact that Barack Hussein Obama, with his ever-outstretched hand, would not attack Iran, no matter how real and present a danger the Iranian nuclear program turned out to be. That left it up to Israel to do the job—if Israel was not to be impeded in that by Obama himself.

On the panel, Bolton said that force was "required" to keep Iran from getting nuclear weapons. What about Obama's outstretched hand? Bolton said that solutions other than taking out Iran's nuclear facilities "have failed, are failing and will fail." UN resolutions, he noted, had "no material impact on Iran's nuclear weapons program," and "the prospect of sanctions in the future is illusory. . . . The combination of Russian and Chinese action in the Security Council on any hypothetical fourth resolution would end up watering it down just like the first three."

Yet despite the fact that an Israeli strike at Iran's nuclear facilities could save the free world (and much of the unfree world), Bolton predicted that such an attack would "cause a very dramatic break in the relationship between the Obama administration and Israel."

No big surprise there.

Was there any alternative? Bolton said that "the ideal outcome is regime change"—and never was the Islamic Republic of Iran closer to that possibility than in the summer of 2009 during the demonstrations against the election results.[56]

But Barack Obama did nothing. The president was naked at the feast.

Only Israel was ready to act. Israeli deputy foreign minister Danny Ayalon demonstrated in a November 2009 interview that he was not nearly as overawed by the mullahs as Barack Obama appeared to be. "The one who's bluffing," said Ayalon, "is Iran, which is trying to play with cards they don't have. All the bravado that we see and the testing and the very dangerous and harsh rhetoric are hiding a lot of weaknesses."[57]

Strong words—so unlike Barack Obama's.

When I interviewed Ambassador Bolton on July 30, 2009, he said: "For me the real long-term answer to the Iranian nuclear weapons program is a change of regime. Again, not just a change of Ahmadinejad, the overthrow of the Islamic revolution of 1979. If Obama and the United States are not willing to work for that end, then we can count on not just the mullahs being in charge for a long time, but possibly even worse, the Islamic Revolutionary Guards Corps, who are more fanatic, more militaristic, and the ones in charge of the nuclear program."[58]

Obama's missed opportunity looked worse by the minute.

THE UN WATCHPUPPY

With an impotent president at the helm of the most powerful country in the world, the powers arrayed against that country behaved as if they had been given a free hand. Obama clung desperately to his naïve belief that if he begged the Iranians often enough, and received with patience their slights, their insults, their slaps to the face, he would eventually be able to blunt the force of their jihad.

And meanwhile, the Iranians continued to pursue their nuclear aspirations, without any indication whatsoever that Barack Hussein Obama was deterring them from doing so. In fact, at one terrible historic moment at the United Nations, Obama gave the mullahs every reason to believe that he would do nothing to impede their nuclear ambitions. In September 2009, Obama chaired a session of the United Nations Security Council. According to Anne Bayefsky, "he turned it into a summit of heads of state and chose the agenda. He insisted—in the words of the advance American 'concept paper'—that 'The Security Council Summit will focus on nuclear non-proliferation and nuclear disarmament broadly and *not focus on any specific countries.*' Obama pushed hard for the adoption of a new Security Council resolution, which was passed unanimously, and *which never mentions Iran or North Korea.*"[59]

To speak about nuclear nonproliferation and nuclear disarmament without ever once mentioning Iran and North Korea is only to demonstrate your fear of standing up to either one.

For the leader of the free world to manifest such fear was disappointing, especially coming when it did. When Obama chaired the Security Council session, it was only weeks after the United Arab Emirates had informed the council that it had taken control of a ship that had been sailing under the flag of the Bahamas and was full of North Korean–made weapons and explosives—bound for Iran in defiance of UN sanctions. The Security Council committee that oversees sanctions wrote to both Tehran and Pyongyang asking for explanations, and received no response.

Chairing the Security Council, Barack Obama could have challenged the North Koreans and the Iranians about their defiance of the sanctions, as well as about their nuclear programs in general.

Instead, he only reinforced their perception of him as weak and unwilling to stand up to them.

In our July 2009 interview Ambassador Bolton spoke critically of "the inexperience and naïveté, really, of the Obama administration." He said that "statesmanship, if it's anything, is looking decades into the future trying to identify risks and challenges and opportunities and structuring events as they develop to maximize the opportunities and minimize the risks."

But Obama had done nothing like this: "So when you hear Obama during the campaign saying, 'Well, Iran is a small country . . . it doesn't represent a big threat,' you know that may be true today, with respect to the United States, but Iran [and] North Korea are not small threats to our friends and allies in their area—Japan and South Korea with respect to North Korea, Israel and the Arab states in the Persian Gulf when they look at Iran. And moreover . . . you have to go longer than just the next six month or twelve months, you have to say, 'What are the implications for the world at large if Iran gets nuclear weapons?'"

Bolton continued:

And it's not simply the threat of a nuclear Iran, well, that's bad enough; it's the consequences of a nuclear Iran. Saudi Arabia will get nuclear weapons, possibly Egypt, possibly Turkey, possibly others in the region, that's what we mean by proliferation. A nuclear Iran actually leads to a more dangerous, more unstable situation with possibly several nations having small numbers of nuclear weapons, thus increasing the likelihood that somebody is going to use them. So this issue of a nuclear Iran is critical for Israel, the Persian Gulf states in the short term, possibly critical to the world as a whole over a longer period.[60]

Barack Obama never showed any signs of having considered any of that. And in March 2009, Ambassador Bolton summed up the weakness of his position: "There is no evidence that Mr. Obama knows substantively how to stop Iran, which senses the palpable vulnerability inherent in his pell-mell rush to the bargaining table. More importantly, his disjointed diplomacy masks a profound strategic disorder, one potentially far more damaging than the photo op urge to shake hands with an Iranian."[61]

INTERNATIONALLY IMPOTENT

Speaking in Prague, a city that lived under the shadow of the Cold War for decades, Obama in April 2009 unveiled an ambitious plan to divest the world of nuclear weapons and usher in a new era of peace. But, of course, since Obama controlled only the American nuclear arsenal, that was the only one he could dismantle. And he announced his intention to do just that.

"The United States," he declared, "has a moral responsibility to act. We cannot succeed in this endeavor alone, but we can lead it, we can start it." Alone. "I'm not naïve," he hastened to assure the world, but he certainly gave the impression that he was.

"To put an end to Cold War thinking," Obama said, "we will reduce the role of nuclear weapons in our national security strategy, and urge others to do the same." We *will* reduce the role of nukes in our own defense, and *urge* others to do likewise. "We will," the president added, "begin the work of reducing our arsenal."[62]

Obama's plan essentially amounted to disarming free, rational nations and allowing rogue nuclear proliferators to run wild—after all, this was the man who said two months after this speech in Prague that oil-rich Iran "has legitimate energy concerns, legitimate aspirations" that made its intention to become a nuclear power reasonable and justifiable.[63]

So apparently in Barack Obama's ideal world, the United States would divest itself of nuclear weapons just as Iran developed the use of nuclear energy, and the United States would trust Iran to abide by international nonproliferation agreements and refrain from weaponizing its new energy source.

And the international agencies in which Obama placed so much hope only mirrored his impotence. So it was that in November 2009 the International Atomic Energy Agency, universally known as the "UN's nuclear watchdog," discovered that the Iranians had conducted tests of a nuclear warhead design that is so advanced, and so top secret, that officially the United States and Britain do not even acknowledge that it exists. But it does exist, and Iran has apparently tested it.

This was still more unmistakable evidence that the Iranians have been lying to the world for months and years on end as they have repeatedly insisted that their nuclear program is peaceful in intent, and that they have no intention of manufacturing nuclear warheads at all. It was proof of the duplicity and untrustworthiness of the Islamic regime, and of its constituting a danger to Israel (which has repeatedly been threatened by Iranian leaders) and to the world at large.

It was a challenge, and an opportunity. Obama could have dropped his beggar's pose and asked the UN for an immediate stiffening of sanctions. He could have put Iran on notice that the United States—not Israel alone—would destroy Iran's nuclear weapons program before Iran got anywhere close to the capability of sending a nuke into Tel Aviv.

But Obama still did nothing. The only response came from the IAEA. Brave, fearless, and courageous as ever, the agency asked Iran for . . . an explanation.[64]

That's it. No sanctions. No condemnation. Certainly no threat of war backed by the will to follow through on that threat if necessary.

An explanation.

With a weak president in the White House, there was a vacuum, a void—one that evil was only too happy to fill.

On Friday, November 27, 2009, the IAEA called on the Iranian mullahs to stop their uranium-enrichment activities. And so on Sunday, showing how much they feared the wrath of the United Nations and the post-American president, Barack Hussein Obama, the mullahs gave the green light to a plan to build ten new uranium-enrichment plants.

This is the same IAEA whose chief, Mohamed Mostafa ElBaradei, said in October that "Israel is No. 1 threat to Middle East."

The American economist Thomas Sowell said that Obama is "heading this country toward disaster on many fronts, including a nuclear Iran, which has every prospect of being an irretrievable disaster of almost unimaginable magnitude. We cannot put that genie back in the bottle—and neither can generations yet unborn. They may yet curse us all for leaving them hostages to nuclear terror."[65]

If history has taught us anything, it's that if weapons are produced, they are used, and if war is talked into the people, one day it becomes a reality. And this is what we are witnessing with Iran. America has always been the force for good that has kept evil in check. Iran's goal is a world living under Islamic law. In a post-American world, what at once seemed impossible is eminently possible.

A world made secure by America so far appears to be comfortable throwing off our cloak of protection. Yet the only reason there is any semblance of peace and tranquility around the world today is because of the military presence of the United States at points across the globe. Iran and the other members of the axis of evil are now working to take advantage of regional and international opportunities that will arise if the United States is not there to stop them.

And they are likely to succeed.

A nuclear Iran in a post-American world would change the geopolitical landscape overnight. A nuclear Iran in a post-American world would result in an immense power shift in the Middle East and elsewhere. The balance of power would shift from democratic and free forces to the forces of Islam and Sharia.

And it is not just the Jewish state that is in Islam's crosshairs; it is the whole of the West.

SIX

A POST-AMERICAN
PRESIDENT WAGES WAR

ON DECEMBER 1, 2009, BARACK OBAMA MADE A MUCH-ANTICIPATED SPEECH AT THE UNITED STATES MILITARY ACADEMY AT WEST POINT ON what he had decided to do in Afghanistan. After considerable deliberation, he had determined to commit an additional 30,000 troops to that troubled nation, and then withdraw them by 2011. This was months after Gen. Stanley McChrystal requested over 60,000 troops, or at least 40,000. McChrystal said if the American presence in Afghanistan was not boosted, the United States could face "mission failure" in that nation.[1]

The speech had been a long time coming: the post-American president, elected by a core constituency of hard-core antiwar Leftists, was clearly reluctant to alienate his base by furthering one of George W. Bush's wars. However, he was also unwilling to pay the political price of withdrawing from Afghanistan at the same time as he was withdrawing from Iraq.

His ambivalence manifested itself as silence and dithering in the face of requests from American commanders in Afghanistan for more troops. The commander of American troops in Afghanistan, Gen. Stanley McChrystal, said in an interview in late September 2009: "I've talked to the president, since I've been here, once on a VTC [video teleconference]."

CBS's David Martin asked a follow-up question: "You've talked to him once in seventy days?" McChrystal said: "That is correct."[2]

On August 30, 2009, McChrystal asked Obama for reinforcements. Between that day and Obama's December 1 speech on Afghanistan, 116 American troops were killed in Afghanistan.[3] But in his speech Obama defended himself against charges that he had endangered American troops already in Afghanistan by delaying his decision on whether to send more troops: "There has never been an option before me that called for troop deployments before 2010, so there has been no delay or denial of resources necessary for the conduct of the war during this review period. Instead, the review has allowed me to ask the hard questions, and to explore all the different options, along with my national security team, our military and civilian leadership in Afghanistan, and our key partners. And given the stakes involved, I owed the American people—and our troops—no less."[4]

And to be sure, Obama had not always seemed to be as indifferent as he appeared during the summer and fall of 2009. During the 2008 election he had banged repeatedly on the Afghan war drum. Afghanistan, in his construction, was the "good" war, Iraq the "bad" war.

Afghanistan, he said, was neglected. That's where the real action was, according to General Obama: it was the place where the war on jihad, the war on terror, the overseas contingency operation (as the Obama administration, ever mindful of politically correct niceties, memorably renamed it) really was. Afghanistan was where Obama would redeploy our troops, while withdrawing from the great mistake that was George W. Bush's venture in Iraq.

And so, committed once again to pursuing the war in Afghanistan, finally Barack Obama went to West Point to explain to the nation and the world what he hoped to accomplish in Afghanistan, and how he intended to go about it.

It was a singularly uninspiring speech, perhaps reflecting the post-American president's postmodern, post-American distaste for the Manichaeism and carnality of warfare. He identified the enemy—if this word could be rightly used while Obama never spoke of "victory," or explained in any detail what he would consider to be a successful outcome in Afghanistan at all—as "Al-Qaeda," whom he described as "a group of extremists who have distorted and defiled Islam, one of the world's great religions, to justify the slaughter of innocents." In keeping with this whitewash of the militaristic Islamic texts and teachings that jihadists use to justify violence, and with his own pronounced affinity with Islam, Obama also characterized the Taliban as "a ruthless, repressive and radical movement." Radical what? He didn't say.

Of course, this soft-pedaling of the Islamic character of the jihadist war against the United States was little different from language George W. Bush had used for eight years. But coming from as Islamophilic a president as Barack Hussein Obama, it signaled more than simply a desire to make common cause with moderate elements within the Islamic world (if such allies in reliable enough supply could truly be found), as it did with Bush. For Barack Obama, in contrast, it was a manifestation of a myopia of immense proportions.

OBAMA AND THE "MODERATE TALIBAN"

This myopia first became glaringly apparent in March 2009, when Obama stated a desire to open negotiations with moderate factions of the Taliban. On first reflection, that actually sounded reasonable. Something like it had worked in Iraq, after all, even if the victory was short-lived. Obama spoke explicitly about wanting to duplicate that success, saying that "part of the success in Iraq involved reaching out to people that we would consider to be Islamic fundamentalists, but who were willing to work with us because they had been completely alienated by the tactics of Al Qaeda in Iraq." And "there may be some comparable opportunities in Afghanistan and the Pakistani region," although he granted that "the situation in Afghanistan is, if anything, more complex."

And it was, for at least two reasons.

First, the Iraqi Sunni insurgents among whom Gen. David Petraeus, the American commander in Iraq, was able to gain confidence had turned against the Al-Qaeda elements for their own pragmatic reasons. Al-Qaeda in Iraq had forced themselves into the communities, onto the tribes, and even demanded local sheikhs' daughters in marriage. Despite whatever ideological affinities the populace may have had with Al-Qaeda (which always appeals to peaceful Muslims by reference to an imperative rooted in the Qur'an and Sunnah), they were overridden, at least temporarily, by the jihadis' boorish behavior. Second, Petraeus had enough troops at the time to provide local security to the former insurgents and their tribal leaders.

Neither of those conditions pertained in Afghanistan; nor would Obama's thirty thousand new troops significantly change that fact. There were still too few American troops to provide local security beyond the capital city, and the Taliban remained the strongest faction among the many mountain tribes.

So who were Obama's "moderate Taliban"? Where could they be found? Waheed Mozhdah, the director of the Afghan Foreign Ministry's Middle East and Africa department when the Taliban were in power, dismissed the post-American president's hopes as "a dream more than reality," asking derisively: "Where are the so-called moderate Taliban? Who are the moderate Taliban?" Newspaper editor Muhammad Qaseem Akhgar declared: "'Moderate Taliban' is like 'moderate killer.' Is there such a thing?"[5]

Obama offered no details as to why he believed in these fantastical creatures, but Vice President Joe Biden, ever helpful, chimed in with some statistics manifesting his confidence in their existence. "Five percent of the Taliban is incorrigible," he explained, "not susceptible to anything other than being defeated. Another 25 percent or so are not quite sure, in my view, of the intensity of their commitment to the insurgency. Roughly 70 percent are involved because of the money."[6] He didn't explain how he arrived at these figures, but one would think that if they were remotely accurate, we would have seen some evidence of dissension within Taliban ranks in Afghanistan and Pakistan, with moderate elements objecting to their colleagues' more extreme behavior.

In late September 2009, for example, Taliban commander Mohammed Ibrahim Hanafi told CNN that the Taliban considered foreign-aid workers to be spies, and was planning to execute them. "Our law," he declared, "is still the same old law which was in place during our rule in Afghanistan. Mullah Mohammad Omar was our leader and he is still our head and leader and so we will follow the same law as before."[7] That law included prohibiting the education of girls, destroying girls' schools all over the country, and even throwing acid in the faces of girls who dare to try to get an education. The Taliban in the Swat Valley in northwest Pakistan bombed or burned down around 300 girls' schools, affecting over 100,000 students. And in Afghanistan over 600 schools did not open in 2009 because they could not guarantee their students' security.

There was no record of any "moderate Taliban" elements speaking out against either the execution of foreign aid workers or the closing of girls' schools and the terrorizing of female students.

The Taliban had also targeted police stations—because they are considered outposts of the central government in Kabul—as well as video and CD stores, since Islamic law forbids music and images of human beings. Pakistan's *News International* reported last month that "two police stations, 12 police posts, 80 video centres, around 300 CD shops, 25 barbershops, 24 bridges, 15 basic health units, an electricity grid station and a main gas supply line were either destroyed or severely damaged" by the Taliban as it has moved in recent months to gain control of Swat—which was once a thriving tourist spot.[8]

There was no record of any moderate Taliban elements speaking out against any of this, or lifting a finger to stop it. One would think that if these reasonable elements who could be negotiated with really constituted over two thirds of those who identify themselves as Taliban, as Biden claimed, there would be some trace of their existence somewhere—even a minute indication that they dissented from the harsh vision of draconian Sharia law that the Taliban imposed upon Afghanistan when it was in power in Kabul, and which it continues to impose upon those areas of Afghanistan and Pakistan that it currently controls.

INTERNATIONALISM IN AFGHANISTAN

Obama, in his December 2009 speech announcing the sending of more troops to Afghanistan, spent a good deal of time recounting the history of how the United States got involved militarily in Afghanistan in the first place. Ever the internationalist, he recalled that "the United

Nations Security Council endorsed the use of all necessary steps to respond to the 9/11 attacks. America, our allies and the world were acting as one to destroy Al-Qaeda's terrorist network and to protect our common security." Obama emphasized that the United States entered Afghanistan in the first place only "under the banner of this domestic unity and international legitimacy."

The Karzai government, he further noted, was also the fruit of international cooperation, having been established "at a conference convened by the U.N." Once it was up and running, "an International Security Assistance Force was established to help bring a lasting peace to a war-torn country."

But disrupting this vision of an internationalist paradise was Bush's other war: "The decision to go into Iraq caused substantial rifts between America and much of the world." He also obliquely blamed the Bush administration for the resurgence of the Taliban in Afghanistan: "Commanders in Afghanistan repeatedly asked for support to deal with the reemergence of the Taliban, but these reinforcements did not arrive." Former defense secretary Donald Rumsfeld, however, sharply disputed this, calling the post-American president's claim a "bald misstatement." Rumsfeld declared: "I am not aware of a single request of that nature between 2001 and 2006. If any such requests occurred, 're- peated' or not, the White House should promptly make them public. The President's assertion does a disservice to the truth and, in particular, to the thousands of men and women in uniform who have fought, served and sacrificed in Afghanistan."[9]

In any case, Obama announced his intention to reverse what he undoubtedly saw as Bush's cowboy unilateralism and irresponsibility: "Today, after extraordinary costs, we are bringing the Iraq war to a responsible end." He announced: "We will remove our combat brigades from Iraq by the end of next summer, and all of our troops by the end of 2011." And likewise in Afghanistan: while announcing that he would send thirty thousand fresh American troops to Afghanistan, he declared in the very next breath that "after 18 months, our troops will begin to come home." He gave the specific date of July 2011, meaning that the troops would leave Afghanistan before they would leave Iraq.

Why a time limit? "The absence of a time frame for transition would deny us any sense of urgency in working with the Afghan government. It must be clear that Afghans will have to take responsibility for their security, and that America has no interest in fighting an endless war in Afghanistan."

Once again, he emphasized that this would be "an international effort," and so "I've asked that our commitment be joined by contributions from our allies. . . . We must come together to end this war successfully. For what's at stake is not simply a test of NATO's credibility—what's at stake is the security of our allies, and the common security of the world." He declared that as American troops left Afghanistan, he would once again consult with the international partners of the United States: "[W]e will work with our partners, the United Nations, and the Afghan people to pursue a more effective civilian strategy, so that the government can take advantage of improved security."

And recalling his outreach to the "moderate Taliban," he added: "We will support efforts by the Afghan government to open the door to those Taliban who abandon violence and respect the human rights of their fellow citizens." Apparently, if they renounced violence and worked toward the same goals through nonviolent means, the post-American president would have no problem with that. Meanwhile, despite having nothing whatsoever to show for his many overtures to the Islamic world, Obama declared his outreach a victory: "[W]e have forged a new beginning between America and the Muslim world—one that recognizes our mutual interest in breaking a cycle of conflict, and that promises a future in which those who kill innocents are isolated by those who stand up for peace and prosperity and human dignity."[10]

WAR AND INTERNATIONALISM IN OSLO

Less than two weeks after his Afghanistan speech, Obama traveled to Oslo to accept his Nobel Peace Prize—a prize that many thought the Nobel Committee gave him as a criticism of George W. Bush's foreign policy and an endorsement of Obama's socialist internationalism.

Speaking of Obama's Afghanistan speech, *National Review*'s Andrew McCarthy pointed out that hard-core Alinskyites "reserve the right to take any position on any matter, to say anything at any time, based on the ebb and flow of popular opinion." As if to confirm this observation, during his Nobel acceptance speech Obama retailed some themes that had become extraordinarily rare during his post-American presidency: the necessity to wage war in some circumstances, and the right of the United States to defend itself. "I face the world as it is," said the dreamy internationalist, "and cannot stand idle in the face of threats to the American people."

Obama even reminded the assembled elites that "it was not simply international institutions—not just treaties and declarations—that brought stability to a post–World War II world. Whatever mistakes we have made, the plain fact is this: The United States of America has helped underwrite global security for more than six decades with the blood of our citizens and the strength of our arms." Sounding an Ayn Randian note, Obama said that the United States had done all this "out of englightened self-interest."

He did not, however, disappoint those who were counting on him to subject America to the governance of international bodies, and had awarded him the Nobel Peace Prize in furtherance of that hope. "I— like any head of state—reserve the right to act unilaterally if necessary to defend my nation," said Obama. However, no sooner had he stated this than he undercut it: "America cannot act alone."

Not *should not*. "Cannot."

"If we want a lasting peace," Obama asserted, "then the words of the international community must mean something." The world, he said, must stand "together as one." And of course, he was careful to note that "the world must come together to confront climate change."[11]

John Bolton observed that the speech "followed the standard international leftist line. He played to the crowd and filled the speech with clichés from the American and international left by saying 'America cannot act alone' and that he 'prohibited torture.' The speech was also typical of Obama in its self-centeredness and 'something for everybody' approach."[12]

ALINSKY DOES AFGHANISTAN

Andrew McCarthy in *National Review* dubbed Obama's speech on troop escalation in Afghanistan "Alinsky Does Afghanistan," and remarked: "If there is one word that captures President Obama's much-anticipated Afghanistan speech, it is 'cynical.' Yes, the speech was also internally contradictory, counter-historical, and premised on fatally flawed assumptions about Islam and the Afghan people."

The post-American president's cynicism in his Afghanistan speech primarily manifested itself in his attempt to co-opt his conservative opposition by appearing to act in favor of America's interests and boosting the U.S. military presence in Afghanistan. "He also frames national security," McCarthy observed, "as a distraction from his more important work socializing our economy. He knows that as long as he is tepidly supportive of a military mission—even one that neither aims to achieve nor can possibly achieve victory over America's enemies—

conservatives will not only overlook the slights; they will anxiously commend him and help the *New York Times* take the lash to those who won't."[13]

Yet given that during his campaign Obama used Afghanistan to criticize the American presence in Iraq, he couldn't back out now. But his hard-left internationalism and socialism made him unwilling to fight a real war in Afghanistan, either. So after his long months of dithering, Obama hit on the solution: he would commit enough troops to Afghanistan to keep up the appearance that he was defending America there, while never explaining in any precise terms what would constitute a successful mission—"success" being all that Americans could reasonably hope for, since the post-American president had already ruled out "victory." In June 2009, General McChrystal on video link from Kabul joined a meeting in the White House Situation Room. In the course of the meeting, he presented a slide containing a pithy "mission statement": "Defeat the Taliban. Secure the Population."

One of the Obama aides in the Situation Room took exception to the idea that American troops were in Afghanistan to defeat the Taliban, asking the general: "Is that really what you think your mission is?" Another Obama adviser said that the meeting really began making progress when the import of this question sunk in with everyone in the Situation Room: "The big moment when the mission became a narrower one was when we realized we're not going to kill every last member of the Taliban."[14]

Speaking of military victory as an endeavor to "kill every last member" of the opposition seemed to be a peculiarly leftist caricature, spoken of by someone who was sure that military men were bloodthirsty hoodlums who delighted in mayhem. In any case, the troops, freed from the obligation of actually trying to defeat the Taliban—

particularly while Obama searched for "moderates" among them—could occupy themselves building schools and roads until they began to leave in July 2011.

Would they even be able to defeat the Taliban if they wanted to? Only if they could do it by that deadline. By setting deadlines in both Iraq and Afghanistan, Obama had ensured that the American troops would not be able to make any meaningful progress toward neutralizing the jihadist and anti-American forces in either nation; all they had to do was hold out for eighteen months, and the field would be theirs.

Military analyst Max Boot remarked that there was "plenty of reason to doubt Obama's resolve in Afghanistan. On the plus side, he committed to sending more troops than some White House aides wanted. . . . But then he undercut some of the urgency he conveyed by pledging 'to begin the transfer of our forces out of Afghanistan in July of 2011.' If this is such a vital national interest—and it is—why is our commitment so limited? How can he be so confident that the extra 30,000 troops—who will be lucky to arrive in their entirety by next summer—can accomplish their ambitious mission in just a year?" [15]

Obama's contempt for the military was palpable. Since he took office, American forces had been experiencing the highest U.S. troop casualty rate ever in Afghanistan, month after month. Why, then, did Obama keep our finest young Americans there when victory was not the objective? Obama's aimless, useless operation in Afghanistan was a death trap. British journalist Melanie Phillips observed trenchantly: "The American President is cynically offering up American soldiers' lives as a fig leaf to disguise the fact that he is giving up and getting out. Obama has now compromised the safety of every single American and British soldier, given not just the Taleban but every watching jihadi a terrific shot in the arm and undermined the very difficult mission in Afghanistan." [16]

Obama is not a wartime president, and certainly no commander in chief. He was sending thousands to their death in Afghanistan for no purpose, no objective, other than to disarm his domestic opposition.

It was the post-American president's way of waging war.

Ayn Rand once said, "When a country doesn't recognize the individual rights of their own citizens, it cannot claim any national or international rights. Therefore, anyone who wants to invade a dictatorship or semi-dictatorship is morally justified in doing so, because he is doing no worse than what that country has accepted as its social system." [17]

With any totalitarian ideology—fascism, communism, or Islam—you must attack the root cause. You can't wish it away or pretend it doesn't exist. We don't send precious lives into war *not to win*. That is not, or should not be, an option. We have the power to fight and win. Not to use this power, while squandering American lives, is monstrous. The idea that America cannot defeat the Taliban is absurd and the entire world knows it. Why are we not allowed to use our power? It is morally bankrupt—this absence of the courage of our convictions. The rules of engagement forced upon our troops are morally repugnant.

Rand said this of our capitulation to leftist thuggery in American politics during the Vietnam era: "Since the world knows we are not physically weak, it would be an admission of moral corruption that we do not possess a primitive dignity that any nation should have—to its own dead, if nothing else—that if it is involved in a war, it should finish it. It must win or be defeated." [18]

We must win.

SEVEN

OBAMA AND ISLAMIC POLITICS

We either live under the light of Islam or we die with dignity
. . . brace yourselves for a long war against the world's infidels
and their agents.

—Osama bin Laden, June 3, 2009 [1]

America is not—and never will be—at war with Islam.

—Barack Obama, Cairo, June 4, 2009

OBAMA'S OVERTURES TO THE ISLAMIC WORLD WERE A HIGH PRIORITY FOR HIM FROM THE MOMENT HE BECAME PRESIDENT OF THE UNITED

States. Before he was inaugurated, he announced his intention to move with deliberate speed. "Very early in the administration," he said in an interview four days before he took office, "I will announce a team and an approach that allows us to get engaged in the Middle East on Day One. And when we do that we'll be naming, you know, the people who are going to be leading that effort. . . . Here's my commitment:

Very early on, the American people, but also the players in the region, are going to know that we are serious about dealing with the Middle East, dealing with Iran, dealing with Afghanistan and Pakistan on the diplomatic front and not just on the military front. We've got a regional set of problems. They're not going to be solved in isolation."[2]

Then in his Inaugural Address, he addressed Muslims worldwide: "To the Muslim world," he said, "we seek a new way forward, based on mutual interest and mutual respect."[3]

"Mutual respect" became a watchword of his appeals to the Islamic world. In his first interview as president, which he gave, with a careful eye for symbolism, to Dubai's Al-Arabiya News Channel on January 26, 2009, he used the phrase again: "And what I've said, and I think Hillary Clinton has expressed this in her confirmation, is that if we are looking at the region as a whole and communicating a message to the Arab world and the Muslim world, that we are ready to initiate a new partnership based on mutual respect and mutual interest, then I think that we can make significant progress."[4]

Appealing to Iran in March 2009, Obama said: "We have serious differences that have grown over time. My administration is now committed to diplomacy that addresses the full range of issues before us, and to pursuing constructive ties among the United States, Iran and the international community. This process will not be advanced by threats. We seek, instead, engagement that is honest and grounded in mutual respect."[5]

It was an ongoing preoccupation. In his principal appeal to the Islamic world, his Cairo address on June 4, 2009, he declared: "I've come here to Cairo to seek a new beginning between the United States and Muslims around the world, one based on mutual interest and mutual respect, and one based upon the truth that America and Islam are not exclusive and need not be in competition."[6]

On November 4, 2009, the thirtieth anniversary of the takeover of the U.S. Embassy in Tehran and the beginning of the Iranian hostage crisis, Obama again issued his increasingly plaintive plea for respect: "This event helped set the United States and Iran on a path of sustained suspicion, mistrust and confrontation. I have made it clear that the United States of America wants to move beyond this past, and seeks a relationship with the Islamic Republic of Iran based upon mutual interests and mutual respect."[7]

And a month later, when he announced his intention to send thirty thousand troops to Afghanistan, he declared: "And we will seek a partnership with Afghanistan grounded in mutual respect—to isolate those who destroy; to strengthen those who build; to hasten the day when our troops will leave; and to forge a lasting friendship in which America is your partner, and never your patron."[8]

With his continual repetition of this phrase, Obama seemed anxious to reassure Islamic nations that the United States—or at least the post-American president—would respect them. Everything his hard-left mentors had told him about American history would have reinforced in him the idea that the respect was lacking on the American side, not on the Muslim side. Indications of this presupposition showed up in several of the speeches in which he mentioned this need to establish "mutual respect."

In Cairo in June 2009, he listed three causes for the tensions between the West and the Islamic world: "Tension has been fed by colonialism that denied rights and opportunities to many Muslims, and a Cold War in which Muslim-majority countries were too often treated as proxies without regard to their own aspirations. Moreover, the sweeping change brought by modernity and globalization led many Muslims to view the West as hostile to the traditions of Islam."

Each of these was the fault of the West, not of the Islamic world.

The respect was lacking from the West toward Muslims, not the other way around. Obama listed only ways in which the West has, in his view, mistreated the Islamic world. Not a word about the jihad doctrine, not a word about Islamic supremacism and the imperative to make war against and subjugate non-Muslims as dhimmis. Not a word about the culture of hatred and contempt for non-Muslims that existed long before the spread of American culture ("modernity and globalization") around the world, which Obama suggested was responsible for the hostility Muslims have for the West.

In a similar vein, at West Point in December 2009, he offered what Andrew McCarthy of *National Review* called "a laughable history of the Afghan people. They're a peaceful bunch who were just minding their own business when, out of the blue, they were 'ravaged by Soviet occupation.' (Actually, the Soviets intervened when the country disintegrated into chaos after Afghan Marxists tried to remake Afghanistan's tribal Muslim society.) Then, Obama's story goes, they somehow became the passive victims of their own civil war. In Obama's telling, the Taliban is 'a ruthless, repressive, and radical movement' that emerged, seemingly out of nowhere, because America—who else?— was inattentive. In fact, the Taliban is an Afghan movement, sprung quite naturally from the Islamic fundamentalism rampant in Pashtun society. It was strategically nurtured by Pakistan and Saudi Arabia, our supposed allies against what Obama can't bring himself to call jihadist terrorism."[9]

In short, the chaos and violence in Afghanistan had nothing to do with the beliefs or actions of the Afghans themselves. It was all due to interference from or bungling by big bad neocolonial powers, including the United States.

Seeking a new accord with the Islamic world, this new way forward had long been one of the chief items on the post-American president's to-do list—as he himself put it shortly before his inauguration, he wanted to "reboot America's image in the world and also in the Muslim world in particular." [10]

Obama thought of himself as uniquely equipped to do this. He explained early in his presidential campaign that "I think the world would see me as a different kind of president, somebody who could see the world through their eyes. . . . If I convened a meeting with Muslim leaders around the world, to discuss how they can align themselves in our battle against terrorism, but also put our, the relationship between the West and the Islamic world on a more productive footing, I do so with the credibility of somebody who actually lived in a Muslim country for a number of years." [11]

He remained consistent in this belief. The *Times* of London reported two days before the inauguration that Obama "believes a personal initiative will dramatise his wish to reassure Muslims, and intends to give a speech in an Islamic capital during his first 100 days in office as a sign of his engagement." [12]

Reassure Muslims? But who would seek to reassure non-Muslims alienated by jihad aggression and Islamic supremacism? Why, no one, of course. That would be "Islamophobic." Rather than confront the doctrines of jihad and Islamic supremacism that fueled jihad activity worldwide, Obama seemed prepared from the very beginning of his presidency to submit to the rules demanded by the Islamic world.

Barack Obama was elected promising change, and a new direction in both domestic and foreign policies. His statements about meeting the challenge of the global jihad, however, were a de facto form of submission, an implementation of a soft Sharia: the quiet and piece-meal implementation of Islamic laws that subjugate non-Muslims. There was the capitulation on free speech at the UN, the respect of a brutal mullahcracy in Iran, and the demand to expel Jews from Israel and ethnically cleanse parts of Jerusalem of Jews. This was change— a fundamental change for America from being a singular force for good and individual rights to capitulating to collectivism and subjugation.

The centerpiece of his "outreach" to the Islamic world was the Cairo speech of June 2009. In it, he was determined to show how much he "respected" the Islamic world—even to the point of twisting history and present-day reality.

CLICHÉS AND ANTI-AMERICANISM: THE CAIRO SPEECH

Obama's much-anticipated Cairo speech to the Islamic world was widely hailed as a major breakthrough in U.S. relations with the Islamic world. But in reality, it was an exercise in pandering, appeasement, historical revisionism, leftist platitudes, and alarming naïveté.

Could any good policy come out of such a foundation?

Obama began with a bit of pandering: "I am honored to be in the timeless city of Cairo, and to be hosted by two remarkable institutions. For over a thousand years, Al-Azhar has stood as a beacon of Islamic learning." He said nothing about the fact that Al-Azhar's Grand Sheikh, Muhammad Sayyid Tantawi, has given his approval—on Islamic grounds—to suicide bombing.[13]

It was no surprise, then, when he characterized jihad violence as emanating from "a small but potent minority of Muslims." The idea that the jihadists are a "small but potent minority of Muslims" is universally accepted dogma, but has no evidence to back it up. The evidence that seems to establish it is highly tendentious—Obama adviser Dalia Mogahed, working on survey data for the Gallup organization with Saudi-funded academic John Esposito, cooked survey data from the Islamic world to increase the number of "moderates."[14]

Bat Ye'or, the world's leading scholar of dhimmitude, the institutionalized mistreatment of non-Muslims in Islamic societies, said this of Obama's speech in Cairo:

President Barack Obama was elected, by an overwhelming majority, on a program in which America's rapprochement with Islam stands pre-eminent. This is a legitimate political aim in the quest for world peace. The questions are: how to achieve it, and why there is no recip-rocal effort from the Muslim world represented by the Organization of the Islamic Conference (OIC). This body could express its regrets for over a millennium of jihad wars, land expropriations, enslave-ments, and humiliations of the conquered non-Muslim populations on three continents.

Obama's Cairo discourse fits perfectly into his agenda. It flatters Muslim sensibilities and expresses the Muslim view of historical toler-ance and cultural superiority over infidel civilizations. When Obama mentioned the "Isra" event, he referred to Muhammad's ascension to heaven and his return in one night on a winged mule named Buraq. There he greets two Muslim prophets, Moses and Jesus/Isa, who are not the biblical figures. The image used here by the American presi-dent as a symbolic interfaith reconciliation between the three faiths is a meeting between three Muslim prophets and not the figureheads of the three monotheistic religions. Besides, the Isra event is not recog-nised by non-Muslims, and it didn't happen in Jerusalem, as this name does not appear once in the Koran.

The president's speech is similar to many such declarations by Eu-ropean leaders. The question it raises is how much the West is ready to forgo truth and its basic principles in its supplication for obtain-ing peace with Islam. Clearly, the full Islamization of the West is the quickest way to obtain it. Obama's political program in connection with the Alliance of Civilizations conforms to an OIC strategy that has already been accepted by the EU. In history, this policy has a name: the dhimmitude syndrome.[15]

Obama demonstrated a continual unwillingness to acknowledge plain facts, asserting that "the attacks of September 11th, 2001, and the continued efforts of these extremists to engage in violence against civilians has led some in my country to view Islam as inevitably hostile not only to America and Western countries, but also to human rights." He predictably ignored the fact that the Islamic texts and teachings that inspired those attacks have fueled this perception. Of course, Obama was not singular in declining to acknowledge the existence of such texts and teachings. In that he was following virtually every influential American politician, diplomat, and analyst.

But here again, the policies Obama has pursued since he became president give an ominous cast to his tendency to exonerate the Islamic world and blame America for the conflict between the two. While speaking a great deal about human rights and even vowing to fight for the right of Islamic women in the West to wear the Islamic headscarf, he said nothing throughout his speech about the Sharia laws that impugn the dignity of women and non-Muslims by denying them various basic rights. "The U.S. government has gone to court to protect the right of women and girls to wear the hijab, and to punish those who would deny it," Obama said proudly. "I reject the view of some in the West that a woman who chooses to cover her hair is somehow less equal."

To this the columnist Mark Steyn responded acidly: "My oh my, he's a profile in courage, isn't he? It's true that there have been occasional frictions over, say, the refusal of Muslim women to reveal their faces for their driver's licenses—Sultaana Freeman, for example, sued the state of Florida over that 'right.' But the real issue in the Western world is 'the right of women and girls' *not* 'to wear the hijab.' A couple of weeks ago in Arizona, a young woman called Noor Almaleki was fatally run over by her father in his Jeep Cherokee for becoming 'too Westernized.' If there were a Matthew Shepard–style gay crucifixion every few months, liberal columnists would be going bananas about the 'climate of hate' in America. But you can run over your daughter, decapitate your wife, drown three teenage girls and a polygamous spouse (to cite merely the most lurid recent examples of North American 'honour killings'), and nobody cares. Certainly, there's no danger of Barack Obama ever standing up for the likes of poor Miss Almaleki to a roomful of A-list imams." [16]

Indeed not.

Obama even went so far as to say: "I consider it part of my responsibility as President of the United States to fight against negative stereotypes of Islam wherever they appear."

Assuming that such stereotypes actually exist, and that negativity toward Islam among non-Muslims isn't entirely a reaction to jihad violence and Islamic supremacism, why was this his responsibility? Was it his responsibility as president to fight against negative stereotypes of Christians as ignorant racist yahoos? Was it his responsibility as president to fight against negative stereotypes of Hindus? Jews? Black Americans? American Southerners? Californians? Or was it only his responsibility to fight against negative stereotypes of Islam? If the latter, why? On what basis? By what justification?

In any case, Obama indulged in a bit of negative stereotyping of his own—against Israel. "Palestinians must abandon violence. Resistance through violence and killing is wrong and does not succeed. For centuries, black people in America suffered the lash of the whip as slaves and the humiliation of segregation. But it was not violence that won full and equal rights. It was a peaceful and determined insistence upon the ideals at the center of America's founding."

His comparison of the Palestinians with black Americans was

unconscionable. Were the Israelis Bull Connor and George Wallace? For the comparison to hold, black Americans must have been launching daily rocket attacks against white civilians, and blowing themselves up at those segregated lunch counters during crowded lunch hours.

Obama took another flight of fancy when he said: "Islam has a proud tradition of tolerance. We see it in the history of Andalusia and Cordoba during the Inquisition." (Obama clumsily pronounced the latter "Cordóba" rather than "Córdoba," demonstrating a closer acquaintance with Ricardo Montalban's Chrysler commercials from the 1980s than with the actual history and geography of Spain.)

This is sheer historical myth. Even Maria Rosa Menocal, in her hagiographical treatment of Muslim Spain, *The Ornament of the World*, admits that non-Muslims did not enjoy equality of rights with Muslims in Andalusia and Cordoba: "The dhimmi, as these covenanted peoples were called, were granted religious freedom, not forced to convert to Islam. They could continue to be Jews and Christians, and, as it turned out, they could share in much of Muslim social and economic life. In return for this freedom of religious conscience the Peoples of the Book (pagans had no such privilege) were required to pay a special tax—no Muslims paid taxes—and to observe a number of restrictive regulations: Christians and Jews were prohibited from attempting to proselytize Muslims, from building new places of worship, from displaying crosses or ringing bells. In sum, they were forbidden most public displays of their religious rituals."[17]

So much for that "proud tradition of tolerance." But on this farrago of historical myth, anti-Americanism, and shameless pandering, Barack Obama set out to build a foreign policy. He abandoned Israel, appeased Iran, and took steps to enable the spread of Islamic supremacism around the world.

STATE DEPARTMENT'S RAMADAN OUTREACH

In August 2009, a State Department cable went out with this announcement: "The Bureau of International Information Programs (IIP) has assembled a range of innovative and traditional tools to support Posts' outreach activities during the Islamic holy month of Ramadan."

State Department outreach during the Islamic holy month? The First Amendment to the U.S. Constitution says that "Congress shall make no law respecting an establishment of religion," and official government activities on behalf of a particular religion have been found to be in violation of that clause in recent years. However, when it comes to Islam all that seemed to go out the window.

The State Department's Ramadan programs were wide-ranging. "On August 10," the cable continues, "America.gov will publish a 'Multicultural Ramadan' feature. American Muslims trace their ancestry to more than 80 countries and the feature will highlight the richness of these various cultural traditions through the lens of Ramadan and Eid. Content will include essays by young Muslims who are part of Eboo Patel's Interfaith Youth Core (IYC). Contact: Alexandra Abboud (AbboudAM@state.gov)."

Still more was planned. The Bureau of International Information Programs was set to "publish three articles for Ramadan 2009 addressing the concept of an Islam in America 'brand'; advocacy (civic and political) of the Muslim American community; and community innovation/community building. The writer will contact Muslim American experts in each of these fields. These articles will be available on America.gov in English, Arabic, and Persian."

The main publication was entitled *Being Muslim in America*: "Conceived as IIP's flagship print publication on the rich and varied experiences of the nation's growing Muslim population, this lavishly illustrated new book links the Muslim-American experience to those of other American racial, religious, and immigrant groups as they moved into the American 'mainstream.' " [18]

Such was the State Department during the post-American presidency.

Can you imagine every American embassy and consulate putting up a menorah and having some rabbis as speakers via a Webcast?

Can you imagine if we had the Stations of the Cross put on the walls of all our embassies, consulates, and other posts, as well as the many Department of State buildings across the country, including C Street?

Why aren't priests and pastors invited during Christmas to give blessings or talk about Christianity in the United States?

Can you imagine if some Buddhist monks came to do a meditation session with the officers of each embassy and consulate?

Can we get printed and distributed Hare Krishna posters for all our posts, so as to reach massive audiences?

In Barack Obama's State Department, of course, only Islam merited such marginally constitutional privileges.

Perhaps the State Department Ramadan outreach was the brainchild of Obama's office for outreach to the *ummah* at State—an office that had existed for less than two months when notice went out of the State Department Ramadan initiatives. In June 2009, Obama had the secretary-general of the Organization of the Islamic Conference, Ekmeleddin Ihsanoglu, at the White House. Ihsanoglu urged Obama to appoint a U.S. ambassador to the Islamic world—and Obama immediately created a new State Department Office for Muslim Outreach, with a Muslim woman of Indian descent, Farah Pandith, serving as the new U.S. special representative for Muslim outreach.

In keeping with Obama's U.S.–Muslim Engagement Project, a charter of dhimmitude, we were to be conditioned to respect Muslim immigrants and accept their culture—and any suspicion regarding terrorist activities among them was to be rejected for fear of being charged with "Islamophobia."

Obama appeared to be more than comfortable with this deal with the devil as he abetted the replacement of America's Judeo-Christian ethic with an Islamo-Christian ethic—which would ultimately destroy the very foundation of this country. Muslims persecute Christians in every country they finally dominate—never in world history have Muslims coexisted as equals with Christians in any Islamic land. The Christians are always subjugated as inferiors, in accord with directives of Islamic law that are still in place.

But none of that appears to be at all important to Barack Hussein Obama.

Why was this immense effort necessary? Columnist Burt Prelutsky said it best: "The Islamists have been actively at war with us for 30 years and generally at war with western civilization for well over a thousand years, and still we pay lip service to these people in a way we never did with Nazi Germany, Imperial Japan or the Soviet Union. Is it because the Muslims commit sadism and murder in the name of religion and not country? If anything, I would think that would make their evil acts all the more contemptible." [19]

HAJ GREETINGS FROM BARACK HUSSEIN

The Islamophilic president went so far as to issue a heartfelt special greeting and best wishes to the Muslim pilgrims in Mecca for the Haj . . . on Thanksgiving Day 2009. Obama asserted that "the rituals of Haj and Eid al-Adha both serve as reminders of the shared Abrahamic roots of three of the world's major religions." And he noted: "Muslims around the world will celebrate Eid-al-Adha and distribute food to the less fortunate to commemorate Abraham's willingness to sacrifice his son out of obedience to God."

191

In this Obama yet again exacerbated tensions instead of calming them. The Islamic Feast of Eid al-Adha commemorates the end of the pilgrimage to Mecca, the haj, and Abraham's willingness to sacrifice his son—Ishmael in the Muslim version. In thinking of Abraham, most Americans think of the biblical figure. In Genesis 22:15–18, Abraham is rewarded for his faith and told he will become a blessing to the nations: "By your descendants shall all the nations of the earth bless themselves, because you have obeyed my voice."

But the Muslim audiences that Obama addressed in this message did not read Genesis. They read the Qur'an, in which Allah says that Abraham was an "excellent example" for the believers only when he told his pagan family that "there has arisen, between us and you, enmity and hatred for ever, unless ye believe in Allah and Him alone" (60:4). The same verse says that Abraham is *not* an excellent example, however, when he tells his pagan father, "I will pray for forgiveness for you." [20]

Thus the Qur'an, in its picture of Abraham—the man Obama invoked as the quintessential symbol of the common elements of the three faiths—held up hatred as exemplary, while belittling the virtue of forgiveness. Obama thereby reinforced a worldview that took for granted the legitimacy of everlasting enmity between Muslims and non-Muslims—and did so while attempting to build bridges between Muslims and non-Muslims.

He also retained, as his chief liaison to the Islamic world, a defender of Sharia: the draconian Islamic law that mandates stoning of adulterers, amputation of thieves' hands, and legal discrimination against women and non-Muslims.

DEFENDING SHARIA

Dalia Mogahed, Barack Obama's adviser on Muslim affairs, appeared on British television in October 2009, where she said: "Sharia is not well understood and Islam as a faith is not well understood." How have we misunderstood Islamic law? We have associated it with "maximum criminal punishments" and "laws that . . . to many people seem unequal to women." The Western view of Sharia was "oversimplified," said Obama's adviser on Muslim affairs; most Muslim women worldwide, she said, associate it with "gender justice."

Here's some gender justice straight out of the Qur'an, the Islamic holy book that forms the basis of Sharia. The Qur'an declares that a woman's testimony is worth half that of a man (2:282). It rules that a son's inheritance should be twice the size of that of a daughter (4:11). The Qur'an tells husbands to beat their disobedient wives (4:34). It also allows for marriage to prepubescent girls, stipulating that Islamic divorce procedures "shall apply to those who have not yet menstruated" (65:4).

All these stipulations—about testimony, inheritance, wife beating, marriage, and divorce—remain part of Sharia to this day. So does the law that a wife must not refuse sex to her husband, no matter where or when he makes the demand. This is based on a saying of the Islamic prophet Muhammad: "If a husband calls his wife to his bed [i.e., to have sexual relations] and she refuses and causes him to sleep in anger, the angels will curse her till morning." And another: "By him in Whose Hand lies my life, a woman can not carry out the right of her Lord, till she carries out the right of her husband. And if he asks her to surrender herself [to him for sexual intercourse] she should not refuse him even if she is on a camel's saddle."

Gender justice. And that's not all. Mogahed, a member of the president's Council on Faith-Based and Neighborhood Partnerships, made

193

her defense of Sharia on a TV show hosted by a member of Hizb ut Tahrir. This is an international organization that is banned as a terrorist group in many nations, and which is openly dedicated to the worldwide imposition of Sharia and the destruction of all governments that are constituted according to any other political philosophy—including constitutional republics that do not establish a state religion.

On the show with Mogahed were two Hizb ut Tahrir representatives, who repeatedly attacked "man-made law" and the "lethal cocktail of liberty and capitalism" one encounters in Western societies. They said Sharia should be "the source of legislation." Not "a" source. "The" source.

Obama's adviser Mogahed, for her part, offered no contradiction to any of this. Should an adviser to the president of the United States really have given her sanction to such a group? Apparently she has no problem with its goal, since instead of defending the American system of government, she maintained that Sharia was popular among Muslim women: "I think the reason so many women support Sharia is because they have a very different understanding of Sharia than the common perception in Western media."

On the same show, Dalia Mogahed described her job in the Obama administration as involving efforts "to convey . . . to the president and other public officials what it is Muslims want." What Muslims want. Not what America might want from Muslims—i.e., a recognition of the ways in which Sharia contradicts the Constitution regarding the equality of all people before the law, and a forthright rejection of those elements of Sharia. No one, Muslim or non-Muslim, seems concerned about any challenge to those provisions from the adherents of Sharia.

Perhaps they should have listened more closely to Dalia Mogahed.

MUTUAL RESPECT?

Obama spoke often about establishing "mutual respect" with the Islamic world. But that respect seemed to be a one-way street. In denigrating his own country and retailing historical myths about the Islamic world, he was only augmenting the haughtiness that was a centerpiece of Islamic supremacism. In endeavoring at least ostensibly to take away the impetus for Islamic terrorism around the world, he was fueling some of its core assumptions: that America was an evil polity, responsible for the conflicts and tensions roiling the world; that Islam was a great civilization, destined to shine again as it once had in the misty distant past—a beacon of light to the world.

Barack Obama, son and stepson of two Muslims, raised a Muslim himself, seemed determined to be the engine of that resurgence.

What was peculiar in all this was that many who were raised Muslim but left Islam—scholars such as Ibn Warraq, politicians such as Ayaan Hirsi, doctors such as Wafa Sultan—were quite vocal about the violations of human rights, the misogyny, the oppression, the child marriages, that they witnessed in Muslim societies. Obama must have seen such things while growing up in the largest Muslim country in the world and attending Qur'anic classes and Islamic study. But they fight against these human-rights abuses, while he embraces the Islamic world uncritically. He respects it, human-rights abuses and all.

THE U.S.–MUSLIM ENGAGEMENT PROJECT: CHARTER FOR DHIMMITUDE

Why was Obama acting this way? The answer lay in his unshakable commitment to the U.S.–Muslim Engagement Project, a multifaceted initiative designed, in its own words, to "create a coherent, broad-based and bipartisan strategy and set of recommendations to improve relations between the U.S. and the Muslim world; and communicate and advocate this strategy in ways that shift U.S. public opinion and contribute to changes in U.S. policies, and public and private action."[21]

This strategy and series of recommendations was laid out in two principal documents. One was the George Soros–funded Report of the Leadership Group on U.S.–Muslim Engagement: *Changing Course: A New Direction for U.S. Relations with the Muslim World*, from September 2008. The other was closely related to the U.S.–Muslim Engagement initiative: *The Doha Compact: New Directions: America and the Muslim World*, from the Saban Center of the Brookings Institution's Project on U.S. Relations with the Islamic World. *The Doha Compact* appeared in October 2008.

No outreach or integration of societies similar to that suggested in *Changing Course* and *The Doha Compact* is ever suggested in any official policy document for any other culture, or religion. Both of these documents, meanwhile, are generally silent about, if not downright hostile toward, the American commitment to Israel—except for their insistence upon the two-state solution, which in reality amounts to nothing more than a call for the destruction of Israel, since a Palestinian state would be nothing more than a base for further jihad attacks against Israel. Pursuing this policy thus constitutes abandonment of a strategic ally in one of the most hostile and belligerent hotspots in the world—an ally that has been a cornerstone of U.S. diplomacy since the late 1940s, through Republican and Democratic administrations alike, from Harry Truman going forward.

Jews, of course, should pay attention to all this, and understand that not only does it undermine the stability and security of the Jewish homeland, but it also has grave implications for Jews in America. For Islamic political influence is always hostile to the Jews, the worst enemies of the Muslims according to the Qur'an (5:82).

Obama's adviser for Muslim affairs, Dalia Mogahed, is listed as a member of the U.S.–Muslim Engagement Project's "Leadership Group," and is a signatory to the *Doha Compact*. Frank Gaffney of the Center for Security Policy noted in March 2009 that *Changing Course* was being "aggressively promoted to the Obama administration and Congress by a number of its non-Muslim participants," including former secretary of state Madeleine Albright, who presented it to the Senate Foreign Relations Committee, and former congressman Vin Weber.[22]

Also part of the Leadership Group is Ingrid Mattson of the Islamic Society of North America (ISNA), an organization that is linked to the Muslim Brotherhood. And the Brotherhood is, in its own words, dedicated in America to "a kind of grand Jihad in eliminating and destroying the Western civilization from within and 'sabotaging' its miserable house by their hands and the hands of the believers so that it is eliminated and Allah's religion is made victorious over all other religions."[23]

So committed was Obama to this strategy and course of action that two documents that set out in detail how this improvement of relations was to be achieved served as virtual templates for the post-American president's action plan, rhetoric, and strategy. His statements hewed so closely to the recommendations in these documents that it sometimes seemed as if Obama's speechwriters were lifting copy straight from the documents.

DICTATING OBAMA'S POLICY
TOWARD THE ISLAMIC WORLD

Changing Course, for example, called on the incoming president to "elevate diplomacy as the primary tool for resolving key conflicts involving Muslim countries, engaging both allies and adversaries in dialogue" and to "engage with Iran to explore the potential for agreements that could increase regional security, while seeking Iran's full compliance with its nuclear nonproliferation commitments." Obama has attempted indefatigably to do both. It further recommended that the new president "work intensively for immediate de-escalation of the Israeli-Palestinian conflict and a viable path to a two-state solution, while ensuring the security of Israelis and Palestinians."

This also was identical to Obama's playbook, as were calls to "promote broad-based political reconciliation in Iraq, and clarify the long-term U.S. role," "renew international commitment and cooperation to halt extremists' resurgence in Afghanistan and Pakistan;" and "provide top-level U.S. leadership to resolve regional conflicts and to improve coordination with international partners."

Changing Course anticipated Obama's language directly in calling upon the U.S. leader to "improve mutual respect and understanding between Americans and Muslims around the world."[24] *The Doha Compact* likewise stated: "Repairing the rift between the United States and the Muslim world must begin with respect. Lack of mutual respect has been an important driver behind the deterioration of relations between the United States and the Muslim world since 9/11."[25] As we have seen, Obama often spoke of restoring "mutual respect" with the Islamic world, including in his Inaugural Address—in line with the *Changing Course* recommendation that the new president "speak to the critical importance of improving relations with the global Muslim community in his 2009 inaugural address."[26]

Changing Course also recommended efforts to "deepen mutual understanding and challenge stereotypes."[27] Obama duly said in his June 2009 Cairo speech that he considered it part of his "responsibility as president of the United States to fight against negative stereotypes of Islam wherever they appear."

The U.S.–Muslim Engagement document called upon the incoming president to reaffirm "the U.S. commitment to prohibit all forms of torture," which Obama did in connection with the Guantánamo Bay detention camp. It recommended that "within the first three months of the Administration," the new president should "initiate a major and sustained diplomatic effort to resolve regional conflicts and promote security cooperation in the Middle East, giving top priority to engagement with Iran and permanent resolution of the Israeli-Palestinian conflict."[28] And Obama has duly reached his outstretched hand to Iran, and put pressure on the Israelis to make further concessions to the Palestinians.

The correspondence between all this and Obama's policies were exact, and there was more. *Changing Course* "supports engagement with groups that have clearly demonstrated a commitment to nonviolent participation in politics."[29] So also *The Doha Compact*: "the United States should be more willing to reach out to Islamist parties that genuinely demonstrate their readiness to embrace the democratic rules of the game and reject violence."[30] This referred primarily to the Muslim Brotherhood, which is attached to Sharia but willing to work for it through the ballot box and cultural initiatives. Obama made sure that Brotherhood members were in the audience when he gave his Cairo speech in June 2009.[31] The call to support nonviolent pro-Sharia parties may also have fueled Obama's fantasies of the "moderate Taliban."

Changing Course warns against supplying "ammunition to extremists by linking the term 'Islam' or key tenets of the religion of Islam with the actions of extremist or terrorist groups."[32] *The Doha Compact* agrees: "Ill-considered terms like 'Islamofascism,' 'Islamic terrorism,' and 'Islamic jihadist' tend to alienate potential friends, while implicitly endorsing the worldview of extremists like bin Laden by suggesting they are true Muslims."[33]

The fact that it is Islamic jihadists, not antiterror analysts, who have energetically equated the texts and teachings of Islam with violence and terrorism was, as usual, glossed over—and Obama was happy to abet this disconnect from reality. In his Nobel Peace Prize acceptance speech he spoke of "the way that religion is used to justify the murder of innocents by those who have distorted and defiled the great religion of Islam, and who attacked my country from Afghanistan." Engaging in another historical flight of fancy, Obama added: "These extremists are not the first to kill in the name of God; the cruelties of the Crusades are amply recorded."[34]

That Islamic jihad aggression preceded the Crusades by 450 years seems to have escaped him.

The Doha Compact directed that the president who took office in January 2009 should "close down the detention facility in Guantánamo Bay, which has unfortunately become a symbol of American excesses and extralegal maneuvers in the war on terror" and "should ban the use of torture in the interrogation of terrorist suspects."[35] Obama set out to do those things from the beginning of his presidency. "The next American president," *The Doha Compact* also declared, "should travel to the region early in his or her term, meeting not only with leaders, but also visiting mosques."[36]

Obama did that, too.

He didn't seem concerned with the Muslim Brotherhood ties of both initiatives, or with how their dictates weakened the United States. He didn't even seem concerned about the fact that the more he accommodated the Islamic world, the angrier and more demanding Islamic states seemed to become.

No wonder jihad terror activity spiked within the United States itself.

EIGHT

AN ISLAMO-CHRISTIAN NATION

IN BARACK OBAMA'S INAUGURAL ADDRESS HE SAID: "WE ARE A NATION OF CHRISTIANS AND MUSLIMS, JEWS AND HINDUS, AND NONBElievers."[1]

The displacement of the Jews from the second position after Christians in Obama's listing had to be intentional. Then, just six days later, Obama restored the Jews to the second position, but after the Muslims: when the post-American president gave his first televised interview as president to Dubai's Al-Arabiya News Channel, he made a point of calling America "a country of Muslims, Jews, Christians, nonbelievers."[2] In that order.

The casual abandonment of the longtime workaday phrase "a

Judeo-Christian nation" was portentous. In one broad stroke Obama sought to diminish, if not completely obliterate, the enormous part the Jews played in the American success story. Obama has never spoken about the inestimable contribution the Jews made to the birth of America or to its subsequent unparalleled historical achievements. Obama never spoke of, say, Haym Solomon, the Jewish patriot and member of the Sons of Liberty who was captured and tortured by the British in the early days of the American Revolution. Solomon loaned as much as $800,000 to the revolutionary cause; in today's dollars, that's about $40 billion. Solomon himself died in poverty after giving everything he had for the cause of American freedom.

Why the reclassification of Jews and Christians? And why would Obama make this his first order of business as soon as he took office? That it was his top priority was made painfully clear when he gave his first interview as president to the Arab world on Al-Arabiya. It would become increasingly clear in the ensuing weeks and months that Barack Hussein Obama was attempting to shift the American paradigm. What was once a given was to be taken. The Judeo-Christian tradition, the essential DNA of American principles, thought, and governance was to be replaced with a false narrative and a dangerous idea—an "Islamo-Christian" ethic.

Were Christians who might be indifferent to such an idea aware of the status of Christians in Islamic countries? Were Christians aware that there was no pluralism in Islamic nations? Traditional Islamic law called for Jews and Christians in Islamic lands to live in a state of chastened subservience to Muslims, denied basic rights in an attempt to ensure that they always remembered their renegade status as those who had rejected the truth of Islam. The hallmark of this mistreatment was a special tax, *jizya*, mandated in the Qur'an (9:29). The Muslims could revoke this contract of "protection" (*dhimma*) at any time if the protected people (dhimmis) got out of line. While the institutionalized discrimination and harassment of this state of dhimmitude is not fully enforced in most Muslim countries today, it remains a part of Islamic law—and a cultural hangover that results in numerous forms of discrimination for non-Muslims in Islamic countries today.

AMERICA'S ISLAMIC HISTORY

These were facts of Islamic history. Obama, bent on fashioning some new accord with the Islamic world, ignored them—but he did not ignore history altogether. In the infancy of his presidency, he seemed to be intent upon rewriting American history. Just as he retailed historical myths about Muslim Spain in his June 2009 speech in Cairo, here he created, out of whole cloth, an Islamic history in America:

> I know, too, that Islam has always been a part of America's story. The first nation to recognize my country was Morocco. In signing the Treaty of Tripoli in 1796, our second President John Adams wrote, "The United States has in itself no character of enmity against the laws, religion or tranquility of Muslims." And since our founding, American Muslims have enriched the United States. They have fought in our wars, served in government, stood for civil rights, started businesses, taught at our Universities, excelled in our sports arenas, won Nobel Prizes, built our tallest building, and lit the Olympic Torch. And when the first Muslim-American was recently elected to Congress, he took the oath to defend our Constitution using the same Holy Koran that one of our Founding Fathers—Thomas Jefferson—kept in his personal library.[3]

It was exaggerated to the point of fiction, or distorted almost beyond recognition—for one thing, Jefferson most likely had a Qur'an not because he respected or revered Islam, but because he wanted to understand the belief system of the Barbary Pirates who were bedeviling American ships in those days, and to whom the United States had been paying tribute—a practice Jefferson ended. But Obama had made it clear, repeatedly: this fictionalized history would henceforth take precedence over the real thing.

In his overwhelming desire to submit to and appease the Islamic world, Obama more than once trafficked in such fulsome historical fictions that may have bolstered the egos of his audience as well as his own, but they did nothing to blunt the force of the global Islamic jihad. If anything, they did just the opposite. Obama emboldened and empowered the *ummah* (the worldwide Islamic community). They were winning, just as their prophet predicted, with this strategy for installing a global caliphate.

"We will convey," said Barack Obama to the Turkish Parliament in April 2009, "our deep appreciation for the Islamic faith, which has done so much over the centuries to shape the world—including in my own country."[4]

Undeniably the Islamic faith has done a great deal to shape the world—a statement that makes no value judgment about exactly *how* it has shaped the world. It has formed the dominant culture in what is known as the Islamic world for centuries. But what on earth could Obama mean when he says that Islam has also "done so much" to shape his own country?

ISLAM SHAPED AMERICA?

Unless he considered himself an Indonesian, Obama's statement was extraordinarily strange. After all, how has the Islamic faith shaped the United States? Were there Muslims along Paul Revere's ride, or standing next to Patrick Henry when he proclaimed, "Give me liberty or give me death"?

Were there Muslims among the framers or signers of the Declaration of Independence, which states that all men—not just Muslims, as Islamic law would have it—are endowed by their Creator with certain unalienable rights, including life, liberty, and the pursuit of happiness?

Were there Muslims among those who drafted the Constitution and vigorously debated its provisions, or among those who enumerated the Bill of Rights, which guarantees—again in contradiction to the tenets of Islamic law—that there should be no established national religion, and that the freedom of speech should not be infringed?

There were not.

Did Muslims play a role in the great struggle over slavery that defined so much of our contemporary understandings of the nature of this republic and of the rights of the individual within it? They did not. In fact, Muhammad owned slaves, and the Qur'an takes the existence of slavery for granted—making abolition movements virtually impossible in an Islamic context. Muslim countries have abolished slavery under pressure from the non-Muslim West, not because of any impulse arising from Islam itself.

Bat Ye'or, the paramount historian of the treatment of non-Muslims in Islamic societies, saw larger issues at play in this: "Freedom of discussion and criticism (forbidden in Islamic countries) brought reforms (non-existent in Islam). The concepts of human rights, freedom and democracy, and the abolition of slavery come from the Judeo-Christian tradition."[5]

Did the Islamic faith shape the way the United States responded to the titanic challenges of the two World Wars, the Great Depression, or the Cold War? It did not. Did the Islamic faith, with its legal apparatus that institutionalizes discrimination against non-Muslims, shape the civil rights movement in the United States?

Did the mainstream media, on which the American people rely to vet our candidates, question Barack Hussein Obama on this? Did they even superficially ask the most cursory of questions? Or ask Obama to provide empirical evidence? No. Chris Matthews's leg couldn't handle the electroshock to answer such questions.

The Civil Rights Act of 1964 mandated equality of access to public facilities—a hard-won victory that came at a great cost, and one that Muslim groups have tried to roll back in the United States recently. One notable example of such attempts was the alcohol-in-cabs controversy at the Minneapolis–St. Paul international airport, when Muslim cabdrivers began to refuse service to customers who were carrying alcohol, on Islamic religious grounds. The core assumption underlying this initiative—that discrimination on the basis of religion is justified—cut right to the heart of the core principle of the American polity, that "all men are created equal," that is, that they have a right to equal treatment in law and society. Alcohol might seem to be a trivial matter; the threatening of the principle of equal access to services is not.

Surveying the whole tapestry of American history, one would be hard-pressed to find any significant way in which the Islamic faith has shaped the United States in terms of its governing principles and the nature of American society. Meanwhile, there are numerous ways in which, if there had been a Muslim presence in the country at the time, some of the most cherished and important principles of American society and law may have met fierce resistance, and may never have seen the light of day.

So in what way has the Islamic faith shaped Obama's country? The most significant event connected to the Islamic faith that has shaped the character of the United States was the attack on the World Trade Center and the Pentagon on September 11, 2001. Those attacks have shaped the nation in numerous ways: they've led to numerous innovations in airline security, which in generations to come—if today's politically correct climate continues to befog minds—may be added to future versions of the "1001 Muslim Inventions" exhibition.[6]

The Islamic faith has shaped the United States since 9/11 in leading to the spending of billions on antiterror measures, and to the ventures in Iraq and Afghanistan, and to Guantánamo, and to so many features of the modern political and social landscape that they cannot be enumerated.

Of course, it is certain that Obama had none of that in mind. But what could he possibly have had in mind? His statement was either careless or ignorant, or both—not qualities we need in a commander in chief even in the best of times.

AMERICA, A MUSLIM COUNTRY

Obama got even more careless and ignorant in a June 1, 2009, interview with the French press. Sounding one of his favorite themes, he said: "I think that the United States and the West generally, we have to educate ourselves more effectively on Islam." Apparently the post-American president's idea of effective education was to depart from reality altogether: "And one of the points I want to make is, is that if you actually took the number of Muslim Americans, we'd be one of the largest Muslim countries in the world."[7]

It was one of the most bizarre statements of a bizarre presidency—and it wasn't remotely true. Indonesia has a population of over 200 million Muslims; India is second with over 160 million Muslims, and Pakistan has 150 million Muslims. The United States, by contrast, is home to 2.3 million Muslims, according to the Pew Research Center.

No mainstream media reporter, not surprisingly, ever challenged Obama about this, and so he never explained what might have motivated him to make this odd assertion. But it was all the more noteworthy in light of the fact that two months earlier, Obama had said that "one of the great strengths of the United States is . . . we have a very large Christian population—we do not consider ourselves a Christian nation or a Jewish nation or a Muslim nation. We consider ourselves a nation of citizens who are bound by ideals and a set of values."[8]

Yet less than eight weeks later, America had become a Muslim nation. Obama was just about to make his major speech in Cairo, and perhaps he wanted to impress his Muslim hosts. And he may well have done so. But he also opened the door to more accommodation of Islam, including—if not especially—its political and supremacist aspects, than had ever before been seen in the United States of America.

Some of it was symbolism, like Obama's abrupt cancellation of the National Day of Prayer, hitherto a White House event with a pronounced Christian flavor.[9] However, it would have been imprecise to say that it was "mere" symbolism. The symbolism, like Obama's statement about America being one of the world's largest Muslim countries, carried important implications.

OBAMA ABANDONS THE JEWS AND LEGITIMIZES "KAPO COUNCILS"

The post-American president in April 2009 hosted a Passover seder at the White House—the first seder ever hosted by a sitting president. But it was a small, muted affair: the White House announced that "President Obama and his family will mark the beginning of Passover with a seder at the White House with friends and staff."[10] Valerie Jarrett attended, as well as Obama's personal aide Reggie Love; an aide to David Axelrod; White House videographer Arun Chaudhary; and some other family members and friends. The guests all sat around one large table with the president.[11]

The smallness of the affair confused some Jewish Obama supporters. One White House staffer revealed that when the seder was announced, "apparently Jewish [residents] here and in neighboring states are now calling wondering why they have not been invited." [12]

No such hurt feelings attended Obama's September 2009 Ramadan iftar dinner: there was plenty of room for everyone. The Obama Ramadan bash was a lavish affair, attended by three Cabinet members, senators, congressmen (including, of course, the nation's two Muslim congressmen, Keith Ellison (D-MN) and André Carson (D-IN)), seventeen ambassadors and six other diplomats, and over thirty invited guests, including Ingrid Mattson of the Islamic Society of North America (ISNA), an unindicted coconspirator in a Hamas terror funding case. [13]

At the Ramadan iftar, Obama went out of his way to praise the Muslim contribution to American society: "Islam, as we know, is part of America. . . . Indeed, the contribution of Muslims to the United States are too long to catalog because Muslims are so interwoven into the fabric of our communities and our country. American Muslims are successful in business and entertainment; in the arts and athletics; in science and in medicine. Above all, they are successful parents, good neighbors, and active citizens." [14]

His Passover greetings contained no similar praise for Jewish citizens; instead, Obama included a veiled call for further Israeli concessions to the Palestinians: "As Jewish families gather across America to enjoy the magnificent and hard-earned gift of freedom, let us all be thankful for the gifts that have been bestowed upon us. And at the same time, let us also work to alleviate the suffering, poverty, and hunger of those who are not yet free." [15]

It was in these seemingly small details that much was revealed: Obama's priorities, his predilections, and his prejudices. And he made no secret of them.

Worse still, on September 11, 2009, the eighth anniversary of the worst terror attack ever on American soil, an attack carried out by devout Muslims, the post-American State Department sent out an invitation to employees from the South Asian–American Employee Association (SAAEA) for a screening of the film *Inside Islam: What a Billion Muslims Really Think*. This film, a soothing whitewash of the jihadist sentiments among Muslims worldwide, premiered in June 2009—and all State Department employees got an invitation to attend that screening as well.[16]

This is systemic. Employees are encouraged and rewarded for abetting the spread of comforting half-truths and outright deceptions about Islam and terrorism. And some of the statements on the department's blog were unsettling (all spelling and grammar is as in the originals). One official suggested that the film screening be turned into a "public diplomacy event by inviting foreign diplomats and representatives from civil society." Another suggested: "I like the idea to bring back having Iftars at the white House or even at the department of state for Muslim civil employees." Separation of religion and state? That is so twentieth century! Another State official wrote: "Happy Ramadan to everyone. I think it would be a great idea to have an Iftar party from DOB or WH not only to celebrate the Muslim's holy month, but also to support the 'Diversity' initiative is currently being taken by Secretary Clinton."[17]

A QUIET HANUKKAH

The State Department was busy actively cultivating Muslim goodwill. And so it came as no surprise, then, in November 2009, when the news was leaked that the White House Hanukkah party guest list was to be cut to half of its 2008 number. *The Jerusalem Post* reported: "Though several Jewish leaders expressed understanding for the economic and other reasons behind the cut, they acknowledged that it would likely help feed feelings in some quarters of the American Jewish community that the White House is giving them the cold shoulder."[18]

There was blowback to this Hanukkah snub after an opinion piece appeared in the Jewish Telegraphic Agency. Tevi Troy, who had been a liaison to Jewish groups in the Bush administration, suggested that Obama was taking Jewish votes for granted, citing as evidence the administration's call for a freeze on Jewish settlements in the West Bank. The Hanukkah guest list cuts, according to Troy, left "a nagging sense that there may be a studied callousness at work here."[19]

It wasn't lost on those who watched such things that the Ramadan iftar celebration was a spectacular gala event. Barack Obama never gave any quarters of the American Muslim community any cause to think that he was giving *them* the cold shoulder. His overtures to them that began on his Inauguration Day, during his Inaugural Address, continued throughout his first year in office.

MUSLIMS IN HIGH PLACES

In June 2009, Obama appointed a Muslim, Kareem Shora, to the Homeland Security Advisory Council. Shora had been executive director of the American-Arab Anti-Discrimination Committee, a group that had generally opposed antiterror efforts since 9/11. But more worrisome was Obama's appointment of another Muslim, Arif Alikhan, to be assistant secretary for policy development at the Department of Homeland Security.

These appointments were obvious attempts to show the Muslims of the United States and the world that antiterror efforts were not anti-Islam or anti-Muslim. Shora and Alikhan would stand as moderate Muslims within the DHS, living illustrations of the iron dogma that all Muslims aside from a tiny minority were loyal Americans who abhorred Osama bin Laden and everything he stood for.

But when he made the appointment, Obama didn't notice, or didn't care, that as deputy mayor of Los Angeles, Alikhan (who has referred to the jihad terrorist group Hizbullah as a "liberation movement") had blocked an effort by the Los Angeles Police Department to gather information about the ethnic makeup of area mosques.[20] This was not an effort to close down Los Angeles mosques, or to conduct surveillance of them. There was no wiretapping or interrogation involved. No one would be jailed or even inconvenienced. Los Angeles deputy chief Michael P. Downing explained in 2007: "We want to know where the Pakistanis, Iranians and Chechens are so we can reach out to those communities."[21] But even outreach was too much for the hypersensitive Muslim leaders of Los Angeles: they cried racism, discrimination, and "Islamophobia" until the LAPD dropped the plan.[22]

And Arif Alikhan spearheaded their drive against this initiative.

Would he bring to the Department of Homeland Security a similar sensitivity to the quickly wounded feelings of Muslims?

JUSTICE DEPARTMENT ENFORCING SHARIA

In Cairo on June 4, 2009, Obama boasted that "the U.S. government has gone to court to protect the right of women and girls to wear the hijab, and to punish those who would deny it. . . . I reject the view of some in the West that a woman who chooses to cover her hair is somehow less equal." Five days later, as if to show that Obama was serious about what he said in Cairo, his post-American Justice Department filed a lawsuit against Essex County, New Jersey, charging that the county had discriminated against a Muslim woman, Yvette Beshier.

Beshier was a corrections officer, and had been forbidden to wear her khimar, or headscarf, while working. When she refused to comply, the Essex County Department of Corrections (DOC) first suspended and then fired her—the khimar was not part of the uniform, and corrections officers were expected to conform to uniform policy. But such policies, of course, were drawn up before the days of politically correct multiculturalism. Instead of simply expecting employees to conform to company rules, now the company had to adapt to the religious particularities of its Muslim employees: Barack Obama's Justice Department sued on Beshier's behalf.[23]

When Obama in Cairo boasted about fighting for hijab-wearing women in the United States, he promised to "punish" infidels for not submitting to the dictates and whims of Islam. The lawsuit that followed less than a week later showed that he was in earnest.

It was almost certainly the first time that the United States Justice Department had filed a lawsuit in order to enforce an element of Sharia, Islamic law.

On duty, Yvette Beshier, like all her fellow corrections officers, should have worn religiously neutral garb. Off duty, she could have dressed any way she wanted. But ultimately the Justice Department's suit wasn't really about the dress code at the Essex County Department of Corrections at all. It was about asserting Islamic practices in the United States, and establishing and reinforcing the precedent that when Islamic law and American law and custom conflicted, it was American law that had to give way. As of this writing, the suit is still pending in federal court.

ENABLING JIHAD FINANCE

In his June 2009 Cairo speech, Obama said: "Freedom of religion is central to the ability of peoples to live together. We must always examine the ways in which we protect it. For instance, in the United States, rules on charitable giving have made it harder for Muslims to fulfill their religious obligation. That's why I'm committed to working with American Muslims to ensure that they can fulfill *zakat*." [24]

Zakat, one of the Five Pillars of Islam, is the Islamic obligation to give alms. Since jihad is also a key obligation for Muslims, it should not be surprising that all too often Islamic charities in the United States have been found to be funneling charitable contributions to jihad groups. Former prosecutor and terror analyst Andrew McCarthy explained several days after Obama's Cairo address: "The inconvenient fact is that numerous Islamic charities have proved to be fronts for terrorist activity, at least in part. These include the Holy Land Foundation (whose top operatives were recently convicted for underwriting Hamas in a prosecution that exposed CAIR [the Council on American-Islamic Relations] as an unindicted co-conspirator) and the al-Haramain Islamic Foundation, one of the world's largest Muslim charities, headquartered in Saudi Arabia (which hosted the president for private talks last week)."[25]

In light of these inconvenient facts, Obama's claim that "in the United States, rules on charitable giving have made it harder for Muslims to fulfill their religious obligation" strained credulity. This fantastic assertion was right out of the Frank Marshall Davis/ JeremiahWright playbook, as if some inherent racism and xenophobia in the American system were hamstringing innocent, pious Muslims who were simply trying to fulfill their duty before God. Asked McCarthy: "Do we really have 'rules on charitable giving' that, as the president claims, make it especially difficult for Muslims—as opposed to others—to give? No. What we have are federal laws against material support for terrorism. These were enacted by Congress in 1996. They have been the bedrock of the DOJ's anti-terrorism enforcement ever since."[26] Do they target Muslims? Of course not. They target anyone and everyone who is trying to give financial support to terrorists.

But in Cairo, Obama told the world that he intended to remove those safeguards. The only beneficiaries, in the long run, would be the

Islamic jihad terrorists who would once again be able to receive support from their well-heeled American coreligionists.

It was all part of a larger pattern.

RUSH TO JUDGMENT

When news broke about the massacre at Fort Hood, Texas, on November 5, 2009, in which thirteen people were killed and thirty-nine wounded, Barack Obama advised the nation not to rush to judgment. "We don't know all the answers yet," the president said. "And I would caution against jumping to conclusions until we have all the facts." Obama delivered this statement from the Rose Garden—while, incidentally, George W. Bush was visiting wounded victims in Fort Hood.

Over the next few days, it became clear, despite the mainstream media's obfuscations and denials, that the shootings were a terrorist attack by an Islamic jihadist, Maj. Nidal Malik Hasan. Yet Obama never acknowledged this, and the Department of Homeland Security refused to classify the shootings as a terrorist attack. Obama would apparently have preferred that the American people forget that Hasan screamed "Allahu akbar" before he mowed down scores of patriotic Americans, and that he gave away Qur'ans with his business card before his act of jihad. Hasan also gave his landlord two weeks' notice—showing that he had planned this for a long time. He didn't just snap.

Obama seemed to want Americans to ignore the fact that Hasan went to a mosque where a jihadist imam preached hatred of America. The same imam, Anwar al-Awlaki, was "spiritual adviser" for three of the hijackers who attacked America on September 11, 2001, and praised Hasan's mass murders as a sterling example of Islamic jihad. Obama apparently preferred that Americans didn't know that, when Hasan was asked his nationality, he didn't identify himself as an American, but as a Palestinian.

Obama didn't want Americans to rush to judgment about how Hasan spoke approvingly of the shooting death by an Islamic jihad terrorist of a Little Rock Army recruiter in June. Obama didn't want anyone to draw any conclusions from how Hasan reportedly was heard saying, "maybe people should strap bombs on themselves and go to Times Square."

Obama didn't want Americans to rush to judgment.

The post-American president was not so circumspect when he spoke out about professor Henry Louis Gates's arrest by Cambridge, Massachusetts, police sergeant James Crowley. Obama incited hatred on national television, rushing to judgment against a white cop who was just doing his job. Obama tried to incite racial division and wrongly criticized the police during a news conference: "But I think it's fair to say, No. 1, any of us would be pretty angry; No. 2, that the Cambridge police acted stupidly in arresting somebody when there was already proof that they were in their own home; and, No. 3 . . . that there's a long history in this country of African-Americans and Latinos being stopped by law enforcement disproportionately."

The incident, Obama said, showed "how race remains a factor in this society."

A few days later, after an avalanche of criticism, Obama backtracked, saying: "In my choice of words, I unfortunately, I think, gave an impression that I was maligning the Cambridge Police Department or Crowley specifically."

But he did not apologize for *his* rush to judgment. Apparently jumping to conclusions was wrong only when it led to the conclusion that there had been another Islamic terror attack on American soil.

But to come to that conclusion really didn't involve any "rush to judgment" at all. What became known about Hasan made that abundantly clear. He wrote "Allah" on his door, according to a neighbor, in Arabic. During his postgraduate work at the Uniformed Service

University of the Health Sciences, he was reprimanded for preaching Islam to his patients and other doctors. He drew attention from law enforcement officials with Internet postings under his name that praised suicide bombing, saying that their intention was to "save Muslims by killing enemy soldiers," and that "if one suicide bomber can kill 100 enemy soldiers because they were caught off guard that would be considered a strategic victory." He turned a grand round session in which he was supposed to be teaching about a topic in psychiatry into a session of Islamic proselytizing, complete with an unusually forthright avowal of the Islamic teachings mandating warfare against unbelievers.

His attack at Fort Hood was not the act of a crazy person. This was not the random act of a nutcase. According to Maj. Gen. Robert Scales at Fort Hood, Hasan committed murder, execution-style, at close range. He shot 44 to 50 rounds, which is a great deal of ammunition to use in a short period. He said that the murders were clearly premeditated.[27]

By not rushing to judgment, Obama could sweep the issue under the carpet.

MAKING AMERICANS LESS SAFE

Meanwhile, Barack Hussein Obama was making Americans less safe than we were before he was president.

In August 2009 his administration made it official, banning government spokesmen and analysts from using the terms "war on terrorism," "jihadists," and "global war."[28] The war on terror was over, and as far as official Washington was concerned, the jihad never was on in the first place.

The only people who didn't get the memo were the Islamic jihadists themselves. Or maybe they did get it, and they understood it all too clearly: they realized that the Obama administration was weak and anxious to accommodate the Islamic world, and surmised that it would do little or nothing to resist Islamic jihad activity in the United States. Like Osama bin Laden observing Bill Clinton's withdrawal of American troops from Somalia in the 1990s after the Black Hawk incident, they sensed that the Americans were a weak horse, and that it was time for their strong opponents to step up operations.

And step them up they did. In a three-month period in the late summer and early fall of 2009, there was an extraordinary proliferation of jihad attacks, attempted attacks, and exposed plots in the United States or involving American nationals abroad. In December 2009, a Pakistani Muslim living in Chicago, David Headley (whose original name was Daood Gilani, but who changed it so as to avoid suspicion in the United States), was arrested and charged with aiding in the planning of the jihad massacre in Mumbai in November 2008. Headley visited all the sites of the massacre beforehand, reporting back to his fellow jihadists about logistics of the attack.[29] The same week five American citizens were arrested in Pakistan for their involvement with violent jihadist groups.[30]

Also that same week, a Muslim graduate student from Saudi Arabia stabbed to death a seventy-seven-year-old professor, Richard Antoun. One of the student's roommates had gone to authorities to report him: "I said he was acting oddly, like a terrorist. When I informed them, it was for them to understand that the guy was violent or he may be violent."[31] But as in the case of Maj. Nidal Hasan, warnings went unheeded. Perhaps officials in Barack Obama's America were more afraid of being charged with "bigotry" and "Islamophobia" and so quietly sat on the roommate's warning, hoping that it wouldn't blow up in their faces.

But it did.

In August 2009, seven Muslims in North Carolina were charged with aiding terrorists; a month later, it came to light that they had planned a jihad attack against the Marine Corps base in Quantico, Virginia.[32] In September, a New York–based Muslim, Najibullah Zazi, was arrested as he plotted to set off a weapon of mass destruction in a sporting event or some other crowded area.[33] Another Islamic jihadist, Hosam Maher Husein Smadi, was arrested after placing an inert car bomb at a sixty-story office tower in downtown Dallas.[34] Yet another jihadist, an American convert calling himself Talib Islam, was arrested for plotting to blow up the Paul Findley Federal Building in Springfield, Illinois.[35] In October, Luqman Ameen Abdullah, a Detroit imam who taught his followers that they should wage jihad warfare against the United States, was killed in a shootout with the FBI.[36] Also in October, a Muslim in Boston, Tarek Mehanna, was arrested for plotting to massacre American civilians in a shopping mall, as well as to murder "members of the executive branch" whom law enforcement officials declined to identify.[37]

The reason there was no major Islamic jihad attack in America after 9/11 was because of President George W. Bush, his team, and his policies. Now Obama is dismantling those very same policies, emasculating the CIA, trying to close Gitmo, and creating walls between agencies—restoring many of the same terrible policies of Bill Clinton that made 9/11 possible.

Obama seemed all too willing to abet the imposition of a soft Sharia in America. Refusing to call Hasan's attack on Fort Hood what it really was, a jihad attack, was to accept the laws of dhimmitude, which forbid the dhimmis from speaking ill of Islam, Allah, or Muhammad. And so, an avowed Islamic jihadist shot over fifty people at Fort Hood, and Obama seemed intent most of all on making sure that no one got the idea that the shootings had anything to do with Islam. This was Sharia. This was dhimmitude.

The crowning capitulation came in February 2010, when the

Obama Defense Department released its Quadrennial Defense Review (QDR), a report on security threats to the United States that it is required to issue every four years. In 128 pages, Obama's QDR doesn't mention the threat of Islamic jihad at all—not even with the popular weasel words such as "radical," "Islamist," or "extremist." However, the report devotes eight pages to an exhaustive discussion of the security threat posed by . . . climate change.[38]

How long do you think you will remain safe while Obama ignores the jihad threat, and meanwhile triples the number of "diversity" visas and "religious" visas from the fiercest jihad hotspots in the world: Somalia, Gaza, Pakistan, Afghanistan, and more?[39]

One thing is certain: Obama's appeasement of the Islamic jihad both internationally and inside America will bear fruit. Bitter fruit.

NINE

DESTROYING THE PRESTIGE OF AMERICA

IN DUE COURSE, THE POST-AMERICAN PRESIDENT TURNED AGAINST HIS OWN PEOPLE (ALTHOUGH IT SEEMS INCREASINGLY UNLIKELY THAT HE ever really considered them his people): those who had dedicated their lives to protecting this nation after the September 11 terror attacks. He announced his intention to close down the Guantánamo Bay detention camp during his presidential campaign and reiterated this goal many times after becoming president, despite the embarrassing fact that many former Gitmo detainees returned to jihad after being released from the camp.

Obama accepted at face value the leftist claim that Guantánamo was a torture camp. Even as late as his December 1, 2009, speech announcing his troop escalation in Afghanistan, he reiterated this: "And finally, we must draw on the strength of our values—for the challenges that we face may have changed, but the things that we believe in must not. That's why we must promote our values by living them at home—which is why I have prohibited torture and will close the prison at Guantánamo Bay. And we must make it clear to every man, woman and child around the world who lives under the dark cloud of tyranny that America will speak out on behalf of their human rights, and tend to the light of freedom and justice and opportunity and respect for the dignity of all peoples. That is who we are. That is the source, the moral source, of America's authority."[1]

But Obama's pledge to speak out on behalf of human rights everywhere rang hollow almost immediately. It was bitterly ironic that just over a week later, the Cairo Institute for Human Rights Studies found in a survey of twelve Arab countries—Algeria, Bahrain, Egypt, Iraq, Lebanon, Morocco, Palestine, Saudi Arabia, Sudan, Syria, Tunisia, and Yemen—that the human-rights situation in virtually all of them had deteriorated markedly in the preceding year. "Arab governments remained wedded to a broad array of repressive laws that undermine basic liberties," said the report—and it accused the Obama administration of abetting the repression. American policies toward these nations, it said, were "wholly inimical to reform and human rights in the region." Obama had abandoned reform initiatives: "The last spark of life in the initiatives was quashed once and for all with the arrival of a new US administration."[2]

Why was Obama mum about the deteriorating human-rights situation in these Muslim countries? Did he harbor hopes that he would be able to induce them to change by heaping praise and concessions upon them? Or was he simply indifferent to the human-rights situation in those nations, for while the alleged torture at Gitmo served his political purposes in numerous ways, human-rights abuses in Syria or

Yemen could not either do him damage or afford any significant political gain?

Obama tried to maximize public outrage over the "torture" at Guantánamo. In April 2009, the Obama administration announced that it intended to release a series of photos that supposedly depicted this torture.[3] This would, of course, have handed America's enemies a huge propaganda opportunity and eroded the nation's moral authority to act in the world perhaps for generations. But the ensuing public outcry was so great that ultimately the post-American president, choosing his battles, quietly let the issue drop.[4]

Nevertheless, the damage had been done: the president of the United States was spreading the notion that American officials had engaged in torture at Guantánamo Bay. Even without actually releasing the photos, he had provided ample grist for Islamic jihadist propaganda mills.

Why did Obama indulge moral outrage over the alleged torture at Gitmo, while ignoring much worse actual torture that was going on in countries he was approaching with outstretched hand?

PROSECUTING AMERICA'S DEFENDERS

On August 24, 2009, Attorney General Eric Holder appointed John Durham as a federal prosecutor to investigate CIA officers who might have abused suspected terrorists. With a fine grasp of understatement, Holder conceded: "I fully realize that my decision to commence this preliminary review will be controversial." But that wasn't going to stop him: "As attorney general, my duty is to examine the facts and to follow the law. In this case, given all of the information currently available, it is clear to me that this review is the only responsible course of action for me to take."[5]

Why?

The Washington Post reported that in appointing this prosecutor, Holder "shook off warnings from President Obama to avoid becoming mired in past controversies." The article went on to note the "respect that Obama says he maintains for the role of an independent attorney general."[6]

But insiders and those close to the administration knew that Holder was executing a policy Obama had long wanted.

Nonetheless, this decision was so politically charged—and so radical in the specter it provided of the U.S. government potentially accusing itself of and confessing to war crimes—that it was hard to believe that Obama left it to Holder, much less dissented from it. Obama would not take the heat for his egregious and enormously hostile policy toward America. Holder was the fall guy for Obama.

Alarmed by how this move cast enemies of the United States in the role of victims and demonized law enforcement, handing a potentially overwhelming propaganda victory to Islamic jihadists worldwide, seven former CIA directors tried to stop the Obama administration from opening investigations on CIA agents who tried to get information out of jihad terrorists. The former CIA chiefs said that "further investigations would demoralize current CIA officers and might also lead allied intelligence services to suspend or scale back cooperation with the United States because the judicial probes could disclose joint operations and activities."[7]

No doubt.

And as foreign governments moved also to prosecute Bush administration officials, Obama did nothing—leading John Bolton to point out that while Obama's prosecution plan may have been "smart politics within the Democratic Party," it risked "grave long-term damage to the United States. Ironically, it could also come back to bite future Obama administration alumni, including the president, for their current policies in Iraq, Afghanistan and elsewhere."

Bolton also noted that "morale at the CIA is at record lows." No surprise there. Holder even opened the door for Obama administration cooperation with a foreign trial of Bush officials: "Obviously, we would look at any request that would come from a court in any country and see how and whether we should comply with it." Remarked Bolton: "This is deeply troubling. Obama appears to be following the John Ehrlichman approach, letting the U.S. lawyers 'twist slowly, slowly in the wind.'"

The people twisting in the wind to whom Bolton was referring were the Bush administration lawyers who wrote legal opinion memos to the effect that waterboarding and similar interrogation procedures did not constitute "torture" as defined by international law. The Obama administration initiated prosecutions of John Yoo and Jay Bybee, who wrote the "torture memos," as trial balloons in a cynically calculated effort to intimidate the entire cadre of ex-Bush administration people into silence on a host of issues—by threatening the low men on the totem pole of Bush officials who were linked to Guantánamo. This effort didn't get far: Yoo and Bybee were cleared by the Justice Department's Office of Professional Responsibility (OPR) in January 2010.[8] But the fact that the attempt to prosecute them was made was disquieting enough.

When the Obama camp began this initiative, former vice president Dick Cheney had had enough, and went public with his fight. "One of the things I find disturbing about this recent disclosure," he explained when Obama released so-called "torture memos" in April 2009, "is they put out the legal memos but they didn't put out the memos that show the success of the effort. There are reports that show specifically what we gained as a result of this activity. . . . I have now formally asked that they be declassified now. . . . They are not telling the whole story. . . . If you're going to have this debate, let's have an honest debate."[9]

But Obama wasn't interested in honest debate. That was never his goal. Bolton explained the point of all such prosecutions: "The real aim is to intimidate U.S. officials into refraining from making hard but necessary decisions to protect our national security."[10]

GOING AFTER THE SEALS

But the post-American president wasn't chastened. In November 2009 three Navy SEALs captured Ahmed Hashim Abed, the mastermind of the killing and horrible mutilation of Americans in Fallujah, Iraq, in 2004. But instead of being hailed as heroes, the SEALs faced court-martial—because Abed emerged, according to Rowan Scarborough of Fox News, with a bloody lip.[11]

A high-placed military source said that the SEALs were so angry about these court-martial proceedings, they were talking about not taking any more prisoners. And who could blame them? So the internationalist Obama managed in one fell swoop not only to demoralize the SEALs, but to make Americans that much less safe.

Even worse, the military source said that the prosecution of the SEALs was a cause dear to the White House, which pursued it relentlessly as payback for an earlier action taken by the SEALs: killing the Somali jihadist pirates who held hostage Capt. Richard Phillips of the *Maersk Alabama* in April 2009. Obama, ever the internationalist, had set the rules of engagement in such a way as to preclude killing the pirates: a shot could be fired only if Phillips seemed to be in imminent danger of death. The SEALs were on site for thirty-eight hours and had several chances to take out the pirates, but were held back. Finally, the on-site commander determined that Phillips was indeed in danger of death, and ordered the SEALs to fire.

According to a retired military intelligence officer who called in to

Rush Limbaugh with the information, Obama was privately furious, although publicly he claimed that he ordered the shot in order to gain public support. But he did not forget the incident, and the prosecution of the SEALs was payback.[12] There was no way to verify this information, but there was also no doubt that it was plausible, particularly given Obama's other actions and habits of mind.

And as we have seen, in August 2009 Secretary of State Clinton said that it was a matter of "great regret" that the United States did not accept the authority of the International Criminal Court (ICC)—which dearly wanted to try American soldiers for war crimes.[13]

It could happen.

Obama seemed preoccupied with—and angry about—the treatment of jihadi terrorists, and was going after those who put protecting Americans first. The hypocrisy of the administration was devastating.

KSM TO NEW YORK

Not long after that, Holder and Obama found a way both to discredit and weaken America at the same time.

In a stunning act of sedition and capitulation to Islamic jihad, the Obama administration announced in November 2009 that it intended to bring the masterminds of the shocking invasion of America on September 11, 2001, into a New York courtroom. Obama was going to try in a U.S. court the Muslim masterminds of the most brutal attack on American soil in modern history—joining what historian Bat Ye'or has termed "over a millennium of jihad wars, land expropriations, enslavements, and humiliations of the conquered non-Muslim populations on three continents."

Obama was determined to prosecute the September 11 act of war as a law enforcement issue. And so our wartime enemy would face a civilian trial in New York City. Congressman Peter King (R-NY) said "it may be the worst decision by a U.S. president in history." Conservative activist David Horowitz agreed with King: "It sends a signal to terrorists everywhere to attack civilians."

There is a United States Supreme Court holding from 1942 regarding six German Nazi saboteurs who had been apprehended on the eastern seaboard during World War II. As they were not military personnel, they asked to be given civilian trials, rather than trials before military panels. The Supreme Court ruled against them, noting that as spies and saboteurs they were enemy combatants, and would thus go before military tribunals under that system.

End of discussion.

That should be ample authority to establish a jurisdictional basis to try Khalid Sheikh Mohammed and his fellow jihadis in a military tribunal. The holding in the Nazi saboteur case noted that Congress had declared war on Germany, but other statutory and historical references would apply very easily to a finding that Mohammed and his henchmen were "unlawful combatants," and therefore subject to trial by military tribunals if so directed by the president.[14]

The precedent is clear. But Holder and Obama, of course, had other priorities.

Consider that the greatest act of war, the most devastating attack on American soil in U.S. history, would be turned over to civilian courts with the enemy mastermind given the constitutional rights of an American citizen.

In a civilian court in New York, the mass-murdering jihadis would not have been put on trial; Bush, Cheney, Rumsfeld, and the military would have been the real defendants in what would certainly have turned out to have been a show trial. It would have been a veritable jihad circus, in which Khalid Sheikh Mohammed could have propagandized the whole world in a courtroom in the shadows of the once towering, majestic symbol of American fiscal greatness and superiority, the World Trade Center.

The terrorists had confessed and would have pled guilty in a military tribunal had the Obama administration not announced that a civilian trial would be held in New York.

The consequences could have been even more devastating. Andrew McCarthy, who prosecuted the jihadists who bombed the World Trade Center in 1993, recalled that one of them told another: "Tell them, 'I don't know. I'm not talking to you. Bring my lawyer.' Never talk to them. Not a word. 'My lawyer'—that's it! That's what's so beautiful about America."

As defendants in a civilian trial, the 9/11 masterminds would be granted access to material from American intelligence services about jihad activity in the United States. They would be granted a look at everything the United States knows about Al-Qaeda and its allied groups, and would be able to pass this information on to active jihadists.

Said McCarthy: "They will get a year or more to sift through our national defense secrets. . . . In the military system, we could have denied them access to classified information, forcing them to accept military lawyers with security clearances who could see such intelligence but not share it with our enemies. In civilian court, the Supreme Court has held an accused has an absolute right to conduct his own defense. If KSM asserts that right—as he tried to do in the military commission—he will have a strong argument that we must surrender relevant, top-secret information directly to him. And we know that indicted terrorists share what they learn with their confederates on the outside." [15]

How much intelligence would be compromised when these jihad barbarians are all lawyered up? They should be tried as war criminals at Gitmo—in a military court.

Sarah Palin called it an atrocious decision: "The trial will afford Mohammed the opportunity to grandstand and make use of his time in front of the world media to rally his disgusting terrorist cohorts. It will also be an insult to the victims of 9/11, as Mohammed will no doubt use the opportunity to spew his hateful rhetoric in the same neighborhood in which he ruthlessly cut down the lives of so many Americans." Palin pointed out that "the mastermind of the 9/11 attacks may walk away from this trial without receiving just punishment because of a 'hung jury' or from any variety of courtroom technicalities."

And the ex-Muslim freedom fighter Nonie Darwish, author of an exposé of Sharia, *Cruel and Usual Punishment*, explained what Obama's decision was really all about: "The purpose of the trial is to embarrass the Bush administration and America itself and to give Arabs a golden opportunity to indulge in propaganda to convince the West with falsehoods regarding the root causes of Islamic terrorism; mainly that it is the consequence of US foreign policy, old grievances and America's support of Israel."

This happened because Obama wanted to propagate the idea that Khalid Sheikh Mohammed and others were tortured at Guantánamo on George W. Bush's watch. Who would have been on trial? KSM, the devout Muslim murderer, or Bush and those who "waterboarded"? Too bad that the thousands of people whose lives were saved in LA can't hop a red-eye to New York and testify. According to a Justice Department memo dated May 30, 2005, waterboarding "led to the discovery of a KSM plot, the 'Second Wave,' 'to use East Asian operatives to crash a hijacked airliner into' a building in Los Angeles."[16] That building was the Liberty Tower, the tallest building in the West.

"There is also no question," Obama claimed in May 2009, "that Guantánamo set back the moral authority that is America's strongest currency in the world."[17]

I disagree. For America to prosecute those who kept this country safe from people like Khalid Sheikh Mohammed, as Obama seems to intend to do, sets back our moral authority. America turning her back on the jihad against women, Christian, Jews, and nonbelievers sets back America's moral authority.

Obama sweated the treatment of Khalid Sheikh Mohammed while setting up our boys and girls in Afghanistan. We were experiencing the highest number of deaths in the war against the global jihad month after month over there because, in Obama's words, "I'm not interested in victory."[18]

When he was concerned about the alleged injustices at Gitmo, it was obvious that Obama wanted very much to take the American eye off his failed policies. He wanted Americans to ignore his foreign-policy realignment with despots and mullahs. He wanted to distract us from his abandonment of our allies and his promotion of jihad. Obama turned a blind eye in the summer of 2009 to the worst and most brutal crackdown imaginable in Iran, but was shocked and dismayed that we may have been too tough on the jihadis who planned to overthrow and defeat America.

Obama dropped the plan for a New York trial of the 9/11 plotters after a sustained public outcry, but he still continued with plans to try these terrorists in civilian courts.[19] He even said in February 2010 that the trial could still ultimately be held in New York City: "I have not ruled it out."[20]

It was yet another appalling chapter in the Obama presidency.

BLAMING AMERICA FOR 9/11

None of this came as any surprise to those who had been following Barack Hussein Obama's career. For as long ago as September 2001, in the wake of the worst terrorist attack on American soil in U.S.

history, Barack Obama set a pattern he would repeat again and again: he blamed America, and prescribed as a solution to the problem the transfer of wealth from Americans to Third Worlders. Speaking just eight days after the 9/11 jihad terror attacks, when America's righteous indignation and will to fight were at their peak, Obama termed the attacks a "tragedy"—as he would many years later as president, when another Islamic jihadist murdered thirteen people at Fort Hood in Texas.

"The essence of this tragedy," Obama said, "it seems to me, derives from a fundamental absence of empathy on the part of the attackers: an inability to imagine, or connect with, the humanity and suffering of others. Such a failure of empathy, such numbness to the pain of a child or the desperation of a parent, is not innate; nor, history tells us, is it unique to a particular culture, religion, or ethnicity. It may find expression in a particular brand of violence, and may be channeled by particular demagogues or fanatics. Most often, though, it grows out of a climate of poverty and ignorance, helplessness and despair."

So in other words, poverty, ignorance, hopelessness, and despair had caused 9/11, and it was up to those deep-pocketed Americans to be empathetic enough to transfer their wealth to these poor, ignorant, despairing people to make sure that such an attack would not happen again. In the socialist Obama's eyes, 9/11 was another occasion for the poor of the world to soak the rich.

Obama also included a warning to Americans: "We will have to make sure, despite our rage, that any U.S. military action takes into account the lives of innocent civilians abroad. We will have to be unwavering in opposing bigotry or discrimination directed against neighbors and friends of Middle Eastern descent. Finally, we will have to devote far more attention to the monumental task of raising the hopes and prospects of embittered children across the globe—children not just in the Middle East, but also in Africa, Asia, Latin America, Eastern Europe and within our own shores."[21]

"Embittered children."

In the cynical and depraved bloodlust of the 9/11 jihadists, Obama saw the cry of lost children. And eight years later, as president of the United States, he demonstrated again and again his solicitude for these brutal and hateful "children."

TEN

FREEDOM OF SPEECH IN THE AGE OF JIHAD

SOON AFTER HE BECAME PRESIDENT, BARACK HUSSEIN OBAMA WENT TO WAR. BUT NOT AGAINST THE GLOBAL JIHAD, OR THE ROGUE STATE of North Korea, or any other enemy of the nation he had sworn to protect.

Instead, Barack Obama went to war against the freedom of speech, the most basic, fundamental, unalienable right of every individual who lives and breathes the air of America's exceptionalism and rule of law.

America is the most magnificent experiment in human history. A novel, moral form of governance that stands on the rights of the individual, freedom of speech, freedom of religion, freedom to dissent.

There was not before, and not since, a country built so completely upon capitalism, the most benevolent human system in the world, in which the individual was protected by rule of law against both mob rule (majority rule) and minority plotting (special interests). The United States of America boasted the first government founded on the rights of the smallest minority in the world, the individual.

The Bill of Rights reads: "Congress shall make no law abridging the freedom of speech or of the press."

It is our foremost safeguard against tyranny. The most basic tenet of our great and noble nation is freedom of speech. It is the cement that holds together the bricks of life, liberty, and the pursuit of happiness. There is no possibility of a constitutional republic without freedom of speech. If one group is allowed to suppress the speech of another, the suppressing group has achieved total hegemony: and more to the point, in the words of Ayn Rand, the principle of free speech is "not concerned with the *content* of a man's speech and does not protect only the expression of *good* ideas, but of *all* ideas. If it were otherwise, who would determine which ideas are good and which to be forbidden? The government?"[1]

Yes, the government. In August 2009, just as the national debate over health care was ramping up, House Speaker Nancy Pelosi (D-CA) and House Majority Leader Steny Hoyer (D-MD) said this in a *USA Today* op-ed about those who were protesting against the plan: "Drowning out opposing views is simply un-American. Drowning out the facts is how we failed at this task for decades."[2]

But who was really trying to drown out the opposition?

Three days before Pelosi and Hoyer branded opponents of Obama's health-care plan as "un-American," Obama spoke at a campaign rally for Virginia gubernatorial hopeful Creigh Deeds. Speaking also of the opponents of his health-care plan, Obama declared: "I don't want the folks who created the mess to do a lot of talking. I want them to get out of the way so we can clean up the mess. I don't mind cleaning up after them, but don't do a lot of talking. Am I wrong, Virginia?"[3]

Yes, Virginia, Barack Obama was wrong. Talking—dissent, debate, and loyal political opposition—is the very heart, the lifeblood, of the American Republic. Freedom of speech not only protects popular ideas, it protects all ideas. If Pelosi, Hoyer, and Obama succeeded in silencing dissent to the Democrats' health-care proposals, the life of that republic would be effectively over.

THE HATRED OF THE GOOD FOR BEING THE GOOD

But surely they did not intend to demonize and silence dissent, did they?

Yes, they did.

It started even before Barack Obama became president. Columnist Michael Barone noticed it in October 2008. After recounting how Obama told a Nevada crowd to "talk to your friends and talk to your neighbors," and to "argue with them and get in their face," Barone noted that "actually, Obama supporters are doing a lot more than getting into people's faces. They seem determined to shut people up."

Barone recalled that when Obama opponent Stanley Kurtz, a writer for the conservative *National Review* who had been exploring ties between Obama and sixties terrorist William Ayers, appeared on radio host Milt Rosenberg's show in Chicago, "Obama fans jammed WGN's phone lines and sent in hundreds of protest emails. The message was clear to anyone who would follow Rosenberg's example. We will make trouble for you if you let anyone make the case against The One."[4]

That same month, the governor of Missouri, Matt Blunt, issued a statement on the Obama campaign's "abusive use of Missouri law enforcement." Blunt charged that three Missouri state officials, St. Louis county circuit attorney Bob McCulloch, St. Louis city circuit attorney Jennifer Joyce, and Jefferson County sheriff Glenn Boyer, along with the leader of Obama's campaign in Missouri, Sen. Claire McCaskill, had "attached the stench of police state tactics to the Obama-Biden campaign." They had announced the formation of "Truth Squads" in Missouri that would track down people who stated publicly what they considered to be falsehoods about Obama, and would initiate proceedings against them for slander or libel. In this, said Blunt, they were "abusing the justice system and offices of public trust to silence political criticism with threats of prosecution and criminal punishment."

Such behavior, said Blunt, was "scandalous beyond words." Obama and his supporters, he said, were trying to "frighten people away from expressing themselves, to chill free and open debate, to suppress support and donations to conservative organizations targeted by this anticivil rights, to strangle criticism of Mr. Obama, to suppress ads about his support of higher taxes, and to choke out criticism on television, radio, the Internet, blogs, e-mail and daily conversation about the election."

"Barack Obama," he declared, "needs to grow up."[5]

But when Barack Obama became president, he was empowered. The Obama administration embarked upon a campaign of demonizing dissenters, eagerly abetted by his corrupt, morally bankrupt, activist propaganda arm, the mainstream media. These were primarily Obama's willing serfs and useful idiots. Secondarily, they hoped for a government bailout for their failing publications as their circulation and readership were falling precipitously. They were quickly being relegated to the trash bin. But Obama was doing his best to keep them alive. Clearly, his Marxist views would lead him to take the media under his wing and shape it according to his own opinion and discourse. It is no wonder that he was so anxious to meet and hug

Venezuelan tyrant Hugo Chávez. Chávez took over all the media in Venezuela. No worries that way.

The New York Times's opinion makers began not long after Barack Obama took office to warn its dwindling readership about the evils of those who opposed the new president. Within one eight-day span in June 2009, Bob Herbert warned about "right-wing hate-mongers" and "gun crazies"; Frank Rich sounded the alarm about "far-right rage"; Paul Krugman claimed that "right-wing extremism is being systematically fed by the conservative media and political establishment"; and Tobin Harshaw also muttered about the "rise of right-wing extremism."[6]

But above all, there was the race card. The demonization of Obama's opponents was illustrated vividly in the summer of 2009, when there appeared in Los Angeles the now-notorious "socialism" poster of Barack Obama made up as The Joker. But although this poster depicted Obama, not his opponents, it was they who ended up being demonized, not the president. Predictably, opponents of the president's policies were branded as "racists." Steven Mikulan said in the *LA Weekly* that the poster "has a bit of everything to appeal to the drunk tank of California conservatism: Obama is in white face, his mouth (like Ledger's Joker's) has been grotesquely slit wide open and the word 'Socialism' appears below his face. The only thing missing is a noose."[7] And *Bedlam Magazine* charged: "The Joker white-face imposed on Obama's visage has a sort of malicious, racist, Jim Crow quality to it."[8]

How disingenuous this was. For years, those of us who chronicled the relentless Bush bashing of the Left documented innumerable instances at rallies, on Internet posts, and in articles, in which Bush was vilified and smeared in the most lurid terms—far worse than the Obama Joker poster. This abuse was never even noted, much less covered by the media. Yet the depth and breath of the invective against Bush was stunning. It is also ironic that *Vanity Fair* published an iconic cartoon of President Bush in white face, as The Joker. In the case of Bush, it was all in good fun, all just for laughs. But it was dead serious when Obama was depicted that way.

This favorite tactic of the Left began in the opening months of the Obama administration to verge on self-parody. Any criticism of Obama, no matter what it was or how legitimate it may have been, was labeled racism. Tea party? Racism! Opposition to socialism? Racism! Opposition to nationalized health care? Racism! Opposition to cap and tax? Racism! Opposition to the ethnic cleansing of Jewish people in Israel? Racism!

Nobel Prize–winning *New York Times* columnist Paul Krugman epitomized this absurdity in an August 2009 column when he linked health-care protesters to those who questioned Obama's American citizenship, as well, of course, to racism. "The driving force behind the town hall mobs," Krugman claimed, "is probably the same cultural and racial anxiety that's behind the 'birther' movement, which denies Mr. Obama's citizenship." The Obama propagandists deliberately coined the pejorative tag of "birther" to sound similar to "truther." This, of course, was a terrible smear. Truthers are conspiracy theorists who actually believe that Bush and members of his administration were the real perpetrators of the September 11 Islamic attacks on America. The birthers, on the other hand, simply wanted Obama to release his long-form birth certificate.

"Senator Dick Durbin has suggested," Krugman continued, "that the birthers and the healthcare protesters are one and the same; we don't know how many of the protesters are birthers, but it wouldn't be surprising if it's a substantial fraction." It is, he said, "a strategy that has played a central role in American politics ever since Richard

Nixon realized that he could advance Republican fortunes by appealing to the racial fears of working-class whites." Krugman thought we were beyond all that as a nation: "Many people hoped that last year's election would mark the end of the 'angry white voter' era in America." But alas, "the angry right is filled with a passionate intensity."[9]

And they're all racists.

Times columnist Maureen Dowd made the same charge after Rep. Joe Wilson (R-SC) shouted "You lie!" at Obama during the president's September 9, 2009, speech defending his plan to nationalize health care. Dowd made Wilson's objection to Obamacare sound like something only Bull Connor would love: "Surrounded by middle-aged white guys—a sepia snapshot of the days when such pols ran Washington like their own men's club—Joe Wilson yelled 'You lie!' at a president who didn't. But, fair or not, what I heard was an unspoken word in the air: You lie, boy!"

Unspoken indeed it was, but that didn't stop Dowd. She went on to explain that Wilson "belonged to the Sons of Confederate Veterans, led a 2000 campaign to keep the Confederate flag waving above South Carolina's state Capitol and denounced as a 'smear' the true claim of a black woman that she was the daughter of Strom Thurmond, the '48 segregationist candidate for president. Wilson clearly did not like being lectured and even rebuked by the brainy black president presiding over the majestic chamber."[10]

Former president Jimmy Carter agreed with Dowd, sanctimoniously opining that Wilson's outburst was "based on racism. There is an inherent feeling," Carter asserted, "among many in this country that an African-American should not be president."[11]

And while the media wrung its hands about Wilson, unnoticed in the hubbub was the two-thousand-page elephant in the room. There was no serious debate about the merits of the government takeover of health care. No debate at all.

OBAMA INCITES RACE HATRED TO
DEMONIZE HIS OPPONENTS

In July 2009, Black Studies professor (and friend of Barack Obama) Henry Louis Gates was arrested at his home in Cambridge, Massachusetts, by a white police sergeant, James Crowley, after Gates created a disturbance when police showed up at his home to investigate an alleged break-in. The Gates affair became a national story because the president used it to make a statement inciting hatred on national television.

At a press conference on health care, Obama passed over the reporter whose turn it was for him to recognize, going out of his way to call on Lynn Sweet of *The Boston Globe*, who asked him about Gates. Obama admitted that he had not seen "all the facts," but still charged that "the Cambridge police acted stupidly." Then he played the race card: "What I think we know separate and apart from this incident is that there is a long history in this country of African-Americans and Latinos being stopped by law enforcement disproportionately. That's just a fact." He suggested that Gates's arrest was significant because it "shows that race is still a troubling issue." [12]

But Americans soon showed themselves to be tired of the African-American president calling them racists, and after being roundly criticized, Obama began to try to backtrack on his racist demagoguery. "In my choice of words," he said a few days after the incident, "I unfortunately, I think, gave an impression that I was maligning the Cambridge Police Department or Crowley specifically." [13] But he did not apologize, and invited both Crowley and Gates to visit the White House—which they duly did, and the incident was over.

But its effects lingered. Obama needed the bogeyman of lingering racism in the United States, and where he didn't find it, he invented it. The monotony of the racism charge was understandable; this

241

tactic had once been effective. One prime example was the 2006 Virginia Senate race, and the destruction of George Allen's reelection campaign by the "macaca" incident.[14] A presidential contender was destroyed by a racism charge, despite the fact that it was utter nonsense. Meanwhile, Joe Biden's insult to Indian people ("You cannot go to a 7-Eleven or a Dunkin' Donuts unless you have a slight Indian accent") went largely unremarked and unnoticed in the mainstream media, and Biden, unlike Allen, was given a full opportunity to explain and defend his remarks.[15]

The media also ignored the real significance of the Obama Joker poster. It wasn't racism; it was a sign of America's rude awakening. The editor of the online journal *American Thinker*, Thomas Lifson, observed that the poster showed that the inevitable backlash against Obama's far-left policies has begun: "It is starting. Open mockery of Barack Obama, as disillusionment sets in with the man, his policies, and the phony image of a race-healing, brilliant, scholarly middle-of-the-roader." But Lifson noted that "the president's supporters have condemned the image, calling it 'mean-spirited and dangerous.'"[16]

Mean-spirited? Dangerous? Racist?

For years the Left engaged in spiteful and malicious attacks on President George W. Bush. He was likened to Hitler. "Bushitler" was so commonly heard, it became a cliché. Leftists compared the jihadi attack on the twin towers to the Reichstag fire. And other motifs came into play as well: When *Vanity Fair* published the image of Bush as The Joker, no one said a word. Instead, we were told that dissent was the highest form of patriotism.

And indeed it can be. After eight years of relentless Bush bashing and America hating, the *Times* published a column by Charles M. Blow that went the whole way, calling for the shutting down of dissent and coming out more or less openly for a police state: "Society needs to do a much better job of creating an environment where hateful beliefs are never ignored and suspicious behavior never goes unreported."[17]

What kind of "hateful beliefs"?

Being American, standing for the fundamental values and our inalienable rights, was now deemed racism. This was a full-scale attack on the American people by Obama, Reid, and Pelosi—an attack against people who were daring to protest against a $14 trillion deficit, the bankrupting of our nation, and the enslaving of our children and grandchildren.

Nancy Pelosi gave a strong hint of what the Democratic party leadership and the administration thought of its opponents, and what it considered "hateful," when she claimed that protesters against Obama's health-care plan were "carrying swastikas and symbols like that to a town meeting on healthcare"—as if the only people opposing Obamacare were white supremacists and neo-Nazis.[18]

As soon as she made this charge, leftist bloggers rushed to try to substantiate it. The online journal *The Huffington Post* ran a closely cropped picture with this caption: "In one image, a young man with a shirt that reads 'Hitler Gave Great Speeches Too' is photographed making what looks like a Hitler salute. TalkLeft blogger Jeralyn Merritt interviewed the teen, who told her [he] was 16 and hailed from former Gov. Sarah Palin's hometown of Wasilla, Alaska."[19] The boy was actually holding his arm up, carrying a sign. *The Huffington Post* modified this article later to remove the preposterous claim that the boy was making the Hitler salute, but by then it was too late. The story had already spread all over the Internet. The damage was done.

Leftist columnists and pundits climbed on. Radio host Bill Press wrote of the town hall protesters: "Taking a page right out of a Nazi playbook, organizers bus in professional protestors and arm them with instructions on how to take over meetings, shut down discussion, shout over any pro–health care reform speakers, and then post video of the resulting chaos on YouTube. It's mob rule, pure and simple."[20]

Nonetheless, it was unlikely that the American people would fall in large numbers for such tricks. With the Tea Party and town hall protests, ordinary Americans could see for themselves what the administration and its supporters were doing. It was no longer a media story they never heard or saw. The victim of this thuggery was the American citizen. The average American was being smeared.

Accordingly, one thing was clear in the summer and fall of 2009: the Left's libelous smear of racism had lost its sting. If everything was racism, then nothing was. The more that Leftists pulled this trick, the more ordinary folks shrugged. The sad and terrible thing was that by using this tactic, the Left obscured the true evil of genuine racism. The fact is, when the Left makes everything about race, and sees everything through a prism of "racism," it shows us who the real racists are.

VIOLENCE AT TEA PARTIES AND TOWN HALLS

White House press secretary Robert Gibbs admonished demonstrators: "Behave yourselves like your mom would probably tell you to do."[21]

The only real thuggery, however, was coming from his side. White House deputy chief of staff Jim Messina told Senate Democrats facing hostile audiences at town hall meetings, "If you get hit, we will punch back twice as hard."[22] Some apparently took these words to heart, not taking Messina to be referring to rhetorical hits at all.

At Rep. Kathy Castor's (D-FL) town hall meeting in Tampa on August 6, 2009, the hall was packed with union and ACORN (Association of Community Organizers for Reform Now) members who had been ushered in through a back door. Castor's security personnel, meanwhile, shut the doors on opponents of Obama's health-care plan, and pro-Obama union thugs roughed up a protester, Randy Arthur. Fifteen hundred people were present, but only about seventy-five were allowed in—only to find ACORN and union members occupying seats that had been reserved for them in the front of the room. A YouTube video recorded the scuffling as all this took place, and notes that according to an eyewitness, Castor squandered the opportunity to stage a rally before a handpicked crowd, leaving after taking no questions and claiming she "couldn't hear."[23]

Meanwhile, in Missouri, over a thousand people were locked out of Rep. Russ Carnahan's (D-MO) town hall meeting in South St. Louis— while members of the Service Employees International Union (SEIU) were let in a side door marked "handicapped."[24] SEIU thugs attacked Kenneth Gladney, a St. Louis conservative activist—and Carnahan promptly blamed Gladney himself for the altercation. Gladney's attorney, David B. Brown, explained:

Kenneth was attacked on the evening of August 6, 2009 at Rep. Russ Carnahan's town hall meeting in South St. Louis County. I was at the town hall meeting as well and witnessed the events leading up to the attack of Kenneth. Kenneth was approached by an SEIU representative as Kenneth was handing out "Don't Tread on Me" flags to other conservatives. The SEIU representative demanded to know why a black man was handing out these flags. The SEIU member used a racial slur against Kenneth, then punched him in the face. Kenneth fell to the ground. Another SEIU member yelled racial epithets at Kenneth as he kicked him in the head and back. Kenneth was also brutally attacked by one other male SEIU member and an unidentified woman. The three men were clearly SEIU members, as they were wearing T-shirts with the SEIU logo. Kenneth was beaten badly. One assailant fled on foot; three others were arrested. Kenneth was admitted to St. John's Mercy Medical Center emergency room, where he was treated for his numerous injuries. Kenneth was merely expressing his freedom of speech by handing out the flags. In fact, he merely asked people as they exited the town hall meeting whether they would like a flag. He in no way provoked any argument or altercation, as evidenced by the fact that three assailants were arrested.

We hope that Kenneth fully recovers from his injuries; however, he is in great pain at this time. We will be pursuing legal action at our discretion. This was a truly senseless hate crime carried out by racist union thugs. Regretfully, Representative Carnahan's statements blaming Kenneth for being a disruptive force are wholly untrue and slanderous. We would like to think that an elected official in Representative Carnahan's position would gather accurate information before carelessly rushing to judgment. Kenneth supports conservative ideals, although he subscribes to no particular political party. We are calling on the SEIU, Representative Carnahan, and President Obama to condemn the racist actions of these union thugs. In the days to come, we will be investigating whether these thugs are working at the behest of Representative Carnahan and how strong their alliances to various organizations—such as ACORN—may be. We hope the St. Louis Tea Party and tea party organizations around the country will protest Representative Carnahan's offices and also protest SEIU offices in every major city across the U.S. These Democratic strong-arm tactics must end now.[25]

Gladney himself observed, "It just seems there's no freedom of speech without being attacked."[26]

Not for conservatives. Not for free Americans. Not in Barack Obama's America.

Obama and the SEIU are closely linked. According to the Federal Election Commission, the SEIU's Committee on Political Education spent $18,818,358.97 on Obama's behalf through December 2008.[27]

This money went for, among other things, door-to-door canvassing for Obama, voter identification and registration, and phone banks. The total SEIU expenditure for Obama was much higher: Andy Stern, the Service Employees International Union president, said in May 2009: "We spent a fortune to elect Barack Obama—$60.7 million to be exact—and we're proud of it."[28] For his part, Obama paid at least $2,250,000 to the SEIU over the last few months of his election campaign: reimbursement for travel, per diem, and other expenses—even reimbursement for staff salaries and benefits.[29]

Obama continued to pound the American people. The majority of Americans—those who lived by the ideals of individualism, self-reliance, and capitalism—were relentlessly demonized. In November 2009, as Americans continued to voice their opposition to Obamacare, the president's national health-care program, Obama smeared his opponents as "extremists." *The New York Times* reported: "According to Representative Earl Blumenauer of Oregon, who supports the health care bill, the president asked, 'Does anybody think that the teabag, anti-government people are going to support them if they bring down health care? All it will do is confuse and dispirit' Democratic voters 'and it will encourage the extremists.'"[30]

DESTROYING OBAMA'S OPPONENTS

One of Obama's foremost critics is the popular radio and TV host Glenn Beck, who ignited a firestorm in July 2009 when, in the wake of the Gates affair, he called the president a "racist" with a "deep-seated hatred for white people or the white culture."[31] A black activist group, Color of Change, began calling for a boycott of Beck's advertisers—and several of those advertisers withdrew their advertising from Beck's program.

As it happened, Color of Change was cofounded by Van Jones, who served for six months in mid-2009 as Obama's special advisor for green jobs, enterprise and innovation at the White House Council on Environmental Quality (CEQ). Jones resigned under fire in September 2009 after Beck and others revealed his inflammatory rhetoric against Obama's congressional opponents and his deep involvement with radical causes. By the time he resigned, the fact that an organization founded by a White House official was leading a campaign against a primary critic of the administration seemed to be the least of Van Jones's sins. But for defenders of free speech and republican government, it was one of the most disquieting.

OBAMA'S WAR ON FOX NEWS

Aside from its connection with Jones, the war on Beck had no direct connection to the Obama White House. But the larger assault on Beck's employer, Fox News, was thoroughly a White House production.

It started out as a joke. But soon it turned out that only Barack Obama wasn't laughing.

At the annual White House Correspondents' Association dinner in May 2009, Obama acknowledged the important role that the cheerleader media played in getting him elected president of the United States: "Most of you covered me," he quipped, "all of you voted for me. Apologies to the Fox table." [32]

It was true: coverage of Obama was three times more positive than coverage of John McCain during the 2008 election, and it was clear virtually every night that the mainstream media was happily in the tank for Obama, regularly skewing stories his way while doing all it could to undermine McCain and Sarah Palin. [33]

According to Mark Halperin of *Time* magazine, liberal media bias marred the presidential campaign of 2008 far more severely than it had other recent presidential campaigns. Halperin was unequivocal: "It was extreme bias, extreme pro-Obama coverage." Halperin invoked one notorious example: "At the end of the campaign, was the two profiles that *The New York Times* ran of the potential first ladies. The story about Cindy McCain was vicious. It looked for every negative thing they could find about her and it cast her in an extraordinarily negative light. It didn't talk about her work, for instance, as a mother for her children, and they cherry-picked every negative thing that's ever been written about her."

The profile of Michelle Obama, on the other hand, was "like a front-page endorsement of what a great person Michelle Obama is."[34]

And so it went, day after day, night after night, in all the newspapers and on all the television networks—warm praise for Barack Obama, sympathetic explanations of his positions, with caustic criticism and even ridicule reserved for his opponents. A Pew Research Center poll found that the American public was getting the message loud and clear: 70 percent of the American electorate believed that the media wanted Obama to win, with only 9 percent believing that the media was favoring McCain, and only 8 percent still buying the myth of media objectivity.[35] A Sacred Heart University poll released the following September reported that 89.3 percent of Americans believed that the mainstream media's coverage of Obama played a large role in electing him president.[36]

So Obama was probably very near right at the White House Correspondents' Association dinner when he said that "all of you voted for me."

But not at Fox News. Alone among the news networks, Fox did not retail wholly hagiographical material about candidate Obama. Rather than applaud the freedom of the press and the robust give-and-take of American politics, however, Obama took a different course once he became president—one with ultimately ominous implications for the freedom of speech and the freedom of the press. Not long after the Correspondents' Association dinner, it became clear that Barack Obama was intent on making Fox pay for not marching in lockstep with the rest of the mainstream media—and with him.

In June 2009, Obama complained about Fox: "I've got one television station that is entirely devoted to attacking my administration. . . . You'd be hard-pressed if you watched the entire day to find a positive story about me on that front."[37] By October 2009 this complaint had escalated to a full-out war. In an attack that was bitterly ironic in light of the relentless leftward tilt of the media, White House communications director Anita Dunn declared: "What I think is fair to say about Fox—and certainly it's the way we view it—is that it really is more a wing of the Republican Party. They take their talking points, put them on the air; take their opposition research, put them on the air. And that's fine. But let's not pretend they're a news network the way CNN is."[38]

The following weekend, Rahm Emanuel, the White House chief of staff, declared that Fox wasn't actually a news organization at all: "The way we—the president looks at it and we look at it, is, it is not a news organization so much as it has a perspective."[39] Obama adviser David Axelrod agreed: "A lot of their news programming, it's really not news. It's pushing a point of view."[40] He added a threat, telling a CNN reporter: "Other news organizations like yours ought not to treat them that way. We're not going to treat them that way."[41]

The substance of the threat manifested itself quickly. Although Axelrod said that Obama spokesmen would "appear on shows and participate" on Fox despite the administration's criticism of the network, they didn't.[42] Fox itself reported the same weekend that Emanuel and Axelrod delivered their remarks on the Sunday morning news shows: "Despite calls to the White House this week, the administration did not offer a guest for this weekend's 'Fox News Sunday' to talk about Dunn's comments, although administration officials appeared on all four Sunday morning shows to speak on various issues."[43]

Dunn and Emanuel had emphasized that they were enunciating the administration's position, and Obama himself soon made that clear, saying on October 21 that he didn't consider Fox a news organization either: "If media is operating, basically, as a talk-radio format, then that's one thing. And if it's operating as a news outlet then that's another. But it's not something I'm losing a lot of sleep over."[44]

Maybe he wasn't, but free Americans ought to have been losing sleep over the implications of his war on Fox News for the freedom of speech. In November 2009 Obama's White House actually warned a Democratic strategist to stop appearing on Fox—or else. According to the *Los Angeles Times*, "shortly after an appearance on Fox," the strategist—who remained anonymous out of fear of Obama—"got a phone call from a White House official telling him not to be a guest on the show again. The call had an intimidating tone, he said." The Obama official told him: "We better not see you on again." Implicit but unmistakable was the threat that "clients might stop using you if you continue."

In strong-arming Democratic consultants to ban Fox, the *Los Angeles Times* explained: "Obama's White House sought to isolate it and make it look more partisan." Pat Caddell, Jimmy Carter's former pollster, said that Democratic spokesmen had told him that Obama's White House had warned them to stay away from Fox. "I find it appalling," said Caddell. "When the White House gets in the business of suppressing dissent and comment, particularly from its own party, it hurts itself."[45]

Indeed. When the president of the United States enjoyed the support of 80 to 90 percent of those who reported the news, and then he directed his energy and made full use of his bully pulpit to discredit and marginalize the remaining 10 to 20 percent, it was hard to avoid the conclusion that he simply was not a strong supporter of the right to dissent.

Without Fox News, what outlet would those who dissented from Obama's policies have? The answer to that was the Internet—but the Obama administration had plans to take care of that also.

CASS SUNSTEIN: FREE SPEECH CZAR?

In April 2009, Sen. John Rockefeller (D-WV) introduced into his Senate Committee on Commerce, Science, and Transportation a "cyber-security" bill that contained this language: "The President may . . . order the limitation or shutdown of Internet traffic to and from any compromised Federal government or United States critical infrastructure information system or network."

Compromised in what way? By whose determination? This appeared to give the president power to shut down any portion of the Internet that displeased him. But after a public outcry, the bill was revised to read in this way: the president, in view of "strategic national interests involving compromised Federal Government or United States critical infrastructure information system or network," may "direct the national response to the cyber threat" along with "relevant industry sectors." It still gives the president the authority to direct the "timely restoration of the affected critical infrastructure information system or network."[46]

This still appears to give the president the sole authority to decide when and whether certain information systems or networks would *ever* come back online. A conflict with the First Amendment and a dangerous abridgement of the freedom of speech? Sure. But with a compliant Supreme Court behind Obama and an indifferent public before him, what would stop such a measure from becoming law?

Nor was this an isolated initiative. In August 2009 *Computerworld* reported that "the Department of Homeland Security's Privacy Office has approved the controversial searches, copying and retention of laptops, PDAs, and other digital devices without cause at U.S. borders."[47] The problem with such sweeping measures was that while they were intended to address security issues, they could all too easily be used to stifle political dissent.

But surely Obama wasn't interested in doing that, was he? If he wasn't, he gave supporters of free speech no comfort when he appointed Cass Sunstein, a professor of law at Harvard University, to head the White House Office of Information and Regulatory Affairs.

With conservative blogs serving as key sources of information for Obama's opponents, it wasn't hard to imagine which blogs Sunstein might think needed to be corralled. In his book *On Rumors: How Falsehoods Spread, Why We Believe Them, What Can Be Done*, which was published in September 2009, Sunstein complained that "people's beliefs are a product of social networks working as echo chambers in which false rumors spread like wildfire." This problem was squarely the fault of the unfettered Internet: "We hardly need to imagine a world, however, in which people and institutions are being harmed by the rapid spread of damaging falsehoods via the Internet. We live in that world. What might be done to reduce the harm?" Sunstein recommended changing libel laws to make it easier to convict someone of libel. "A 'chilling effect' on those who would spread destructive falsehoods can be an excellent idea." Why would such a chill be so urgently needed? Because "falsehoods can undermine democracy itself."[48]

New York Post reporter Kyle Smith observed: "What Sunstein means by that sentence is pretty clear: He doesn't like so-called false rumors about his longtime University of Chicago friend and colleague, Barack Obama."[49] And he means to stop them not just by the compelling force of sweet reason, but by the force of law. But who would decide, in such an eventuality, what was a false rumor and what was legitimate political dissent? Why, the very ones from whom the dissenters were dissenting. And that would be the end of the freedom of speech in America.

In initiatives to block free speech on the Internet, Sunstein might find an ally in another Obama appointee, Attorney General Eric Holder, who said on NPR's *Morning Edition* as far back as 1999 that the Internet would have to be restricted: "It is gonna be a difficult thing," said Holder, "but it seems to me that if we can come up with reasonable restrictions, reasonable regulations in how people interact on the Internet, that is something that the Supreme Court and the courts ought to favorably look at."[50]

Now's his chance.

With Sunstein's friend the president saying that he didn't want "the folks who created the mess to do a lot of talking," in the first year of the Obama administration there was nothing farfetched about concerns over the very survival of the right of free speech.

OBAMA MOVES TO SHUT DOWN FREE SPEECH

The Obama administration's apparent disdain for free speech and dissent from his policies wasn't limited to rhetoric alone, or to campaigns against dissenters in the mainstream media, or even to the occasional resort to strong-arm tactics. He also moved on the legislative front. In the first months of Barack Obama's presidency, the new administration indicated in numerous ways, large and small, that it was hardly a champion of the robust debate and hearty rough-and-tumble involved in defending one's views in the public square. On the contrary, it gave numerous indications that dispensing with the freedom of speech altogether would suit it just fine.

An especially Orwellian touch came on August 4, 2009, just days before Obama, Pelosi, and Hoyer spoke out against dissent. The

White House blog "The Briefing Room" posted an item asking Americans to report on "casual conversation" that included "disinformation" or anything "fishy" said about the health-care debate: "There is a lot of disinformation about health insurance reform out there, spanning from control of personal finances to end of life care. These rumors often travel just below the surface via chain emails or through casual conversation. Since we can't keep track of all of them here at the White House, we're asking for your help. If you get an email or see something on the web about health insurance reform that seems fishy, send it to flag@whitehouse.gov."[51]

The desired effect of such a request? A chilling assault on free speech. Sen. John Cornyn saw exactly that: "I am not aware of any precedent for a President asking American citizens to report their fellow citizens to the White House for pure political speech that is deemed 'fishy' or otherwise inimical to the White House's political interests. . . . As Congress debates health care reform and other critical policy matters, citizen engagement must not be chilled by fear of government monitoring the exercise of free speech rights."[52]

Yet that kind of monitoring seemed to be exactly the administration's agenda. With the mainstream media solidly in liberal Democratic control, talk radio and the Internet became the primary sources of news and perspectives that differed from the White House party line—and so the administration moved quickly against those two remaining outlets for free discussion and unfettered inquiry.

The blog RedState.com revealed in August 2009 that the Obama administration was using the National Telecommunications and Information Administration to gather data on free citizens: "The NTIA is now requiring internet providers to give the government 'average revenue per end user and data regarding type, technical specification or location of broadband infrastructure,' i.e. your home address, IP address, how much you pay, and where the connection is at your house."

That meant that "we have a White House asking neighbors to turn in neighbors by forwarding emails—some of which will contain IP address information. And we have the White House demanding internet providers provide them with the home addresses corresponding to those IP addresses."[53]

Faced with a public outcry over all this, Obama quickly began backtracking. In the wake of the branding of dissenters as "un-American" by Pelosi and Hoyer, White House deputy press secretary Bill Burton said: "The President thinks that if people want to come and have a spirited debate about health care, a real vigorous conversation about it, that's a part of the American tradition and he encourages that, because people do have questions and concerns. . . . And so if people want to come and have their concerns and their questions answered, the President thinks that's important."[54]

A lot had changed for the man who just three days before this had said that he didn't want "the folks who created the mess to do a lot of talking." Or maybe he was just saving face. For he continued his assault on the freedoms of Americans: *The Washington Times* reported in September 2009 that "the White House is collecting and storing comments and videos placed on its social-networking sites such as Facebook, Twitter, and YouTube without notifying or asking the consent of the site users, a failure that appears to run counter to President Obama's promise of a transparent government and his pledge to protect privacy on the Internet."[55]

Big Brother was watching and waiting.

Why did Obama do all this? The Obama administration had made plain that there was no war on terror, no war on Islamic jihad. As a matter of fact, the word "jihad" had been banned from government lexicon. So why all the spying on American citizens?

And more was in the offing.

LEGISLATING FREE SPEECH AWAY

On April 2, 2009, Rep. Linda T. Sanchez (D-CA) introduced into the House the Megan Meier Cyberbullying Prevention Act, named after a teenage girl who committed suicide after being hounded on the online social networking site MySpace by a friend's mother, who was posing as a teenage boy.[56] The bill accordingly declares that "whoever transmits in interstate or foreign commerce any communication, with the intent to coerce, intimidate, harass, or cause substantial emotional distress to a person, using electronic means to support severe, repeated, and hostile behavior, shall be fined under this title or imprisoned not more than two years, or both."[57]

The free-speech implications are obvious. Who decides what constitutes coercion, intimidation, and harassment? Who determines that sufficient emotional distress has been inflicted upon a plaintiff so as to justify the imprisonment of the defendant for two years?

Attorney and blogger Eugene Volokh painted a troubling scenario: "I try to coerce a politician into voting a particular way, by repeatedly blogging (using a hostile tone) about what a hypocrite / campaign promise breaker / fool / etc. he would be if he voted the other way. I am transmitting in interstate commerce a communication with the intent to coerce using electronic means (a blog) 'to support severe, repeated, and hostile behavior'—unless, of course, my statements aren't seen as 'severe,' a term that is entirely undefined and unclear. Result: I am a felon, unless somehow my 'behavior' isn't 'severe.'"[58]

Representative Sanchez insisted that such concerns were unfounded. "Congress has no interest in censoring speech," she asserted, "and it will not do so if it passes this bill. Put simply, this legislation would be used as a tool for a judge and jury to determine whether there is significant evidence to prove that a person 'cyberbullied'

another. That is: did they have the required intent, did they use electronic means of communication, and was the communication severe,
hostile, and repeated. So—bloggers, emailers, texters, spiteful exes,
and those who have blogged against this bill have no fear—your words
are still protected under the same American values."[59]

Subcommittee hearings were held on the bill on September 30,
2009; it is still under consideration and could become the law of the
land.[60]

NET NEUTRALITY

It sounds like a grand, noble initiative: a "free and open Internet."[61]
The stated idea of net neutrality is for the government to forbid Internet service providers from doing anything to filter or block traffic on
the Internet.

The chairman of the Federal Communications Commission, Julius Genachowski, who went to Harvard Law School with Barack
Obama, came out in September 2009 in favor of the broadest possible net-neutrality legislation. Genachowski explained why net neutrality was needed: "The Internet's creators didn't want the network
architecture—or any single entity—to pick winners and losers," he asserted. "The principles that will protect the open Internet are an essential step to maximize investment and innovation in the network and
on the edge of it—by establishing rules of the road that incentivize
competition, empower entrepreneurs, and grow the economic pie to
the benefit of all."[62]

Who could object? As it turned out, lovers of freedom could—and
did. While net-neutrality advocates advertised their plan as one that
would ensure a "free and open Internet," in reality net neutrality was
an attempt to *limit* the freedom of Internet users by subjecting what
had always been a free-market give-and-take to government regula-

tion: the FCC would control how all information reached personal computers.

"Few proposals in Washington have been sold employing such deceptive language—and that's saying something," observed James G. Lakely, who is the codirector of the Center on the Digital Economy for the Heartland Institute, a free-market think tank. "But few public policy ideas can boast the unashamedly socialist pedigree of net neutrality." Lakely pointed out that "the modern Internet is a creation of the free market, which has brought about a revolution in communication, free speech, education, and commerce." But Genachowski, said Lakely, "apparently doesn't like that. He stated last month the way Internet service providers manage their networks—in response to millions of individual consumer choices—is not sufficiently 'fair,' 'open' or 'free.'"

Genachowski's remedy? Lakely said that he wanted to "claim for the FCC the power to decide how every bit of data is transferred from the Web to every personal computer and handheld device in the nation."

Lakely noted that net neutrality had strong backers among the Hard Left—backers who were generally more forthright than Genachowski about what the measure was really intended to do: "Eben Moglen's 2003 treatise *The dotCommunist Manifesto* is more honest about the thinking behind net neutrality—it's sprinkled throughout with the language of communism's great and bloody revolutionaries. The people must 'struggle' to 'wrest from the bourgeoisie, by degrees, the shared patrimony of humankind' that has been 'stolen from us under the guise of "intellectual property."'"

Robert W. McChesney, who is the cofounder of Free Press—which Lakely describes as "the leading advocacy group in Washington pushing for net neutrality"—said that net neutrality could accomplish nothing less than Marxist "revolution." McChesney's enthusiasm is not misplaced, for net neutrality would do what Marxist revolutions did in Russia, China, North Korea, Cuba, and everywhere else they have triumphed: destroy private ownership and private property, transferring control over to the government.

"And in typical Marxist fashion," Lakely declares, "innocuous words—the language of neutralism and liberty—cloak an agenda that would crush freedom. That's the agenda President Obama's FCC is pushing."[63]

The Megan Meier Cyberbullying Prevention Act. Net neutrality. Cass Sunstein and Eric Holder both on record saying that free speech on the Internet should be restricted. The Obama administration's agenda for the Internet was clear: in an age in which almost all the mainstream media was in the tank for the Democratic party, and the Internet had become virtually the last redoubt for genuine and robust opposition to the Obama agenda, the brave new president had determined that it must be brought to heel. And he was working hard to make that happen.

WILL THE FIRST AMENDMENT GET US OUT OF THIS FIX?

Most, of course, will dismiss such concerns the way they always dismiss them: with a wave of the hand and an invocation of the First Amendment—as if the First Amendment were some kind of inviolate shield that cannot itself ever in any way be impeached or impugned. Would that it were so. But the Obama administration is already showing how little it cares for free speech and open dissent. And with an Obama-compliant Supreme Court (which can be achieved with a retirement or two) judging cases that challenge their actions and interpreting the First Amendment for us, what's to stop the administration from playing ball with the Organization of the Islamic Conference and building wonderful new bridges with the Islamic world in this way, while working to silence dissent at home?

Free speech is our most important right—our fundamental protection against tyranny.

The Democrats' desire to silence dissent and spy on the American people bodes most ill.

In 2003, Hillary Clinton said this: "I am sick and tired of people who say that if you debate and you disagree with this administration somehow you're not patriotic. We should stand up and say we are Americans and we have a right to debate and disagree with any administration."[64]

Does she believe the same thing now? Will she stand up to the president? Will free Americans stand up to him?

In the age of jihad, in the age of Obama, the freedom of speech is under attack everywhere. If Barack Obama championed this freedom, he could change everything. Instead, he has aligned himself with the enemies of free speech. He has reached out to the Organization of the Islamic Conference, which is waging a concerted campaign to extinguish free speech in Western nations.

And the campaign to silence points of view that the elites consider inconvenient is picking up steam in other ways as well. A stultifying leftist orthodoxy is stifling dissenting voices on our nation's campuses. In November 2009, Nonie Darwish, the executive director of Former Muslims United and author of *Cruel and Usual Punishment: The Terrifying Global Implications of Islamic Law*, was scheduled to speak at Columbia and Princeton Universities, but both events were canceled under pressure from Muslim groups on campus.

Columbia, where Ahmadinejad was welcomed like a returning king.

Just hours before Darwish was scheduled to speak at Columbia, the groups that had invited her to come to both universities, the

Whig-Clio student debate society and Tigers for Israel, succumbed to demands from student Muslim groups and canceled her speaking event. The Whig-Cliosophic Society is the oldest debating society in the United States, founded by James Madison in 1765. These are the students who are supposed to be the leaders of the future.

At Princeton, Princeton Arab Society president Sami Yabroudi and former president Sarah Mousa issued a joint statement, claiming: "Nonie Darwish is to Arabs and Muslims what Ku Klux Klan members, skinheads and neo-Nazis are to other minorities, and we decided that the role of her talk in the logical, intellectual discourse espoused by Princeton University needed to be questioned."

KKK? Neo-Nazi? Nonie Darwish was scheduled to speak about Sharia and Israel—standing up for human rights against the jihad.

But the sponsors of her talk immediately caved. Whig-Clio president Ben Weisman said: "Our decision to co-host the event was based on our belief that by extending an offer to speak to Ms. Darwish, members of TFI deemed her views a legitimate element of the mainstream discourse and in part agreed with her incendiary opinions. By rescinding their offer, TFI indicated their understanding that Darwish's views have no place in the campus community."

Tigers for Israel said in a statement: "On Tuesday evening Tigers for Israel and Whig-Clio rescinded our cosponsorship of today's Nonie Darwish Lecture. Tigers for Israel accepted the opportunity for her to speak based on a misconception about what she actually believes.

"After her anti-Islam position was brought to my attention on Tuesday afternoon by the Center for Jewish Life director Rabbi Julie Roth and the Muslim Chaplain Imam Sohaib Sultan, I conducted extensive research and discussed the issue with TFI and Whig-Clio leadership, and we decided to rescind our cosponsorship after concluding that Tigers for Israel disagrees with and does not condone Ms. Darwish and her beliefs on Islam. . . . As President of TFI I take full responsibility for not vetting Ms. Darwish from the beginning, and I sincerely apologize for offending any person or group on campus, especially the Muslim community. Tigers for Israel deeply regrets the initial sponsorship and we do not in any way endorse her views."

Cowards. Have they studied Islam? Jihad?

Here is something they don't know: Sohaib Sultan, who helped get the Darwish lecture canceled, wrote the book *The Koran for Dummies*. In that book he says that the medieval Islamic scholar Ibn Kathir is the "most referred to" authority on Islam "in the Muslim world today." Sultan says that Ibn Kathir offers "an excellent collection of historical analysis on the Koran and his mastery of Islamic law makes his insights especially interesting." Yet Ibn Kathir taught that Muslims should wage jihad war against Jews and Christians and impose laws upon them that would make them "disgraced, humiliated and belittled."

Ibn Kathir said that "Muslims are not allowed to honor the people of Dhimmah [Jews and Christians] or elevate them above Muslims, for they are miserable, disgraced and humiliated."

So who really resembles the KKK or neo-Nazis? A courageous woman standing up for human rights for Muslim women and ex-Muslims, or a Muslim imam who holds up as an authority someone who says that non-Muslims should be "disgraced, humiliated and belittled"? [65]

Darwish told me that she was shocked that just weeks after an Islamic attack on Fort Hood, the largest such attack in U.S. history, activists who speak the truth about Islam are being shut down and marginalized.

In another assault on free speech that same month, they were throwing pies at a Robert Spencer event at New York University. What's next? Grenades? And in the summer of 2009 the American Library Association canceled an appearance by Robert Spencer at their national convention in Chicago when they succumbed to pressure from the Council on American-Islamic Relations (CAIR), an unindicted coconspirator in a Hamas jihad terror funding case. CAIR falsely accused Spencer of bigotry, and instead of allowing him a fair hearing and opportunity for rebuttal, the ALA simply canceled his appearance.[66]

The war against free speech is being waged internationally as well—and here again, if Obama were acting as the leader of the Free World, he could put a stop to this. Instead, he abets it. At the beginning of 2010 the Dutch politician Geert Wilders faced prosecution in the Netherlands for "hate speech" for his elegant and brilliant film exposing the Qur'anic imperative to violence and supremacism, *Fitna*. He was also being sued by a number of European countries, and was barred from entering Britain (although that ban was later overturned) and the Czech Republic.[67] When Dutch authorities disallowed fifteen of the eighteen witnesses Wilders had requested for his defense, Wilders called the court on its obvious intention to railroad him: "This Court is not interested in the truth. This Court doesn't want me to have a fair trial. I can't have any respect for this. This Court would not be out of place in a dictatorship."[68]

It is America that has always stood solid and true. America has stood on the wall protecting these our basic freedoms—freedoms that have been the lifeblood of the greatest constitutional republic ever to have existed.

Until the post-American president took office.

Freedom of speech defines a free people. In the war of ideas, free speech is the foremost defense of a free people against tyranny.

You won't like what comes post-America.

ELEVEN

SOCIALIST AMERICA

BARACK HUSSEIN OBAMA HID THE
FACT THAT HE WAS A HARD-LINE, DOCTRINAIRE
SOCIALIST AND STATIST, WHO BELIEVED IN CENTRAL
planning and government control of the economy as fervently as Stalin
or Mao or Kim Jong Il ever did.

As president in the history of the United States, Barack Obama has
been extraordinarily secretive. Among the many records he has sealed
and never allowed to see the light of day are the infamous long form of
his Hawaii birth certificate; the Indonesian passport he had as a dual
citizen of that country and the United States; the marriage licenses of
his parents and his mother and stepfather, Lolo Soetoro; the papers
pertaining to his adoption by Lolo Soetoro; his application to the Fran-
siskus Assisi School in Indonesia; his academic records at Occidental
College, Columbia, and Harvard; his medical records; his law-practice

client list; and the scholarly articles he produced at the University of Chicago.

Among the many records that never saw the light of day during his campaign or the first months of his presidency was his Columbia thesis—which became the focus of a minor media pseudo-controversy about Obama's socialist leanings late in October 2009. At that time a bit of satire circulated around the Internet, featuring a fake thesis from Columbia University in which Obama criticized the Constitution. Rush Limbaugh, as well as Denis Keohane at *American Thinker* and Michael Ledeen at Pajamas Media, picked it up, only to be pilloried by the Left when it proved to be a hoax.

The fake thesis featured Obama criticizing the Constitution, saying that "the so-called Founders did not allow for economic freedom. While political freedom is supposedly a cornerstone of the document, the distribution of wealth is not even mentioned. While many believed that the new Constitution gave them liberty, it instead fitted them with the shackles of hypocrisy."[1]

While it would have been inconceivable that any president of the United States before Barack Hussein Obama would ever have spoken that way, it wasn't at all out of character for the post-American president. It sounded to many like something Obama would have said. As Michael Ledeen said, "it worked because it's plausible."[2] Was it really unbelievable that a protégé of Frank Marshall Davis, the ideological kin of Alice Palmer, a longtime associate of Bill Ayers, would turn out to be a socialist? It would have been more surprising if he hadn't.

Obama had in fact said things very similar to the ones he was made to say in the satire of his thesis. He said them in a radio interview dating from 2001. The fake thesis just echoed things Obama has already said. In the interview, Obama discusses the best way to bring about a redistribution of wealth. He speaks of the "tendency to lose track of the political and community organizing and activities on the ground that are able to put together the actual coalitions of power through which you bring about redistributive change."[3]

Yes, "redistributive change." He said that it was a tragedy that the Constitution wasn't radically reinterpreted to force redistribution of the wealth: "I am not optimistic," he said, "about bringing about redistributive change through the courts. The institution just isn't structured that way." He praised the civil-rights movement and its "litigation strategy in the court" for succeeding in vesting "formal rights in previously dispossessed peoples."

Yet, for Obama, the civil-rights movement didn't go far enough. "One of the I think tragedies of the civil rights movement was because the civil rights movement became so court focused . . . in some ways we still suffer from that."[4]

This was the fault of the Supreme Court and the Constitution itself: "But the Supreme Court never ventured into the issues of redistribution of wealth and sort of more basic issues of political and economic justice in this society. And to that extent as radical as people tried to characterize the Warren court, it wasn't that radical."[5]

And that was because of the constraints of the Constitution: "It didn't break free from the essential constraints that were placed by the Founding Fathers in the Constitution, at least as it's been interpreted, and the Warren court interpreted it in the same way that generally the Constitution is a charter of negative liberties.

"It says what the states can't do to you, it says what the federal government can't do to you, but it doesn't say what the federal government or the state government must do on your behalf. And that hasn't shifted."[6]

So he doesn't think redistribution of wealth can be accomplished through the courts, but he thinks it can be done legislatively. That is why a liberal supermajority in Congress was crucial to Obama's strategy.

Notice that Obama was not discussing whether redistribution of the wealth is right or wrong—this was a conversation about how to achieve that goal. And this was back in 2001.

Obama has been on record favoring the redistribution of wealth for years. The media just never bothered to notice.

THE NEW PARTY AND THE DEMOCRATIC SOCIALISTS OF AMERICA

When Barack Obama first ran for the Illinois State Senate in 1996, *The Progressive Populist* newspaper noted blandly: "New Party member Barack Obama was uncontested for a State Senate seat from Chicago."[7] According to journalist Stanley Kurtz, "the New Party's agenda was radically redistributionist. More important, the New Party's specific strategy for achieving its economic goals precisely paralleled Obama's now infamous 2001 radio remarks on 'major redistributive change.'"[8]

The Democratic Socialists of America (DSA) endorsed Obama for that State Senate seat. Obama didn't shy away from this association; on the contrary, he cultivated it. In February 1996, State Senate candidate Obama participated in a panel discussion at the University of Chicago, sponsored by the University's DSA Youth Section, the Chicago chapter of the DSA, and the University Democrats. The panel topic was "Economic Insecurity." The DSA newsletter *New Ground* reported that Obama said that "a true welfare system would provide for medical care, child care and job training." It noted: "While Barack Obama did not use this term, it sounded very much like the 'social wage' approach used by many social democratic labor parties. By 'workforce preparation strategy', Barack Obama simply meant a coordinated, purposeful program of job training instead of the ad hoc, fragmented approach used by the State of Illinois today."

In other words, Barack Obama was singing the praises of a centrally planned economy. Obama believed that the state should control the means of production and redistribute the wealth of its citizens. In line with this, *New Ground* reported that Obama also said that "the state government can also play a role in redistribution, the allocation of wages and jobs. . . . The government can use as tools labor law reform, public works and contracts."[9] In March 1998, State Senator Obama spoke at a memorial service for Saul Mendelson, who—again according to *New Ground*—"joined the Socialist movement at the age of 18" and was a lifelong agitator for socialist causes.[10]

NATIONALIZING THE AUTO INDUSTRY

The economic crisis that attended Obama's accession to the presidency enabled him to move swiftly to nationalize large segments of American industry—particularly the flagging auto industry. And once that was done, he wanted more. "Given the Obama administration's rapid takeovers of General Motors and Chrysler," remarked the director of the Center for Investors and Entrepreneurs at the Competitive Enterprise Institute, John Berlau, in June 2009, "it shouldn't come as much of a surprise to conservatives that, in the name of 'financial reform,' President Obama is arguing that government should get vast new powers to seize private firms."[11]

Obama almost immediately announced ambitious new plans for the new government-subsidized auto industry. Pundit Charles Krauthammer explained in May 2009: "Well, with an essentially nationalized auto industry, the president has decreed that by 2016 autos will have exactly on average 39 mpg and trucks 30. Well, if you do the math, it is a seven-year plan. Stalin restricted himself to five-year plans."[12]

There was bite to Krauthammer's quip. Economist John Lott put it succinctly: "Government ownership implies much less efficiency. It implies political decisions in running the company."[13]

It was the problem with the socialist economy in a nutshell—and soon it would become the problem of the United States health-care system.

SOCIALIST HEALTH CARE

Socialized medicine is the keystone to the arch of the socialist state.

—attributed to Lenin

Despite overwhelming and unprecedented opposition to nationalized health care, Democrats in the House of Representatives passed the administration's health-care resolution. Then the Senate quickly voted to consider the bill, which was tantamount to approving it.

And yet few Americans really wanted nationalized health care at all. Again and again America had spoken on this, yet the autocrats in Washington steadfastly ignored the will of the American people. A League of Women Voters/Zogby poll released in November 2009 found that Americans of all ages opposed Obama's health-care proposals. Even those who were assumed to be most solidly in the Obama camp, voters under age thirty, opposed the plan by a 65–25 percent margin in a sampling taken in Arkansas, North Dakota, and Maine. Pollster John Zogby commented: "These results among 18- to 29-year-olds are striking. It puts in jeopardy the whole theory of the new

Democratic majority, because young people are essential to that base."
Nationally, support for the plan had fallen to 38 percent by November
2009.[14]

But Obama and the Democrats appeared intent on steamrolling
over "we, the people." One indication of that was that the administration passed over workable solutions to the health-care mess in favor
of their hypertrophied and unreadable plan. Dr. C. L. Gray, president
of the watchdog group Physicians for Reform, a coalition of working
physicians, patients, and business leaders, proposed a simple, com-
monsense alternative to the elephantine health-care bills that Obama,
Pelosi, and Reid seemed intent to force upon Americans. "Mr. President," Gray wrote, "if you believe so strongly in the principles of
choice and competition, introduce them. *Let individuals and businesses
purchase insurance across state lines.* With one, simple, twenty-five-page
bill—no pork, no slight-of-hand [*sic*], written with clarity the average
American can understand—we can have choice and competition without adding a dime to the federal deficit or asking for a penny of new
taxes."

Yet despite the fact that, as Gray noted, "when Wolf Blitzer
posed this question to David Axelrod, one of your top advisors, even
Mr. Axelrod could find no objection," such a suggestion will gain no
traction with Obama.[15] That's because Obama's health-care reform
plan was not really about improving America's health-care system.
Obama was not searching dispassionately for a plan that he would endorse simply on its merits, because it solved more problems with the
existing system than did other plans. No, he was not doing that, because reforming health care was not really the point.

The point, rather, was controlling one sixth of the American economy. Obama's health-care proposal had little to do with improving
health care and everything to do with control. It offered no genuine
fixes to the weaknesses in an exemplary health-care system, the envy of

the world. Obama's plan was not about making health care healthier; it was about seizing 20 percent of the American economy.

But in response to this unprecedented power grab, for the first time in modern American history tens of thousands of hitherto nonpolitical Americans were taking to the streets, to town hall meetings, and to the Mall in Washington, D.C., to protest against the "stimulus" program and Obamacare. They were derided, dismissed, and summarily ignored—at best. It was a uniquely un-American response to a uniquely American moment. It was a turning point for America.

Interestingly enough, the Democrats' health-care strategy appeared to be the brainchild of Robert Creamer, former head of Citizen Action/Illinois, and yet another Alinskyite socialist in the Obama camp. While serving time in federal prison for bank fraud and tax evasion, Creamer wrote a political manifesto entitled *Listen to Your Mother: Stand Up Straight! How Progressives Can Win*. The book carries an endorsement from, among other top Democrats, Obama aide David Axelrod, who said it provided "a blueprint for future victories."

In the book, Creamer lays out a ten-point plan to compel the American people to accept socialized health care:

- "We must create a national consensus that health care is a right, not a commodity; and that government must guarantee that right."
- "We must create a national consensus that the health care system is in crisis."
- "Our messaging program over the next two years should focus heavily on reducing the credibility of the health insurance industry and focusing on the failure of private health insurance."
- "We need to systematically forge relationships with large sectors of the business/employer community."

- "We need to convince political leaders that they owe their elections, at least in part, to the groundswell of support of [*sic*] universal health care, and that they face political peril if they fail to deliver on universal health care in 2009."
- "We need not agree in advance on the components of a plan, but we must foster a process that can ultimately yield consensus."
- "Over the next two years, we must design and organize a massive national field program."
- "We must focus especially on the mobilization of the labor movement and the faith community."
- "We must systematically leverage the connections and resources of a massive array of institutions and organizations of all types."
- "To be successful, we must put in place commitments for hundreds of millions of dollars to be used to finance paid communications and mobilization once the battle is joined."

And: "To win we must not just generate understanding, but emotion—fear, revulsion, anger, disgust."[16]

This has, of course, been exactly the Democrats' plan of action.

But the American people were in no mood to go gently into the night. This cynical plan was met with informed and passionate opposition.

SARAH PALIN AND THE DEATH PANELS

The Republican Party's 2008 vice presidential candidate, former Alaska governor Sarah Palin, quickly emerged as the most trenchant and effective critic of the Obama administration in its first year.

She embodied the angry patriot fighting for her beloved country. She gave voice to the voiceless. She bypassed a hostile, mendacious media and posted her positions directly to her Facebook page, where no left-wing propagandist editor could slice and dice her remarks.

She embarrassed the post-American president by pointing out that his health-care plan included what came popularly to be known as "death panels"—tribunals that would decide whether elderly and disabled people merited health care at all.

On August 7, 2009, she pointed out that nationalized health care would lead to health-care rationing: "The Democrats promise that a government health care system will reduce the cost of health care, but as the economist Thomas Sowell has pointed out, government health care will not reduce the cost; it will simply refuse to pay the cost. And who will suffer the most when they ration care? The sick, the elderly, and the disabled, of course. The America I know and love is not one in which my parents or my baby with Down Syndrome will have to stand in front of Obama's 'death panel' so his bureaucrats can decide, based on a subjective judgment of their 'level of productivity in society,' whether they are worthy of health care. Such a system is downright evil."

Palin said that the stakes couldn't be higher: "Nationalizing our health care system is a point of no return for government interference in the lives of its citizens. If we go down this path, there will be no turning back. Ronald Reagan once wrote, 'Government programs, once launched, never disappear. Actually, a government bureau is the nearest thing to eternal life we'll ever see on this earth.'"[17]

Obama shot back three days later with a response out of the Alinsky playbook, laced with ridicule: "The rumor that's been circulating a lot lately is this idea that somehow the House of Representatives voted for death panels that will basically pull the plug on grandma because we've decided that we don't . . . it's too expensive to let her live anymore." He said that such fears were completely groundless: "It turns out that I guess this arose out of a provision in one of the House bills that allowed Medicare to reimburse people for consultations about end-of-life care, setting up living wills, the availability of hospice, etc. So the intention of the members of Congress was to give people more information so that they could handle issues of end-of-life care when they're ready on their own terms. It wasn't forcing anybody to do anything."[18]

Palin, however, replied that the section of the House bill to which Obama was referring, Section 1233 of HR 3200, entitled "Advance Care Planning Consultation," authorized "advanced care planning consultations for senior citizens" that would ultimately have a "coercive effect." She said that it was understandable that "senior citizens might view such consultations as attempts to convince them to help reduce health care costs by accepting minimal end-of-life care." She quoted New York state senator Ruben Diaz, a Democrat and chairman of the New York State Senate Aging Committee: "Section 1233 of House Resolution 3200 puts our senior citizens on a slippery slope and may diminish respect for the inherent dignity of each of their lives. . . . It is egregious to consider that any senior citizen . . . should be placed in a situation where he or she would feel pressured to save the government money by dying a little sooner than he or she otherwise would, be required to be counseled about the supposed benefits of killing oneself, or be encouraged to sign any end of life directives that they would not otherwise sign."[19]

Palin wasn't the only one concerned about the death panels. *The Wall Street Journal* backhandedly agreed with her, noting in an editorial that "elderly Americans are turning out in droves to fight ObamaCare," and that while it believed that "claims about euthanasia and 'death panels'" were "over the top," nonetheless, "senior fears have exposed a fundamental truth about what Mr. Obama is proposing: Namely, once health care is nationalized, or mostly nationalized, rationing care is inevitable, and those who have lived the longest will find their care the most restricted." The *Journal* acknowledged that "Mrs. Palin has also exposed a basic truth. A substantial portion of Medicare spending is incurred in the last six months of life. From the point of view of politicians with a limited budget, is it worth spending a lot on, say, a patient with late-stage cancer where the odds of remission are long? Or should they spend to improve quality, not length, of life? Or pay for a hip or knee replacement for seniors, when palliative care might cost less? And who decides?"[20]

In Barack Obama's socialist America, the government would decide. Benevolent Big Brother would take your life in his hands.

RATIONING HEALTH CARE

The "death panels" weren't by far the only problem with Obama's health-care plan, nor the only sign that under the post-American president's plan, health care would be rationed. In November 2009 the Heritage Foundation pointed out that "both the House and Senate versions of Obamacare create detailed new federal regulations that micromanage all health insurance decisions." Fundamental to this micromanagement would be "cost control rationing," which would be "the very heart of Obamacare's promise to control health care costs." This would necessitate the rationing of basic services; even before Obama's plan became the law of the land, in that same month "the United States Preventive Services Task Force issued new guidelines recommending that women in their 40s no longer have annual mammograms and that women ages 50 to 74 have them only every other year, instead of annually." According to the Heritage Foundation, this was in line with the classification of mammograms as a "C" service (not recommended) rather than an "A" or "B" service (recommended).[21]

It was becoming increasingly clear that Sarah Palin had been right all along: Obama's health-care plans would mean the rationing of basic health-care services, so that its cumulative effect would be not the extension of health-care benefits to all Americans, but rather their restriction from people who had once had access to them.

Obama's "reforms" would cripple the health-care system and the American economy in general.

HEALTH-CARE REFORM BUT NO TORT REFORM?

Palin also observed that while many Americans favored health-care reform, "current plans being pushed by the Democratic leadership represent change that may not be what we had in mind—change which poses serious ethical concerns over the government having control over our families' health care decisions. In addition, the current plans greatly increase costs of health care, while doing lip service toward controlling costs." She pointed out that much of the high cost of medical care stemmed from the cost of the malpractice insurance that doctors had to buy to protect themselves from (often frivolous) lawsuits.

"Excessive litigation and waste in the nation's current tort system," said Palin, "imposes an estimated yearly tort tax of $9,827 for a family of four and increases health care spending in the United States by $124 billion." Therefore, "you would think that any effort to reform our health care system would include tort reform, especially if the stated purpose for Obama's plan to nationalize our health care industry is the current high costs. So I have new questions for the president: Why no legal reform? Why continue to encourage defensive medicine that wastes billions of dollars and does nothing for the patients? Do you want health care reform to benefit trial attorneys or patients?"[22]

The answer was clear. Obama included no legal reform in his health-care plan because he didn't care about improving health care for ordinary Americans at all.

JAIL FOR HEALTH-CARE DISSENTERS

Socialism is coercive by its very nature. The only way economic equality can be achieved in any population is through force. And Obama's health-care plan, true to its thoroughgoing socialism, was ready to use that force in the name of the "basic human right" of health care.

The plan that the House of Representatives passed in November 2009 contained provisions for penalties of up to five years in prison for Americans who refused to buy health insurance that had been approved by the government. House Speaker Nancy Pelosi said that jail for health-care miscreants would be "very fair in this respect."[23] Asked about this, Obama saw nothing wrong with it, either: "What I think is appropriate is that in the same way that everybody has to get auto insurance and if you don't, you're subject to some penalty, that in this situation, if you have the ability to buy insurance, it's affordable and you choose not to do so, forcing you and me and everybody else to subsidize you, you know, there's a thousand dollar hidden tax that families all across America are—are burdened by because of the fact that people don't have health insurance, you know, there's nothing wrong with a penalty."[24]

In saying that, Obama reversed himself on a position he had taken during his campaign. In a debate with his rival for the Democratic presidential nomination, Hillary Clinton, Obama said in 2008: "And I think that it is important for us to recognize that if, in fact, you are going to mandate the purchase of insurance and it's not affordable, then there's going to have to be some enforcement mechanism that the government uses. And they may charge people who already don't have health care fines, or have to take it out of their paychecks. And that, I don't think, is helping those without health insurance."[25]

But Barack Obama disagreed with Hillary Clinton only in order to curry favor with certain voters. Once elected, he changed his mind about mandates.

THE CULT OF PERSONALITY

Socialist states from the Soviet Union under Stalin and Communist China under Mao to Hitler's National Socialist Germany are more often than not constructed around a cult of personality. The socialist paradise has to have a socialist hero, the perfect man who fully and completely embodies the ideals of the state.

And so it happened in September 2009 that videos began to surface of children in public schools being made to sing songs of fulsome praise for . . . Barack Hussein Obama. It smacked of Stalinism and Goebbels-style indoctrination, and was a stunning indictment of how dangerously politicized the public education system had become.

Perhaps worst of all was that Obama had no rebuke for this cultish adulation. He had nothing to say about it at all. He could have and should have reminded these students and teachers about the dangers of such idolization and the merits of republican government with its orderly transitions from leader to leader.

It was yet another missed opportunity for Barack Hussein Obama.

The first public school Obama-worship to be revealed came from an elementary school in New Jersey. Children sang to their dear leader with as much ardor as any child in Pyongyang ever sang to Kim Jong Il:

Mmm, mmm, mm!

Barack Hussein Obama

He said that all must lend a hand

To make this country strong again

Mmm, mmm, mm!

Barack Hussein Obama

He said we must be fair today

Equal work means equal pay

Mmm, mmm, mm!

Barack Hussein Obama

He said that we must take a stand

To make sure everyone gets a chance

Mmm, mmm, mm!

That was bad enough, but the rest was positively messianic. It had become commonplace for Obama's critics to deride the adulation of his followers by referring to him as "the Messiah," but this song cast Obama more or less overtly as the savior, borrowing lyrics from "Jesus Loves the Little Children":

Barack Hussein Obama

He said red, yellow, black or white

All are equal in his sight

Mmm, mmm, mm![26]

Another song children sang at the same school went this way: "Hello, Mr. President we honor you today! / For all your great accomplishments, we all doth say 'hooray!'"[27]

Accomplishments? What accomplishments?

The New Jersey school's Obama-adulation was no isolated incident. At Giffen Elementary School in Albany, New York, fifth and sixth graders sang a "Barack Obama Rap" accompanied by Obama's recorded voice talking about himself in speeches. The students sang:

We're here to tell you about the man.
His name is Barack Obama he's the leader of this land.
He was born in Hawaii then he lived in Illinois.
His father moved to Africa when he was a little boy.
He got into some trouble when he was 17 and he has come clean now . . .
He fights for civil rights and better health care.
He wants to make sure that we all will have care. . . .
He's very educated and he's got a lot of rhythm.
First black President with a heart that's only true,
he wants to make the world better for me and you. . . .[28]

These were not the only public schools indoctrinating their children in Obama-worship just months after he was elected.

The Left refuses to recognize the need for objectivity among men—particularly men of different views and opinions. It's good that people in this great nation have varying opinions, provided we respect each other's rights. But the Left is incapable of this. It wasn't very long ago that a photo of George W. Bush was not allowed in many private schools. It would have been too "controversial." But teaching classrooms of prepubescent children to sing songs praising Barack Obama? No problem!

Schools have no right playing politics with our children. It's a terrible infringement of rights. And Obama's cult of personality in public schools is nothing short of ominous.

RECRUITING FOR OBAMA IN THE SCHOOLS

Barack Obama is using our public school system to recruit for his next campaign. In January 2010 I broke the story that Organizing for America (OFA), formerly Obama For America, is recruiting in our high schools to "build on the movement that elected President Obama by empowering students across the country to help us bring about our agenda."

An eleventh-grade teacher in a government class in a public high school, Perry Local in Massillon, Ohio, passed out a propaganda recruiting paper—headed with Obama's distinctive "O" logo—asking students to sign up as interns for Organizing for America.

The form carried a recommended reading list, including *Rules for Radicals* by the notorious hard-left community organizer and Obama mentor Saul Alinsky, and two *Huffington Post* articles by Zack Exley, "The New Organizers" and "Obama Field Organizers Plot a Miracle." The first of those, published in October 2008, enthuses about "an insurgent generation of organizers" inside the Obama campaign that has, "almost without anyone noticing . . . built the Progressive movement a brand new and potentially durable people's organization, in a dozen states, rooted at the neighborhood level."

During the 2000 presidential campaign, Exley operated the Web site www.gwbush.com, which was filled with lies about George W. Bush that were designed to kill his chance to become president. The site's headline was "Just Say 'No' to a Former Cocaine User for President."

Also included on the OFA internship recommended reading list were *Stir It Up: Lessons from Community Organizing and Advocacy* by the leftist activist Rinku Sen, and sections of Obama's book *Dreams from My Father* dealing with his days as a community organizer in Chicago.

And what is the point of all this propaganda and community organizing? To elect more Democrats, of course. This internship program is geared toward the 2010 elections. The form begins with a nakedly partisan and propagandistic appeal: "Organizing for America, the successor organization to Obama for America, is building on the movement that elected President Obama by empowering students across the country to help us bring about our agenda of change. OFA is launching a national internship program connecting students all over the country with our organization on the ground—working to make the change we fought so hard for in 2008 a reality in 2010 and beyond."[29]

Obama is using the public school system to help ensure Democratic victories in 2010, 2012, and thereafter.

SOCIALIST PROPAGANDA THROUGH THE NEA

A few overzealous schoolteachers, nothing more? Such was the claim on the left. But there was no mistaking the post-American president's insidious manipulation of the National Endowment for the Arts. On August 10, 2009, the White House Office of Public Engagement, the National Endowment for the Arts, and an ostensibly nonpartisan volunteer group called United We Serve hosted a conference call. According to Patrick Courrielche of Big Hollywood, who was invited to participate, "the call would include 'a group of artists, producers, promoters, organizers, influencers, marketers, taste-makers, leaders or just plain cool people to join together and work together to promote a more civically engaged America and celebrate how the arts can be used for a positive change!"

What kind of positive change? What else but promoting the socialist agenda of the post-American president? "We were encouraged," Courrielche explains, "to bring the same sense of enthusiasm to these 'focus areas' as we had brought to Obama's presidential campaign, and we were encouraged to create art and art initiatives that brought awareness to these issues."

In other words, the participants were encouraged to create art to further the Obama agenda. The ballot box wasn't enough. The mainstream media wasn't enough. The appeal to reason and proven success would fail the post-American president and his allies, and apparently they knew it—so they wanted to resort to more subtle means of persuasion. Courrielche warned of "the danger of the use of the art community as a tool of the state."[30] There was no attempt to hide the manipulative and politicized aspect of the "art" the conference call participants were being urged to produce: "Throughout the conversation," recalled Courrielche, "we were reminded of our ability as artists and art professionals to 'shape the lives' of those around us. The now famous Obama 'Hope' poster, created by artist Shepard Fairey and promoted by many of those on the phone call, and will.i.am's 'Yes We Can' song and music video were presented as shining examples of our group's clear role in the election."[31]

The official story was that Michael Skolnik, the political director for hip-hop entrepreneur Russell Simmons (why does a music-industry leader need a "political director"?), organized the call out of sheer public-spiritedness. However, John Nolte of Big Hollywood explained that "all evidence points to the fact that the conference call was a ruse, a front for a White House using Skolnik as a kind of beard in order to put an innocent spin on their abuse of the NEA and two non-partisan volunteer organizations (United We Serve—an initiative overseen by The Corporation for National and Community Service—a federal agency, and the White House's Office of Public Engagement)." Nolte said that the goal of all this was "to motivate a group of hand-picked pro-Obama artists (grant recipients or those wanting grants) to push the President's flagging agenda, especially health care—and to funnel this promotion through the ACORN-related Serve.gov website."[32]

American taxpayers of all political persuasions subsidize the National Endowment for the Arts (and, of course, have no choice not to do so), supposedly so that art will be created that will enrich all citizens and American culture in general. Barack Obama was attempting to use it to further one political perspective. Yet when art becomes the handmaiden of politics, it is no longer art at all—it is propaganda. He was attempting to compel the NEA to start turning out a softer version of the socialist realism that put a confident, muscular face on Stalin's tyranny.

The August 10 call was not the Obama administration's only attempt to corral the art world into becoming propagandists for the regime. Culture critic Lee Rosenbaum, who blogs about the art world, reported on September 2, 2009, that Kalpen Modi, the associate director of the White House Office of Public Engagement, in an August 27 conference call "sought to rally the artworld troops behind President Obama's call for Americans to engage in public service." Rosenbaum, who noted that she "supported and (with reservations) still support the agenda of the new President," saw the ominous implications of this for the integrity of the art world: "It's a worthwhile objective, to be sure. But government exhortations for artists to join the United We Serve brigade makes me more than a little uneasy. . . . More government oversight will inevitably lead to more government interference and control."[33]

ONE-PARTY STATE

And for the post-American president, more government interference and control meant Democrat Party interference and control. On November 5, 2009, John Berry, the director of the United States Office of Personnel Management (OPM), which oversees personnel appointments for the federal bureaucracy, issued a directive: "Beginning

January 1, 2010, agencies must seek prior approval from OPM before they can appoint a current or recent political appointee to a competitive or non-political excepted service position at any level under the provisions of title 5, United States Code."[34] In plain English, this meant that former political appointees could not be appointed to civil service positions without special approval—and the memo directed that this provision was to be made retroactive going back five years. Pundit Mark Tapscott explained that this directive "effectively establishes a partisan political factor in hiring for career civil service positions in the federal bureaucracy. . . . In other words, if you worked for President Bush in the executive branch at any time during his second term in the White House, you may not be approved. The same applies if you worked for a Republican Member of Congress at any point during the past five years."[35]

According to political blogger Erick Erickson of RedState.com, it amounted to an attempt to "purge the federal government of Republican civil servants. . . . The memorandum goes on to apply this change to civil servants who were political appointees in the last five years, in effect freezing these employees out of other positions, denying them promotions, and forcing them out of their jobs."[36]

For Erickson, there was more than a whiff of the one-party state to this Obama initiative: "This is what happens in third world kleptocracies and totalitarian regimes. This is scary stuff."[37]

Even that was not all. Any decent socialist propaganda needs a socialist hero. And some were anxious to cast the post-American president himself in that role.

SOCIALIST HERO

Louis Farrakhan proclaimed Obama to be the messiah back in October 2008: "You are the instruments that God is gonna use to bring about universal change, and that is why Barack has captured the youth. And he has involved young people in a political process that they didn't care anything about. That's a sign. When the Messiah speaks, the youth will hear, and the Messiah is absolutely speaking."[38] It became a joke, particularly among Republicans and conservatives, to call Obama the Messiah in view of the extravagant praise—and extravagant hopes—that were attached to him during the campaign.

But there was also a serious cultic edge to some of the adulation.

The chairman of the National Endowment for the Arts, Rocco Landesman, provoked ridicule when he said in October 2009 that "Barack Obama is the most powerful writer since Julius Caesar." He didn't mean that Barack Obama is a literary titan who doth bestride the narrow world like a colossus while petty men like Chaucer, Shakespeare, and Tolstoy walk under his huge legs and peep about to find themselves dishonorable graves. But what he did mean, while no less fatuous, was also disquieting in its implications: for the first time, the United States of America had a president whose supporters talked about him in the same effusive and worshipful tones usually reserved for the likes of Stalin, Mao, and Kim Jong Il.

What Landesman really meant was that since Obama was the most powerful man in the world and a writer as well, the president was the most politically powerful writer since Caesar. "This is the first president," Landesman asserted, "that actually writes his own books since Teddy Roosevelt and arguably the first to write them really well since Lincoln." Landesman is wrong about this in several ways: as Scott Johnson at the popular "Powerline" blog pointed out, Lincoln never actually wrote a book, and Theodore Roosevelt, Woodrow Wilson, Herbert Hoover, and Richard Nixon wrote books without employing ghostwriters. Johnson also mentions Bill Clinton and John F. Kennedy, whose *Profiles in Courage* was ghostwritten; "my guess," Johnson concludes, "is that JFK and Obama share the attribute of authorship in roughly equal measure."

Probably so. But that didn't stop Landesman from exulting: "If you accept the premise, and I do, that the United States is the most powerful country in the world, then Barack Obama is the most powerful writer since Julius Caesar. That has to be good for American artists." Ludicrous? Yes. After all, the inevitable question was, "What has he done to deserve this?" Did *Dreams from My Father* and *The Audacity of Hope* really merit being placed above Churchill's *The Second World War, The Personal Memoirs of Ulysses S. Grant*, or even Theodore Roosevelt's *The Strenuous Life*?

Landesman's ridiculously exaggerated praise recalled the Soviet literary establishment's hailing of Stalin's turgid *Marxism and Problems of Linguistics* and *Economic Problems of Socialism in the USSR* as "works of genius." Every German home once had a copy of *Mein Kampf*, even if nobody in the house read it, and every Chinese citizen once knew that he better own a copy of Chairman Mao's *Little Red Book*—if he knew what was good for him. Landesman has given Barack Obama the perfect companion to his spurious Nobel Prize: the fulsome and empty literary praise usually reserved for totalitarian autocrats of little or no actual literary accomplishment.

At a time when the Obama administration was relentlessly demonizing dissenting voices and manifesting a shaky (at best) commitment to the freedom of speech, it was hardly a reassuring message to send. It demonstrated once again this administration's utter tone deafness and apparent indifference to genuine concerns about its commitment to core principles of the U.S. Constitution—witness Nancy Pelosi's incredulous response of "Are you serious?" to a questioner who asked her about the constitutionality of nationalizing health care.

With free speech under attack everywhere—attacks that were sometimes abetted by the Obama administration—it was not the time to be inviting comparisons with history's greatest oppressors. Even comparisons on the absurdity meter.

Writing in 1962, Ayn Rand foresaw the disaster the Obama administration was bringing upon the nation:

A "mixed economy" [socialism/capitalism] is a society in the process of committing suicide.

A nation cannot survive half-slave, half-free. Consider the condition of a nation in which every other social group becomes both the slave and the enslaved of every other group. Ask yourself how long such a condition can last and what its inevitable outcome will be.[39]

TWELVE

THE RED CZARS

ON THE CAMPAIGN TRAIL, PRESIDEN-
TIAL CANDIDATE BARACK OBAMA WARNED
ABOUT THE ARROGATION OF POWER IN THE EXECUTIVE
branch: "The biggest problems that we're facing right now have to do
with George Bush trying to bring more and more power into the executive branch and not go through Congress at all. And that's what I
intend to reverse when I'm president of the United States."[1]

When he did become president, however, he did just the opposite.
He took steps to centralize power in the executive branch that George
W. Bush would never have dreamed of taking. Working at a furious pace, he appointed an unprecedented proliferation of officials—
known popularly as "czars"—with a huge array of responsibilities
over immense swaths of domestic and foreign policy. These appointments bypassed the legislative branch altogether, for while conven-

tional Cabinet appointments required the approval and oversight of Congress, these czars were accountable to no one except Barack Hussein Obama.

The czars all have Cabinet counterparts, also—people who should be doing their jobs, and as far as the general public is concerned, *are* doing their jobs. Yet while Cabinet members are subject to confirmation hearings and public scrutiny, the czars perform many of their ostensible duties—out of the public eye and far away from any accountability.

Obama wasn't the first president to appoint "czars" answerable only to himself. The media first used the term in connection with World War II–era Roosevelt administration officials overseeing various emergency programs, and revived it during the Nixon administration; it has been around ever since. But many of these earlier czars were performing special duties, without having responsibilities that overlapped with those of other officials. And none of his predecessors could match the post-American president in his proliferation of czars—Obama appointed thirty-two during his first months in office, and showed no sign of stopping.

It was an all-out assault on the American system of checks and balances, and a concentration of power in the executive branch unmatched by anything in American history.

Rep. Eric Cantor (R-VA), the House minority whip, pointed out in August 2009 that "by appointing a virtual army of 'czars'—each wholly unaccountable to Congress yet tasked with spearheading major policy efforts for the White House—the president has made an end-run around the legislative branch of historic proportions. . . . Vesting such broad authority in the hands of people not subjected to Senate confirmation and congressional oversight poses a grave threat to our system of checks and balances."

Even Sen. Robert Byrd (D-WV), the dean of Democrats in the

Senate, was upset. In February 2009 he wrote to Obama about several of the czars, saying: "I am concerned about the relationship between these new White House positions and their executive branch counterparts. Too often, I have seen these lines of authority and responsibility become tangled and blurred, sometimes purposely, to shield information and to obscure the decision-making process." Like Cantor, he warned: "The rapid and easy accumulation of power by White House staff can threaten the Constitutional system of checks and balances."[2]

This isn't the way it's supposed to be. Cantor declared that, by appointing so many czars, Obama has departed from constitutional mandates: "The Constitution mandates that the Senate confirm Cabinet-level department heads and other appointees in positions of authority. This gives Congress—elected by the people—the power to compel executive decision-makers to testify and be held accountable by someone other than the president. It also ensures that key appointees cannot claim executive privilege when subpoenaed to come before Congress."[3]

Likewise Byrd: "If the czars are working behind the scenes and the secretaries will be the mouthpieces of the administration, it calls into question who is actually making the policy decision. "Whoever is making the policy decisions needs to be accountable and available to Congress and the American public."[4] But by contrast, Cantor says, Congress has "not been able to vet" Obama's czars, "and we have no idea what they're doing."[5]

The post-American president may have a very good reason for that: much of what they're doing is not good, and several among them are committed socialists: red czars.

OBAMA'S HARD-LEFT INTERNATIONALIST SCIENCE CZAR

John P. Holdren, the Teresa and John Heinz Professor of Environmental Policy at the Kennedy School of Government at Harvard University, is Obama's assistant to the president for Science and Technology, director of the White House Office of Science and Technology Policy, and cochair of the President's Council of Advisors on Science and Technology (PCAST)—that is, the science czar. As he announced Holdren's appointment, Obama, never a reliable friend of the freedom of speech, indulged in some bitterly ironic pieties: the post-American president said that "the truth is that promoting science isn't just about providing resources—it's about protecting free and open inquiry. It's about ensuring that facts and evidence are never twisted or obscured by politics or ideology."[6]

Yet John P. Holdren was a relentlessly politicized ideologue—so much so that one could find more fervent true believers only in a Soviet Politburo meeting, or, more recently, staffing other positions in the Obama administration. Holdren was, not surprisingly, a true believer in global government and tight controls on free citizens. A longtime and deeply committed Leftist, he participated in the Pugwash Conferences on Science and World Affairs. Joseph Rotblat, Barack Obama's fellow Nobel Peace Prize winner, founded the Pugwash Conferences (named after the Nova Scotia site of the first conference) in the 1950s to enable Western and Soviet scientists to meet together. Rotblat himself was a nuclear scientist who had been part of the Manhattan Project, but who left the project and devoted himself to nuclear disarmament when it became clear that a post–World War II America would use nuclear weapons as a deterrent against the Soviet Union. The Pugwash Conferences Web site still contains a tribute to him.[7]

Jay Nordlinger, *National Review*'s senior editor, identifies these conferences as more political than scientific—and decidedly pro-communist: "Ostensibly, this was an anti-nuclear group, but somehow they managed to serve the Soviet agenda, whatever it was that year. The Pugwashers declared themselves completely opposed to the concept of deterrence—and everything else that eventually ended the Cold War, and won it for freedom. Before Rotblat received the Nobel Prize, he and the Pugwashers were decorated by such peace-lovers as Husak, the Czechoslovakian dictator, and Jaruzelski, the Polish dictator. In fact, the Pugwashers were pleased to hold their conference in Warsaw after Jaruzelski imposed martial law."

Like Barack Obama, Holdren was from early in his career an advocate of the redistribution of wealth. In 1977 he coauthored the book *Ecoscience* with Paul and Anne Ehrlich, which espouses "the neo-Malthusian view." This view, according to the Ehrlichs and Holdren, proposes "population limitation and redistribution of wealth," and "on these points, we find ourselves firmly in the neo-Malthusian camp."[8] They recommended that the "de-development of overdeveloped countries . . . be given top priority," and called on the United States and other First World nations to "divert their excess productivity into helping the poorer people of the world rather than exploiting them." ("Excess" according to whom?) How much of their excess productivity? Oh, 20 percent of their gross national products would be about right—indeed, necessary: "We believe an effort of this magnitude is not only justified but essential."[9]

They also advocated a "considerably more equitable distribution of wealth and income" within America itself, suggesting: "Possibly this would be achieved by some formal mechanism."[10]

The future president who lamented the fact that "the Supreme Court never ventured into the issues of redistribution of wealth and sort of more basic issues of political and economic justice in this society" would undoubtedly have approved—as his later appointment of Holdren made abundantly clear.[11]

Holdren and his coauthors also came out for government controls on population growth—controls so strict that they might have made the most committed Maoist blush. "There exists ample authority," they asserted, "under which population growth could be regulated." They even claimed that "compulsory population-control laws, even including laws requiring compulsory abortion, could be sustained under the existing constitution if the population crisis became sufficiently severe to endanger the society." And they recommended that the United Nations step in to enforce such laws if American authorities failed to do so.[12]

The Erlichs and Holdren advocated more than just a role for the UN in internal U.S. affairs. They called for the establishment of a "comprehensive Planetary Regime" that would essentially control everything: it would "control the development, administration, conservation, and distribution of all natural resources, renewable or nonrenewable . . . not only in the atmosphere and oceans, but in such freshwater bodies as rivers and lakes." It would also "be a logical central agency for regulating all international trade" and would be "given responsibility for determining the optimum population for the world and for each region and for arbitrating various countries' shares within their regional limits . . . the Regime would have some power to enforce the agreed limits."[13] They would enforce these limits by means of a global police force: "Security might be provided by an armed international organization, a global analogue of a police force. . . . The first step necessarily involves partial surrender of sovereignty to an international organization."[14]

When he accepted the Nobel Prize that was awarded to both Rotblat and Pugwash in 1995, Holdren demonstrated that he still held these views. "The post-Cold-War world," he said, "needs a more powerful United Nations, probably with a standing volunteer force—owing loyalty directly to the UN rather than to contingents from individual nations."[15] And in a January 2008 address to the American Association for the Advancement of Science (AAAS), he called for "a universal prohibition on nuclear weapons, coupled with means to ensure confidence in compliance."[16]

Global warming offered him an opportunity to reaffirm his commitment to internationalism and the destruction of American sovereignty. In response to climate change, he recommended in February 2007 that the UN establish a "global framework" for enforcement of various restrictions, including a global emissions tax: "a requirement for the early establishment of a substantial price on carbon emissions in all countries, whether by a carbon tax or a tradable permit approach."[17]

CAROL BROWNER, SOCIALIST CLIMATE CZAR

Among Obama's czars, Holdren wasn't alone way out on the far left. He shared a great ideological affinity with Carol M. Browner, the assistant to the president for energy and climate change—that is, the global-warming czar. Right up until Obama appointed her, she was publicly listed as one of the leaders of the Socialist International's Commission for a Sustainable World Society, a socialist organization that advocates "global governance" and calls upon First-World nations to commit economic suicide in order to put an end to global warming—the greatest fraud in human history. Never before has so much been spent, reallocated, and redistributed on the basis of . . . nothing. Once Obama's appointment became public, however, the socialists hastily removed mention of Browner from their Web site.

Guilty conscience?

Browner was one of many socialist internationalists closely associated with the post-American president. The American representative of the Socialist International is the Democratic Socialists of America (DSA). The DSA, of course, endorsed Barack Obama when he first ran for the Illinois State Senate, and he appeared for them on a panel discussion at the University of Chicago in 1998—on which he praised the virtues of a centrally planned economy: "The state government can . . . play a role in redistribution, the allocation of wages and jobs." [18]

The Socialist International in 2008, while Browner was still listed among its leaders, declared that "market solutions alone are insufficient and will not provide the financial support and resources necessary to achieve the required combination of deep emission reduction, adaptation to already changing climate conditions, energy security and equitable and environmentally sound economic development." If market solutions are insufficient, government controls must supply what is lacking.

And that, of course, was just what Barack Obama wanted to impose. *The Washington Examiner* said in an editorial: "By appointing Browner to a White House post, Obama has at the least implicitly endorsed an utterly radical socialist agenda for his administration's environmental policy. The incoming chief executive thus strengthens critics who contend environmental policies aren't really about protecting endangered species or preserving virgin lands, but rather expanding government power and limiting individual freedom." [19]

Nevertheless, according to the Obama camp, Browner's socialism came to them as a complete surprise. *The Washington Times* reported: "An aide on the Obama team said its information shows that Mrs. Browner resigned from the organization in June 2008. The aide, who asked not to be named because he was discussing internal matters, said the transition team was aware she had been a member of the group when she was vetted." [20]

But even if this was true and the White House didn't know of Browner's socialist ties, would those ties really have bothered them—or was this statement just window dressing for an adulatory press and an indifferent public? With Obama's own socialist leanings and so many other socialists among his friends and associates, why would Browner's socialism suddenly raise eyebrows among the Obamaites?

It strained credulity.

However, Tony Shapiro, spokesman for the Obama transition, said just before Obama became president that Browner was picked "to help the president-elect coordinate energy and climate policy because she understands that our efforts to create jobs, achieve energy security and combat climate change demand integration among different agencies; cooperation between federal, state and local governments; and partnership with the private sector." He didn't say anything about her being picked because she was ideologically simpatico with the post-American president. Still, it was hard to escape that conclusion.

And Shapiro's description of her duties was noteworthy in itself. A socialist coordinating cooperation between various levels of government might reasonably be tempted to centralize. And apparently that would be just fine with Barack Hussein Obama.

THE REGULATORY CZAR

The administrator of the White House Office of Information and Regulatory Affairs, or regulatory czar, is Cass Sunstein. Sunstein is also, like Obama himself, as well as Holdren and Browner, a socialist and redistributionist.

And again like Holdren and Browner, Sunstein sees the global-warming scam as opening the door to full socialism in the United States: "It is even possible that desirable redistribution is more likely to occur through climate change policy than otherwise, or to be accomplished more effectively through climate policy than through direct foreign aid."

Sunstein thought international climate-change regulations were acceptable simply because of their socialist character—apparently aside from the question of whether environmental changes actually showed that they were warranted: "We agree that if the United States does spend a great deal on emissions reductions as part of an international agreement, and if the agreement does give particular help to disadvantaged people, considerations of distributive justice support its action, even if better redistributive mechanisms are imaginable."

In Sunstein's view, wealthy nations have a duty to poor nations: "If we care about social welfare, we should approve of a situation in which a wealthy nation is willing to engage in a degree of self-sacrifice when the world benefits more than that nation loses."[21]

VAN JONES

The most notorious socialist among Obama's czars was one who served for less than six months: Van Jones. A radical black nationalist as well as a socialist hard-liner, Jones was Obama's special advisor for green jobs, enterprise and innovation at the White House Council on Environmental Quality (CEQ)—the environment czar—from March 16 to September 5, 2009, when he resigned under pressure after the full extent of his ties to socialism and race-baiting hate politics was revealed.

Jones was radicalized by the acquittal of the white cops who had beaten a black man, Rodney King, in 1992. He remembered later: "I was a rowdy nationalist on April 28th, and then the verdicts came down on April 29th. By August, I was a communist." Arrested at a mass rally shortly thereafter, he recalled his jail experience fondly: "I met all these young radical people of color—I mean really radical, communists and anarchists. And it was, like, 'This is what I need to be a part of.' . . . I spent the next ten years of my life working with a lot of those people I met in jail, trying to be a revolutionary." [22]

In those days Jones probably never dreamed that he would one day become a top White House official. He might have thought he would have had to sell out his principles to white, capitalist America in order to attain such a position. But instead, the White House came to him. The post-American president brought black nationalism and socialism to the heart of American power. The pose was different, the substance was the same: as Jones himself once put it, "I'm willing to forgo the cheap satisfaction of the radical pose for the deep satisfaction of radical ends." [23]

He could have been describing the career trajectory of Barack Hussein Obama.

After a public outcry led by television personality Glenn Beck, who called public attention to Jones's hard-left leanings, Jones resigned. But if all the socialists, race baiters, and communists were removed from the Obama high command, there would be no one left.

THE PAY CZAR

Among Obama's many socialist czars was Kenneth Feinberg, the special master for TARP executive compensation, or pay czar. Feinberg had sweeping and final authority to set salaries for executives at corporations including Bank of America, Citigroup, General Motors, and Chrysler—the large corporations receiving "bailouts" from the federal government in exchange for government control. [24]

Columnist David Harsanyi warned that "this unprecedented intrusion into the economy accomplishes nothing—well, other than setting an array of dangerous precedents." Among them, never-ending government control: "Yes, these companies were at the taxpayer trough.

Which means that firms that accept aid from Washington should consider the 'assistance' analogous to the help offered by The Godfather at his daughter's wedding. You're in for life. Existing contracts have no real value. A single political appointee may have the power to decide what you're worth."[25]

That's exactly what Feinberg did. In October 2009 he slashed executive salaries, and in December 2009 he did it again, announcing a pay cut for mid-level executives at his pet corporations that left fewer than 10 out of 450 executives being allowed salaries over $500,000 a year.[26] He turned a deaf ear to complaints that he was thereby rendering these corporations uncompetitive in a tough market. And what if the executives decided to leave the corporations under Feinberg's control in order to earn higher salaries elsewhere? Economist Alex Tabarook predicts: "Chaos will be created at these firms as top people leave in droves. Will the administration then order people back to work?"[27]

The appointments of all these socialists to key positions removed from conventional means of accountability was one more indication of the hard-left political convictions of the president who appointed them.

THIRTEEN

ACORN: FEDERALLY FUNDED FRAUD

ACORN FUNCTIONS AS IF IT WERE THE PROVO ARM OF THE DEMOCRAT PARTY. ACORN PERFORMS ALL OF THE ILLEGALITIES—PHONY VOTER registrations, dummied-up fronts for laundered money, and worse. ACORN has specialized, along with the Black Panthers and the SEIU, in voting booth intimidation, blocking people from access, and the like. And when somebody gets caught, or a scam gets uncovered, the Democrats scramble and cover for their provo.

The wheels started to come off the ACORN bus in September 2009, when a video came to light of a young man and woman posing as a thirteen-year-old prostitute and her pimp, discussing with ACORN officials how to set up a house of prostitution staffed with underage, illegal prostitutes. Helpful ACORN staffers advise the couple on how they can deceive the police and launder the money from this enterprise.[1]

But that was just the straw that broke the camel's back. The Association of Community Organizers for Reform Now (ACORN) had a long record of voter fraud, going back years. According to journalist Amanda Carpenter, ACORN's taste for fraud appears to be growing rather than diminishing: in 2004, two Colorado ACORN officials submitted false voter registrations and were ultimately convicted of perjury. In 2006, ACORN submitted fraudulent voter registrations in five states.[2] In November 2006, a Missouri grand jury indicted four ACORN workers for submitting over fifteen thousand phony voter-registration forms.[3]

Then during the 2008 presidential campaign, ACORN faced voter-registration-fraud accusations in *thirteen* states. An ACORN staffer convinced one Ohio teenager to register to vote no fewer than seventy-three times. Every member of the Dallas Cowboys football team registered to vote in Nevada.[4]

Over half of the voter applications ACORN submitted in Indiana had to be thrown out.[5] This problem was not restricted to Indiana alone: according to former ACORN employee Anita MonCrief, more than 50 percent of voter registrations that ACORN submitted nationwide during the 2008 election were fraudulent.[6]

ACORN is also a radical socialist, hard-left organization. A 2003 exposé of ACORN called it "the largest radical group in the country," with "120,000 dues-paying members, chapters in 700 poor neighborhoods in 50 cities," promoting "a 1960s-bred agenda of anti-capitalism, central planning, victimology, and government handouts to the poor" and sometimes even "undisguised authoritarian socialism."[7] ACORN is dedicated to stealth revolution, communism, demonizing honest American businesses and businessmen, ripping off the American taxpayer, and subverting free markets—among other similar objectives.

IT'S A POWER THING

Barack Obama once worked as an ACORN "leadership trainer." He hired ACORN affiliates for voter registration. Obama was a speaker at ACORN seminars. Obama was their lawyer.[8] The *Illinois Times* reported in 2008: "Fresh out of Harvard Law School, Obama moved to Chicago to head up the local branch of Project Vote, a D.C.-based nonpartisan voter-registration organization focused on low-income communities of color. Recruiting staff and volunteers from community groups and black churches, he helped train 700 deputy registrars and devised a comprehensive media campaign based on the slogan 'It's a Power Thing.' His volunteers hit the streets and registered more than 150,000 black voters in only six months. According to a 1993 report published in Chicago magazine, the elections 'turned on these totals.'"[9]

Obama continued to use the tactics he learned in the "It's a Power Thing" media campaign during his presidential run, as the *Illinois Times* noted: "Vote for Change is the latest iteration of the Obama campaign's comprehensive electoral ground game, one that will build on the methodical and underreported registration efforts staged by Obama supporters during the primary season. Just in the late contests alone, campaign volunteers enlisted 200,000 new Democrats in Pennsylvania, 165,000 in North Carolina, and more than 150,000 in Indiana."[10]

When ACORN's federal funding began to be challenged, journalist John Fund observed that Obama "carefully declined to say whether he would approve a federal cutoff of funds to the group," and that the president "took great pains to act as if he barely knew about Acorn. In fact, his association goes back almost 20 years. In 1991, he took time off from his law firm to run a voter-registration drive for Project Vote, an Acorn partner that was soon fully absorbed under the Acorn umbrella."

His success in that drive led to the election of Democrat senator Carol Moseley Braun, and made Obama "a hot commodity on the community organizing circuit. He became a top trainer at Acorn's Chicago conferences. In 1995, he became Acorn's attorney, participating in a landmark case to force the state of Illinois to implement the federal Motor Voter Law. That law's loose voter registration requirements would later be exploited by Acorn employees in an effort to flood voter rolls with fake names."[11]

Through ACORN, Obama established numerous long-standing political associations. "He met people not just in the African-American community but in the progressive white community," David Axelrod recalled. "The folks who funded Project Vote were some of the key progressive leaders."[12]

At a December 2007 ACORN rally, Obama was effusive about the important role the organization would play when he became president: "Before I even get inaugurated, during the transition, we're going to be calling all of you in to help us shape the agenda. We're gonna be having meetings all across the country with community organizations so that you have input into the agenda of the next presidency of the United States of America."[13]

And in February 2008, Obama acknowledged his personal debt to the organization:

I come out of a grassroots organizing background. That's what I did for three and half years before I went to law school. That's the reason I moved to Chicago was to organize. So this is something that I know personally, the work you do, the importance of it. I've been fighting alongside ACORN on issues you care about my entire career. Even before I was an elected official, when I ran Project Vote voter registration drive in Illinois, ACORN was smack dab in the middle of it, and we appreciate your work.[14]

In December 2009, Rep. Steve King (R-IA) said he was certain that any investigation of ACORN would "lead to the White House." King pointed out that "Obama has worked for ACORN, and he has been part and parcel of that—Project Vote in particular. That entire network is something the Chicago Organization that now sits in the White House knows a lot about." King also noted a spectacular example of Obama administration hypocrisy: White House counsel Robert Bauer called last year for George W. Bush and John McCain to be investigated for "alleging that ACORN was promoting fraudulent voter registration activities."[15]

Despite everything that is unsavory about the organization, however, the ostensibly nonpartisan ACORN really does indeed want people to register to vote—as long as they're Democrats. Republican registrations go into the trash.

REGISTER AS MANY VOTERS AS YOU CAN— AS LONG AS THEY'RE DEMOCRATS

In February 2008, Fathiyyah Muhammad of Jacksonville, Florida, heard that ACORN was paying people three dollars for each voter they could register. ACORN paid her three dollars for each voter she registered, but Fathiyyah Muhammad says that the group threw out her votes and fired her when she brought them registrations of *Republican* voters.

Fathiyyah Muhammad voted for Obama. "I'm a Republican," she

says, "and this was the first time that I voted for a Democrat since JFK. . . . I'm one of those rare birds, a black conservative Republican, and actually this is the black conservative capital of the country, Jacksonville, Florida."

She is an entrepreneur and a great American: she makes custom hats for her businesses Bilal's Custom Caps and Only in America. She and her husband, James, have made custom caps for politicians, sports heroes, musicians, and others. "America," she says, "is the place you can live your dreams if you work at it." She's a can-do woman with a great American spirit, and when she saw what was breaking in the news about ACORN, she came forward; I interviewed her in October 2009.

"This is my first experience" with ACORN, Muhammad said. "This was before Obama got the nomination, long before then. . . . I heard about this group that was paying three dollars per person, to go out and to get people to sign up to vote. So I went over, I thought that well this is a good way to make some money because I know everybody, you know. I went over there and this guy signed me up and everything, and gave me my little pad, all this stuff."

Muhammad went to the ACORN office in Jacksonville. There she encountered a young man speaking to a room of about twenty people. "He was telling us, you know, about his experience, he was from Brooklyn, he wasn't from this area. He was just here recruiting people to register people to vote. They had a big office here, and I would say maybe about ten or twelve people at there."

She went to work: "Well, I went out and got a lot of people, homeless people, but of course I signed everybody up as a Republican, and I would have put people had they been Democrats." She was not forcing people to sign up as Republicans: "You could put down anything you wanted." But when she got back to ACORN, a group leader was not pleased: "So I showed what I had, and he said, 'No, no, you a fraud, there can't be any black Republicans,' and oh, he just kind of hung me out to dry. . . . But of course their main aim was to register only Democrats. They're not interested in registering Republicans."

She saw ACORN officials in Jacksonville throw out the Republican registrations she made. "They just discarded those, they weren't valid. All of the registrations . . . they just threw those out." Yet she says that she is sure that the people she registered were actually going to vote: "Yes, they all were going to vote, I just didn't want to get anybody just to get the three dollars, I wasn't desperate for three dollars."

ACORN did not honor its agreement to pay three dollars for each registered voter. "He took my papers," says Muhammad, "didn't pay me anything and I just left, I just figured that this is just another scam. . . . Everyone else got paid, all the other people got paid, but I didn't. And I didn't make a big deal about it, I just figured that it was another one of life's experiences."

Fathiyyah Muhammad didn't know anything about ACORN at that time. She didn't know that ACORN has been doing this for a long time. As far back as November 2006 the organization was indicted for some forty thousand illegal voter registrations, and that was before any of the recent revelations.

Looking back on it all, Fathiyyah Muhammad mused: "I can't believe that they got away with it for so long." And she wanted her story to be told: "How are you going to shine a light on the laundry if you don't want to come out and say what happened?"[16]

Fathiyyah Muhammad was unafraid to shine that light. And her testimony was another nail in the coffin of the community organizers of ACORN and their stealth agenda. But ACORN, of course, still had powerful friends. And they had been in damage control mode for quite some time.

So was Barack Hussein Obama.

OBAMA LIED

As scandalous ACORN stories began to be virtually a daily news feature, the potential for Barack Obama to be seriously embarrassed—and even the possibility that his political career could be damaged—began to grow.

And so he lied.

During his presidential campaign, his Fight The Smears Web site contained a preposterous claim: "Fact: Barack was never an ACORN trainer and never worked for ACORN in any other capacity." Yet Toni Foulkes, a leader in Chicago's ACORN chapter, wrote an article in 2004 in which she spoke proudly about Obama's role as an ACORN trainer, and emphasizes that Obama's Project Vote activities were done in conjunction with ACORN.[17]

Representative King charged in November 2009 that Obama had appointed Robert Bauer to be White House counsel in order to gain his help in deflecting scrutiny away from Obama's ties to ACORN: "Bauer's hiring," said King, "appears to be a tactical maneuver to strategically defend the White House exactly one week after Louisiana attorney general Buddy Caldwell raided ACORN's national headquarters in New Orleans and seized paper records and computer hard drives that may lead to the White House."

Bauer, incidentally, is married to former White House communications director Anita Dunn, who caused controversy in June 2009 when she called a murderous totalitarian communist, Mao Tse Tung, one of her "favorite political philosophers."[18]

BRAZENING IT OUT

ACORN has received over $53 million in federal money—taxpayer money—since 1994.[19] The feds gave ACORN $2.6 million in 2003 and

2004 just for the organization's housing programs alone.[20] And the stimulus package that the post-American president rammed through Congress in his first days in office contained the staggering sum of $5.2 *billion* for ACORN.[21] ACORN was eligible to receive the funds, but they declared bankruptcy and rebranded themselves so that they could masquerade as a different group and steal under a new name.[22]

But in late September 2009, after the prostitution video and other corruption scandals, ACORN lost its federal funding in a congressional vote that was not even close: in the Senate the vote was 85–11, and in the House it was 345–75.[23] Around the same time, Barack Obama gave five interviews to the Sunday morning news shows, and only one interviewer bothered to ask him about ACORN. Obama's answer? He brazened it out: "You know, if—frankly, it's not really something I've followed closely. I didn't even know that ACORN was getting a whole lot of federal money." And he downplayed the importance of the issue: "This is not the biggest issue facing the country. It's not something I'm paying a lot of attention to."[24]

Taking him at his word, what exactly *was* Obama paying attention to? Nationalizing a perfectly good private health-care system, the best in the world? Outreach to the *ummah* (the worldwide global Muslim community)? What was he paying attention to? Mounting a Department of Justice witch hunt, a persecution of CIA agents whose crime was keeping us safe from the worldwide jihad in the immediate aftermath of 9/11? What was he paying attention to? Ethnically cleansing Israel of the Jewish people? Or facilitating a nuclear Iran? Sanctioning Islamic law there and snuffing out the people marching for freedom in Iran? Lest we forget his priority of crushing democracy in Honduras.

Yet Barack Obama *was* ACORN. Remember, this was the same Barack Obama who said, in an address to ACORN in 2008, "I have been fighting alongside ACORN on issues you care about my entire career." And Obama was still fighting alongside ACORN: after both the Senate and the House voted overwhelmingly to cut off ACORN's federal funding, his post-American Justice Department found legal cover to continue giving taxpayer dollars to ACORN—and congressional Democrats shot down Republican attempts to stop this.[25]

This is madness. ACORN's massive voter fraud constitutes a coup on the American electoral system, a usurpation of the will of the people: government by the people and for the people made into a sham. It's a government by the moochers and the looters, for the moochers and the looters, stolen from the good, hardworking Americans.

And worse, the American people sat by and let it happen. Obama's presidency was not an accident of history. It was a very deliberate assault by the Hard Left on the foundation of the greatest country in human history.

If we purged the illegals, the dead, and the fraudulent whom ACORN has placed on the voting rolls, we would have honest leadership that reflected the real landscape of this great nation.

ACORN is a racketeering criminal organization whose specialty is sedition—overthrowing the good governance of this great nation. Why hasn't it been stripped of its funding and rendered illegal like the Cosa Nostra? What's the difference, except that the Mafia was patriotic?

Investigative journalist Stanley Kurtz, noting that Obama's links to ACORN are "wide, deep, and longstanding," draws the inescapable conclusion: "If Acorn is adept at creating a non-partisan, inside-game veneer for what is in fact an intensely radical, leftist, and politically partisan reality, so is Obama himself."

Intensely radical, leftist, and fanatically partisan: it was a profile of the post-American president.

FOURTEEN

THE ENERGY SHELL GAME

OBAMA'S ENERGY POLICY, LIKE HIS HEALTH-CARE POLICY, IS ABOUT BIG GOVERN-MENT CONTROL AND GLOBAL GOVERNANCE. OUR EN-ergy needs are easily solved. I'll restate the obvious: drill, baby, drill. America has enormous resources that we deny to ourselves. Democrats, Leftists, and environmentalists have blocked development of new sources of energy; drilling for oil in Alaska, off the Florida coast, and anywhere else; the construction of new oil refineries; and the expanded use of clean nuclear energy and clean coal. In October 2009, the post-American Interior Department froze oil and gas development at sixty (out of a total of seventy-seven) drilling sites in Utah.[1]

Obama doesn't seem to mind building "peaceful" nuclear plants in the oil-rich Islamic dictatorship in Iran, but he and his radical leftist cronies prohibit the building of new nuclear plants here. Instead of fostering traditional American self-reliance, we depend on foreign oil, selling out our principles, our politics, and our foreign policy to our enemies.

Sarah Palin has counted the cost: "Think about how much of our trade deficit is fueled by the oil we import—sometimes as much as half of the total. Through this massive transfer of wealth, we lose hundreds of billions of dollars a year that could be invested in our economy. Instead it goes to foreign countries, including some repressive regimes that use it to fund activities that threaten our security. Reliance on foreign sources of energy weakens America." If not for the American dollar, the global jihad would be relegated to the cave from whence it came and where it belongs. In the largest transfer of wealth in human history, we are committing economic suicide while effectively funding a movement whose sole objective is establishing a worldwide caliphate that will impose upon societies the most brutal, misogynistic, antihuman ideology in history.

This situation has no doubt been long in the making. But the Obama administration and the Democrats are now ramming through an unprecedented energy policy that seems designed to cripple the nation. And it is completely unnecessary. Palin pointed out that drilling to augment our domestic energy problem would not only help lessen our energy dependence upon hostile states; it would also pull America out of the current economic malaise. "Building an energy-independent America," said Palin, "will mean a real economic stimulus. It will mean American jobs that can never be shipped overseas."[2]

In contrast, Obama's energy plan mandated scarcity in the richest country in the world.

CAP AND TRADE

On June 26, 2009, the House of Representatives passed by seven votes the American Clean Energy and Security Act of 2009, known popularly as the Waxman-Markey Cap-and-Trade bill—a massive, thousand-page-long bill that would place limits on the greenhouse gas emissions that supposedly caused global warming.

Would climate justice ensue? Normalized temperatures? Cleaner air? Healthier forests, lakes, and streams?

Don't hold your breath. Despite Obama's pious public rhetoric, the bill was unlikely to bring any of that about, or do much of anything except bleed American taxpayers dry. The plan supposedly would reduce emissions by 17 percent from their 2005 levels by 2020, and by 83 percent by 2050.[3] In reality, Obama's cap-and-trade plan was a gigantic shell game, in which the government sold businesses emission rights—licenses to give off certain amounts of gases deemed harmful to the environment.

If you had the cash, you could be as big a polluter as you cared to be. Emissions rights could be bought, sold, traded. *The Wall Street Journal* explained that this would result simply in higher costs for ordinary Americans: "As the cap is tightened and companies are stripped of initial opportunities to 'offset' their emissions, the price of permits will skyrocket beyond the CBO estimate of $28 per ton of carbon. The corporate costs of buying these expensive permits will be passed to consumers."[4]

The idea was to give the federal government enormous power to regulate the activity of American businesses—and to open up a lucrative new tax revenue stream. Obama was banking on bringing $300 billion to the elephantine and hypercentralized U.S. government by 2022.[5] The tax burden from the cap-and-trade plan was so large that a Treasury Department estimate showed that it would place an additional $200 billion annual burden on American taxpayers, raising every taxpayer's personal income taxes by 15 percent—an average of $1,761 annually from every household in the United States.[6]

A Heritage Foundation estimate saw the plan as even more prohibitive than that, costing $1,870 for every family of four in the United States by 2020, and $6,800 per family of four by 2035, as some of the end-loaded restrictions came into effect.[7] Another dire estimate came from Ben Lieberman, senior policy analyst for energy and environment in the Thomas A. Roe Institute for Economic Policy Studies at the Heritage Foundation. In testimony before the House and Senate Western Caucus on July 30, 2009, Lieberman declared: "The higher energy costs kick in as soon as the bill's provisions take effect in 2012. For a household of four, energy costs go up $436 that year, and they eventually reach $1,241 in 2035 and average $829 annually over that span. Electricity costs go up 90 percent by 2035, gasoline by 58 percent, and natural gas by 55 percent by 2035. The cumulative higher energy costs for a family of four by then will be nearly $20,000. But direct energy costs are only part of the consumer impact. Nearly everything goes up, since higher energy costs raise production costs. If you look at the total cost of Waxman-Markey, it works out to an average of $2,979 annually from 2012–2035 for a household of four. By 2035 alone, the total cost is over $4,600."

Lieberman called cap and trade "nothing more than an energy tax in disguise," and labeled the bill "the most convoluted attempt at economic central planning this nation has ever attempted." He said that "cap and trade works by raising the cost of energy high enough so that individuals and businesses are forced to use less of it. Inflicting economic pain is what this is all about." He said that over a million jobs would be lost, "while others will be outsourced to nations like China and India that have repeatedly stated that they'll never hamper their own economic growth with energy-cost-boosting global-warming measures like Waxman-Markey."

Lieberman's conclusion was ominous: "Overall, Waxman-Markey reduces gross domestic product by an average of $393 billion annually between 2012 and 2035, and cumulatively by $9.4 trillion. In other words, the nation will be $9.4 trillion poorer with Waxman-Markey than without it."[8]

In fact, the burden that Waxman-Markey would place on American individuals and businesses would be so crushing that the bill was a hard sell even among the Leftists and moderate Democrats. *The Wall Street Journal* observed in June 2009 that "despite House Energy and Commerce Chairman Henry Waxman's many payoffs to members, rural and Blue Dog Democrats remain wary of voting for a bill that will impose crushing costs on their home-district businesses and consumers. The leadership's solution to this problem is to simply claim the bill defies the laws of economics."[9]

That sleight of hand worked on House Democrats. It won't work, however, to stave off economic disaster for the American people. Republican critics were scathing. Said Karl Rove: "Cap-and-trade would not achieve its goals—and it would put America on a ruinous course. . . . Putting a tax on carbon means that every American who flips a light switch, turns a car key, or buys anything made or shipped in this country will pay more."[10]

Rove also observed that cap and trade "would require a larger, more intrusive government bureaucracy, regulating vast swatches of our economy and diminishing innovation, flexibility, and enterprise."

That sounded like just the thing that would warm the heart of the socialist post-American president. "Businesses," Rove continued, "would reduce their cap-and-trade costs by moving jobs to countries without a tax on carbon or a cap on greenhouse emissions."[11] So more businesses would move out of the United States, to the benefit of overseas competitors.

Once again, it sounded like something right up the alley of the internationalist ideologue Obama.

Obama's most determined, formidable, patriotic, and populist critic, Sarah Palin, was as unimpressed as Rove. "I am deeply concerned about President Obama's cap-and-trade energy plan," she wrote in July 2009, "and I believe it is an enormous threat to our economy. It would undermine our recovery over the short term and would inflict permanent damage. . . . The president's cap-and-trade energy tax would adversely affect every aspect of the U.S. economy."

Palin pointed out that the framers of the bill seemed to realize that it would result in Americans losing their jobs, making it all the more bitterly ironic that Obama was actually calling this a jobs bill: "Job losses are so certain under this new cap-and-tax plan that it includes a provision accommodating newly unemployed workers from the resulting dried-up energy sector, to the tune of $4.2 billion over eight years. So much for creating jobs."[12] Commented Chris Tucker of the Institute for Energy Research: "Can you name another jobs-creation bill that was so concerned about its potential impact that it preemptively included a benefits program for the millions of workers it expected to displace?"[13]

Palin asked a question that Obama the internationalist might have been reluctant to answer (and not surprisingly, he ignored it): "We have an important choice to make. Do we want to control our energy supply and its environmental impact? Or, do we want to outsource it to China, Russia and Saudi Arabia? Make no mistake: President Obama's plan will result in the latter."[14]

An Exxon Mobil executive with three decades of experience attended a presentation on the bill given by Richard Igercich, a refinery manager for Chalmette Refining, L.L.C., a joint venture of Exxon

Mobil PDVSA, Venezuela's state oil company; Dan Borne, president of the Gulf South Chemical Plants Association; and an Exxon Mobil political analyst. The executive emerged from this presentation with the conviction that "the Bill is a very complex one and offers devastating results to you, me, our generations to come and every business in America."

The executive said that the bill would deprive ordinary Americans of gasoline, diesel, kerosene, jet fuel, pharmaceuticals, medical supplies, and heating oil, and dramatically increase the costs of electricity, coal, and natural gas. He said that this was part and parcel of Obama's plan: to wean America off crude oil petroleum products simply by making them too expensive for Americans to afford. "The bill in its present form," he said, "targets Oil Refineries and Chemical Plants as the most dangerous contributors to Global Warming," while there are "no scientific facts to support that accusation."[15]

It was all political.

OBAMA'S ENABLING ACT?

One ominous detail in the cap-and-trade bill was that it gave the president emergency powers to act to stop global warming. The bill lays out a series of conditions that would be considered to constitute such an emergency—most notably, if global greenhouse gas levels rise above 450 parts per million. But it is a very real possibility that greenhouse gas levels could rise above 450 parts per million as early as 2010.

If they do, the president must "direct all Federal agencies to use existing statutory authority to take appropriate actions" to lower emissions levels. "The bill's language," according to investigative journalist David Freddoso, "places an unusually broad mandate upon the president to act in the event of this 'emergency' situation." He explains that "declaration of this 'climate emergency' could result in federal agencies denying all discretionary permits for carbon-emitting industries."[16]

The president, in short, could destroy whole American industries that refused to tow his political and environmental line. And with broad and vaguely defined "emergency powers," he could destroy the American system of checks and balances, and the restraints on executive authority that have always been the hallmark of the American Republic.

With his taste for socialism and authoritarianism, however, Barack Obama never much cared much for those restraints. And so constitutional rule was imperiled as never before in American history—and all for what turned out to be a completely fabricated crisis.

THE GLOBAL WARMING COVER-UP: "A MIRACLE HAS HAPPENED"

Fresh on the heels of Lord Christopher Monckton's declaration about Obama's plans to sign away American sovereignty for global warming came a blockbuster exposé that blew the lid off the climate-change hoax.

Obama had been poised to sign away American sovereignty for that hoax.

Suspicions had been mounting throughout the first year of Obama's presidency about the supposedly assured results that purported to establish global warming as fact. In July 2009 Peter Ferrara, director of entitlement and budget policy at the Institute for Policy Innovation and general counsel of the American Civil Rights Union, expressed the growing skepticism of many when he wrote in *The American Spectator* that "the science behind global warming is now collapsing. The most reliable satellite weather data shows that global atmospheric

THE POST-AMERICAN PRESIDENCY

temperatures have *declined* over the last 11 years, with the trend downward accelerating. Even global warming advocates are now conceding that this trend may continue for decades." [17]

But real cracks in the edifice didn't start appearing until several months later. It all started with four words that shook the world. "A miracle has happened," a writer cryptically posted to Climate Audit, a Web site devoted to showing that climate-change science was junk science.

The cryptic writer followed those four words with a link to another site, Real Climate. There, on the morning of November 17, 2009, was a veritable treasure trove for scientists and citizens who had long been skeptical about mankind's role in global warming.

The computers of the Hadley Climate Research Unit of the University of East Anglia, England, were hacked, whereupon over a thousand e-mails and over four thousand extraordinarily revealing documents were made public, showing how global warming advocates plotted to deceive the public about the holes in the theory. The miracle had indeed happened: it was revealed not only that "global warming" was a hoax, but that its foremost advocates knew it was a hoax, and strategized on how to keep that information from the American people.

According to Dr. Tim Ball, an environmental consultant and former climatology professor at the University of Winnipeg, the Hadley Unit controlled the Intergovernmental Panel on Climate Change (IPCC) Reports and prepared the Summary for Policymakers (SPM). These reports were the linchpin of the efforts to convince the public that rapid action had to be taken by governments to reverse the effects of man-made global warming. [18]

The scientists who prepared these reports were lying, and they knew they were lying. In one of the e-mails Phil Jones, the head of the Climate Research Unit (CRU) and—up to this point—one of the most respected global warming advocates internationally, casually tells his colleagues how he manipulated data to hide evidence that average temperatures are actually decreasing, not increasing: "I've just completed Mike's Nature trick of adding in the real temps to each series for the last 20 years (ie from 1981 onwards) amd [*sic*] from 1961 for Keith's to hide the decline." Another scientist admits that the data don't fit the theory for which Obama was ready to subject America to international authorities: "The fact is that we can't account for the lack of warming at the moment and it is a travesty that we can't."

The scientists discussed at length how to close their fellow scientists who were skeptical about global warming out of the climate-change debate, and ultimately discredit them completely: "This was the danger of always criticising the skeptics for not publishing in the 'peer-reviewed literature'. Obviously, they found a solution to that—take over a journal! So what do we do about this? I think we have to stop considering 'Climate Research' as a legitimate peer-reviewed journal. Perhaps we should encourage our colleagues in the climate research community to no longer submit to, or cite papers in, this journal. We would also need to consider what we tell or request of our more reasonable colleagues who currently sit on the editorial board. . . . What do others think?"[19]

Ball concludes: "Of course the IPCC Reports and especially the SPM Reports are the basis for Kyoto and the Copenhagen Accord, but now we know they are based on completely falsified and manipulated data and science. It is no longer a suspicion. Surely this is the death knell for the CRU [Climatic Research Unit at the University of East Anglia], the IPCC, Kyoto and Copenhagen and the Carbon Credits shell game."[20]

Even *The New York Times*, while remaining smug about the total victory of global warming advocates, revealed that it was shaken: "The evidence pointing to a growing human contribution to global warming is so widely accepted that the hacked material is unlikely to erode the overall argument. However, the documents will undoubtedly raise questions about the quality of research on some specific questions and the actions of some scientists." Yet it quoted one climatologist whose assessment was a bit more honest: "This is not a smoking gun; this is a mushroom cloud."[21]

The corrupt, activist media worked hard to bury this explosive story. Environmental reporter Andrew Revkin explained primly in *The New York Times* why the Paper of Record was not printing the e-mails: "The documents appear to have been acquired illegally and contain all manner of private information and statements that were never intended for the public eye, so they won't be posted here."[22]

"Acquired illegally"? "Statements that were never intended for the public eye"? Funny how that never seemed to bother them when they published *The Pentagon Papers*.

Yet despite the "mushroom cloud" hanging over what had been the assured proof of man-made global warming, Obama headed to Europe at the end of November to accept his Nobel Peace Prize and make what he promised would be a major address on global warming. Many of us have exposed the hoax of climate change as revealed by legitimate, responsible scientists for years, but still Obama and the socialist elites were determined to rob us blind and torment us with legislation and regulation on what they continued to call "the greatest threat facing humanity."

As Obama headed to Copenhagen, White House press secretary Robert Gibbs dismissed the leaked e-mails and the fraud they revealed: "I think there's no real scientific basis for the dispute of this"—that is, anthropogenic global warming.[23] "There is nothing in the hacked e-mails that undermines the science upon which this decision is based," Environmental Protection Agency chief Lisa Jackson gamely asserted.[24] Global warming czar Carol Browner likewise clung doggedly to her tattered faith: "There has been for a very long time a very small group of people who continue to say this isn't a real problem, that we don't need to do anything. On the other hand, we have 2,500 of the world's foremost scientists who are in absolute agreement that this is a real problem and that we need to do something and we need to do something as soon as possible. What am I going to do, side with the couple of naysayers out there, or the 2,500 scientists? I'm sticking with the 2,500 scientists. I mean, these people have been studying this issue for a very, very long time, and agree that the problem is real."[25]

That they might have come to such an agreement based on fraudulent data didn't seem to trouble her.

The irony was thick. When Barack Obama appointed his science czar, John P. Holdren, he declared that "promoting science isn't just about providing resources." Rather, "it's about ensuring that facts and evidence are never twisted or obscured by politics or ideology. It's about listening to what our scientists have to say, even when it's inconvenient—especially when it's inconvenient."[26]

Except, apparently, when the inconvenient truths involved the fraud of global warming. In that event, it was no longer important to listen to "our scientists" at all, or to read their embarrassing e-mails.

Sarah Palin urged Obama to reconsider and boycott the Copenhagen conference, and skewered his hypocrisy: "Policy should be based on sound science, not snake oil. . . . Policy decisions require real science and real solutions, not junk science and doomsday scare tactics pushed by an environmental priesthood that capitalizes on the public's worry and makes them feel that owning an SUV is a 'sin' against the planet. In his inaugural address, President Obama declared his intention to 'restore science to its rightful place.' Boycotting Copenhagen while this scandal is thoroughly investigated would send a strong message that the United States government will not be a party to fraudulent scientific practices. Saying no to Copenhagen and cap and tax are first steps in 'restoring science to its rightful place.'"[27]

Palin kept up the pressure, writing a week later in *The Washington Post* that "what Obama really hopes to bring home from Copenhagen is more pressure to pass the Democrats' cap-and-tax proposal. This is a political move. The last thing America needs is misguided legislation that will raise taxes and cost jobs—particularly when the push for such legislation rests on agenda-driven science."[28]

But Barack Hussein Obama paid no heed. And so, with the prospect of international climate controls looming, American sovereignty was once again threatened.

E P I L O G U E

WHAT LOVERS OF FREEDOM *MUST* DO

When the history of the Obama administration is written, one of its most heinous crimes will be its deliberate policy of destroying American superiority.

We are living at a time of so many firsts, it is difficult to get one's arms and one's mind around it. As I said at the beginning of this book, America is being tested in a way she has never been tested before—and you won't like what comes after America.

In the first year of the post-American presidency, both Iran and North Korea were emboldened to press forward with their nuclear-weapons programs. At the end of December 2009, Gao Shangtao, a professor of international relations at Beijing's China Foreign Affairs University, was blunt: "The world is worse off than a year ago." Iran and North Korea "will not give up."

Mark Fitzpatrick of the London-based International Institute for Strategic Studies said flatly about Iran and North Korea: "Nothing seems to have worked." UN sanctions proved powerless even to slow them down. Obama's repeated calls for negotiations came to nothing. Nations that have depended upon the United States to aid in their defense—notably Israel and the Asian states surrounding North Korea—are quietly exploring other options in the new, post-American world.[1]

And that's after a year of Obama. Imagine what the world will be like after four years of the post-American presidency.

Obama has moved against free speech and free media, raised taxes, and moved to nationalize the health-care system. In what arena has he ever endorsed independence of thought, action, or property?

America is not dead. But it is time to stand up.

Fight! Defiance is our answer. This is the quintessentially American answer to overwhelming government authority.

For the first time in modern history, during the first months of the Obama administration millions of Americans took to the streets to protest big government. The protesters came in all races, creeds, colors, and ages. This was not a movement limited to one demographic group; it was a distinctly American movement. And while the media tried to pigeonhole it with limiting labels like tea parties, town hall meetings, or 912ers, in reality it was a singular expression of outrage that heralded the beginning of a new American revolution. It was an ordinarily docile population motivated to take to the streets of their towns and cities or jump into the car and head to D.C. to try to stop Obama and the Democrats from plunging the freest nation on earth down the road to serfdom.[2]

These protests were a great American moment. And they were ignored in official Washington. The will of the people was dismissed the way an autocratic ruler would turn away supplicants with haughty indifference. It spoke volumes as to what we were dealing with in the White House, the Senate, and the House.

America is under siege. The people are peacefully rebelling and are being summarily ignored. So what is to be done?

First, we must vote them out. We must kick them out in 2010. We must do this overwhelmingly. We must get involved in local politics. Start with your school boards and city councils. Become a precinct captain. This is what the Left has done. They run Democrats on Republican tickets while we busy ourselves with work, family, hearth, and home. We must take their game plan and use it for the good.

We have been co-opted and conquered while we slept. We cannot take the greatest country in the history of the world for granted. Do we mean for our children and grandchildren to be held hostage to nuclear terrorists and live as slaves to a crushing debt that cannot be paid?

Is that who we are? Is that our legacy?

Our parents and grandparents are thought of as the "greatest generation." They saved the free world. They destroyed the Third Reich. How will we fight this century's Nazis? Will we continue to shun our responsibilities to protect and defend our political and economic freedom? If we do, we will go down in history as the "worst generation"—as cowards and degenerate spenders. Our children and our grandchildren will hate us unless we stand up and fight for our freedoms, and practice peaceful civil disobedience against laws that are coercive and unconstitutional.

Samuel Adams said it in the days of the Revolution: "The liberties of our country, the freedoms of our civil Constitution are worth defending at all hazards; it is our duty to defend them against all attacks. We have received them as a fair inheritance from our worthy ancestors. They purchased them for us with toil and danger and expense of treasure and blood. It will bring a mark of everlasting infamy on the present generation—enlightened as it is—if we should suffer them to be wrested from us by violence without a struggle, or to be cheated out of them by the artifices of designing men."

This does not have to happen. We must choose our candidates wisely and educate the people. You must teach. People need to know who Saul Alinsky was and why his teachings are so dangerous. People need to know exactly what is wrong with socialism and statism, and why the freedom of speech is so important. People need to know why Islamic supremacism is subversive, threatening the core principles upon which our freedoms are based.

We have to get behind politicians who understand political freedom, capitalism, and Sharia. We need rugged individualists like Sarah Palin, Rep. Michele Bachmann (R-MN), and Florida congressional candidate Lt. Col. Allen West. Find ideal men and women in your community and get behind them. Men and women as they ought to be in this low state of the world. They exist.

We must elect candidates in 2010 and 2012 who oppose Obama's socialist and internationalist policies—candidates in sufficient numbers to enable us simply to refuse funding to the post-American president's most destructive policies.

This will be an uphill battle with the mainstream media shilling for Obama. The media has abdicated its role as public servant. The mainstream media is a corrupt, activist arm of the Hard Left. They no longer cover the news. So you must fight in that arena also. You must choose who edits your news. Find reliable news sources you trust. Become acquainted with the alternative media, the new media, the free media.

Take nothing at face value. Many of our institutions are beyond infiltration—the enemy is in charge (the State Department is a perfect example). They must be rooted out, but this cannot happen until the treasonous clowns who allowed them this access in the first place are voted out. That is what must be done or America cannot be saved.

There is no doubt in my mind that we will win, that good will triumph over evil. But at what cost?

Former Democratic National Committee chairman Howard Dean made it explicit in an April 2009 speech:

There's not so much of a debate on the left anymore about capitalism, whether we should have it or not. There's a debate about how to have it. I think capitalism is always going to be with us because capitalism represents part of human nature, but the other part of human nature is communitarianism. There's a natural tendency of human beings—in addition to wanting to do things for themselves, they feel a great responsibility in wanting to be part of the community. So I think the debate for the new generation, instead of capitalism or socialism, is we're going to have both, and then which proportion of each should we have in order to make this all work. It's a much more sensible debate.[3]

And a mixed economy is exactly what Obama has planned.

You cannot have both capitalism and socialism. It's just that simple. To attempt this is to sign the death warrant of a free nation. And so now, if America ain't dead yet, the patient is surely on life support. Think Obama's health-care plan: the problem is the doctor who has vowed to nurse the patient back to health, but is choosing remedies that will only make the sickness worse.

"The fundamental principle of capitalism," says Ayn Rand, "is the *separation of* State and Economics—that is: the liberation of men's economic activities, of production and trade, from any form of intervention, coercion, compulsion, regulation, or control by the government."[4]

Now Obama is doing all he can to discard that fundamental principle, while rendering us subject to international authorities that do not have America's best interests at heart, and rolling back our defenses against enemies newly emboldened by his weakness.

After just one year of the post-American presidency, on January 29, 2010, Solidarity hero and former Polish president Lech Walesa spoke of the new post-American world: "The United States is only one superpower. Today they lead the world. Nobody has doubts about it—militarily. They also lead economically, but they're getting weak. They don't lead morally and politically anymore. The world has no leadership. The United States was always the last resort and hope for all other nations. There was the hope, whenever something was going wrong, one could count on the United States. Today, we lost that hope."[5]

Our enemies could never have defeated us; we can only defeat ourselves.

Whether Barack Hussein Obama succeeds in destroying America or not, those words could be the epitaph of his post-American presidency.

N O T E S

PREFACE

1. Nicholas Kristof, "Obama: Man of the World," *New York Times,* March 6, 2007.
2. Ayn Rand, *The Ayn Rand Letter 1971–1976* (New Milford, Conn.: Second Renaissance Press, 1990), pp. i, 5, 24.
3. "Could US elect a Luo before Kenya?" BBC News, January 3, 2008.
4. Kirsten Scharnberg and Kim Barker, "The Not-So-Simple Story of Barack Obama's Youth," *Chicago Tribune,* March 25, 2007.
5. "President Barack Obama's Inaugural Address," WhiteHouse.gov, January 21, 2009, http://www.whitehouse.gov/blog/inaugural-address.
6. Mark Silva, "Cheney: Obama 'More Radical' Than Seen," *Chicago Tribune,* December 8, 2009, available at http://www.swamppolitics.com/news/politics/blog/2009/12/cheney_obama_radical.html.
7. "*The Post-American World* by Fareed Zakaria," FareedZakaria.com, http://www.fareedzakaria.com/books/index.html.
8. Silva, "Cheney: Obama 'More Radical' Than Seen."
9. "Interview of the President by Laura Haim, Canal Plus," WhiteHouse.gov, June 1, 2009, http://www.whitehouse.gov/the_press_office/Transcript-of-the-Interview-of-the-President-by-Laura-Haim-Canal-Plus-6-1-09; "Remarks by President Obama to the Turkish Parliament," WhiteHouse.gov, April 6, 2009, http://www.whitehouse.gov/the_press_office/Remarks-By-President-Obama-To-The-Turkish-Parliament.

ONE: OBAMA AND AMERICAN EXCEPTIONALISM

1. Barack Obama, "Remarks by the President to the United Nations General Assembly," WhiteHouse.gov, September 23, 2009, http://www.whitehouse.gov/the_press_office/Remarks-by-the-President-to-the-United-Nations-General-Assembly.
2. Jamil Dakwar, "Protecting the Constitution, At Home and Abroad," ACLU.org, September 17, 2008, http://www.aclu.org/blog/human-rights/protecting-constitution-home-and-abroad.

331

3. "Bolder Bolton," National Rifle Association Institute for Legislative Action, May 7, 2009, http://www.nraila.org/Issues/Articles/Read.aspx?id=355&issue=015.

4. John Bolton, *Surrender is Not an Option* (New York: Threshold Editions, 2007), p. 89.

5. "US wins first seat on UN rights council," Associated Press, May 12, 2009.

6. Harvey Morris, "Obama to Seal US-UN Relationship," *Financial Times,* September 8, 2009.

7. Randall Mikkelsen, "U.S. drops 'enemy combatant' as basis for detention," Reuters, March 13, 2009.

8. Daniel Schwammenthal, "Prosecuting American 'War Crimes,'" *Wall Street Journal,* November 26, 2009.

9. Gerald Warner, "Barack Obama May Subject US Troops to International Criminal Court," *Telegraph,* March 6, 2009.

10. Schwammenthal, "Prosecuting American 'War Crimes.'"

11. Ibid.

12. Warner, "Barack Obama May Subject US Troops to International Criminal Court."

13. Phillip Barea, "Obama to Promote International Law and Diplomacy: Future American President has Progressive World View," Suite101.com, November 6, 2008, http://international-politics.suite101.com/article.cfm/obama_to_promote _international_law_and_diplomacy.

14. John B. Bellinger III, "A Global Court Quandary for the President," *Washington Post,* August 10, 2009.

15. Warner, "Barack Obama May Subject US Troops to International Criminal Court."

16. Frank Jordans, "UN body OKs call to curb religious criticism," Associated Press, March 26, 2009.

17. "Outcome Document of the Durban Review Conference," Durban Review Conference, http://www.un.org/durbanreview2009.

18. Rukmini Callimachi, "Defame Islam, Get Sued?" Associated Press, March 14, 2008.

19. Ariel Rabkin, "Who Controls the Internet?" *Weekly Standard,* May 25, 2009.

20. "Obama says US can work with Muslims: OIC," Agence France-Presse, February 1, 2009.

21. "The Secretary Announces the Office of the United States Special Representative to Muslim Countries (S/SRMC)," United States Department of State Department Notice, June 23, 2009; Patrick Goodenough, "Islamic Bloc Chief Urges Appointment of New US Envoy, But Is This It?" CNSNews.com, June 26, 2009.

22. "Biography: Farah Anwar Pandith, Special Representative to Muslim Communities," U.S. Department of State, http://www.state.gov/r/pa/ei/biog/125492.htm.

23. Stuart Taylor Jr., "Troubling Signals On Free Speech," *National Journal,* October 31, 2009.

24. Eugene Volokh, "Is the Obama Administration Supporting Calls to Outlaw Supposed Hate Speech?" Huffington Post, October 1, 2009, http://www.huffington post.com/eugene-volokh/is-the-obama-administrati_b_307132.html.

25. Ibid.

26. Ekmeleddin Ihsanoglu, "Speech of Secretary General at the thirty-fifth session of the Council of Foreign Ministers of the Organisation of the Islamic Conference," June 18, 2008, http://www.oic-oci.org/topic_detail.asp?t_id=1144&x_key=.

27. "Obama: 'Peace requires responsibility,'" CNN, December 10, 2009, http://www
    .cnn.com/2009/POLITICS/12/10/obama.transcript/index.html.

28. Sher Zieve, "Obama Begins Turnover of USA Sovereignty to International Body,"
    Canada Free Press, April 3, 2009, http://www.canadafreepress.com/index.php/
    article/9908.

29. Matthew Day, "President of Poland Signs Lisbon Treaty," *Telegraph,* October 10,
    2009.

30. "Barack Obama Praises EU's Lisbon Treaty Agreement," *Telegraph,* November 3,
    2009.

31. Simon Johnson, "John Bolton: Lisbon Treaty Will Undermine Democracy," *Tele-
    graph,* June 8, 2008.

32. "AIM Says Media Cover-Up Obama's Socialist-Oriented Global Tax Bill," Accu-
    racy In Media, February 13, 2008, http://www.aim.org/press-release/aim-says-media
    -cover-up-obamas-socialist-oriented-global-tax-bill.

33. David Adam, "Copenhagen Negotiating Text: 200 Pages to Save the World?"
    Guardian, September 28, 2009.

34. Lord Christopher Monckton, address at Bethel University, St. Paul, Minnesota, Oc-
    tober 14, 2009, http://www.youtube.com/watch?v=PMe5dOgbu40&feature=player
    _embedded.

35. Mark Steyn, "The 'Science' of Global Warming," *Maclean's,* December 3, 2009,
    http://www2.macleans.ca/2009/12/03/the-science-of-global-warming.

36. Daniel Terris, Cesare P.R. Romano, and Leigh Swigart, *The International Judge: An
    Introduction to the Men and Women Who Decide the World's Cases* (Waltham, Mass.:
    Brandeis University Press, 2007), p. ix.

37. Collin Levy, "Sotomayor and International Law," *Wall Street Journal,* July 14, 2009.

38. Nathan Figler, "Obama's Supreme Pick," American News Inc., May 26, 2009, avail-
    able at http://jumpinginpools.blogspot.com/2009/05/sotomayor-gun-ownership.html
    #ixzz0YVlcoSQC.

39. M. Edward Whelan III, "Harold Koh's Transnationalism," *National Review On-
    line*'s Bench Memos, April 16, 2009, available at http://www.eppc.org/publications/
    pubID.3793/pub_detail.asp#Part10.

40. Eric Lichtblau, "After Attacks, Supporters Rally Around Choice for Top Adminis-
    tration Legal Job," *New York Times,* April 1, 2009.

41. Whelan III, "Harold Koh's Transnationalism."

42. Meghan Clyne, "Obama's Most Perilous Legal Pick," *New York Post,* March 30,
    2009.

43. Ibid.

44. Robin Reeves Zorthian, letter to the *New York Post,* April 1, 2009.

45. "Sharia law in UK is 'unavoidable,'" BBC News, February 7, 2008.

46. "The UN And International Treaties," National Rifle Association Institute for
    Legislative Action, November 25, 2009, http://www.nraila.org/Legislation/Read
    .aspx?ID=5224.

47. "Bolder Bolton," National Rifle Association Institute for Legislative Action.

48. Ayn Rand, *Capitalism: The Unknown Ideal* (New York: Signet, 1986), p. 148.

49. Andrew Bostom, "From Communism as 'The 20th Century Islam,' to 'Islam as
    the 21st Century Communism'?" AndrewBostom.com, December 5, 2009, http://
    www.andrewbostom.org/blog/2009/12/05/from-communism-as-%E2%80%9Cthe

-20th-century-islam%E2%80%9D-to-%E2%80%9Cislam-as-the-21st-century
-communism%E2%80%9D/.

TWO: THE INDOCTRINATION OF BARACK OBAMA

1. Ryan Lizza, "Making It: How Chicago Shaped Obama," *New Yorker,* July 21, 2008.
2. Kirsten Scharnberg and Kim Barker, "The Not-So-Simple Story of Barack Obama's Youth," *Chicago Tribune,* March 25, 2007.
3. Barack Obama, *The Audacity of Hope* (New York: Three Rivers Press, 2006), p. 274.
4. Ibid., pp. 278–279.
5. Ibid., pp. 274–275.
6. Andrew Walden, "What Barack Obama Learned from the Communist Party," *American Thinker,* July 8, 2008.
7. Dan Boylan, " '08: Year of Obama," *MidWeek,* January 2, 2008.
8. Walden, "What Barack Obama Learned from the Communist Party."
9. Barack Obama, *Dreams from My Father* (New York: Crown Publishers, 1995), pp. 46–47.
10. Amanda Ripley, "The Story of Barack Obama's Mother," *Time,* April 9, 2008.
11. Tim Jones, "Obama's Mom: Not Just a Girl from Kansas: Part 2," *Chicago Tribune,* March 27, 2008.
12. Morgan Reynolds, "Timothy Geithner and the Ruling Class," LewRockwell.com, February 12, 2009.
13. "Barack Hussein Obama," Discover the Networks, http://www.discoverthenet works.org/individualProfile.asp?indid=1511.
14. Obama, *Dreams from My Father,* p. 98.
15. *Unfit for Publication: An Investigative Report on the Lies in Jerome Corsi's "Obama Nation,"* pamphlet published by Obama for America, 2008, p. 9, available at http://www.google.com/url?sa=t&source=web&ct=res&cd=1&ved=0CAsQFjAA&url=htt p%3A%2F%2Fobama.3cdn.net%2Fa74586f9067028c40a_5km6vrqwa.pdf&rct=j&q =%22Unfit+for+Publication%22+Obama&ei=7ZmWS6XiIJGXtgeLjaXtDQ&usg =AFQjCNFrAQV7ys8YYaLtgMIqIzpEiILXjw.
16. James A. Miller, "Frank Marshall Davis: Black Moods: Collected Poems," *African American Review,* Summer-Fall, 2003.
17. Gerald Horne, "Rethinking the History and Future of the Communist Party," *Political Affairs,* March 28, 2007, http://www.politicalaffairs.net/article/articleview/ 5047/1/32.
18. Ibid.
19. Toby Harnden, "Frank Marshall Davis, Alleged Communist, was Early Influence on Barack Obama," *Telegraph,* August 22, 2008.
20. Ibid.
21. Horne, "Rethinking the History and Future of the Communist Party."
22. Abul A'la Maududi, *Jihad in Islam* (Beirut: The Holy Koran Publishing House, n.d., originally published 1939), p. 10.
23. Art Moore, "Did CAIR founder say Islam to rule America?" WorldNetDaily, December 11, 2006.
24. Mohamed Akram, "An Explanatory Memorandum on the General Strategic Goal for the Group in North America," May 22, 1991, Government Exhibit 003-0085, *U.S. vs. HLF,* et al., p. 7(21).

25. Ahmed ibn Naqib al-Misri, *Reliance of the Traveller ('Umdat al-Salik): A Classic Manual of Islamic Sacred Law,* transl. Ha Mim Keller (Beltsville, MD: Amana Publications, 1999), o11.10.

26. Bat Yeor, "Geert Wilders and the Fight for Europe," *National Review,* February 16, 2009.

27. *'Umdat al-Salik,* o4.9.

28. "McCain supporter plays up 'Hussein,'" MSNBC First Read, February 26, 2008, http://firstread.msnbc.msn.com/archive/2008/02/26/702467.aspx.

29. Nathan Thornburgh, "Why Is Obama's Middle Name Taboo?" *Time,* February 28, 2008.

30. Juan Cole, "Obama should be proud to be named Hussein," Salon, February 28, 2008.

31. Lynn Sweet, "Obama at Florida Fund-raiser Says GOP Will Go After Him Because He is Black. Pool report," *Chicago Sun-Times,* June 20, 2008.

32. Jake Tapper and Sunlen Miller, "The Emergence of President Obama's Muslim Roots," ABC News, June 2, 2009.

33. Christi Parsons, John McCormick, and Peter Nicholas, "Barack Obama Plans to Reach Out to Muslim World," *Chicago Tribune,* December 10, 2008.

34. Barack Obama, "Remarks By The President On A New Beginning," June 4, 2009, http://www.whitehouse.gov/the_press_office/Remarks-by-the-President-at-Cairo-University-6-04-09.

35. "Obama's Verbal Slip Fuels His Critics," *Washington Times,* September 7, 2008.

36. "Obama asked about connection to Islam," MSNBC First Read, December 22, 2007, http://firstread.msnbc.msn.com/archive/2007/12/22/531492.aspx.

37. Tapper and Miller, "The Emergence of President Obama's Muslim Roots."

38. Ibid.

39. "Obama asked about connection to Islam."

40. Aaron Klein, "Obama anti-smear site: 'He was never a Muslim,'" WorldNetDaily, June 12, 2008.

41. Nicholas D. Kristof, "Obama: Man of the World," *New York Times,* March 6, 2007.

42. Obama, *Dreams from My Father,* p. 154.

43. Kim Barker, "Obama Madrassa Myth Debunked," *Chicago Tribune,* March 25, 2007.

44. Kim Barker, "History of Schooling Distorted," *Chicago Tribune,* March 25, 2007.

45. "Tracking Down Obama in Indonesia—Part 5," An American Expat in Southeast Asia, January 28, 2007, http://laotze.blogspot.com/2007/01/tracking-down-obama-in-indonesia-part-5.html.

46. "Obama and the Inconvenient Truth," An American Expat in Southeast Asia, January 10, 2008, http://laotze.blogspot.com/2008/01/obama-and-inconvenient-truth.html.

47. "Tracking Down Obama in Indonesia—Part 3," An American Expat in Southeast Asia, January 24, 2007, http://laotze.blogspot.com/2007/01/tracking-down-obama-in-indonesia-part-3.html; Nedra Pickler, "Obama Debunks Claim About Islamic School," The Associated Press, January 24, 2007. Photo of registration card at http://www.daylife.com/photo/01u33pL9Ns06D.

48. Paul Watson, "As a Child, Obama Crossed a Cultural Divide in Indonesia," *Los Angeles Times,* March 15, 2007.

49. Jodi Kantor, "A Candidate, His Minister and the Search for Faith," *New York Times,* April 30, 2007.

50. "Obama and the Inconvenient Truth."

51. David A. Patten, "Obama 'Lying' About Muslim Past, Expert Says," Newsmax, October 9, 2008.

52. "The Truth About Barack's Faith," FightTheSmears.com, http://fightthesmears.com/articles/3/baracksfaith.

53. "Obama Has Never Been A Muslim, And Is a Committed Christian," dated November 12, 2007, but containing numerous later revisions, http://www.barackobama.com/factcheck/2007/11/12/obama_has_never_been_a_muslim_1.php.

54. Katharine Houreld, "Obama's grandma slams 'untruths,'" Associated Press, March 5, 2008.

55. "Obama's Grandmother to Perform Haj," Daily Times (Pakistan), May 3, 2009.

56. "Obama's Church," *Investor's Business Daily,* January 15, 2008.

57. "'Meet the Press' transcript for Oct. 19, 2008," MSNBC, October 19, 2008, http://www.msnbc.msn.com/id/27266223.

58. Obama, *The Audacity of Hope,* p. 261.

59. That Muslims recite the Fatihah seventeen times daily: Abdullah Rahman, "Surat al-Fatihah," Quran-Tafsir.org, http://www.quran-tafsir.org/; that it refers to Jews and Christians: Ibn Kathir, *Tafsir Ibn Kathir* (abridged), vol. 1 (Houston: Dar-us-Salam Publications, 2000), p. 87. This is the view of Tabari, Zamakhshari, the *Tafsir al-Jalalayn,* the *Tanwir al-Miqbas min Tafsir Ibn Abbas,* and Ibn Arabi, as well as Ibn Kathir.

60. Obama, *Dreams from My Father,* p. 100.

61. Ibid., pp. 100–01.

62. Adam Schatz, "Frantz Fanon: The Doctor Prescribed Violence," *New York Times,* September 2, 2001.

63. Deborah Lambert, "Obama, A College Marxist?" Accuracy in Academia, February 22, 2010, http://www.academia.org/obama-a-college-marxist-2/.

64. "Barack Hussein Obama," Discover the Networks, http://www.discoverthenetworks.org/individualProfile.asp?indid=1511.

65. Ibid.

66. David Moberg, "Obama's Community Roots," *Nation,* April 3, 2007, http://www.thenation.com/doc/20070416/moberg.

67. Ryan Lizza, "The Agitator: Barack Obama's Unlikely Political Education," *New Republic,* March 19, 2007.

68. Andrew Walden, "What Barack Obama Learned from the Communist Party," *American Thinker,* July 8, 2008.

69. Michael Dobbs, "Obama's 'Weatherman' Connection," *Washington Post,* February 19, 2008.

70. Stanley Kurtz, "Chicago Annenberg Challenge Shutdown?" *National Review,* August 18, 2008.

71. George Neumayr, "Guilt by Agreement," *American Spectator,* October 9, 2008.

72. Aaron Klein, "Obama worked closely with terrorist Bill Ayers," WorldNetDaily, September 23, 2008; Aaron Klein, "Meet Obama's new Bill Ayers associate," WorldNetDaily, September 14, 2008.

73. Chris Fusco and Abdon M. Pallasch, "Who is Bill Ayers?" *Chicago Sun-Times,* April 18, 2008.

74. Sammy Benoit, "White House Releases Visitors List. Soros, ACORN/SEIU and

Others," The Lid, October 30, 2009, http://yidwithlid.blogspot.com/2009/10/white-house-releases-visitors-listayers.html.

75. Norm Eisen, "75,000 White House Visitor Records Posted Online," The White House Blog, January 29, 2010, http://www.whitehouse.gov/blog/2010/01/29/75000-white-house-visitor-records-posted-online.

76. Bill Dedman, "Obama blocks list of visitors to White House," MSNBC, June 16, 2009, http://www.msnbc.msn.com/id/31373407.

77. Bill Dedman, "Group sues for Obama White House visitor list," MSNBC, December 9, 2009, http://www.msnbc.msn.com/id/34347510.

78 Lizza, "The Agitator: Barack Obama's Unlikely Political Education."

79. Ashahed M. Muhammad, "Farrakhan: America's Time Is Up," The Final Call, December 2, 2009.

80. Thomas Lipscomb, "Did Bill Ayers Write Obama's Book?" Accuracy In Media, November 27, 2009, http://www.aim.org/aim-report/did-bill-ayers-write-obamas-book.

81. Klein, "Obama anti-smear site: 'He was never a Muslim.'"

82. Jodi Kantor, "Barack Obama's Search for Faith," *New York Times,* April 30, 2007.

83. Lisa Miller and Richard Wolffe, "Finding His Faith," *Newsweek,* July 12, 2008.

84. "Obama's Church."

85. Michael Tomasky, "Wright and Wrong," *Guardian,* March 14, 2008.

86. Pamela Geller, "Obama Refuses to Say Bombing Hiroshima Was the 'Right Decision,'" AtlasShrugs.com, November 14, 2009, http://atlasshrugs2000.typepad.com/atlas_shrugs/2009/11/obama-refuses-to-say-bombing-hiroshima-was-the-right-decision.html.

87. Sammy Benoit, "White House Releases Visitors List. Soros, ACORN/SEIU and Others."

88. Lynn Sweet, "Senator Rebukes Kenya's Corruption," *Chicago Sun-Times,* August 29, 2006.

89. Mark Hyman, "Obama's Kenya Ghosts," *Washington Times,* October 12, 2008.

90. Sweet, "Senator Rebukes Kenya's Corruption."

91. "Obama's Kenya 'honeymoon' ends abruptly after graft rebuke," Agence France-Presse, August 29, 2006.

92. Thomas Mukoya and Leon Malherbe, "Some Kenyans forget crisis to root for Obama," Reuters, January 8, 2008.

93. Xan Rice, "Loud and Populist, but No Political Outsider," *Guardian,* December 29, 2007; "About Raila," Raila2007.com, http://www.raila07.com/about.html.

94. Hyman, "Obama's Kenya Ghosts."

95. "The Golden Chain," Wikipedia, accessed November 23, 2009, http://en.wikipedia.org/wiki/The_Golden_Chain.

96. "How rich is Raila, the ODM-Kenya Presidential aspirant," African Press International, April 26, 2007.

97. Stephen Mbogo, "Outcome of Kenyan Election Could Impact Anti-Terror Cooperation," CNSNews.com, October 17, 2007.

98. Joshua Hammer, "The African Front," *New York Times,* December 23, 2007.

99. Daniel Blake, "Concerns Raised Over Alleged Vow to Enforce Islamic Law in Kenya," Christian Post, December 18, 2007.

100. Ibid.

101. Hyman, "Obama's Kenya Ghosts."
102. Blake, "Concerns Raised Over Alleged Vow to Enforce Islamic Law in Kenya."
103. Bernard Namunane, "Kenya: Revealed—Raila's Real MoU With Muslims," *Daily Nation,* November 28, 2007.
104. Ibid.
105. Blake, "Concerns Raised Over Alleged Vow to Enforce Islamic Law in Kenya."
106. Ibid.
107. David Lewis, "Violence we fled was planned, say Kenyan refugees," Reuters, January 26, 2008.
108. Hyman, "Obama's Kenya Ghosts."
109. "Mob burns Kenyans seeking refuge in church," CNN, January 1, 2008.
110. Sam Kiplagat, "Kenya: Violence Planned Before Poll, Says Report," *Daily Nation,* March 18, 2008.
111. David Lewis, "Violence we fled was planned, say Kenyan refugees," Reuters, January 26, 2008.
112. Mike Pflanz, "I'm Barack Obama's Cousin, Says Raila Odinga," *Telegraph,* January 8, 2008.
113. "Odinga says Obama is his cousin," BBC News, January 8, 2008.
114. Laura Blue, "The Demons That Still Haunt Africa," *Time,* January 10, 2008.
115. "Change and Hope: Iranian President Mahmoud Ahmadinejad Meets With Obama's Cousin in Kenya," Audacity of Hypocrisy, February 25, 2009, http://www.audacityofhypocrisy.com/2009/02/25/change-and-hope-iranian-president-mahmoud-ahmadinejad-meets-with-obamas-cousin-in-kenya/.

THREE: OBAMA AND THE JEWS

1. Caroline B. Glick, "Obama's Failure, Netanyahu's Opportunity," Jewish World Review, November 13, 2009.
2. Ali Abunimah, "How Barack Obama learned to love Israel," The Electronic Intifada, March 4, 2007.
3. Pamela Geller, "Obama's Anti-Semitic Perspective . . . Show me your friends and I'll show you who and what you are," AtlasShrugs.com, October 7, 2009, http://atlasshrugs2000.typepad.com/atlas_shrugs/2009/10/obamas-antisemitic-perspective.html.
4. Peggy Shapiro, "Reverend Wright: The Bible and No Jews," *American Thinker,* March 19, 2008.
5. Ryan Lizza, "The Agitator: Barack Obama's Unlikely Political Education," *The New Republic,* March 19, 2007.
6. Tony Vega, "Barack Obama's Church Honors Nation of Islam Leader Louis Farrakhan," Associated Content, January 8, 2008.
7. Richard Cohen, "Obama's Farrakhan Test," *Washington Post,* January 15, 2008.
8. Robert Wistrich, *Hitler's Apocalypse: Jews and the Nazi Legacy* (New York: St. Martin's Press, 1986), pp. 189–90.
9. "Farrakhan In His Own Words," Anti-Defamation League, May 5, 2009, http://www.adl.org/special_reports/farrakhan_own_words2/farrakhan_own_words.asp.
10. Ibid.
11. Stanley Kurtz, "History of Wright and Farrakhan," *National Review*'s The Corner, April 29, 2008.

12. Dana Milbank, "Could Rev. Spell Doom for Obama?" *Washington Post,* April 28, 2008.

13. Nathan Guttman, "Farrakhan Casts Long Shadow on Campaign Trail," Jewish Daily Forward, March 7, 2008.

14. Rev. Jeremiah Wright, "War On Iraq IQ Test," Mindfully.org, 2003. Quoted in Ed Lasky, "Barack Obama and Israel," *American Thinker,* January 16, 2008.

15. David Squires, "Rev. Jeremiah Wright Says 'Jews' Are Keeping Him from President Obama," *Newport News (VA) Daily Press,* June 10, 2009.

16. "Obama: Israeli Settlement Construction Could be 'Dangerous,' " VOA News, November 18, 2009.

17. Cohen, "Obama's Farrakhan Test."

18. Kenneth R. Timmerman, "Obama Had Close Ties to Top Saudi Adviser at Early Age," Newsmax, September 3, 2008.

19. Jacob Gershman, "Saudis Funded Columbia Program At Institute That Trained Teachers," *New York Sun,* March 10, 2005.

20. Adam Daifallah, "Said Chair At Columbia Also Backed By Saudis," *New York Sun,* July 23, 2003.

21. Gershman, "Saudis Funded Columbia Program At Institute That Trained Teachers."

22. Aaron Klein, "Obama worked with terrorist: Senator helped fund organization that rejects 'racist' Israel's existence," WorldNetDaily, February 24, 2008.

23. Ed Lasky, "The Said-Khalidi-Obama Connection," *American Thinker,* October 22, 2008.

24. Klein, "Obama worked with terrorist: Senator helped fund organization that rejects 'racist' Israel's existence."

25. "McCain Campaign Accuses L.A. Times of 'Suppressing' Obama Video," *Los Angeles Times,* October 29, 2008.

26. Peter Wallsten, "Allies of Palestinians see a friend in Obama," *Los Angeles Times,* April 10, 2008.

27. Wallsten, "Allies of Palestinians see a friend in Obama."

28. Federal Election Commission, "Foreign Nationals," July 2003, http://www.fec.gov/pages/brochures/foreign.shtml.

29. "Obama's Gazan Contributions," AtlasShrugs.com, July 31, 2008; Pamela Geller, "Obama's Foreign Donors: The media averts its eyes," *American Thinker,* August 14, 2008.

30. Video at http://www.youtube.com/watch?v=21YF7ggCG6g.

31. http://watchdog.net/p/barack_obama.

32. Mohamed Akram, "An Explanatory Memorandum on the General Strategic Goal for the Group in North America," May 22, 1991, Government Exhibit 003-0085, *U.S. vs. HLF,* et al, pp. 7–8 (21–22).

33. Ibid.

34. Glenn R. Simpson, "Tangled Paths: A Sprawling Probe Of Terror Funding Centers in Virginia," *Wall Street Journal,* June 21, 2004.

35. "Muslims in fed terror probe making donations to Obama," WorldNetDaily, August 29, 2008.

36. "Gaza's Obama campaign," Al-Jazeera English, March 31, 2008, http://www.youtube.com/watch?v=21YF7ggCG6g.

37. "Obama advisor calls for a military invasion of Israel," YouTube, September 7, 2008, http://www.youtube.com/watch?v=2oFkmcZT4OO.

38. Shmuel Rosner, "Obama's Top Adviser Says Does not Believe in Imposing a Peace Settlement," *Haaretz,* August 27, 2008.

39. Michael Rubin, "Obama Adviser Samantha Power on Israel, 'Jenin Massacre,'" *National Review*'s The Corner, February 11, 2008.

40. Sholto Byrnes, "Interview: Samantha Power," *New Statesman,* March 6, 2008.

41. "Statement by Press Secretary Robert Gibbs on the Appointment of Two Senior Officials Responsible for Iraqi Refugees and Internally Displaced Persons," White House press release, August 14, 2009, http://www.whitehouse.gov/the_press_office/Statement-by-Press-Secretary-Robert-Gibbs-on-the-Appointment-of-Two-Senior-Officials-Responsible-for-Iraqi-Refugees-and-Internally-Displaced-Persons/.

42. Aaron Klein, "Obama Policy Adviser Raises Israeli Concerns," *Jewish Week,* January 30, 2008.

43. Tom Baldwin, "Barack Obama Sacks Adviser Over Talks with Hamas," *Times* (London), May 10, 2008.

44. "Obama Promises Improved Ties With Egypt, Syria," *Middle East Newsline,* November 5, 2008.

45. Klein, "Obama Policy Adviser Raises Israeli Concerns."

46. Alex Spillius, "Obama supporter accuses Jews of 'McCarthyism,'" Independent.ie, May 27, 2008.

47. Gerald Posner, "How Obama Flubbed His Missile Message," The Daily Beast, September 18, 2009.

48. Rosa Brooks, "Israel Can't Bomb Its Way to Peace," *Los Angeles Times,* January 1, 2009.

49. Rosa Brooks, "Criticize Israel? You're an Anti-Semite!," *Los Angeles Times,* September 3, 2006.

50. "Obama Names Israel Critic to Intelligence Board," *Jerusalem Post,* October 29, 2009.

51. "Indecisive Senator Hagel has Questionable Israel Record," National Jewish Democratic Council, March 12, 2007, http://njdc.typepad.com/njdcs_blog/2007/03/indecisive_sena.html.

52. "Obama Names Israel Critic to Intelligence Board."

53. Sammy Benoit, "Obama Appoints Another Israel-Hating Adviser: Chuck Hagel," The Lid, October 28, 2009, http://yidwithlid.blogspot.com/2009/10/obama-appoints-another-israel-hating.html.

54. "Terms of Service," Organizing for America, http://www.barackobama.com/terms/.

55. Tom Burnett, "Open discussion includes all points of view," Organizing for America, June 23, 2008, http://my.barackobama.com/page/community/post/tcburnett/gG5hnt; Pamela Geller, "Obama Bans His Own Words But Sanctions Overthrow Of Congress & Jew Hate," AtlasShrugs.com, July 1, 2008, http://atlasshrugs2000.typepad.com/atlas_shrugs/2008/07/obama-deletes-h.html.

56. Bill Levinson, "Obama's Web Site Blows its Disclaimer, Now Responsible for All Hate Speech," Israpundit, June 28, 2008, http://www.israpundit.com/2008/?p=1427.

57. Bill Levinson, "Obama Blogger: 'Jews owe Africa and Africans everything they have today,'" Israpundit, April 7, 2008, http://www.israpundit.com/2008/?p=687.

58. Bill Levinson, "'Nazi Israel:' Obama's Official Web Site Equates Israel to Nazi Germany," Israpundit, October 4, 2009, http://www.israpundit.com/2008/?p=17346.

59. "Israeli intel warns Netanyahu on Obama policy: 'We have become an obstacle,'" *World Tribune,* April 21, 2009.

FOUR: OBAMA AND ISRAEL

1. Caroline Glick, "Our World: Obama's New World Order and Israel," *Jerusalem Post,* February 9, 2009.

2. Helene Cooper, "U.S. to Give $900 Million in Gaza Aid, Officials Say," *New York Times,* February 23, 2009.

3. Josef Federman, "UN halts aid to Gaza, cites Hamas disruption," Associated Press, February 6, 2009.

4. Caroline Glick, "Column One: Obama's Green Light to Attack Iran," *Jerusalem Post,* May 7, 2009.

5. Barak Ravid and Natasha Mozgovaya, "Obama Gets Tougher with Israel on Palestinians, Iran," *Haaretz,* May 5, 2009.

6. Glick, "Column One: Obama's Green Light to Attack Iran."

7. Louis Charbonneau, "U.S. wants Israel, India in anti-nuclear arms treaty," Reuters, May 5, 2009.

8. "Sen. Obama's Letter to U.N. Ambassador Zalmay Khalilzad," Organizing for America, January 22, 2008, http://my.barackobama.com/page/community/post/adamweissmann/g G5hjN.

9. "Obama under fire for comment on Palestinians," Associated Press, March 15, 2007.

10. Justin Elliott, "Obama's Israel Shuffle," *Mother Jones,* February 2008.

11. Lynn Sweet, "Obama's AIPAC speech: Text as prepared for delivery," *Chicago Sun-Times,* March 2, 2007.

12. "Obama under fire for comment on Palestinians"; "Democratic Candidates Debate," FactCheck.org, April 27, 2007, http://www.factcheck.org/elections-2008/democratic_candidates_debate.html.

13. Thomas Beaumont, "Obama Urges More Compassion in Mideast," *Des Moines Register,* March 12, 2007.

14. "Transcript: Obama's Speech at AIPAC," National Public Radio, June 4, 2008, http://www.npr.org/templates/story/story.php?storyId=91150432.

15. Sarah Silverman, "Sarah Silverman and The Great Schlep," YouTube, September 25, 2008, http://www.youtube.com/watch?v=AgHHX9R4Qtk.

16. Josh Gerstein, "U.S.: Facts Tie Muslim Groups To Hamas Front Case," *New York Sun,* July 11, 2008.

17. "ISNA Admits Hamas Ties," IPT News, July 25, 2008.

18. "Hamas Charter: The Covenant of the Islamic Resistance Movement (Hamas)," MidEast Web Historical Documents, August 18, 1988, http://www.mideastweb.org/hamas.htm.

19. Mohamed Akram, "An Explanatory Memorandum on the General Strategic Goal for the Brotherhood in North America," May 19, 1991, http://www.investigativeproject.org/document/id/20.

20. Charles A. Radin, "Islamic Leader Urges Jews be Wary of Fundamentalists," *Boston Globe,* March 14, 2007.

21. "Valerie Jarrett, Ingrid Mattson: White House Opens Wider to Islam," Maggie's Note-

book, July 23, 2009, http://maggiesnotebook.blogspot.com/2009/07/valerie-jarrett
-ingrid-matton-white.html.

22. "State Sponsors of Terrorism," U.S. Department of State, http://www.state.gov/s/ct/
c14151.htm.

23. "Ahmadinejad, Hezbollah chief Nasrallah meet in Damascus," *Haaretz,* July 19,
2007.

24. "Iran's Larijani meets Hamas in Damascus," Reuters, January 7, 2009.

25. "Obama returns US ambassador to Syria," FOXNews.com, June 24, 2009.

26. "Obama preparing to lift sanctions against Syria," World Tribune, February 9,
2009.

27. "Obama returns US ambassador to Syria."

28. "Syrian envoy: 'US lifts ban on air industry,'" *Jerusalem Post,* July 27, 2009.

29. Aaron Klein, "Obama opens up billions in business for Syria: Damascus gets crucial deal without promising to drop alliance with Iran," WorldNetDaily, October 9,
2009.

30. "Remarks by President Obama and Prime Minister Netanyahu of Israel in Press
Availability," WhiteHouse.gov, May 18, 2009, http://www.whitehouse.gov/the
_press_office/Remarks-by-President-Obama-and-Israeli-Prime-Minister-Netan
yahu-in-press-availability/

31. Khaled Abu Toameh, "Hamas reiterates its refusal to recognize Israel," *Jerusalem
Post,* May 16, 2009.

32. "Hamas: We won't accept two-state solution," Deutsche Presse-Agentur, May 9,
2009.

33. "Palestinian Ambassador to Lebanon Abbas Zaki: Two-State Solution Will Lead
to the Collapse of Israel," Middle East Media Research Institute, Special Dispatch
No. 2358, May 14, 2009.

34. Tzvi Ben Gedalyahu, "Rocket Attack on Sderot Home," Israel National News, May
19, 2009.

35. Farah Stockman, "Obama, Abbas talk peace," *Boston Globe,* May 28, 2009.

36. David Bedein, "US Admits Training Palestinian Armed Forces While PA Negoti-
ates With Hamas," *Bulletin* (Philadelphia), May 18, 2009.

37. Khaled Abu Toameh, "'Fatah has never recognized Israel,'" *Jerusalem Post*, July 22,
2009.

38. Glick, "Column One: Obama's green light to attack Iran."

39. "Transcript: Obama's Speech at AIPAC."

40. "Report: US seeks to aid Hamas-backed gov't," Ynet News, April 27, 2009.

41. Ibid.

42. "Gen. Jim Jones Reiterates US Commitment to Peace, Palestinian State at ATFP
Gala," American Task Force for Palestine, October 15, 2009, http://www.american
taskforce.org/in_media/pr/2009/10/16/1255665600.

43. Itamar Marcus and Nan Jacques Zilberdik, "Palestinian children learn: English is
the language of the enemy," Palestinian Media Watch, October 18, 2009.

44. "Warith Deen Umar: Jews 'Have Control of the World,'" The Investigative Project
on Terrorism, July 5, 2009, http://www.investigativeproject.org/1081/warith-deen
-umar-jews-have-control-of-the-world.

45. U.S. State Department, "'Palestine' Proposal Cable—Documentary & Series on
Muslims in America for Palestinians," available at http://atlasshrugs2000.typepad

.com/atlas_shrugs/2009/07/us-government-welcomes-hamas-mouthpiece-alquds-tv
-to-dc-to-film-propaganda.html.

46. Ibid.

47. Pamela Geller, "'Palestinian' Poll: 'How to Improve US Image'—Demands More Money! More R-E-S-P-E-C-T! Jerusalem!," AtlasShrugs.com, November 2, 2009, http://atlasshrugs2000.typepad.com/atlas_shrugs/2009/11/palestinian-poll-how-to-improve-us-image-demands-more-money-more-respect-jerusal em.html.

48. Gil Troy, "Center Field: Honoring Mary Robinson, Obama honors appeasement of anti-Semitism," *Jerusalem Post,* August 2, 2009.

49. Isi Liebler, "J Street's 'Pro-Israel' Stance is Phoney," *Guardian,* October 26, 2009.

50. Philip Klein, "Obama National Security Adviser to Speak at Anti-Israel Conference," *American Spectator,* October 16, 2009.

51. Liebler, "J Street's 'Pro-Israel' Stance is Phoney."

52. Hilary Leila Krieger, "Muslims, Arabs among J Street donors," *Jerusalem Post,* August 14, 2009.

53. Liebler, "J Street's 'Pro-Israel' Stance is Phoney."

54. Klein, "Obama National Security Adviser to Speak at Anti-Israel Conference."

55. Etgar Lefkovits, "Obama fails to name anti-Semitism envoy," *Jerusalem Post,* July 30, 2009.

56. Hannah Rosenthal, "Reclaiming The Pro-Israel Mantle," *Jewish Week* (New York), April 23, 2008.

57. Abraham H. Foxman, "An Open Letter To Hannah Rosenthal," *Jewish Week* (New York), May 1, 2008.

58. Ed Lasky, "Obama's Type of Anti-Semitism Fighter," *American Thinker,* November 11, 2009.

59. Patrick Goodenough, "Islamic Bloc Chief Urges Appointment of New US Envoy, But Is This It?" CNS News, June 26, 2009.

60. Barack Obama, "Remarks by the President to the United Nations General Assembly," September 23, 2009, http://www.whitehouse.gov/the_press_office/Remarks-by-the-President-to-the-United-Nations-General-Assembly/.

61. Aaron Klein, "Official: Obama 'disgusted' with Israel," WorldNetDaily, October 16, 2009.

62. "Clinton calls Israeli concessions 'unprecedented,'" Associated Press, November 1, 2009.

63. John Bolton, remarks on the *Glenn Beck* show, September 23, 2009. Transcribed at http://atlasshrugs2000.typepad.com/atlas_shrugs/2009/09/bolton-on-obama-at-the-un-this-is-the-most-radical-antiisrael-speech-i-can-recall-any-president-maki.html.

64. Efrat Weiss, "Israeli shot in West Bank," Ynet News, September 29, 2009.

65. Herb Keinon and Yaakov Katz, "IDF to remove 100 West Bank roadblocks," *Jerusalem Post,* September 16, 2009.

66. Stephanie Nebehay, "US urges Israel to probe Gaza crimes to boost peace," Reuters, September 29, 2009.

67. Anne Bayefsky, "The Goldstone Mission: The UN Blood Libel," statement at the Human Rights Council, Geneva, Switzerland, September 29, 2009.

68. "OIC initiated Goldstone inquiry," Al-Jazeera, October 28, 2009.

69. Muhammad Humaidan, "Al-Aqsa is the red line, warns OIC," Arab News, November 2, 2009.

70. Hana Levi Julian, "State Dept: US Goal to Expel Jews in 'Occupied' Post-67 Lands," Israel National News, November 11, 2009.

71. David Bedein, "Palestinian Prime Minister Belies Moderate Image With Working Policy Paper About Future Palestinian State," Israel Resource Review, September 17, 2009.

72. Roni Sofer, "Obama sends Israel holiday greeting," Ynet News, September 17, 2009.

73. Hillel Fendel, "Anti-Obama Rally in Jerusalem," Israel National News, July 27, 2009.

FIVE: OBAMA AND IRAN

1. "Obama Officially Abandons Missile Defense in Europe," Heritage Foundation, August 27, 2009, http://blog.heritage.org/2009/08/27/obama-officially-abandons -missile-defense-in-europe/.

2. "In quotes: US missile reaction," BBC, September 17, 2009.

3. Ibid.

4. Paul Kiernan, Jose de Cordoba, and Jay Solomon, "Coup Rocks Honduras," Wall Street Journal, June 29, 2009.

5. Ibid.

6. Mary Anastasia O'Grady, "In Elections, Honduras Defeats Chávez," Wall Street Journal, November 29, 2009.

7. CNN, November 4, 2009, http://www.youtube.com/watch?v=gC5I1ZCb9Do.

8. Michael Muskal, "Obama calls for new relationship with Iran on anniversay [sic] of embassy takeover," Los Angeles Times, November 4, 2009, http://www.latimes.com/news/nationworld/world/la-naw-obama-iran5-2009nov05,0,4668198.story.

9. Thomas Erdbrink and William Branigin, "Iran's Khamenei Rejects U.S. Outreach," Washington Post, November 4, 2009.

10. John Bolton, "Iran Clenches Its Fist," Wall Street Journal, March 2, 2009.

11. Erdbrink and Branigin, "Iran's Khamenei Rejects U.S. Outreach."

12. "President Barack Obama's Inaugural Address," WhiteHouse.gov, January 21, 2009, http://www.whitehouse.gov/blog/inaugural-address/.

13. "Obama must apologize for crimes against Iran: Ahmadinejad," Agence France-Presse, January 28, 2009.

14. "Iran says Obama's offer to talk shows US failure," Agence France-Presse, January 31, 2009.

15. George Jahn, "Tehran wants U.S. to admit 'its mistakes,'" Associated Press, February 7, 2009.

16. "Ahmadinejad: Iran 'Will Never Negotiate' Over Nuclear 'Rights,'" Associated Press, September 7, 2009.

17. Barack Obama, "Happy New Year to Iran," Guardian, March 20, 2009.

18. "Ahmadinejad in Response to Obama: Any Hand Outstretched to Attack Us Will Be Cut Off," Middle East Media Research Institute (MEMRI), Special Dispatch No. 2305, April 2, 2009.

19. "Ahmadinejad to West: You Are Weak, Your Hands Are Empty, And You Can't Force Us to Do Anything; Nearly 7,000 Centrifuges Are Spinning Today at Natanz, Mocking You," Middle East Media Research Institute (MEMRI), Special Dispatch No. 2317, April 17, 2009.

20. Edward Yeranian, "Iran Claims to Have Test-Fired Mid-Range Missile, VOA News, May 20, 2009.

21. Barack Obama, "Remarks By The President On A New Beginning, Cairo University, Cairo, Egypt," WhiteHouse.gov, June 4, 2009, http://www.whitehouse.gov/the_press_office/Remarks-by-the-President-at-Cairo-University-6-04-09/.

22. Lara Setrakian, "Iran Protests Against U.S. and Regime on Hostage Anniversary," ABC News, November 4, 2009.

23. Jay Solomon and Peter Spiegel, "Obama Says Iran Must Pick Its Own Leaders," *Wall Street Journal,* June 16, 2009.

24. "President Obama's Press Briefing," *New York Times,* June 23, 2009.

25. "The President Meets with Prime Minister Berlusconi, Comments on Iran," White House Blog, June 15, 2009, http://www.whitehouse.gov/blog/The-President-Meets-with-Prime-Minister-Berlusconi-Comments-on-Iran/.

26. Nicholas Johnston, "Obama Says 'Dialogue' With Iran Will Continue After Election," Bloomberg, June 16, 2009.

27. Christopher Booker, "Iranian elections a 'loathsome charade,'" *Telegraph,* June 13, 2009.

28. Rana Moussaoui, "Hezbollah accuses West of fomenting Iran turmoil," Agence France-Press, June 24, 2009.

29. Pamela Geller, "The Case for Iran: Fighting for Freedom," *American Thinker,* June 29, 2009.

30. Kenneth Katzman, "Iran: U.S. Concerns and Policy Responses," Congressional Research Service, May 19, 2009.

31. Ibid.

32. Farah Stockman, "US Funds Dry Up for Iran Rights Watchdog: Obama White House Less Confrontational," *Boston Globe,* October 6, 2009.

33. Ibid.

34. Laura Rozen, "Former U.S. diplomat, hostage in Tehran takes up Iran post at State," Politico, November 7, 2009, http://www.politico.com/blogs/laurarozen/1109/Former_US_diplomat_hostage_in_Tehran_takes_up_Iran_post_at_State_.html?showall#.

35. "Act to Stop the Violence in Iran," National Iranian American Council, n.d., http://capwiz.com/niacouncil/issues/alert/?alertid=13659871.

36. "NIAC's Accomplishments," National Iranian American Council, June 24, 2009, http://www.niacouncil.org/index.php?option=com_content&task=view&id=1456&Itemid=28.

37. "Iran Updates—July 1," niacINsight, July 1, 2009, http://niacblog.wordpress.com/2009/07/01/iran-updates-july-1/#more-2915.

38. "NIAC rebuts MKO and FrontPage Magazine's untruths and fabrications," National Iranian American Council, April 20, 2007, http://www.niacouncil.org/index.php?Itemid=59&id=744&option=com_content&task=view.

39. Ibid.

40. Trita Parsi, "NIAC Memo: Ahmadinejad's Little Helpers," National Iranian American Council, June 8, 2009, http://www.niacouncil.org/index.php?option=com_content&task=view&id=1438&Itemid=29.

41. Hassan Daioleslam, "Twelve Years of Iranian Lobby," Global Politician, December 18, 2008, http://www.globalpolitician.com/25328-iran-lobby.

42. Katzman, "Iran: U.S. Concerns and Policy Responses."

43. Jonathan Schanzer, "Obama Attempts To Delay Iranian Sanctions Bill," New Majority, October 13, 2009.

44. Marc Ginsberg, "'Qum' Buy Ya," Huffington Post, November 13, 2009, http://www.huffingtonpost.com/amb-marc-ginsberg/qum-buy-ya_b_357382.html.

45. "Obama: Iran's Secret Nuke Facility 'Inconsistent with a Peaceful Program,'" USA Today, September 25, 2009.

46. Edwin Chen, "Obama Says He's Still Open to 'Meaningful Dialogue' With Iran," Bloomberg, September 26, 2009.

47. "Obama's News Conference at the G-20," New York Times, September 25, 2009.

48. Walter Pincus and Karen DeYoung, "Iran Tests Missiles On Eve Of Talks," Washington Post, September 28, 2009.

49. George Jahn, "U.S., Iran meet directly at nuclear talks in Geneva," Associated Press, October 1, 2009.

50. "Iranian cleric hails 'great victory' in Geneva," PressTV, October 9, 2009, http://www.presstv.ir/sections.aspx?section=351020101.

51. John Bolton, "Iran's Big Victory in Geneva," Wall Street Journal, October 5, 2009.

52. "Former U.N. Ambassador John Bolton on Obama and the Politics of 'Appeasement,'" FOXNews.com, May 20, 2008.

53. Anne Barker, "US warns Israel not to attack Iran," Australian Broadcasting Corporation, May 15, 2009.

54. Hana Levi Julian, "Israel Warns IDF Ready to Roll Against Iran," Israel National News, November 5, 2009.

55. Myra Noveck, "Israeli Navy Captures Arms Shipment," New York Times, November 4, 2009.

56. Tim Mak, "Bolton: Israel Must Bomb Iran," FrumForum, October 23, 2009, http://www.frumforum.com/bolton-israel-must-bomb-iran.

57. Julian, "Israel Warns IDF Ready to Roll Against Iran."

58. John Bolton, interview with Pamela Geller, July 30, 2009.

59. Anne Bayefsky, "Obama's U.N. Double Talk," National Review's The Corner, September 25, 2009.

60. John Bolton, interview with Pamela Geller, July 30, 2009.

61. Bolton, "Iran Clenches Its Fist."

62. "Remarks by President Barack Obama, Hradcany Square, Prague, Czech Republic," WhiteHouse.gov, April 5, 2009, http://www.whitehouse.gov/the_press_office/Remarks-By-President-Barack-Obama-In-Prague-As-Delivered.

63. "Obama: Iran May Have Right To Nuke Energy," Associated Press, June 2, 2009.

64. Julian Borger, "Iran tested advanced nuclear warhead design—secret report," Guardian, November 5, 2009.

65. Thomas Sowell, "Disaster in the Making: Obama's Repeated Demonstrations of His Amateurism and Immaturity," National Review, July 29, 2009.

SIX: A POST-AMERICAN PRESIDENT WAGES WAR

1. Peter Spiegel and Yochi Dreazen, "Top Troop Request Exceeds 60,000," Wall Street Journal, October 9, 2009.

2. Amanda Carpenter, "U.S. Commander in Afghanistan Talked with Obama Only Once," Washington Times, September 28, 2009.

3. Edwin Mora, "116 U.S. Troops Died in Afghanistan While Obama Pondered Reinforcement," CNSNews.com, December 1, 2009.

4. Barack Obama, "Obama's Address on the War in Afghanistan," *New York Times,* December 1, 2009.

5. "Obama's call on moderate Taliban useless: analysts," Reuters, March 9, 2009.

6. Ulrich Speck, "Biden Cites Mounting Problems In Afghanistan, But Says War 'Far From Lost,'" Radio Free Europe/Radio Liberty, October 3, 2009.

7. Robert Spencer, "Where's the Moderate Taliban?" *Human Events,* March 18, 2009.

8. Javed Aziz Khan, "Education for girls prime victim of Swat turmoil," News International, February 10, 2009, http://www.thenews.com.pk/daily_detail.asp?id=161693.

9. Eric Zimmerman, "Rumsfeld questions Obama's claim on troops," The Hill, December 2, 2009, http://thehill.com/blogs/blog-briefing-room/news/70221-rumsfeld-questions-obamas-claim-on-troops.

10. "Obama's Address on the War in Afghanistan."

11. "Obama: 'Peace requires responsibility,'" CNN, December 10, 2009, http://www.cnn.com/2009/POLITICS/12/10/obama.transcript/index.html.

12. Robert Costa, "Bolton: Obama's 'Pedestrian, Turgid, and Uninspired' Address," *National Review,* December 10, 2009.

13. Andrew C. McCarthy, "Alinsky Does Afghanistan," *National Review,* December 4, 2009.

14. Anne E. Kornblut, Scott Wilson, and Karen DeYoung, "Obama Pressed for Faster Surge," *Washington Post,* December 6, 2009.

15. Max Boot, "Three Quarters of the Way There," *Commentary,* December 1, 2009, http://www.commentarymagazine.com/blogs/index.php/boot/184491.

16. Melanie Phillips, "McChrystal Undermined," *Spectator,* December 2, 2009, http://www.spectator.co.uk/melaniephillips/5593271/mcchrystal-undermined.html.

17. Ayn Rand, *Answers* (New York: New American Library, 2005), p. 92.

18. Ibid., p. 87.

SEVEN: OBAMA AND ISLAMIC POLITICS

1. "Osama calls for long war against 'infidels,'" Reuters, June 4, 2009.

2. "'We've been through tougher times,'" interview with Barack Obama, *USA Today,* January 16, 2009.

3. Barack Obama, "President Barack Obama's Inaugural Address," WhiteHouse.gov, January 21, 2009.

4. "Obama Al-Arabiya Interview: Full Text," Huffington Post, January 26, 2009, http://www.huffingtonpost.com/2009/01/26/obama-al-arabiya-intervie_n_161127.html.

5. "Obama offers Iran 'the promise of a new beginning,'" CNN, March 20, 2009, http://www.cnn.com/2009/WORLD/meast/03/20/obama.iran.video/index.html.

6. Barack Obama, Remarks By The President On A New Beginning," WhiteHouse.gov, June 4, 2009, http://www.whitehouse.gov/the_press_office/Remarks-by-the-President-at-Cairo-University-6-04-09.

7. Michael Muskal, "Obama calls for new relationship with Iran on anniversay [*sic*] of embassy takeover," *Los Angeles Times,* November 4, 2009, http://www.latimes.com/news/nationworld/world/la-naw-obama-iran5-2009nov05,0,4668198.story.

8. "Obama's Address on the War in Afghanistan," *New York Times,* December 1, 2009, http://www.nytimes.com/2009/12/02/world/asia/02prexy.text.html.

9. Andrew C. McCarthy, "Alinsky Does Afghanistan," *National Review,* December 4, 2009.

10. Sarah Baxter, "Obama Reaches Out to Muslims," *Sunday Times*, January 18, 2009.

11. Robert Spencer, "Obama's Special Insight," *Human Events*, August 6, 2008.

12. Baxter, "Obama Reaches Out to Muslims."

13. "Egyptian grand shaykh: Islamic law sees suicide-bombers as martyrs," Independent Media Review Analysis, November 3, 2003, http://www.imra.org.il/story .php3?id=18722.

14. Robert Satloff, "Just Like Us! Really? Gallup says only 7 percent of the world's Muslims are political radicals. Yet 36 percent think the 9/11 attacks were in some way justified," *Weekly Standard,* May 12, 2008.

15. Bat Ye'or, Symposium, "Criticism and Conciliation," *National Review,* June 4, 2009.

16. Mark Steyn, "What Signal Does Barbie's Burka Send?" *Maclean's,* December 10, 2009.

17. Maria Rosa Menocal, *The Ornament of the World: How Muslims, Jews, and Christians Created a Culture of Tolerance in Medieval Spain* (New York: Little, Brown, 2002), pp. 72–73.

18. Pamela Geller, "Obama's State Department Submits to Islam," *American Thinker,* August 18, 2009.

19. Burt Prelutsky, "The Straight Poop On Radical Islam," Big Hollywood, August 13, 2009, http://bighollywood.breitbart.com/bprelutsky/2009/08/13/the-straight-poop -on-radical-islam/.

20. "Obama Issues Special Hajj Message to World's Muslims," *Los Angeles Times,* November 25, 2009.

21. "History," U.S.-Muslim Engagement Project, http://www.usmuslimengagement .org/index.php?option=com_content&task=view&id=14&Itemid=43.

22. Frank Gaffney, Jr., "Shariah's Brotherhood," Center for Security Policy, March 16, 2009, http://204.96.138.161/p17940.xml.

23. Mohamed Akram, "An Explanatory Memorandum on the General Strategic Goal for the Group in North America," May 22, 1991, Government Exhibit 003-0085, *U.S. vs. HLF,* et al, p. 7 (21).

24. *Changing Course: A New Direction for U.S. Relations with the Muslim World*, report of the Leadership Group on U.S.-Muslim Engagement Project, second printing, February 2009, p. 5.

25. *The Doha Compact: New Directions: America and the Muslim World*, the Brookings Project on U.S. Relations with the Islamic World, Saban Center at Brookings, October 2008, p. 4.

26. *Changing Course: A New Directions for U.S. Relations with the Muslim World*, p. 6.

27. Ibid., p. 5.

28. Ibid., p. 6.

29. Ibid., p. 61.

30. *The Doha Compact: New Directions: America and the Muslim World*, p. 16.

31. Marc Ambinder, "'Brotherhood' Invited To Obama Speech By U.S.," *The Atlantic,* June 3, 2009.

32. *Changing Course: A New Direction for U.S. Relations with the Muslim World*, p. 77.

33. *The Doha Compact: New Directions: America and the Muslim World*, p. 16.
34. "Obama: 'Peace requires responsibility,'" CNN, December 10, 2009.
35. *The Doha Compact: New Directions: America and the Muslim World*, p. 5.
36. Ibid.

EIGHT: AN ISLAMO-CHRISTIAN NATION
1. "President Barack Obama's Inaugural Address," WhiteHouse.gov, January 20, 2009.
2. "Obama Al-Arabiya Interview: Full Text," Huffington Post, January 26, 2009, http://www.huffingtonpost.com/2009/01/26/obama-al-arabiya-intervie_n_161127.html.
3. "President Barack Obama's Inaugural Address."
4. Jesse Lee, "Crossroads in Turkey," WhiteHouse.gov, April 6, 2009, http://www.whitehouse.gov/blog/09/04/06/Crossroads-in-Turkey.
5. Bat Ye'or, email to Pamela Geller, December 11, 2009.
6. http://www.1001inventions.com/.
7. "Interview of the President by Laura Haim, Canal Plus," WhiteHouse.gov, June 2, 2009, http://www.whitehouse.gov/the_press_office/Transcript-of-the-Interview-of-the-President-by-Laura-Haim-Canal-Plus-6-1-09/.
8. Arthur Delaney, "Obama: U.S. 'Not A Christian Nation Or A Jewish Nation Or A Muslim Nation' (VIDEO)," Huffington Post, April 6, 2009, http://www.huffingtonpost.com/2009/04/06/obama-us-not-a-christian_n_183772.html.
9. Johanna Neuman, "Obama Ends Bush-Era National Prayer Day Service at White House," *Los Angeles Times,* May 7, 2009.
10. Mark Silva, "Obama's Seder: This Year at White House," *Chicago Tribune,* April 8, 2009.
11. "Obama Passover Seder UPDATE: Photo, Guest List, Menu," Associated Press, April 10, 2009.
12. Ben Meyerson, "Obama Hosts a Seder: Who Was Invited?" *Los Angeles Times,* April 10, 2009.
13. Mark Silva, "Obama's Ramadan Dinner: Big Crowd," *Chicago Tribune,* September 1, 2009.
14. Ibid.
15. "2009 US Presidential Passover Greeting," available at http://www.holidays.net/passover/presnote2009.htm.
16. Robert Satloff, "Just Like Us! Really? Gallup says only 7 percent of the world's Muslims are political radicals. Yet 36 percent think the 9/11 attacks were in some way justified," *Weekly Standard,* May 12, 2008.
17. Pamela Geller, "State Department at Work: On 911, 'Islam, What a Billion Muslims Really Think':) Movie Screening and Iftar Dinner for State Department Employees," AtlasShrugs.com, September 21, 2009, http://atlasshrugs2000.typepad.com/atlas_shrugs/2009/09/state-department-at-work-on-911-islam-what-a-billion-muslims-really-think-movie- screening-and-iftar-dinner-for-state.html.
18. Hilary Leila Krieger, "White House Hanukka party guest list to be cut in half," *Jerusalem Post,* November 19, 2009.
19. Rachel L. Swarns, "Washington Fuss Over White House Hanukkah Party," *New York Times,* December 10, 2009.

20. Alan Caruba, "Obama's War On America," Canada Free Press, November 11, 2009, http://canadafreepress.com/index.php/article/16763.

21. "Los Angeles police plan to map Muslims," Associated Press, November 9, 2007.

22. "Muslims Welcome Removal of LAPD's Mapping Program," Muslim Public Affairs Council, November 16, 2007, http://www.mpac.org/article.php?id=563.

23. "Justice Department Files Religious Discrimination Lawsuit Against Essex County, New Jersey," United States Department of Justice, June 8, 2009, http://www.justice.gov/opa/pr/2009/June/09-crt-559.html.

24. Barack Obama, Remarks By The President On A New Beginning, WhiteHouse.gov, June 4, 2009. http://www.whitehouse.gov/the_press_office/Remarks-by-the-President-at-Cairo-University-6-04-09/.

25. Andrew C. McCarthy, "Material Support on the Ropes? Will a key anti-terror tool fall victim to Obama's Muslim outreach?" National Review, June 9, 2009.

26. Ibid.

27. Pamela Geller, "Muslim Terror Attack," AtlasShrugs.com, November 5, 2009, http://atlasshrugs2000.typepad.com/atlas_shrugs/2009/11/seven-shot-dead-at-us-army-base.html.

28. Jon Ward and Eli Lake, "White House: 'War on Terrorism' is Over," Washington Times, August 6, 2009.

29. "Chicagoan charged with aiding deadly Mumbai terror attack," Chicago Breaking News Center, December 7, 2009, http://www.chicagobreakingnews.com/2009/12/chicagoan-charged-with-aiding-deadly-mumbai-terror-attack.html.

30. Mike Levine, "Americans Arrested in Pakistan; FBI Probing," FOXNews.com, December 9, 2009.

31. Michael S. Schmidt and Michael D. Regan, "Binghamton Student Says He Warned Officials," New York Times, December 6, 2009.

32. "U.S. terror suspects accused of targeting Marine base," Reuters, September 24, 2009.

33. Dina Temple-Raston, "Officials: NYC Plot Operational, Not Just Aspirational," National Public Radio, September 28, 2009.

34. Jason Trahan, Todd J. Gillman, and Scott Goldstein, "Dallas Bomb Plot Suspect Told Landlord He was Moving Out," Dallas Morning News, September 26, 2009.

35. "Man accused of plotting to bomb Springfield courthouse," Chicago Breaking News, September 24, 2009, http://www.chicagobreakingnews.com/2009/09/man-accused-of-plotting-to-bomb-springfield-courthouse.html.

36. Paul Egan, "Detroit Mosque Leader Killed in FBI Raids," Detroit News, October 28, 2009.

37. Laura Crimaldi and Laurel J. Sweet, "Beltway Sniper Alleged Inspiration for Terror Suspect," Boston Herald, October 21, 2009.

38. James Corum, "Obama's National Defence Review ignores Iran and Islam in favour of . . . climate change!", Telegraph, February 12, 2010.

39. Pamela Geller, "'Diversity Visas' and 'Religious Visas': Importing Jihad," Atlas Shrugs.com, April 10, 2009, http://atlasshrugs2000.typepad.com/atlas_shrugs/2009/04/diversity-visas-and-religious-visas-.html.

NINE: DESTROYING THE PRESTIGE OF AMERICA

1. Barack Obama, "Obama's Address on the War in Afghanistan," *New York Times,* December 1, 2009.

2. Samer al-Atrush, "Arab countries fail on human rights—report," Agence France-Presse, December 9, 2009.

3. "Obama to release interrogation photos," United Press International, April 23, 2009.

4. "Senators Call on Obama to Resolve Dispute With Pelosi Over 'Torture Photos,'" FOXNews.com, June 11, 2009.

5. Carrie Johnson, "Prosecutor to Probe CIA Interrogations: Attorney General Parts with White House in Approving Preliminary Investigation, *Washington Post,* August 25, 2009.

6. Ibid.

7. Eli Lake, "7 Ex-CIA Chiefs Oppose Detainee Probe," *Washington Times,* September 18, 2009.

8. Michael Isikoff and Daniel Klaidman, "Justice Official Clears Bush Lawyers in Torture Memo Probe," *Newsweek,* January 29, 2010.

9. Pamela Geller, "Why Didn't President Hussein Release *All* of the CIA Memos?" AtlasShrugs.com, April 21, 2009, http://atlasshrugs2000.typepad.com/atlas_shrugs/2009/04/why-didnt-president-hussein-release-all-the-cia-memos.html.

10. John R. Bolton, "Obama's Prosecutions by Proxy," *Washington Post,* May 6, 2009.

11. Rowan Scarborough, "Navy SEALs Face Assault Charges for Capturing Most-Wanted Terrorist," Fox News, November 25, 2009.

12. Pamela Geller, "Justice for America's Hero: After Action Report In Support of Michael Behenna," AtlasShrugs.com, December 6, 2009, http://atlasshrugs2000.typepad.com/atlas_shrugs/2009/12/justice-for-americas-hro-after-action-report-in-support-of-michael-behenna.html?cid=6a00d8341c60bf53ef0120a71df106970b.

13. Daniel Schwammenthal, "Prosecuting American 'War Crimes,'" *Wall Street Journal,* November 26, 2009.

14. U.S. Supreme Court, *Ex Parte Quirin,* 317 U.S. 1 (1942), available at http://caselaw.lp.findlaw.com/scripts/getcase.pl?court=US&vol=317&invol=1.

15. Andrew C. McCarthy, "How Obama is Courting Danger: Civilian Trials Set Back the War on Terror," *Daily News* (New York), November 22, 2009.

16. Marc A. Thiessen, "The CIA's Questioning Worked," *Washington Post,* April 21, 2009.

17. Mimi Hall and Ken Dilanian, "Guantanamo Plan Takes More Shots," *USA Today,* May 22, 2009.

18. "Obama's News Conference at the G-20," *New York Times,* September 25, 2009.

19. Kenneth R. Bazinet, Wil Cruz, and Samuel Goldsmith, "Trial for 9/11 Mastermind Khalid Sheikh Mohammed Won't Happen in New York City, Says Official," *Daily News* (New York), January 29, 2010.

20. Jim Kouri, "Terrorist trials may still be held in Manhattan, says President," Law Enforcement Examiner, February 8, 2010, http://www.examiner.com/x-2684-Law-Enforcement-Examiner~y2010m2d8-Terrorist-trials-may-still-be-held-in-Manhattan-says-President.

21. Ryan Lizza, "Making It: How Chicago Shaped Obama," *New Yorker,* July 21, 2008.

TEN: FREEDOM OF SPEECH IN THE AGE OF JIHAD

1. Ayn Rand, *Ayn Rand Answers—The Best of Her Q & A,* ed. Robert Mayhew (New York: NAL Books, 2005), p. 20.
2. Nancy Pelosi and Steny Hoyer, "'Un-American' Attacks Can't Derail Health Care Debate," *USA Today,* August 10, 2009.
3. Barack Obama, speech in McLean, Virginia, August 7, 2009, http://www.youtube .com/watch?v=jifjRVLVjzA&eurl=http%3A%2F%2Fwww.breitbart.tv%2 Fobama-dont-want-the-folks-who-created-the-mess-to-do-a-lot-of-talking%2 F&feature=player_embedded.
4. Michael Barone, "Obama vs. Free Speech," RealClearPolitics, October 11, 2008.
5. "Gov. Blunt Statement on Obama Campaign's Abusive Use of Missouri Law Enforcement," Office of Governor Matt Blunt, September 27, 2008.
6. Bob Herbert, "A Threat We Can't Ignore," *New York Times,* June 19, 2009; Frank Rich, "The Obama Haters' Silent Enablers," *New York Times,* June 13, 2009; Paul Krugman, "The Big Hate," *New York Times,* June 11, 2009; Tobin Harshaw, "Weekend Opinionator: Is Racist Hate Republican or Democratic?" *New York Times,* June 12, 2009.
7. Steven Mikulan, "New Anti-Obama 'Joker' Poster," *LA Weekly,* August 3, 2009.
8. "Mystery Obama/Joker Poster Appears in L.A.," *Bedlam Magazine,* August 3, 2009.
9. Paul Krugman, "The Town Hall Mob," *New York Times,* August 6, 2009.
10. Maureen Dowd, "Boy, Oh, Boy," *New York Times,* September 12, 2009.
11. Greg Bluestein, "Carter Cites 'Racism' in Wilson Outburst," Associated Press, September 16, 2009.
12. Katharine Q. Seelye, "Obama Wades Into a Volatile Racial Issue," *New York Times,* July 23, 2009.
13. Pamela Geller, "Obama's Race Baiting Must End," Newsmax, July 27, 2009.
14. Tim Craig and Michael D. Shear, "Allen Quip Provokes Outrage, Apology: Name Insults Webb Volunteer," *Washington Post,* August 15, 2006.
15. "Biden explains Indian-American remarks," Associated Press, July 7, 2006.
16. Thomas Lifson, "Barack Obama, Laughingstock," *American Thinker,* August 2, 2009.
17. Charles M. Blow, "Hate in a Cocoon of Silence," *New York Times,* June 12, 2009.
18. Dave Eberhart, "Pelosi Video: Healthcare Protesters Tote Swastikas," Newsmax, August 6, 2009.
19. Sam Stein, "Pelosi Protesters, Including Kid In Stroller, Compare Obama To Hitler," Huffington Post, August 7, 2009, http://www.huffingtonpost.com/2009/08/07/ pelosi-protesters-includi_n_253762.html.
20. Bill Press, "The Tea Baggers Are Back—Crazy as Ever," *Hartford Courant,* August 6, 2009.
21. David Goldstein, "Emotions Spill at Town Halls on Health Care," *Kansas City Star,* August 7, 2009.
22. Carrie Budoff Brown, "White House to Democrats: 'Punch back twice as hard,'" Politico.com, August 6, 2009, http://www.politico.com/news/stories/0809/25891 .html.
23. "Kathy Castor - Healthcare Town Hall Meeting in Tampa - 8/6," YouTube, August 6, 2009, http://www.youtube.com/watch?v=_kxaGfClPws&eurl=http%3A% 2F%2Fatlasshrugs2000.typepad.com%2Fatlas_shrugs%2F2009%2F08%2Fobamas

-union-thugs-are-beating-people-up-at-town-hall-meetings.html&feature=player_embedded#t=217.

24. "Dems Sneak Union Thugs Into Carnahan Town Hall—Tea Party Taxpayers Locked Out!," YouTube, August 6, 2009, http://www.youtube.com/watch?v=ZJhR3T4aw&eurl=http%3A%2F%2Fatlasshrugs2000.typepad.com%2Fatlas_shrugs%2F2009%2F08%2Fthe-obama-auguar-psyop-democrats-begin-to-pack-town-hall-meetings-with-a&feature=player_embedded.

25. "Union Thugs Deliver Unprovoked Beating on Black Conservative at Carnahan Town Hall," St. Louis Tea Party, August 7, 2009, http://stlouisteaparty.com/2009/08/07/union-thugs-deliver-unprovoked-beating-on-black-conservative-at-carnahan-town-hall/.

26. Leah Thorsen, "Six People, Including P-D Reporter, Arrested at Carnahan Meeting," St. Louis Post-Dispatch, August 6, 2009.

27. "Committees And Candidates Supported/Opposed: SEIU COPE (Service Employees International Union Committee on Political Education)," Federal Election Commission, n.d., http://query.nictusa.com/cgi-bin/com_supopp/2007_C00004036.

28. Michael Mishak, "Unplugged: The SEIU Chief on the Labor Movement and the Card Check," Las Vegas Sun, May 10, 2009.

29. Pamela Geller, "Obama and Blago . . . and the SEIU," AtlasShrugs.com, December 10, 2008, http://atlasshrugs2000.typepad.com/atlas_shrugs/2008/12/obama-and-blago.html.

30. Jackie Calmes, "Lawmakers Detail Obama's Pitch," New York Times, November 7, 2009.

31. Helen Kennedy, "President Obama Insult by Glenn Beck has Advertisers Boycotting Show," Daily News (New York), August 18, 2009.

32. Richard Leiby, "Obama Delivers the Zingers at Journalists' Dinner," Washington Post, May 10, 2009.

33. Howard Kurtz, "Study: Coverage of McCain Much More Negative Than That of Obama," Washington Post, October 22, 2008.

34. Alexander Burns, "Halperin at Politico/USC conf.: 'extreme pro-Obama' press bias," Politico, November 22, 2008, http://www.politico.com/news/stories/1108/15885.html#xzz0WPq5PGFN.

35. "Most Voters Say News Media Wants Obama to Win," The Pew Research Center for the People and the Press, October 22, 2008, http://people-press.org/report/463/media-wants-obama.

36. Fred Lucas, "Poll: Big Majorities Say Objective Journalism Is Dead and that Media Back Obama," CNS News, September 25, 2009.

37. Jeff Poor, "Obama Blasts Fox News: 'I've Got One Television Station that is Entirely Devoted to Attacking My Administration,'" Business & Media Institute, June 16, 2009.

38. Brian Stelter, "Fox's Volley With Obama Intensifying," FOXNews.com, October 11, 2009.

39. "Obama Team Continues Effort to Isolate Fox News," FOXNews.com, October 18, 2009.

40. Ibid.

41. Johanna Newman, "The Obama War Against Fox News: Risky Business?" Los Angeles Times, October 19, 2009.

42. James Gordon Meek, "Obama's Team Again Rips Fox News—But Says Aides Will Appear on Shows," *Daily News* (New York), October 19, 2009.

43. "Obama Team Continues Effort to Isolate Fox News."

44. "Obama Compares Fox News to Talk Radio, Says He's Not 'Losing Sleep' Over Controversy," FOXNews.com, October 21, 2009.

45. Peter Nicholas, "Democratic Consultant Says He Got a Warning from White House After Appearing on Fox News," *Los Angeles Times,* November 6, 2009.

46. John Fontana, "Bill giving Obama power to shut Web takes on new tone," Computer-World, August 31, 2009.

47. Jaikumar Vijayan, "Privacy Office approves laptop searches without suspicion at U.S. borders," ComputerWorld, August 31, 2009.

48. Kyle Smith, "Gag the Internet!," *New York Post,* July 11, 2009.

49. Ibid.

50. Kerry Picket, "New AG Choice Advocated To Stifle Speech On Web," News busters.com, November 21, 2008.

51. Macon Phillips, "Facts Are Stubborn Things," WhiteHouse.gov, August 4, 2009, http://www.whitehouse.gov/blog/facts-are-stubborn-things/.

52. "Sen. Cornyn Sends Letter To President Obama About 'Fishy' Activities Program," John Cornyn website, August 5, 2009, http://cornyn.senate.gov/public/index.cfm ?FuseAction=ForPress.NewsReleases&ContentRecord_id=ebc2c77d-802a -23ad-4ae4-6ccf4c7a255c&ContentType_id=b94acc28-404a-4fc6-b143-a9e15bf 92da4&Group_id=24eb5606-e2db-4d7f-bf6c-efc5df80b676&MonthDisplay=8&Year Display=2009.

53. Erick Erickson, "John Cornyn Takes on Obama's flag@whitehouse.gov Program, But Wait! There's More with the NTIA," RedState.com, August 5, 2009, http:// www.redstate.com/erick/2009/08/05/john-cornyn-takes-on-obamas-flagwhitehouse gov-program-but-wait-theres-more-with-the-ntia/.

54. Jake Tapper, "Political Punch," ABCNews.com, August 10, 2009.

55. Audrey Hudson, "EXCLUSIVE: W.H. Collects Web Users' Data Without Notice," *Washington Times,* September 16, 2009.

56. Jacqui Cheng, "EFF: MySpace suicide charges a threat to free speech," Ars Technica, August 4, 2008, http://arstechnica.com/tech-policy/news/2008/08/eff-myspace -suicide-charges-a-threat-to-free-speech.ars.

57. "H.R. 1966 - Megan Meier Cyberbullying Prevention Act," available at http://www .opencongress.org/bill/111-h1966/text.

58. Eugene Volokh, "Federal Felony To Use Blogs, the Web, Etc. To Cause Substantial Emotional Distress Through 'Severe, Repeated, and Hostile' Speech?" Volokh Conspiracy, April 30, 2009, http://volokh.com/posts/1241122059.html.

59. Rep. Linda Sanchez, "Protecting Victims, Preserving Freedoms," Huffington Post, May 6, 2009.

60. "H.R. 1966 - Megan Meier Cyberbullying Prevention Act."

61. Ryan Singel, "FCC Backs Net Neutrality—And Then Some," Wired.com, September 21, 2009, http://www.wired.com/epicenter/2009/09/net-neutrality-announce ment/.

62. Ibid.

63. James G. Lakely, " 'Net Neutrality' Is Socialism, Not Freedom," *Examiner* (Washington), October 20, 2009.

64. Glenn Beck, "The Radicals on the Left Want You to Shut Up," Fox News, August 13, 2009.

65. Pamela Geller, "Free Speech Silenced at Columbia and Princeton," *American Thinker,* November 24, 2009.

66. William J. Becker, Jr., "The American Library Association's Stealth Jihad Against Free Speech," FrontPageMagazine.com, October 9, 2009.

67. Pamela Geller, "Free Speech Code Blue: Geert Wilders Goes on Trial January 2010," AtlasShrugs.com, September 12, 2009, http://atlasshrugs2000.typepad.com/atlas _shrugs/2009/09/free-speech-code-blue-geert-wilders-goes-on-trial-january-2010 .html; Pamela Geller, "Geert Wilders Arrested! Refused Entry," AtlasShrugs.com, February 12, 2009, http://atlasshrugs2000.typepad.com/atlas_shrugs/2009/02/geert -wilders-arrested-refused-entry.html; Pamela Geller, "Wilders Liberated to Travel to UK! Coming to Columbia University Next Week," AtlasShrugs.com, October 13, 2009, http://atlasshrugs2000.typepad.com/atlas_shrugs/2009/10/wilders-liberated-to -travel-to-uk-coming-to-columbia-university-next-week.html; Pamela Geller, "Self Imposed Noose Tightens on the West: Another Wilders Ban," AtlasShrugs.com, November 22, 2009, http://atlasshrugs2000.typepad.com/atlas_shrugs/2009/11/self -imposed-noose-tightens-on-the-west-another-wilders-ban.html.

68. "Reaction to the decision in the pre-trial review," WildersOnTrial.com, February 3, 2010, http://www.wildersontrial.com/index.php?option=com_content&view=section &layout=blog&id=4&Itemid=2.

ELEVEN: SOCIALIST AMERICA

1. "Obama College Thesis: 'Constitution is Inherently Flawed,'" Jumping In Pools, August 25, 2009, http://jumpinginpools.blogspot.com/2009/08/obama-college-thesis -constitution-is.html.

2. Michael Ledeen, "The Obama 'thesis' hoax," Pajamas Media, October 23, 2009, http://pajamasmedia.com/michaelledeen/2009/10/23/the-obama-thesis-hoax/.

3. "Obama Bombshell Redistribution of Wealth Audio Uncovered," Barack Obama interview, WBEZ-FM, 2001, YouTube, October 26, 2008, http://www.youtube.com/ watch?v=iivL4c_3pck&feature=player_embedded.

4. Ibid.

5. Ibid.

6. Ibid.

7. "The next campaign," *Progressive Populist,* November 1996, http://www.populist .com/11.96.Edit.html.

8. Stanley Kurtz, "Life of the New Party," *National Review,* October 30, 2008.

9. Bob Roman, "A Town Meeting on Economic Insecurity: Employment and Survival in Urban America," *New Ground* 45, March-April 1996, http://www.chicagodsa .org/ngarchive/ng45.html.

10. Carl Shier, "So Long, Saul, Old Friend," *New Ground* 58, May-June 1998, http:// www.chicagodsa.org/ngarchive/ng58.html.

11. John Berlau, "Nationalization Review," *American Spectator,* June 23, 2009.

12. "Krauthammer's Take," *National Review,* May 20, 2009.

13. John Lott, "The Nationalization of the US auto industry," John Lott's Website, April 28, 2009, http://johnrlott.blogspot.com/2009/04/nationalization-of-us-auto -industry.html.

14. Dick Morris and Eileen McGann, "The Young Turn Against Obamacare," Dick Morris.com, November 24, 2009.

15. Pamela Geller, "Obamacare DOA: Rx America, A Doctor's Prescription," Atlas Shrugs.com, September 20, 2009, http://atlasshrugs2000.typepad.com/atlas_shrugs/2009/09/obamacare-doa-rx-america.html.

16. Robert Creamer, *Listen to Your Mother: Stand Up Straight: How Progressives Can Win* (Santa Ana, Calif.: Seven Locks Press, 2007); Joel B. Pollak, "Was Democrats' Health Care Strategy Written In Federal Prison?" Big Government, December 7, 2009.

17. Sarah Palin, "Statement on the Current Health Care Debate," Sarah Palin's Notes, Facebook.com, August 7, 2009.

18. Jake Tapper and Sunlen Miller, "President Obama Addresses Sarah Palin 'Death Panels,' 'Wild Representations,'" ABC News, August 11, 2009.

19. Sarah Palin, "Concerning the 'Death Panels,'" Sarah Palin's Notes, Facebook.com, August 12, 2009.

20. "Obama's Senior Moment," *Wall Street Journal*, August 14, 2009.

21. "Morning Bell: The Obamacare Rationing Threat To Your Mammograms," The Heritage Foundation, November 24, 2009, http://blog.heritage.org/2009/11/24/morning-bell-the-obamacare-rationing-threat-to-your-mammograms/.

22. Pamela Geller, "Palin Rules: No Health Care Reform Without Legal Reform," AtlasShrugs.com, August 22, 2009, http://atlasshrugs2000.typepad.com/atlas_shrugs/2009/08/palin-rules-.html.

23. "Video: Pelosi Says Jail 'Very Fair' Punishment For Not Buying Health Insurance," Heritage Foundation, November 13, 2009, http://blog.heritage.org/2009/11/13/video-pelosi-says-jail-very-fair-punishment-for-not-buying-health-insurance.

24. Sunlen Miller, "Interview with the President: Jail Time for Those without Health Care Insurance?" ABC News, November 9, 2009.

25. "Video: Pelosi Says Jail 'Very Fair' Punishment For Not Buying Health Insurance."

26. "Lyrics: Songs About President Obama," FOXNews.com, September 24, 2009.

27. Ibid.

28. John Nolte, "Elementary Epidemic: 11 Uncovered Videos Show School Children Performing Praises to Obama," Big Hollywood, November 4, 2009, http://bigholly wood.breitbart.com/jjmnolte/2009/11/04/elementary-epidemic-11-uncovered-videos-show-school-children-performing-praises-to-obama/#more-251738.

29. Pamela Geller, "Obama Recruiting Radicals in High Schools," Big Government, January 31, 2010, http://biggovernment.com/pgeller/2010/01/31/obama-recruiting-radicals-in-high-schools/.

30. Patrick Courrielche, "The National Endowment for the Art of Persuasion?" Big Hollywood, August 25, 2009. http://bighollywood.breitbart.com/pcourrielche/2009/08/25/the-national-endowment-for-the-art-of-persuasion-patrick-courrielche.

31. Ibid.

32. John Nolte, "Propaganda, Health Care and ACORN: Full Context of NEA Conference Call Reveals Disturbing Pattern," Big Hollywood, September 21, 2009, http://bighollywood.breibart.com/jjmnolte/2009/09/21/propaganda-health-care-and-acorn-full-context-of-nea-conference-call-reveals-disturbing-pattern.

33. Lee Rosenbaum, "'United We Serve': Should the Arts be Politically Exploited?"

CultureGrrl, September 2, 2009, http://www.artsjournal.com/culturegrrl/2009/09/
united_we_serve.html.

34. John Berry, "Memorandum For Heads Of Executive Departments and Agencies,"
United States Office of Personnel Management, November 5, 2009, http://www
.chcoc.gov/Transmittals/TransmittalDetails.aspx?TransmittalId=2588.

35. Mark Tapscott, "Obama to weed out Bush political appointees who careered in; Establishes new political test for career jobs UPDATED!," *Examiner* (Washington),
November 12, 2009, http://www.washingtonexaminer.com/opinion/blogs/beltway
-confidential/Obama-to-weed-out-Bush-political-appointees-who-careered-in
-Establishes-new-political-test-for-career-jobs-69858442.html.

36. Erick Erickson, "Obama Administration Intends to Purge Republicans From
the Civil Service," RedState.com, November 12, 2009, http://www.redstate.com/
erick/2009/11/12/obama-administration-intends-to-purge-republicans-from-the
-civil-service/.

37. Ibid.

38. P. J. Gladnick, "Will MSM Report on Louis Farrakhan Declaration of Obama as the
Messiah?" Newsbusters, October 9, 2008, http://newsbusters.org/blogs/p-j-gladnick/
2008/10/09/will-msm-report-louis-farrakhan-declaration-obama-messiah.

39. Ayn Rand, *The Ayn Rand Column,* ed. Peter Schwartz (New Miford, Conn.: Second
Renaissance Books, 1998), p. 18.

TWELVE: THE RED CZARS

1. Eric Cantor, "Obama and His 32 Czars: President is Skirting Legislative Branch,"
Washington Post, August 1, 2009.

2. Robert Byrd, Letter to Barack Obama, February 23, 2009, available at http://www
.eenews.net/public/25/9865/features/documents/2009/02/25/document_gw_02.pdf.

3. Cantor, "Obama and His 32 Czars."

4. Byrd, Letter to Barack Obama.

5. Eric Cantor, "Obama and His 32 Czars."

6. David Rochelson, "The search for knowledge, truth and a greater understanding
of the world around us," Change.gov, December 20, 2008, http://change.gov/news
room/entry/the_search_for_knowledge_truth_and_a_greater_understanding_of
_the_world_aro.

7. http://www.pugwash.org/.

8. Paul Ehrlich, Anne Ehrlich, and John Holdren, *Ecoscience: Population, Resources,
and Environment,* (New York: W. H. Freeman and Company, 1977), p. 954. Quoted
in Ben Johnson, "Obama's Biggest Radical," FrontPageMagazine.com, February 27,
2009, http://97.74.65.51/readArticle.aspx?ARTID=34198.

9. Ibid.

10. Ibid.

11. "Obama Bombshell Redistribution of Wealth Audio Uncovered," Barack Obama
interview, WBEZ-FM, 2001, YouTube, October 26, 2008. http://www.youtube.com/
watch?v=iivL4c_3pck&feature=player_embedded.

12. Ehrlich, Ehrlich, and Holdren, *Ecoscience: Population, Resources, and Environment,*
pp. 837–38. Quoted in Johnson, "Obama's Biggest Radical."

13. Ibid., p. 943. Quoted in Johnson.

14. Ibid., p. 917. Quoted in Johnson.

15. John P. Holdren, "Arms Limitation and Peace Building in the Post-Cold-War World," Pugwash Online, December 10, 1995, http://www.pugwash.org/award/Holdrennobel.htm. Quoted in Ben Johnson, "Obama's Biggest Radical," Front PageMagazine.com, February 27, 2009, http://97.74.65.51/readArticle.aspx?ARTID =34198.

16. John P. Holdren, "Science and Technology for Sustainable Well-Being," *Science* 25, January 2008: Vol. 319, no. 5862, pp. 424–34. Quoted in Ben Johnson, "Obama's Biggest Radical," FrontPageMagazine.com, February 27, 2009, http://97.74.65.51/read Article.aspx?ARTID=34198.

17. Ben Johnson, "Obama's Biggest Radical," FrontPageMagazine.com, February 27, 2009, http://97.74.65.51/readArticle.aspx?ARTID=34198.

18. Bob Roman, "A Town Meeting on Economic Insecurity: Employment and Survival in Urban America," *New Ground* 45, March-April 1996, http://www.chicagodsa .org/ngarchive/ng45.html.

19. "Browner is an Environmental Radical—and a Socialist (Seriously)," *Examiner* (Washington), January 8, 2009, http://www.washingtonexaminer.com/opinion/Browner_is_an_environmental_radical__and_a_socialist_seriously_010809.html.

20. Stephen Dinan, "Obama Climate Czar has Socialist Ties," *Washington Times,* January 12, 2009.

21. John Griffing, "Watermelon Marxists," *American Thinker,* December 8, 2009.

22. Eliza Strickland, "The New Face of Environmentalism," *The East Bay Express,* November 2, 2005.

23. Aaron Klein, "Will a 'Red' Help Blacks Go Green?" WorldNetDaily, November 5, 2009.

24. Deborah Solomon, "Pay Czar Gets Broad Authority Over Executive Compensation," *Wall Street Journal,* June 11, 2009.

25. David Harsanyi, "The Rise of the Mob Economy," Townhall.com, October 23, 2009, http://townhall.com/columnists/DavidHarsanyi/2009/10/23/the_rise_of_the_mob _economy?page=full&comments=true.

26. Eamon Javers, "'Pay czar' Kenneth Feinberg caps pay of midlevel executives," Politico, December 11, 2009, http://www.politico.com/news/stories/1209/30480.html.

27. Harsanyi, "The Rise of the Mob Economy."

THIRTEEN: ACORN: FEDERALLY FUNDED FRAUD

1. James O'Keefe, "Complete ACORN Baltimore Child Prostitution Investigation Transcript," Big Government, September 10, 2009, http://biggovernment.com/2009/09/10/complete-acorn-baltimore-prostitution-investigation-transcript/.

2. Amanda Carpenter, "ACORN's Rap Sheet," Townhall.com, October 13, 2008, http://townhall.com/columnists/AmandaCarpenter/2008/10/13/acorns_rap_sheet ?page=full&comments=true.

3. Terrence Scanlon, "Is ACORN disenfranchising the process itself?" *Examiner* (Washington), November 6, 2006, http://www.examiner.com/a-381567~Terrence _Scanlon_Is_ACORN_disenfranchising_the_process_itself_.html.

4. Carpenter, "ACORN's Rap Sheet."

5. Ibid.

6. Ronald Kessler, "Former ACORN Employee: More Than Half Voter Registrations Invalid," Newsmax, March 19, 2009.

7. Sol Stern, "ACORN's Nutty Regime for Cities," *City Journal,* Spring 2003, http://www.city-journal.org/html/13_2_acorns_nutty_regime.html.

8. Stanley Kurtz, "Inside Obama's Acorn," *National Review,* May 29, 2008.

9. Adam Doster, "Growing the Pie: How Obama's Voter-Registration Efforts Could Reshape the Electoral Map in November," *Illinois Times,* August 6, 2008.

10. Ibid.

11. John Fund, "Acorn Who? Obama Heads for the High Grass," *Wall Street Journal,* September 21, 2009.

12. Ryan Lizza, "Making It: How Chicago Shaped Obama," *New Yorker,* July 21, 2008.

13. "Obama Caught Saying ACORN and Friends Will Shape His Presidential Agenda," YouTube.com, October 11, 2008, http://www.youtube.com/watch?v=8vJcVgJhNaU&e.

14. Sam Graham-Felsen, "ACORN Political Action Committee Endorses Obama," Organizing For America, February 21, 2008, http://my.barackobama.com/page/community/post/samgrahamfelsen/gGC7zm.

15. "Rep. Steve King Says any ACORN Investigation 'Will Lead to the White House' - Video 12/4/09," Freedom's Lighthouse, December 4, 2009, http://www.freedomslighthouse.com/2009/12/rep-steve-king-says-any-acorn.html.

16. Pamela Geller, "ACORN Throws Out Republican Voter Registrations," Big Government, October 7, 2009, http://biggovernment.com/2009/10/07/acorn-throws-out-republican-voter-registrations/.

17. Thomas Lifson, "Obama Campaign Now Publishing Lies on His Ties to Acorn," *American Thinker,* October 10, 2008.

18. Chad Groening, "Praise of Mao should be White House no-no," One News Now, October 28, 2009, http://onenewsnow.com/Politics/Default.aspx?id=740592.

19. John Boehner, "Dems Vote to Allow Federal Funding for Corrupt ACORN," Big Government, December 9, 2009, http://biggovernment.com/2009/12/09/dems-vote-to-allow-federal-funding-for-corrupt-acorn/.

20. Scanlon, "Is ACORN disenfranchising the process itself?"

21. Matthew Vadum, "ACORN's Stimulus," *American Spectator,* January 27, 2009.

22. Bill Hemmer of FOX News stated on *America's Newsroom,* February 3, 2010: "We're learning the community organizing group ACORN may stand to benefit from this $3.8 trillion proposal." See also Matthew Vadum, "Show ACORN the Money," *American Spectator,* February 2, 2010.

23. Boehner, "Dems Vote to Allow Federal Funding for Corrupt ACORN."

24. George Stephanopoulos, "Obama on ACORN: 'Not Something I've Followed Closely' Won't Commit to Cut Federal Funds," ABCNews.com, September 20, 2009, http://blogs.abcnews.com/george/2009/09/obama-on-acorn-not-something-ive-followed-closely.html.

25. Boehner, "Dems Vote to Allow Federal Funding for Corrupt ACORN."

FOURTEEN: THE ENERGY SHELL GAME

1. John M. Broder, "U.S. Blocks Oil Drilling at 60 Sites in Utah," *New York Times,* October 8, 2009.

2. Sarah Palin, "Drill: Petroleum is a Major Part of America's Energy Picture. Shall We Get It Here or Abroad?" *National Review,* October 16, 2009.

3. John Carey, "House Passes Carbon Cap-and-Trade Bill," *BusinessWeek,* June 26, 2009; Peter Ferrara, "Cap and Trade Dementia," *American Spectator,* July 1, 2009.

4. "The Cap and Tax Fiction," *Wall Street Journal,* June 26, 2009.

5. Tom LoBianco, "Obama Counting On Cap-and-Trade," *Washington Times,* February 25, 2009.

6. Declan McCullagh, "Obama Admin: Cap And Trade Could Cost Families $1,761 A Year," CBS News, September 15, 2009, http://www.cbsnews.com/blogs/2009/09/15/taking_liberties/entry5314040.shtml.

7. "The Cap and Tax Fiction."

8. Pamela Geller, "Obama's Energy Plan: Mandated Scarcity in the Richest Country in the World," AtlasShrugs.com, August 17, 2009, http://atlasshrugs2000.typepad.com/atlas_shrugs/2009/08/obamas-energy-plan-mandated-scarcity-in-the-richest-country-in-the-world.html.

9. "The Cap and Tax Fiction."

10. Karl Rove, "Scrap Cap-and-Trade," *Newsweek,* October 31, 2009.

11. Ibid.

12. On Obama Calling It a Jobs Bill, cf. Peter Ferrara, "Cap and Trade Dementia," *American Spectator,* July 1, 2009.

13. Amanda DeBard, "Energy Job Losers Could Get Windfall," *Washington Times,* July 3, 2009.

14. Sarah Palin, "The 'Cap And Tax' Dead End," *Washington Post,* July 14, 2009.

15. Geller, "Obama's Energy Plan: Mandated Scarcity in the Richest Country in the World."

16. David Freddoso, "Don't Buy Those Carbon Credits Just Yet," *Examiner* (Washington), November 10, 2009, http://www.washingtonexaminer.com/opinion/blogs/beltway-confidential/Dont-buy-those-carbon-credits-just-yet-69645032.html.

17. Peter Ferrara, "Cap and Trade Dementia," *American Spectator,* July 1, 2009.

18. Tim Ball, "The Death Blow to Climate Science," Canada Free Press, November 21, 2009, http://canadafreepress.com/index.php/members/17102/Ball/.

19. James Delingpole, "Climategate: The Final Nail in the Coffin of 'Anthropogenic Global Warming'?" *Telegraph,* November 20, 2009.

20. Ball, "The Death Blow to Climate Science."

21. Andrew C. Revkin, "Hacked E-Mail is New Fodder for Climate Dispute," *New York Times,* November 20, 2009.

22. Andrew C. Revkin, "Private Climate Conversations on Display," *New York Times,* November 20, 2009.

23. "Leaked E-mails Muddy Waters Ahead of Climate Change Conference," FOXNews.com, November 30, 2009, http://www.foxnews.com/politics/2009/11/30/leaked-e-mails-muddy-waters-ahead-climate-change-conference/?utm_source=feedburner&utm_medium=feed&utm_campaign=Feed%253A+foxnews%252Fpolitics+%2528FOXNews.com+-+Politics%2529&utm_content=Google+Feedfetcher.

24. Ben Geman, "EPA chief: The hacked e-mails change nothing," The Hill, December 7, 2009, http://thehill.com/blogs/e2-wire/677-e2-wire/70943-epa-chief-the-hacked-emails-dont-change-a-thing.

25. Jake Tapper, "White House Pushes Back on Climate Change Email Controversy," ABC News, December 3, 2009, http://blogs.abcnews.com/politicalpunch/2009/12/white-house-pushes-back-on-climate-change-email-controversy.html.

26. David Rochelson, "The search for knowledge, truth and a greater understanding of the world around us," Change.gov, December 20, 2008, http://change.gov/news room/entry/the_search_for_knowledge_truth_and_a_greater_understanding_of _the_world_aro.

27. Sarah Palin, "Mr. President: Boycott Copenhagen; Investigate Your Climate Change 'Experts,'" Sarah Palin's Notes, Facebook.com, December 3, 2009.

28. Sarah Palin, "Copenhagen's Political Science," *Washington Post,* December 9, 2009.

EPILOGUE: WHAT LOVERS OF FREEDOM *MUST* DO

1. George Jahn, "Analysis: A year on, Iran, NKorea threats worsen," Associated Press, December 13, 2009.

2. See F. A. Hayek, *The Road to Serfdom* (Chicago: University of Chicago Press, 2007).

3. "Howard Dean has a point on capitalism and socialism," Free Frank Warner, December 5, 2009, http://frankwarner.typepad.com/free_frank_warner/2009/12/ howard-dean-has-a-point-on-capitalism-and-socialism.html?cid=6a00d83451cd37 69e20128761c4ae6970c.

4. Ayn Rand, *For the New Intellectual* (New York: Signet, 1963), p. 46.

5. Kathleen Gilbert, "Lech Walesa: World Has 'Lost Hope' of America's Moral Leadership," LifeSite News, February 5, 2010.

ACKNOWLEDGMENTS

Much thanks to attorney John Jay for helping me parse through the legal language of the Copenhagen climate change documents; to Scott Mendel for his efforts on behalf of this book; and to Mitchell Ivers and his colleagues at Threshold for their excellent work on the manuscript. But most of all, deepest gratitude to my Atlas Shrugs readers, those great Americans and freedom lovers who sent me news tips and other material that helped me expose Obama's agenda and activities— *mwah!*

INDEX